The Epistle of Paul The Apostle
to the
HEBREWS
and The First and Second Epistles of
ST PETER

CALVIN'S COMMENTARIES

CALVIN'S COMMENTARIES

The Epistle of Paul The Apostle

to the

HEBREWS

and

The First and Second Epistles of ST PETER

Translator
WILLIAM B. JOHNSTON

Editors
DAVID W. TORRANCE
THOMAS F. TORRANCE

Wm. B. Eerdmans Publishing Company
Grand Rapids, Michigan

Published *1963*
Fifth reprinting, April 1979

ISBN 0-8028-2052-2

Published in Great Britain by Oliver and Boyd, Edinburgh

Translation © 1963 Oliver and Boyd Ltd.

PHOTOLITHOPRINTED BY EERDMANS PRINTING COMPANY
GRAND RAPIDS, MICHIGAN, UNITED STATES OF AMERICA

TRANSLATOR'S PREFACE

The translation of the Calvin Translation Society which this now replaces was made in 1853 by the Rev. John Owen, vicar of Thrussington in Leicestershire. In the intervening century there has been a great advance in Calvin studies, and in the understanding of the closely knit theological reasoning that is found in his commentaries. This is especially true of the Epistle to the Hebrews where Law and Gospel are considered in their office and their relevance. There are perhaps no more important questions for contemporary theological thinking than those of the divine-human priesthood of Christ, and the relation of the New Testament faith to Old Testament types. To this the Epistle to the Hebrews, and Calvin's careful exegesis of it, are immediately relevant.

The following are the principal editions of the Commentaries on Hebrews and 1 and 2 Peter.

1. In Latin

Composite works:

Commentaries on St Paul's Epistles, 1550, Robertus Stephanus.

In Omnes Pauli Apostoli Epistolas atque etiam in Epistolam ad Hebraeos Commentarii, Geneva 1565.

Works of Calvin, Vignon and Chouet, Geneva 1612, 1617.

Works of Calvin, Amsterdam Edition, vol. VII. J. J. Schipper, Amsterdam, 1667, 1671.

New Testament Commentaries, Halle, 1832; Eichler, Berlin, 1834 and 1838.

Works of Calvin, Brunswick Edition, Bauer, Cunitz and Reuss, 1892, vol. LV. (republished in *Corpus Reformatorum* vol. lxxx)

Epistle to the Hebrews

First edition, dedicated to King Sigismund Augustus of Poland, Geneva, 1549.

1 Peter

First Edition, dedicated to King Edward VI of England, Geneva, 1551.

2. *In French*

Commentaries, Badius, Geneva, 1561, 1562; Paris, 1854; Société calviniste de France, Geneva, 1960.

3. *In English*

A Commentarie on the whole Epistle to the Hebrews, by John Calvin. Translated by Clement Cotton. London, 1605.

Commentaries on the Epistle of Paul to the Hebrews, translated by Rev. John Owen. Edinburgh, 1853 (Calvin Translation Society).

Commentaries on the Catholic Epistles, by John Calvin, translated by Rev. John Owen. Edinburgh, 1855 (Calvin Translation Society).

This translation is made on the basis of the text of the Berlin edition of the Commentaries, 1834. The Scripture text (except where Calvin's own comments demand a variant rendering) is that of the Revised Version.

W. B. J.

THE EPISTLE TO
THE HEBREWS

DEDICATION

JOHN CALVIN
TO THE MOST MIGHTY AND SERENE PRINCE
SIGISMUND AUGUSTUS
BY THE GRACE OF GOD,
KING OF POLAND, GRAND DUKE OF LITHUANIA,
RUSSIA, PRUSSIA, LORD AND HEIR OF MUSCOVY

THERE are today many foolish men who through a vain and constant desire for writing engage the minds of ignorant and thoughtless readers with their trifles. To this evil, most illustrious King, is added a further indignity, that while they inscribe their silly things to kings and princes in order to disguise or at least to cover them by borrowed splendour, they not only profane sacred names, but also besmirch them with some measure of their own unworthiness. The unreasonable rashness of such men makes it necessary for serious and sober writers to frame an excuse when they publicly dedicate their labours to great men, even though there is nothing in them that does not correspond with the greatness of those to whom they are offered. It was necessary to make these introductory remarks in case I should seem to be of the number of those who allow themselves through the example of others to render public anything they please, however foolish it may be. It does not, however, escape me how much appearance it has of foolish confidence, that I (not to speak of other things) who am an unknown and obscure man, should not hesitate to address your royal Majesty. If my reasons be heard, and if you, Your Majesty, approve of what I do, what others may judge will cause me no great anxiety.

Firstly, although I am not unmindful of my insignificance nor ignorant of the reverence due to your Majesty, yet the fame of your piety alone which has reached to almost all who are zealous for the true doctrine of Christ is sufficient to remove any fear. I bring with me a present which that piety will not allow you to reject. Since the Epistle addressed to the Hebrews contains a full discussion of the eternal divinity of Christ, His supreme government, and only priesthood (which are the main points of heavenly wisdom) and as these things are so explained in it, that the whole power and work of Christ are set forth in the most graphic way, it rightly deserves to have the place and honour of an invaluable treasure in the Church. I do not doubt that it will be valued by you also, since you desire the Son of God to reign and to excel over all.

I do not say that I have succeeded in the exposition which I have undertaken, but I feel confident that when you have read it you will at least approve my fidelity and diligence. As I do not claim the praise of great knowledge or of erudition, so I am not ashamed to profess what has been given me by the Lord for the purpose of understanding the Scripture (since this is simply to glory in Him). If I have any talents for assisting the Church of God in this direction, I have endeavoured to give clear proof of it in this study of mine. I therefore hope, as I have said, that this present which I offer will not only avail as an excuse to your Majesty, but also procure for me some of your favour.

Perhaps this will be a new encouragement to your Majesty inasmuch as you are already concerned for the restoration of the kingdom of Christ, and to many who live under your sovereignty to take it up. You have a kingdom which is extensive and renowned, and which contains many glories, but its happiness will only have a firm foundation if it takes Christ as its supreme Governor to be defended by His faith and protection. To submit your sceptre to Him is not inconsistent with the high estate in which you are set, but would be far more glorious than all wordly triumphs. Since it is held among men that gratitude is the proper virtue of the great and noble spirit, what would be less becoming to kings than to show themselves ungrateful to the Son of God by whom they have been raised to the highest point of honour? It is therefore not only an honourable but a more than royal service, which raises us to the ranks of the angels, that the throne of Christ is set up among us so that His heavenly Voice alone becomes the rule for living and dying, alike to the highest and the humblest. Although profession of obedience to the rule of Christ is today commonly made by almost everyone, yet there are very few who show Him the obedience which they boast.

This can happen only where the whole of religion is contained within the infallible rule of His sacred truth. But at this point strange conflicts arise because men who are not only puffed up with pride, but also bewitched by monstrous madness, pay less attention to the eternal teachings of the Heavenly Master than to their own empty inventions. Whatever pretences are urged by those who give their energies to opposing us in favour of the Antichrist of Rome, the source of all the strife by which the Church has been so bitterly torn these thirty years will be found in the fact that those who want to be the chief among the followers of Christ cannot bear to submit to His teaching. So voracious is their ambition and their boldness, that the truth of God lies buried under innumerable lies, that all His institutions are debased by the foulest corruptions, that worship is everywhere profaned, the doctrine of faith utterly overturned, the observance of the sacraments corrupted, the government of the Church turned into a barbarous tyranny, evil trafficking in all things sacred introduced, the power of Christ misused to support the unrestrained tyranny of the ungodly, and terrible profanation of everything full of the most dreadful mockeries has taken the place of Christianity. When we offer for all these many terrible evils the single remedy that those on earth should give ear to the Voice of the Son of God speaking from heaven, instantly there arise those great Atlases, not to support the Church on their shoulders, but to bear on high an idol which they have made for themselves with vain, bombastic titles. Furthermore they make the excuse for their fierce recriminations against us that we have disturbed the peace and equanimity of the Church by our interference. When things are seen as they really are, these resourceful artificers are in fact devising a Church which has a system of government wholly apart from and foreign to that of Christ. What is this but a wicked and sacrilegious attempt to separate the body from its Head? From this it is clear how empty the boast of many people about their Christianity is, since the majority allow themselves by no means to be governed by the pure teaching of the Gospel.

The fact that you recognize, Your Majesty, that for Christ to take full possession of His kingdom there must needs be a complete purge of all superstitions is a mark of your singular wisdom, and that you undertake and attempt what you thus judge to be really necessary for this end is a sign of rare virtue. There are many signs which give an almost certain hope to all good men that you are divinely chosen to be the image of another Hezekiah or Josiah soon to restore in the kingdom of Poland the purer teaching of the Gospel which has been spoiled throughout the whole world by the craft of Satan and the betrayal of men.

Even omitting your other outstanding virtues about which even foreigners declare, and men of your own realm perceive with great advantage, a remarkable zeal for piety has always appeared in you, and even today radiates from you, but the most outstanding thing is that Christ, the Son of Righteousness, has so illumined your mind with the light of His Gospel, that you know the true way of governing the Church which is to be sought from Him alone, and at the same time you see how much difference there is between the true form of religion which He instituted, and this debased and fictitious one which is a later introduction. You understand that the worship of God has been corrupted and deformed because innumerable superstitions have crept into its place, that the grace of Christ has been unworthily overwhelmed by great darkness, that the power of His death has been destroyed, He Himself torn and dishevelled, the assurance of salvation completely overturned, consciences miserably and horribly torn and tormented, men in their wretchedness led away from true and sincere worship of God into all kinds of strange wanderings, the Church oppressed by a cruel tyranny, and in short no part of Christianity left in its purity.

It is incredible, Your Majesty, that you have been endowed with this understanding by God without His purposing for you a service in some great matter. So far it has happened in the marvellous providence of God that in the whole renowned kingdom of Poland no innocent blood of the saints has been shed, not even a drop which might demand vengeance and thus retard its happiness. It was through the clemency and gentleness of King Sigismund of happy memory, your Majesty's father, that, although the infection of savagery took possession of so many parts of the Christian world, yet he kept his hands pure. Now your Honour and some of your excellent princes are not only readily admitting Christ when He presents Himself to them, but are earnestly seeking Him. I see also that John à Lasco, scion of an illustrious family, has carried the torch to other nations also.

All the less tolerable, therefore, is the presumption of Eck, that by dedicating his book on the sacrifice of the mass to king Sigismund, your Majesty's father, he besmirched with an evil stain (so far as he could) such an illustrious kingdom, although there was nothing strange in the behaviour of that fellow Silenus, that, prince of drunkards as he was, he used to be sick as often at the altar as at the dung-heap. If by addressing and dedicating this work of mine to your Majesty I have done something at least to purify the name of Poland of that rotten filth of Eck, so that it does not stick where it was so unworthily thrown, I shall reckon to have achieved something worth while. There is scarcely any book of Scripture that could be more fittingly chosen for this purpose. Here our apostle takes the greatest possible trouble to show that the sacrifice which Eck urges is clearly at variance with the priesthood of Christ. No mention is made here of the mass, which Satan had not yet thrown up from the underworld. In his instruction to the Church to be content with the one, unique sacrifice which Christ made on the Cross, to do away with all sacrificial rites, he has surely barred the road to their new inventions. The apostle proclaims that Christ was sacrificed once for all on the Cross, while Eck invents the idea that this victim is renewed every day. The apostle declares that the Son of God alone was the fitting priest to offer Himself to the Father, and for that was constituted by oath, while Eck says that priesthood does not rest in His Person only, but transfers His office to hired sacrificers. The evasions by which they try to avoid these and other similar arguments do not escape me, but I have no fear that he will deceive any others than those who are self-blinded or who flee the light. He was so intoxicated by his Thrasonic superiority that he took more trouble over his insolent boasting than in careful argumentation. In case I seem to be beating a dead dog to no purpose, I shall add nothing more for the present, except to say that this commentary of mine will be of use to wipe off the stain which that drunken good-for-nothing by producing his miserable book fixed on the name of Poland. I have no fear that those who take the trouble to read will be caught by his baits.

Since by offering this book of mine to your Majesty I do not only wish to provide some mark of regard to your Majesty privately, but also to give testimony to this regard before the whole world, it now remains for me humbly to beseech your Majesty not to reject what little I have done. If I have given any encouragement to you to continue your pious efforts, I shall consider that I have been amply rewarded. Do you, therefore, make it your concern, Your Majesty, with the blessing of Christ, and as is worthy both of your high royal state and of your heroic virtue, that the eternal truth of God in which both the glory and salvation of men are contained, may, wherever your rule extends, recover its rightful place which has been usurped by the robbery of Antichrist. It is indeed a hard task, and one of such magnitude as to fill even the wisest men with anxiety and fear.

But in the first place, there is no danger which we ought not readily to undergo, no difficulty that we should not resolutely bear, and no struggle that we should not boldly engage ourselves in for such a necessary cause. Secondly, because it is the peculiar work of God, we should not have regard here to the extent of our human powers, but to the glory that is due to His power, so that relying on it not only as our help but also as our guide, we may dare things beyond our strength, for Scripture everywhere rightly assigns to God the task of both founding and renewing the Church. Moreover because the work is altogether divine in nature, as soon as any beginning is made Satan marshals whatever damaging stratagems he has in a body either to stop further advance or to delay it. We know that the prince of this world has never any lack of countless henchmen who are always prepared to provide resources to oppose the kingdom of Christ. Some are instigated by ambition, others are impelled by greed. These battles try us to some extent because of our frailty, and no doubt your Majesty will experience far greater difficulties. Anyone who takes it on himself to forward the doctrine of salvation and the safety of the Church must be armed with unconquerable perseverance; but since this is a matter beyond our strength, God will supply us with heavenly weapons.

Meantime it is our duty to have written on our hearts the promises which occur throughout Scripture that as the Lord has laid the foundations of the Church with His own hand, so He will not allow it to remain derelict without being concerned for repairing and restoring its ruins. In so saying He promises that He will never fail us in this work. Just as He does not wish us to be inactive spectators of His power, so by the presence of His aid in supporting the hands which labour He shows clearly that He is the chief architect. This He repeats and emphasises time and again so that we do not fail to remember it however often we have to contend with the enemies who constantly attack us. They are, as has been said, almost inexhaustible in resources and infinite in their variety. But this one thing is abundantly sufficient to encourage us, in that we have a Leader so invincible that the more battles He fights, the more triumphs and victories He gains.

Farewell, Most Invincible Majesty. May the Lord Jesus govern you by the Spirit of wisdom, sustain you by the Spirit of fortitude, follow you with every kind of blessing, long save Your Majesty in health and prosperity, and guard your kingdom. Amen.

GENEVA. 23rd May 1549

THE THEME

VARIOUS opinions were formerly entertained as to the author of this epistle, and it was only at a later period that it was received by the Latin Churches. They suspected that it favoured Novatus in denying pardon to the fallen; but various passages will show that this was a groundless opinion. I class it without hesitation among the apostolical writings; I do not doubt that it has been through the craft of Satan that any have been led to dispute its authority. There is, indeed, no book in Holy Scripture which speaks so clearly of the priesthood of Christ, which so highly exalts the virtue and dignity of that only true sacrifice which He offered by His death, which so abundantly deals with the use of ceremonies as well as their abrogation, and, in a word, so fully explains that Christ is the end of the Law. Let us therefore not allow the Church of God or ourselves to be deprived of so great a benefit, but firmly defend the possession of it.

As to its author, we need not be greatly worried. Some think that the author was Paul, others Luke, others Barnabas, and others Clement, as Jerome says; yet Eusebius, in the sixth book of his *Church History*, mentions only Luke and Clement. I well know that in the time of Chrysostom it was received everywhere by the Greeks as among the Pauline epistles; but the Latins thought otherwise, especially those who were nearest to the apostolic times.

I can adduce no reason to show that Paul was its author; for those who say that he designedly suppressed his name because it was hateful to the Jews, make no relevant case. Why, then, did he mention the name of Timothy? By this he betrayed himself. The manner of teaching and the style sufficiently show that Paul was not the author, and the writer himself confesses in the second chapter that he was one of the disciples of the apostles, which is wholly different from the way in which Paul spoke of himself. Moreover, what is said of the practice of catechizing in the sixth chapter, does not well suit the time of Paul. There are other things which we shall notice in their proper places.

I know the excuse that is usually made as to the style, namely that no opinion can be formed therefrom, because the Greek is a translation made from the Hebrew by Luke or someone else. This conjecture can be easily refuted. I pass by other places quoted from Scripture; but if the Epistle was written in Hebrew, there would have been no allusion to the word Testament, on which the writer so much dwells. What he says of a *Testament*, in the ninth chapter, could not have been drawn from any other source than from the Greek word, for $\delta\iota\alpha\theta\acute{\eta}\kappa\eta$ has two meanings in Greek, while בְּרִית (*berith*) in Hebrew means only a covenant. This reason alone is enough to convince men of sound judgment of what I have said that the epistle was written in the Greek language. The objection on the other hand, that it is more probable that the apostle wrote to the Jews in their own language, has no weight in it; for how few then understood their ancestral language? Each had learned the language of the country where he dwelt. Besides, the Greek was then more widely known than all other languages. We shall proceed now to the Theme.

The object at the beginning is not to show to the Jews that Jesus, the Son of Mary, was the Christ, the Redeemer promised to them. Because he was writing to those who had already made a profession of Christ, that point is taken as granted. The concern of the writer is to prove what the office of Christ is. From this it appears evident, that by His coming an end was put to ceremonies. It is necessary to draw this distinction. As it would have been a superfluous task for the apostle to prove to those who were already convinced that He who had appeared was the Christ, so it was necessary for him to show what He was, because they did not as yet clearly understand the end, the effect, and the advantages of His coming, but being taken up with a false view of the Law, they laid hold on the shadow instead of the substance. Our business with the papists is the same today, for they confess with us that Christ is the Son of God, the Redeemer who had been promised to the world, but when we come to the reality, we find that they rob Him of more than one-half of His power.

He begins from the dignity of Christ; because it seemed strange to the Jews that the Gospel should be preferred to the Law. First he settles that point which was in dispute, that the doctrine brought by Christ had the pre-eminence, because it was the fulfilment of all the prophecies. Since the reverence in which they held Moses might have been a hindrance to them, he shows that Christ was far superior to all others. After he has briefly referred to those things in which He excelled others, he mentions by name the angels, so as to include all the others with them in their proper order. Thus he advances prudently in his course. If he had begun with Moses, his comparison would have been more disliked, but when it is made clear from Scripture that celestial powers are subordinate to Christ, there is no reason why Moses or any mortal being should refuse to be classed with them, so that the Son of God may appear eminent above angels as well as men.

After he has thus brought the angels under the power and dominion of Christ, the apostle having, as it were, gained their confidence, declares that Moses was inferior to Him as a servant is to his master.

THE THEME

In thus setting Christ in the three first chapters in the supreme step of power, he indicates that when He speaks all ought to be silent, and that nothing should prevent us from seriously attending to His doctrine. At the same time he sets Him forth in the second chapter as our Brother in our flesh, and he thus allures us to devote ourselves more willingly to Him. He also blends exhortations and threatenings in order to lead to obedience those who are tardy or who perversely resist; and he continues in this strain nearly to the end of the fourth chapter.

Then he turns to explain the priesthood of Christ, the true, pure understanding of which abolishes all the ceremonies of the Law. After he has briefly showed how welcome that priesthood ought to be to us, and how gladly we ought to acquiesce in it, he turns aside for a bit to reprove the Jews, because they stopped at the first elements of religion like children—and he also terrifies them with a grievous and severe denunciation, because there was danger that if they were slothful to make progress, they might at length be rejected by the Lord. Presently he softens this asperity by saying that he hoped better things of them, in order to encourage those, whom he had depressed, to make progress.

Then he returns to the priesthood, and first shows that it differed from the ancient priesthood under the Law; secondly, that it was more excellent, because it took its place, and was sanctioned by an oath, because it is eternal, and remains for ever efficacious and because he who performs its duties is superior in honour and dignity to Aaron and all the rest of the Levitical tribe, of all of which the type was shadowed forth in the person of Melchizedek.

In order to prove more fully that the ceremonies of the Law were abrogated, he mentions that the ceremonies were appointed, along with the tabernacle, for a particular end, namely to set forth the heavenly prototype. Hence it follows, that they were not to be rested in unless we wish to stop in the middle of our course, and have no regard to the goal. On this subject he quotes a passage from Jeremiah, in which a new covenant is promised, which was simply an improvement on the old. Hence it follows that the old was weak and fading.

Having spoken of the likeness and similitude between the shadows and the reality exhibited in Christ, he then concludes that all the rituals appointed by Moses have been abrogated by the one only true sacrifice of Christ, because the efficacy of this sacrifice is perpetual, and that not only is the sanction of the New Testament made by it complete, but that it is also a true and a spiritual accomplishment of that external priesthood which was in force under the Law.

To this doctrine he again connects an exhortation like a goad that they put aside all impediments and receive Christ with due reverence.

3

With regard to the many examples he mentions in the eleventh chapter concerning the fathers, they seem to me to have been brought forward for this purpose—that the Jews might understand, that if they were led from Moses to Christ they would not be departing from the fathers, but would be especially connected with them. If the chief thing in them was faith, and the root of all other virtues, it follows that this is especially that by which they could be counted the children of Abraham and the Prophets. On the other hand all those who do not follow the faith of the fathers are illegitimate. This is no small commendation of the Gospel, that by it we have union and fellowship with the universal Church, which has been from the beginning of the world.

The last two chapters contain various precepts as to the way in which we ought to live. They speak of hope, of bearing the cross, of perseverance, of gratitude towards God, of obedience, of mercy, of the duties of love, of chastity, and of such like things. Lastly, he concludes with a prayer, and at the same time gives them a hope of his coming to see them.

CHAPTER ONE

God, having of old time spoken unto the fathers in the prophets by divers portions and in divers manners, hath at the end of these days spoken unto us in his Son, whom he appointed heir of all things, through whom also he made the worlds. (1-2)

1. *God of old etc.* The purpose of this introduction is to commend the doctrine of Christ. It teaches that we are not only to receive this doctrine with reverence, but we are to rest in it alone. In order to understand this better, we must note the antithesis of the separate clauses. First, the Son of God is contrasted with the prophets: then we with the fathers: thirdly, the various and manifold forms of speech which God uses in the fathers with the latest revelation which is given us by Christ. Nevertheless in this diversity he sets before us one God, in case anyone should think that the Law is at variance with the Gospel, or that the author of the latter is different from that of the former. In order, therefore, that you may grasp the crux of this contrast, the following tabulation will illustrate—

	God spoke
of old by the prophets:	now by the Son.
then to the fathers:	but now to us.
then at many times:	now as at the end of the times.

With the laying of this foundation the agreement between the Law and the Gospel is established, because God, who is always like Himself, and whose Word is unchanging, and whose truth is unshakeable, spoke in both together. We must notice, however, the difference between us and the fathers, because He addressed them of old differently from us today. Firstly, in the times of the fathers He used the prophets: but to us He has given His own Son as ambassador. Our state is thus in this regard a better one. Furthermore, Moses is included in the ranks of the prophets, as being one of those who are far inferior to the Son. We are better off, too, in the manner of the revelation, for the diversity of visions and of other dispensations which existed in the Old Testament was evidence that there was not yet a firm and stable order of things such as is proper when everything is perfectly settled. That is the meaning of the phrase 'in divers portions and in divers manners'. God would have followed the same pattern in perpetuity right to the end if it had been perfect in every way. It follows, therefore, that this variety was a sign of imperfection. Furthermore, I take these two words in the following sense, namely, that 'in divers portions' refers to the various changes of times. The Greek word is πολυμερῶς which means literally 'in many parts', as, for example, when we intend to speak more fully later: but πολυτρόπως (in my opinion) indicates diversity in the pattern itself. When he says—hath spoken to us at the end of these days, he means that there is no further reason why we should be in doubt whether to expect any new revelation. It was not a part of the Word that Christ brought, but the last closing Word. It is in this sense that the apostles understand 'the last times' and 'the last days'. This too is what Paul understands when he writes that 'upon us the ends of the ages have come' (I Cor. 10.11). If God has now spoken His last Word, it is right to advance thus far, just as we must halt our steps when we arrive at Him. It is very necessary for us to recognize both these aspects: for it was a great drawback on the part of the Jews that they did not reckon with the possibility that God had postponed a fuller teaching to another time. They were content with their own law, and did not hurry on to the goal. On the other hand since Christ appeared the opposite evil has begun to take effect in the world. Men try to go beyond Christ. What else is the whole system of Popery, but the transgression of this limit which the apostle fixed? Therefore, just as the Spirit of God in this passage invites all to come as far as Christ, so He forbids them to overstep this last Word of which He makes mention. In short, the limit of our wisdom is placed here in the Gospel.

2. *Whom he appointed heir.* He glorifies Christ in these praises so as to bring us to reverence Him, for since the Father has made all things subject to Him, we too belong to His kingdom. He declares also that no good can be found outside of Him, since He is the Heir of all things. Hence, it follows that we are most miserable and destitute of all good things, unless He helps us with His riches. Further, he adds that this honour, namely, to have power over all things, belongs by right to the Son of God, because all things were made by Him; although these two attributes are ascribed to Christ for different reasons. The world was created by Him as being the eternal wisdom of God which was the director of all His works from the beginning. That is the proof of the eternity of Christ; He must have existed before the world was created by Him. But if the question be of the duration of time, no beginning will be found. It does not detract from His power to say that the world was created by Him as if He did not create it Himself. It is a usual manner of speaking to call the Father the Creator: and what is added in some passages—by Wisdom (Prov. 8.27) or by the Word (John 1.3), or by the Son (Col. 1.16)—has the same force as if Wisdom itself were

named as Creator. It must be noted that there is a distinction of persons, not only in respect of men, but also in God Himself, between the Father and the Son. Unity of essence requires that what is of the essence of God is as much of the Son as of the Father: and therefore whatever belongs to God alone, is common to both. This does not prevent each having the property of His own person. The name 'heir' is attributed to Christ as manifest in the flesh; for in being made man and putting on the same nature as us, He took on Himself this heirship, in order to restore to us what we had lost in Adam. In the beginning God had established man as His son to be the heir of all good things; but the first man by his sin alienated from God both himself and his posterity, and deprived them both of the blessing of God and of all good things. We begin to enjoy the good things of God by right only when Christ, who is the Heir of all things, admits us to His fellowship. He is the Heir so that He may make us wealthy by His riches. Indeed the apostle gives Him this title so that we may know that without Him we are destitute of all good things. If you take 'all' to be masculine gender, this clause will mean something like this—that we ought to be subject to Christ, because we have been given to Him by the Father. But I prefer to read it as neuter, to mean that we are deprived of lawful possession of heaven and earth and all creatures, unless we have fellowship with Christ.

Who being the effulgence of his glory, and the very image of his substance and upholding all things by the word of his power, when he had made purification of sins, sat down at the right hand of the Majesty on high. (3)

3. *Who being the effulgence of his glory.* This has reference partly to the divine nature of Christ, and partly to His putting on of our flesh. What is described as 'the effulgence of his glory and the very image of his substance' properly belongs to His divinity, the rest refers to His human nature; but it is all set down to show forth the dignity of Christ. By the same token the Son is called the effulgence of His glory and the very image of His substance. Both words are common speech. In matters so great and so profound nothing can be said except by way of analogy (*similitudine*) taken from creaturely things. There is no need for us to discuss too subtly how the Son, who is of one essence with the Father, is the glory shining forth from His brightness. We must allow that there is a measure of impropriety (*improprium quodammodo*) in what is taken from earthly things and applied to the hidden majesty of God. At the same time things which are perceptible by our senses are appropriately applied to God, so that we may know what is to be found in Christ, and what benefits He brings us. This too

should be noted, that this is not the teaching of empty speculations, but the exposition of a firm doctrine of faith. We ought therefore to put these titles of Christ to our own use, inasmuch as they bear a relation to us. When you hear that the Son is the glory of the Father's glory, bear in mind that the glory of the Father is invisible to you until it shines forth in Christ: and that He is called the very image of His substance because the majesty of the Father is hidden, until it shows itself as impressed on His image. Those who ignore this relationship and who speculate more airily vex themselves to no purpose because they do not hold to the apostle's argument. His intention was not to describe the likeness of the Father to the Son within the Godhead, but, as I have said, to build up our faith fruitfully, so that we may learn that God is revealed to us in no other way than in Christ. The radiance in the substance of God is so mighty that it hurts our eyes, until it shines on us in Christ. It follows from this that we are blind to the light of God unless it illumines us in Christ. This is indeed a useful philosophy, that we should learn the excellency of Christ by a true sense of faith and by our own experience. As I have already said we must have a similar understanding of the image: while God is incomprehensible to us in Himself, yet His form appears to us in the Son.

'Ἀπαύγασμα he remeans nothing other than visible light or radiance, of which our eyes are perceptive; and χαρακτήρ means the living form of a hidden substance. The former term reminds us that apart from Christ there is no light, but unbroken darkness. Since God is the only light by which we must all be illumined, so this light is shed on us (so to speak) only by such irradiation. The latter term reminds us that God is known truly and firmly only in Christ. His likeness is not just veiled and concealed, but is an express image which represents God Himself, just as a coin bears the image of the die-stamp from which it is struck. Indeed the apostle goes even further and says that the substance of the Father is in some way engraven on Christ. The word ὑποστάσις which along with others I have translated as substance, denotes (in my opinion) not the *esse* or the essence of the Father, but the person. It would be absurd to say that the essence of God is impressed on Christ, since the one and the same is the essence of both. It is, however, true and appropriate to say that whatever is peculiar to the Father is also expressed in Christ, so that he who knows Him also knows whatever is in the Father. The orthodox fathers also take *hypostasis* in this sense, as being threefold in God, the οὐσία being one. Hilary throughout takes the Latin word *substantia* as equivalent to person. Furthermore, although it is not the apostle's purpose here to discuss the nature of Christ in Himself, but His nature as He reveals it to us, nevertheless he sufficiently refutes the Arians and the Sabellians

8

by attributing to Christ what belongs to God alone, and at the same time distinguishing two separate persons in the Father and the Son. Hence we infer that the Son is one God with the Father, yet is nonetheless to be appropriately distinguished in such a way that each has His own subsistence.

And upholding all things. To uphold is used in the sense of to care for and to keep all creation in its proper state. He sees that everything will quickly disintegrate if it is not upheld by His goodness. The demonstrative pronoun 'His' can be construed equally well as referring either to the Father or to the Son: it can be rendered as 'the Father's' or as 'His own'. I am inclined to accept the latter rendering because it is more widely received and best suits the context. Literally it reads 'by the Word of His power', but the genitive has the force of an adjective in accordance with Hebrew idiom. There is no point in the tortuous explanation of some of the effect that Christ upholds all things by the Word of the Father, that is by Himself, because He is the Word. There is no need of such a forced exposition, for Christ is not called ῥῆμα but λόγος. Word, here, simply means will, and the gist is that Christ who upholds the whole world by His will alone, nevertheless did not refuse the task of accomplishing our purification.

This is the second section of the doctrine which is treated in this epistle. The whole discussion is stated under these two heads—that Christ, to whom is given supreme authority, is to be listened to before all others; and that, because by His death He has reconciled us to the Father, He has put an end to the old sacrifices. That is why this first sentence, which is in the form of a general proposition, is in two parts. When the writer says—by Himself—there is to be understood an implicit antithesis, that He was not helped to His purpose by the shadows of the Mosaic law. He shows a clear difference between Christ and the Levitical priests. True, the latter were said to forgive sins, but they borrowed this power from elsewhere. In short, his intention is to exclude all other means or intermediaries by placing both the price and the power of our purification in Christ.

Sat down on the right hand. This is as though he were saying—when He had given salvation to men in the world, He was received into heavenly glory, so that He might rule over all things. He has added this clause to show that it is not a temporary salvation that He has won for us, for in other respects we are apt to measure His power as it appears to us at present. He cautions us that we are not to make less of Christ because we do not see Him with our own eyes. This is rather the culmination of His glory, that He was received and taken to the very highest pinnacle of empire. *On the right hand* is applied metaphorically (*per similitudinem*) to God, who is neither contained in one place, nor has He a left or a right side. Christ being seated means nothing else than the kingdom which is given to Him by the Father, and that power to which Paul refers, that in His Name every knee shall bow (Phil. 2.10). To sit at the right hand of the Father is simply to rule on the Father's behalf, just as viceroys do, who are granted full powers over everything. To that is added the description—of majesty, and then—on high, to show that Christ is placed on the highest throne from which majesty of God shines forth. As He is to be loved because of His redemption, He is also to be worshipped in this majesty.

. . . having become by so much better than the angels, as he hath inherited a more excellent name than they. For unto which of the angels said he at any time, Thou art my Son, this day have I begotten thee? (Ps. 2.7) and again, I will be to him a Father, and he shall be to me a Son? (II Sam. 7.14). And when he again bringeth in the firstborn into the world, he saith, And let all the angels of God worship him (Ps. 97.7).
(4-6)

4. *having become by so much better.* After preferring Christ to Moses and all the others, the writer now increases His glory still more by comparing Him with the angels. It was a common tradition among the Jews that the Law was given by angels. They heard the honourable things which are said about angels throughout Scripture, and in the way that the world is marvellously prone to fall into superstition, they obscured the glory of God by an over-extolling of angels. They must therefore be restrained within their own order so as not to stand in the way of the glory of Christ. The first argument is from His Name, that Christ is far superior to them, because He is called the Son of God. The writer proves from two scriptural evidences that Christ was distinguished by this title. Both of these we must examine, and then we shall reach the sum of the matter.

5. *Thou art my son.* It is undeniable that this refers to David in so far as he represented Christ (*Christi personam sustinuit*). What is contained in this psalm should have been foreshadowed in David; but they are expressed in Christ. The fact that the former extended the bounds of his kingdom by overcoming many enemies round about was some adumbration of this promise—'I will give thee the heathen for an inheritance.' But how small was this compared with the fulness of the kingdom of Christ, which stretches from east to west? By the same token he was called the son of God, that is, chosen particularly by God to do great things. But this was hardly a modest spark of that glory which shone forth in Christ, in whom the Father has engraven His own image. The name of Son belongs by a singular prerogative to Christ alone, and cannot be transferred to anyone else without

profaning it. It is He and no one else whom the Father has sealed. On the other hand this argument of the apostle seems to be insufficiently founded. On what ground does he maintain that Christ is superior to angels except in having the name of Son? It seems as if He did not have this in common with princes and with others of eminent authority, of whom it is written—Ye are gods, and all of you sons of the Most High; as if the prophet did not speak with greater esteem of all Israel when he called them the firstborn of God (Jer. 31.9). The name son is given to Israel throughout; even apart from the fact that elsewhere David calls the angels themselves the sons of God (Ps. 89.6)—Who, he says, is like Jehovah among the sons of the gods? The answer is easy. It is that the princes are called by this name only in some respects; that in the case of Israel it denotes the common grace of election; that the angels are called the sons of God figuratively because they are heavenly spirits, and are those who in their blessed immortality have some traces of the divine. When David without any qualification calls himself the son of God in the person of Christ, he denotes something outstanding and excelling in honour both angels and princes and indeed all Israel. Otherwise it would be an improper and unfitting way of speaking if he were called the son of God by merit and yet had nothing more than any others; He is in fact taken out of the common herd and from being included in the generality. Since this is said exclusively of Christ— Thou art my Son—it follows that no angel is entitled to such honour. If anyone objects that to say this is to give David a superiority to the angels, I reply that there is nothing out of place in preferring him to the angels, in so far as he is the type of Christ, in the same way as no injustice was done to the angels when the high priest, who made atonement for sins, used to be called the mediator. They did not hold that title in their own right, but as they represented the rule of Christ they also took over the title from Him. The very sacraments, although in themselves they are dead things, are yet distinguished with names which the angels would not claim for themselves without sacrilege. Thus it seems that the argument from the name of the Son is well founded. A brief word must be said about the word *begotten*, to the effect that it is to be taken here relatively. Augustine's subtlety here is quite frivolous in imagining that today means eternity or for ever. Christ is certainly the eternal Son of God, because He is the Wisdom of God born before time was. But this has no connexion with the present passage which refers to men, by whom Christ was recognized as the Son of God only after the Father revealed Him. Hence this declaration which Paul mentions in Romans chapter 1 verse 4 had (so to speak) a kind of form of eternity. The former declaration, which had preceded this one, was hidden and internal, and was unknown to

men; indeed no account could have been taken of it if the Father had
not proved it by a visible revelation.

I will be to him a Father. The same observation as before holds good
for this second citation, though here the reference is to Solomon, who
was in other respects lower than the angels, yet was segregated from
the ranks of the rest of the common herd when God promised that He
would be to him a Father. He was not going to be a Father to him as
being one of Abraham's sons, or one of the patriarchs, but as being one
who has pre-eminence over all the rest. By that same privilege by
which he is made a son, all others are excluded from equal honour. It
is clear from the context of the passage that this is said of Solomon
only in so far as he was the type of Christ; for the kingdom of the
whole world is settled on the Son who is there mentioned, and that
kingdom is claimed as being for ever. On the other hand, it is agreed
that the kingdom of Solomon was confined within narrow boundaries,
and was of so little duration that immediately after his death it was
divided, and then after some time it fell completely. In the psalm the
sun and the moon are cited as witnesses, and the Lord swears that as
long as they shine in the sky that kingdom will stand unharmed. On
the other hand the kingdom of David fell after a short space of time
and in the end disintegrated entirely. Further, it is clear from several
passages in the prophets that that promise was never taken in any other
sense than as referring to Christ, so that no one can object that this is a
new comment. It is from this passage that the common custom of the
Jews of calling Christ the Son of David received its encouragement.

6. *And when he again bringeth in the firstborn into the world.* He now
adduces another argument that Christ is above the angels, namely,
because the angels are commanded to worship Him. It follows, therefore, that He is their Head and Chief. It could appear that this is wrong
and is misapplied to Christ on the ground that it is predicated of God
alone. If we reply that Christ is eternal God, and that what is true of
God is justifiably applied to Him, not everyone will be satisfied. It
would not add strength to the proving of a doubtful proposition to
argue in this cause from the common attributes of God. The apostle
is dealing with the manifestation of Christ in the flesh, and he says
expressly that this was how the Spirit spoke when He was brought
into the world, which would not have been said truthfully, if the psalm
had not properly been speaking of the manifestation of Christ. This is
indeed the case. The beginning of the psalm is a call to rejoice. David
addresses not the Jews, but the whole earth, to the furthest islands, that
is, the lands beyond the seas. The reason given is because the Lord will
reign. If you go through the whole psalm, you will find nothing but
the reign of Christ, which begins with the proclamation of the Gospel;

the theme of the psalm is simply the solemn mission on which Christ is sent to take possession of His kingdom. Why should there be any joy arising from His reign unless it be to save the whole world, that is, Gentiles as well as Jews? Therefore the apostle speaks fittingly when he says that He is brought into the world, because what is described here is His advent among men. The Hebrew word, here rendered 'angels', is *Elohim*, which means 'gods'. There is not the least doubt that the prophet is speaking of angels, because the meaning is that there is no power so exalted as not to be subject to the rule of this King, at whose coming the whole world is to rejoice.

And of the angels he saith (Ps. 104.4) Who maketh his angels winds, And his ministers a flame of fire: but of the Son he saith (Ps. 45.7) Thy throne, O God, is for ever and ever: And the sceptre of uprightness is the sceptre of thy kingdom. Thou hast loved righteousness and hated iniquity: therefore God, thy God, hath anointed thee with the oil of gladness above thy fellows. (7-9)

7. *And to the angels.* To the angels means about the angels. But the passage which he quotes seems to be turned into a different meaning. When David here describes the order which we discern in the government of the world, nothing is more certain than that he makes mention of the winds, which he says are messengers sent by the Lord, because He uses them as His runners. In the same way when He ranges the earth with His lightnings, He shows how quick and speedy His messengers are to obey his orders. None of this has anything to do with angels. Some take refuge in allegory as though the apostle were expounding the clear and literal meaning (as they say) allegorically with reference to angels. It seems more satisfactory to me to adduce this evidence as referring to angels metaphorically in this way, that David compares the winds to angels as performing in this world the duty which the angels perform in heaven; for the winds are a sort of visible spirits. In the same way Moses in describing the creation of the world mentions only the things which are perceptible by our senses, but nevertheless implies that higher things are to be understood. So David in this description of the world and its nature paints for us as if on a canvas what we must understand from the order of heaven. I think that this is a similar argument when the apostle attributes to the angels what is properly said of the winds.

8. *But of the Son.* It must be admitted that this psalm was composed by Solomon to give a picture of marriage, because he is here celebrating his marriage to the daughter of the king of Egypt. But again it cannot be denied that the reference is to something much loftier than simply to Solomon. To avoid having to recognize Christ as God, the Jews

make specious objections to the effect that it is the throne of God that is spoken of, or that the verb 'established' is to be understood. According to the former exposition the noun אלהים would be construed with 'thy throne', the throne of God in the genitive case. The other exposition supposes a defective sentence. It is obvious that these are nothing but evasions. Anyone who reads this verse with a clear mind and without looking for an argument will not be turned aside from calling the Messiah God. There is no need to object that the noun is applied indiscriminately to angels and to judges. It is nowhere attributed simply to one person, except to God alone. Further, not to fight over a word, whose throne will be described as established for ever except God's alone? Therefore the eternity of the kingdom is evidence of divinity.

After that the sceptre of Christ's kingdom is called the sceptre of righteousness. There was some prototype of this in Solomon, though obscurely, to the extent that he showed himself a just king and one who was concerned for what was right. The righteousness of the reign of Christ is more clear, because by His Gospel, which is His spiritual sceptre, He reforms us after the righteousness of God. The same is to be understood of the purpose of His justice. Because He loves His people, He causes it to reign among them.

9. *Therefore God hath anointed thee.* This was truly said of Solomon, who was made king because God preferred him to his other brothers who were his equals in other respects being like him the sons of the king. This again refers more suitably to Christ who has adopted us as his joint-heirs, even though we were without any right of our own. He was anointed over us all, because His is without measure, whereas ours is each according to his portion as He divides it to each one of us. Then He was anointed for our sake, that we might all draw from His fulness. He himself is Christ, we are Christians depending on Him as streams on a fountain. Because Christ has received this anointing in His flesh, He is spoken of as anointed by his God. It would have been absurd to be subject to God except in respect of His human nature.

And, Thou, Lord, in the beginning hast laid the foundation of the earth, And the heavens are the works of thy hands; They shall perish; but thou continuest: And they all shall wax old as doth a garment: And as a mantle shalt thou roll them up, As a garment, and they shall be changed: But thou art the same, and thy years shall not fail (Ps. 102.26-28). But unto which of the angels hath he said at any time, Sit thou on my right hand Till I make thine enemies the footstool of thy feet? (Ps. 110.1). Are they not all ministering spirits, sent forth to do service for the sake of them that shall inherit salvation? (10-14)

10. *And Thou in the beginning.* This evidence may seem at first sight to be applied ineptly to Christ, especially in the doubtful way in which it is adduced. The matter under discussion is not the glory of God, but the proper attributes of Christ: but there is no mention here of Christ, but what is set forth is the plain majesty of God. Indeed I admit that Christ is not mentioned by name in the whole of the psalm. Nevertheless it is clear that the allusion is such that no one can doubt that it is His kingdom that is expressly commended to us. Therefore everything that is contained in this passage is to be applied to His person. Only in Christ has this been fulfilled—Thou shalt arise and have mercy upon Zion, so that the nations shall fear thy name, and all kings of the earth thy glory. Or again—When the peoples are gathered together and the kingdoms, to serve the Lord. We shall look in vain for this God, by whom the whole world is brought into one faith and worship of God, except in Christ. The other things, therefore, which are contained in this psalm are fitly applied to the person of Christ, and among other things this, that He is God everlasting, Creator of heaven and earth; that His being is eternal, free from all change, by which His majesty is exalted to the highest and He is removed from the order of all created things. What David says about the heavens perishing some explain away as a mere possible contingency, as though there was no firm statement. But what is the need for this forced explanation when we know that all creatures are subject to vanity? To what purpose is this renewal which the heavens also await with all expectancy like that of those in travail except that they are now falling to destruction? Against that the eternity of Christ which is here set forth brings special comfort to the righteous. The psalm ends by saying that they will share in this renewal, that Christ communicates Himself and His nature to His body.

13. *But unto which of the angels.* Again the writer extols the excellence of Christ by another piece of evidence to show from it how much He surpasses the angels. The reference is to Ps. 110.1, which can only be expounded with reference to Christ. Since it was unlawful for kings to usurp the priesthood (as in the case of the leprosy of Uzziah—II Chron. 26.18), and it is clear that neither David nor any other of his successors to the kingdom were ordained priest, it follows that both a new kingdom and a new priesthood are here envisaged since the same person is made king and priest. Moreover eternal priesthood belongs to Christ alone.

Right at the very beginning of the psalm He is set at the right hand of God, a manner of speaking which has the force (as I have said above) of giving Him a place second only to the Father. It is a metaphor which means that He is the Father's Representative and His chief

Lieutenant in the exercise of His power, so that the Father reigns through Him. There is no angel who holds such exalted rank; therefore Christ far excels them all.

Till I make. So long as there is never any lack of enemies of Christ who attack His kingdon, it would not seem possible to be out of danger, especially when those who try to overturn it are strong and powerful, employ varying stratagems, and try again and again in all ways with violent force. Certainly if we are to believe what our eyes see, then the kingdom of Christ seems to be on the verge of ruin. But this promise that Christ will never be dragged from His throne but that rather He will lay low all His enemies, banishes from us all fear. Two things are worth noting here: one, that the Kingdom of Christ will never know tranquillity, but that there will always be many enemies who will disturb it. Secondly, that whatever these enemies do, they will never prevail, because Christ's place at the right hand of the Father is not temporary, but to the end of the world. Therefore all those who do not submit to His rule will be trodden down and trampled under His feet. If anyone asks if Christ's kingdom will come to an end when He has trodden down His enemies, I answer that it will last for ever, but in such form as Paul has declared in I Cor. 15.25. It is there stated that God, who wills now to be known only in Christ will then show Himself as very God. Nevertheless Christ will not cease to be the Lord of men and angels, nor will there be any detraction from His honour. The answer to this question must be sought from that passage.

14. *Are they not all . . .* To make the comparison clearer, the writer now reviews the nature and condition of the angels. In calling them 'spirits', he shows their excellence, for in this they are superior to bodily creatures. But the λειτουργια which he immediately goes on to assign to them restrains them in their proper rank, as being one which is the opposite of ruling. He defines it more expressly when he says that they minister. The former description has the force of speaking of them as functionaries: but the word 'ministry' describes something humbler and more lowly. It is indeed an honourable service that God imposes on the angels: but the very fact that they serve makes it clear that they are far different from Christ who is Lord of all. If anyone objects that Christ is similarly described in many places as Servant and Minister not only of God but also of us, the answer is easy, that it is not of His nature, but of His voluntary self-emptying, as Paul testifies in Phil. 2.7. At the same time He retains His sovereignty in no way curtailed. On the other hand, the angels were created for the purpose of serving, and their whole condition is contained within this ministry. There is, therefore, a great difference, because what is natural to them

is adventitious to Christ in respect of our flesh which He took on Himself. What is necessarily theirs, He undertook of His own accord. Moreover Christ is a Servant in such a way that there is no detraction from the majesty of His rule, even in the flesh. From this passage the faithful may take great encouragement when they hear that the heavenly hosts are assigned to be their servants to see to their salvation. It is no ordinary pledge of God's love for us, that He keeps them busily working for our sake. From this there comes an extraordinary confirmation of our faith that our salvation is beyond danger, guarded as it is by such defences. God has the best possible consideration for our infirmity in giving us such helpers to resist Satan with us, and to put forth all their effort in every way to care for us. This blessing is given particularly to His elect: and therefore in order that the angels may be our helpers, we must be members of Christ. It is, of course, possible to produce scriptural evidence to the contrary and from it to argue that angels are sometimes sent forth for the sake of the reprobate. There is mention in Daniel (10.20) of the angels of the Persians and the Greeks. But I reply that such reprobates are helped by the work of the angels so that God may in this way advance the salvation of His own people. The successes and the victories which they obtained were always with reference to the Church as their proper aim. This is certain, that because we are outcasts from the kingdom of God by our sin we have no communion with the angels except through the reconciliation effected in Christ, and that this can be seen in the ladder which the patriarch Jacob saw set up in his vision.

CHAPTER TWO

Therefore we ought to give the more earnest heed to the things that were heard, lest haply we drift away from them. For if the word spoken through angels proved stedfast, and every transgression and disobedience received a just recompense of reward; how shall we escape, if we neglect so great salvation? which having at the first been spoken through the Lord, was confirmed unto us by them that heard; God also bearing witness with them, both by signs and wonders and by manifold powers, and by gifts of the Holy Ghost, according to his own will. (1-4)

1. *Therefore we ought.* He now makes clear, what he has up to this point had in view by comparing Christ to the angels, namely that he gives the highest authority to this doctrine. If the Law, which was given by angels, was not to be lightly accepted, and transgression of it was visited with heavy penalties, what will happen, he asks, to those who despise the Gospel which has the Son of God as its Author and which was confirmed by so many miracles? This is the sum of the matter; the greater the rank of Christ above the angels, the more reverence is to be paid to the Gospel than to the Law. It is the person of its Author that commends the doctrine. If it seems absurd to anyone that since the doctrine both of the Law and the Gospel is alike from God one should be preferred to the other, as if the majesty of God would be lessened by relegating the Law to second place, the answer is easy; it is that He is always to be heard with equal attention whenever He speaks; that the more fully He manifests Himself to us it is clear that the reverence for and desire to obey His revelation increases proportionately. It is not that God is less than Himself at one time rather than at another, but that we do not always equally realize His greatness. This question then arises whether the Law was not given by the hand of Christ? If so, the apostle's argument seems invalid. I reply that in this comparison he is concerned with two forms of revelation, on the one hand a hidden one, and on the other hand one that is manifest. Since in the giving of the Law Christ showed Himself only obscurely and as it were all covered up, it is no wonder that no mention is made of Him, and it is said that the Law was given by angels. He did not appear openly. On the other hand in the proclamation of the Gospel, His glory was fully revealed, so that He is rightly accounted its Author.

Lest haply we drift away from them. If you prefer, drift past them:

although there is little importance in the word, because the true
meaning can be gathered from the contrast. To 'hold to' and to 'drift
past' are antonyms. The former means to hold, the latter to pour out
like a sieve or a perforated cask whatever is poured in. I do not agree
with the view of those who take this as meaning 'to perish', as we find
in the second book of Samuel chapter 14 verse 14—'We all perish and
vanish like water.' As I have said, the antithesis is rather to be considered as one between holding and pouring. A retentive mind is like
a vessel that is well sealed: a wandering and lazy one is like a vessel
that is full of holes.

2. *Was stedfast.* That is, kept its weight, because God authenticated
its faithfulness. This is made clearer by its penalties, because no one
disregarded the Law with impunity. This firmness shows its authority;
and the further clause about the penalties is to be understood as
explanatory, because the doctrine of which God shows Himself to be
the vindicator is certainly not empty or ineffectual.

3. *if we neglect so great salvation.* It is not only the rejecting of the
Gospel, but even the neglecting of it that deserves the severest penalty
in view of the greatness of the grace which is offered in it. Therefore
he says—*so great salvation.* God wishes His gifts to be valued by us at
their proper worth. The more precious they are, the baser is our
ingratitude if they do not have their proper value for us. In accordance
with the greatness of Christ, so will be the severity of God's vengeance
on all despisers of the Gospel. Notice that the word 'salvation' is
applied here by metonymy to the doctrine, because, just as God wills
that men should be saved in no other way than through the Gospel, so
when it is neglected the whole salvation of God is rejected. For it is
the power of God unto salvation to everyone that believeth (Rom.
1.16). Whoever seeks salvation elsewhere, seeks to find it in a power
other than that of God; which is the height of madness. This eulogy
indeed has not only the force of commending the Gospel, but it is also
an outstanding support for our faith, because it testifies that the Word
is by no means empty, but contains in itself our sure salvation.

Which having at first been spoken. Now he contrasts the Son of God
as the first Herald of the Gospel with the angels, and at the same time
in anticipation removes a doubt which could have occurred to many.
They were not instructed by the mouth of Christ Himself, whom for
the most part they had never seen. Therefore if they had considered
only the men by whose guidance they were led to faith, they would
have made less of what they learned from them. For that reason the
apostle reminds us that this doctrine which has been handed down by
other hands has none the less proceeded from Christ. He says that the
disciples of Christ were those who held faithfully to the instructions

given by Christ Himself. He uses the word 'confirmed' as if to say that it was no vague rumour without an author, nor the story of witnesses of doubtful credibility, but a report which had as its authors responsible men. This passage is an indication that this epistle was not written by Paul. He is not accustomed to speak so humbly as to admit to being one of the apostles' disciples. He did not do this out of ambition, but because wicked men used this as a pretext to try to detract from his doctrine. It is clear, therefore, that it is not Paul who writes that he received the Gospel by hearing, and not by revelation.

4. *God also bearing witness.* In addition to receiving the message which they preached from the Son of God, God also set His seal on the apostles' preaching by miracles, as though by a solemn subscription. Those, therefore, who do not reverently receive the Gospel, commended as it is by such evidences, do wrong not only to the Word of God, but also to His works. To increase their importance he describes the miracles by three words. First, they are called signs, because they urge the minds of men to look for something higher than mere appearance: then, wonders, because they include what is new and unusual: and powers, because in them the Lord shows a special and extraordinary mark of His power. The word 'bearing witness' denotes the proper use of miracles, namely that they ought to serve the establishing of the Gospel. We find that almost all miracles, in whatever age they were performed, have had as their purpose to be seals of the Word of God. All the more absurd, then, is the Papist superstition by which they distort their own fictitious miracles to weaken the truth of God. The conjunction σύν, 'together with', means that we are confirmed in the faith of the Gospel by a harmony of God and men, since God's miracles as it were harmonize with the voice of men by their complementary evidences. He adds, 'by the gifts of the Holy Ghost', by which the doctrine of the Gospel has been adorned, these being the appendices. Why has God distributed the gifts of His Spirit, if not partly to be aids to proclaiming the Gospel, and partly by admiration to move the minds of men to obey? Hence Paul says that the gift of tongues was a sign to unbelievers. The phrase, 'according to His will' reminds us that those powers to which he refers cannot be ascribed to anyone except God, and that they have not been made known casually, but in His definite purpose to set the seal on the credibility of the Gospel.

For not unto angels did he subject the world to come, whereof we speak. But one hath somewhere testified, saying, What is man that thou art mindful of him? Or the son of man that thou visitest him? Thou hast made him a little lower than the angels; Thou crownedst him with glory and honour, And didst set him over the works of thy hands: Thou didst put all things in subjection under his feet. For in that he subjected all things unto him, he left nothing that is not subject to him. But now we see not yet all things subjected to him. But we behold him who hath been made a little lower than the angels, even Jesus, because of the suffering of death crowned with glory and honour, that by the grace of God he should taste death for every man. (5-9)

5. *Not unto angels.* The writer again shows by another argument that Christ is to be obeyed—namely, because the Father has conferred on Him sovereignty over the whole world, from which honour the angels are far removed. Hence it follows that there should be no angelic impediment to prevent the pre-eminence of Him who alone holds the highest place. In the first place we must examine the psalm which he quotes, because it seems ineptly applied to Christ. David is here recounting the blessings which God bestows on the human race. After considering the power of God in the heavens and in the stars, he comes to man, in whom His wonderful goodness particularly appears. He is not, therefore, speaking of one man, but of all mankind. I reply that all this is no reason why these words should not be applied to the person of Christ. I certainly admit that in the beginning man was put in possession of the world to have lordship over all the works of God; but then by his rebellion he deserved the disowning of this dominion. This is a just punishment for ingratitude on the part of a beneficiary that God, whom he refuses to acknowledge or to worship with due faith, should deprive him of the right which He had previously given him. As soon as Adam cut himself off from God by his sin, he was rightly deprived of all the good things which he had received: not in losing the use of them, but in forfeiting the legitimate right to them, after he left God. In the very use of them God has willed that there should be signs of this deprivation, as for example, the fact that wild beasts attack us fiercely, and that when they ought to be awed by our presence they are instead terrifying to us; or the fact that some can never be trained to obey and others only with difficulty; or the fact that they hurt us in various ways; or the fact that the earth does not respond to our cultivation; or that sky, air, sea and other elements are often hostile to us. Indeed even where every creature remains in a state of subjection, whatever the sons of Adam claim, it is reckoned as obtained by theft. What will they say is their own when they themselves are not of God? From this foundation so laid it is clear that that blessing of God has no application to us until what we have lost in Adam has been restored to us through Christ. It is in this sense that Paul teaches (I Tim. 4.5) that food is sanctified to us by faith: and elsewhere (Titus 1.15) he declares that nothing is clean to un-

believers because they have a defiled conscience. This is the teaching
which we found at the beginning of this epistle that Christ has been
ordained by the Father to be Heir of all things. By thus assigning the
whole inheritance to one Heir, he excludes all the rest as strangers, and
rightly so; for we are all exiles from the kingdom of God. It is not
lawful for us to seize for ourselves the food which He has intended for
His own household. But Christ by whom we are adopted into the
family also admits us into the fellowship of this right, so that we may
enjoy the whole world with God's blessing. Paul also teaches that
Abraham was made the heir of the world by faith (Rom. 4.13), because
obviously he was implanted into the body of Christ. If men are
excluded from every blessing of God until they are made partakers of
it through Christ, it follows that we lost in Adam that lordship of
which the psalm speaks, and therefore the gift of it must be renewed
to us afresh. This restoration originates from Christ as the fountain-
head. There is no doubt, then, that we ought to look to Him whenever reference is made to the primacy of man over all creatures.

What the apostle refers to expressly as 'the world to come' has
relevance here; for he takes it in the sense of the renewed world. To
make it clearer, let us imagine a twofold world—first the old one,
which was corrupted by the sin of Adam; secondly the one later in
time as it is renewed through Christ. The state of the first creation has
decayed, and has fallen with man as far as man himself. Until there is
a new restoration through Christ, this psalm has no place. Hence it is
now clear that the world to come is so described not only as that which
we hope for after the resurrection, but as that which begins from the
rise of the kingdom of Christ, and it will find its fulfilment in the final
redemption. It is not clear to me why he has suppressed the name of
David. Certainly he refers to 'one' not contemptuously but as a mark
of respect as if he were one of the prophets or the famous writers.

7. *Thou hast made him a little lower than the angels.* A new difficulty
now emerges in the exposition of these words. I have already shown
that the passage is properly to be expounded as referring to the Son
of God, but the apostle now seems to use the words in a different sense
from that in which David understood them. The phrase 'a little'
($\beta\rho\alpha\chi\acute{u}\ \tau\iota$) seems to refer to time, as meaning for a little while, and
denotes the humiliation when Christ emptied Himself, and restricts
His glory to the day of resurrection, whereas David extends it in
general to the whole life of man. I answer that it was not the purpose
of the apostle to give an accurate exposition of the words. There is
nothing improper if he looks for allusions in the words to embellish
the case he is presenting, as Paul does in Rom. 10.6 when he cites
evidence from Moses—'Who shall ascend into heaven', etc.—adding

the words about heaven and hell not as an explanation but as an embellishment. David's meaning is this: Lord Thou hast raised man to such dignity that he is very little distant from divine or angelic honour, since he is given authority over the whole world. The apostle has no intention of overthrowing this meaning or of giving it a different turn; but he only bids us consider the humiliation of Christ, which was shown forth for a short time, and then the glory with which He is crowned for ever, and he does this more by alluding to the words than by expounding what David meant. He takes 'to be mindful' and 'to visit' as meaning the same thing, except that the second is somewhat fuller, because it describes the presence of God by its results.

8. *In that he subjected all things unto him.* Someone may think that the argument runs thus—All things are subject to the man about whom David speaks; all things are not subject to the human race; therefore he is not referring to any and every man. But this argument will not stand, because even the minor premise is applicable to Christ. All things are not yet subject even to Him, as Paul shows in I Cor. 15.28. Therefore there is a different context. After he has established the fact that Christ is the Lord of all creatures without exception, he adds in turn the contrary objection: But all things do not yet obey the rule of Christ. To meet this objection he teaches that what is not seen to be completed in Christ is what immediately afterwards follows about 'glory and honour', as if he had said: Although that universal subjection is not yet clear to us, we should be content that He has conquered death and been raised to the highest honour; and what is still lacking will be fulfilled in its own time. This first clause offends some on the ground that the apostle makes a too facile inference that there is nothing not subject to Christ since David embraces all things generally. The various species which he afterwards enumerates—beasts of the field, fish of the sea and birds of the air—show no such subjection. I answer that the general statement should not be confined to these species, because David's only purpose was to show an example of that domination in the most outstanding cases, or to extend it to the very lowest forms of existence, so that we might know that nothing is ours other than by the goodness of God and our participation in Christ. Therefore we may paraphrase the passage as follows: Thou hast made all things subject, not only those which bring about eternal blessedness, but the very least of those which serve our physical needs. Whatever it be, the inferior lordship over the animals derives from the superior. The question may now be asked, why he denies that we see all things subject to Christ. You will find the answer to this question in the passage from Paul quoted above: and we touched somewhat on this in the first chapter of this epistle. Because Christ is waging a constant

war against various enemies, He has clearly no peaceful possession of His kingdom as yet. He is, of course, not compelled to wage war of necessity, but does this of His will, that His enemies are not overcome until the last day, so that He may prove us by our exercises against them.

9. *Jesus, who hath been made a little lower.* Because the meaning of the phrase βραχύ τι (a little) is ambiguous he looks rather at the matter itself as it exists in the person of Christ than at the real meaning of the words, as I have already said. He sets out for our consideration the resurrection glory which David extends to all the gifts which God in His goodness has bestowed on man. There is nothing improper in this embellishment which leaves the literal meaning unaffected.

Because of the suffering of death has the force as if it had been said that Christ has conquered death and has been raised to this glory which He has reached, as Paul says in Phil. 2.8-11: not that Christ has obtained anything for Himself privately, according to the fiction of the sophists, that He first earned eternal life for Himself, and then for us. It is only the means (so to speak) of His obtaining glory that is indicated here. Christ is crowned with glory so that every knee may bend before Him (Phil. 2.10). One may therefore reason from the final cause that all things are given into His hand.

That by the grace of God. He refers to the cause and effect of the death of Christ in case he should be thought to detract at all from His dignity. When we hear that so much good has been bestowed on us, there is no place left for contempt, because admiration of the divine goodness fills everything. When he says *for every man,* he does not just mean that He should be an example to others, in the way that Chrysostom adduces the metaphor of a physician who takes the first sip of a bitter draught, so that the sick man will not refuse to drink it. He means that Christ died for us, because He took on Himself our lot, and redeemed us from the curse of death. So there is added that this was done by the grace of God, because the ground of our redemption is that immense love of God towards us by which it happened that He did not even spare His own Son (Rom. 8.32). What Chrysostom expounds as tasting death, as if He touched it with the edge of his lips to the point where Christ emerged from death as victor, I neither refute nor disapprove, although I do not know whether the apostle intended to speak so subtly.

For it became Him, for whom are all things, and through whom are all things, in bringing many sons unto glory, to make the author of their salvation perfect through sufferings. For both He that sanctifieth and they that are sanctified are all of one: for which cause He is not ashamed to call them brethren, saying (Ps. 22.23) I will declare Thy name unto my brethren, In the midst of the congregation will I sing Thy praise. And again (Ps. 18.3), I will put my trust in him. And again (Isa. 8.18), Behold, I and my children which God hath given me. (10-13)

10. *For it became him.* The purpose here is to render Christ's humiliation as glorious to the godly. When He is said to put on our flesh, He seems to be classed with common humanity. The Cross humbles Him below all men. We must therefore beware lest Christ is made of less account because of His own accord He emptied Himself for our sake. And this is what is now done. The apostle shows that this very act ought to be honourable for the Son of God, because He is thus consecrated as the captain of our salvation. First he takes it for granted that we are to hold fast to God's decree, because just as all things are upheld by His power, so they ought to serve His glory. Therefore no better ground is to be found other than that it thus pleased God. Hence the point of the circumlocution which he uses—*for whom and by whom are all things.* He could in one word say God, but his purpose was to remind us that what God Himself decides must be deemed best, whose will and glory is the proper end of all things.

Nevertheless it does not yet seem to be established what he means that it was right for Christ to be consecrated in this way. This depends on the ordinary way which God holds to in dealing with His people. His will is for them to be exercised by various tribulations, and to spend their whole life under the Cross. Therefore it was necessary for Christ, as being the Firstborn, to be installed to His primacy by the Cross, since that is the common law and condition of all. This is the conforming of the head to the members of which Paul speaks in Rom. 8.29. This is an exceptional consolation in mitigation of the bitterness of the Cross, when the faithful hear that by their miseries and tribulations they are sanctified for glory along with Christ, and thus they see that there is a reason why they should lovingly kiss the Cross rather than shudder at it. This cannot happen without the shame of the Cross of Christ being absorbed and its glory shining forth. Who could think cheaply of what is sacred, indeed of what God sanctifies? Who could hold as ignominious that by which we are prepared for glory? Both these propositions are here made about the death of Christ.

Through whom are all things. When creation is dealt with it is attributed to the Son as His own, because all things were created by Him; but here the apostle simply means that all creatures exist or are preserved in their station by the power of God. Where we have translated 'to consecrate', others have rendered 'to make perfect'.

Since the word πλειῶσαι, which he uses, is of doubtful meaning, I think it is clear that the meaning I have posited is better suited to the context. It is noted that there is a certain solemn and rightful ordination by which the sons of God are initiated, so that they may reach their proper state and thus be separated from the rest of the world. Thus mention is thereupon made of sanctification.

11. *For both he that sanctifieth.* He shows that it was fitting that what He had said should be fulfilled in the person of Christ because of His relationship with the members. In so doing he teaches that it is an outstanding example of the divine loving-kindness that He put on our flesh. He says 'are all of one', that is that the Author of our salvation and we who share in it are of one nature (as I understand it). This is generally understood as meaning of one Adam; but some apply it to God, and this is not unreasonable. I am inclined to think that the nature described is one and the same, and I take one as being in the neuter gender, as if he were saying that we are all made of one and the same stuff. This is a strong support for our faith that we are united to the Son of God by a bond of necessity so tight that we may find in our nature the holiness which we need. It is not only that He sanctified us inasmuch as He is God, but the power of sanctification lies in our human nature, not because it has it of itself, but because God pours into our nature the whole fulness of holiness so that we may all draw from it. That is the meaning of the sentence (John 17.19), 'For their sakes I sanctify myself.' If we are sinful and unclean, the remedy is not far to seek, because it is offered to us in our flesh. If anyone prefers to take this as referring to a spiritual unity which the godly have with the Son of God differently from that which men have commonly among each other, I do not object. Nevertheless I prefer to follow the meaning that is more generally accepted, where that is not disagreeable to reason.

He is not ashamed to call them brethren. This passage is taken from Ps. 22.23. The evangelists are the chief witnesses that Christ is here introduced, or David speaking in the person of Christ, for they quote more verses from the same psalm, as, for example—'They parted my garments among them': and again, 'They gave me gall for my meat': and again, 'My God, my God, why hast thou forsaken me?' Thereafter the same truth is shown. One can see in the story of the passion the living expression of everything that is narrated here. The end of the psalm which is concerned with the calling of the Gentiles can only be applied to Christ—'All the ends of the earth shall . . . turn unto the Lord: and all the kindreds of the nations shall worship before thee. For the kingdom is the Lord's, and he is the ruler over the nations.' The fulfilment of all this is in Christ alone who enlarged the kingdom of God not over a small area (as David did), but extended it over the whole world, when formerly it has been as it were shut up within defined limits. There is no doubt, too, that it is His voice which is referred to in this passage. It says appropriately and significantly that He is not ashamed. How great a difference is there between us and Him? He greatly humbles Himself when He honours us with the name of brethren; otherwise we are not worthy to be considered less than His servants. Moreover this great honour of His towards us is made greater by the circumstances, for Christ speaks here no more as a mortal man in the form of a servant but as He who has put on immortal glory after the resurrection. This title has the force of His carrying us up with Him into heaven. Whenever we hear ourselves called brethren by Christ, let us remember that He has clothed us (so to speak) with this quality so that we may obtain along with the name of brethren eternal life and every heavenly blessing.

Moreover we must notice the functions that Christ takes on Himself, namely, those of declaring the Name of God, which began to be done in the preaching of the Gospel, and continues daily in the pastoral ministry. Hence we conclude that the Gospel is offered to us for this end, that it may lead us to the knowledge of God by which His goodness is made known among us; thence that Christ is the Author of the Gospel in whatever way it is brought among men. This is what Paul says (II Cor. 5.20) that he and others act as the ambassadors of Christ and exhort as in the Name of Christ. This ought to add not a little to our respect for the Gospel, that we must think of it as told not so much by men themselves as by Christ with their lips. At the time when He promises that He will declare the name of God to men, He has ceased to be in the world; and yet He does not discharge this office in vain. He has in very truth fulfilled it through His disciples.

In the midst of the congregation. This shows even more clearly that the proclaiming of the praises of God is contained in the Evangelical teaching, because as soon as God becomes known to us His infinite praises resound in our hearts and ears. And Christ encourages us by His example to sing them publicly, so that they may be heard by still more. It would not be enough for each one individually to be grateful to God for the benefits he has received without giving public evidence of our gratitude and thus mutually encouraging each other to the same purpose. This teaching is the very strongest encouragement to us to bring yet more fervent zeal to the praise of God, when we hear that Christ heeds our praise, and is the chief Conductor of our hymns.

13. *I will put my trust in him.* Since this sentence is found in Ps. 18.3 we must believe that it has been quoted here from that source.

Except for the fact that Paul in Rom. 15.9 applies another verse about the calling of the Gentiles to the kingdom of Christ the steps of the argument themselves sufficiently show that David is here speaking in another guise. There appears indeed in David a faint shadow of that greatness which is here so magnificently set forth. He boasts that he has been made 'the head of the nations' (v. 43), and that foreigners and strangers have come in submission at the mere fame of his name. David certainly subdued by force a few neighbouring and well-known tribes, and made them his vassals, but what was this compared with the greatness of many other kings? Where was this voluntary submission? Where were these peoples so remote that he did not know them? Where was the solemn proclamation of the grace of God among the Gentiles which the end of the psalm mentions? It is therefore Christ who is made Head over the various peoples, to whom strangers from the furthest borders of the earth submit, and who are impelled solely by hearing of him, because they are not driven to take his yoke by force of arms, but are compelled by his teaching to offer themselves in spontaneous obedience.

That kind of feigned and false profession of obedience which is here noted is seen even in the Church, because many people every day call themselves Christians, but not with their hearts. Be it, therefore, beyond argument that the psalm is fittingly applied to Christ. But what has this to do with our present purpose? It does not seem to follow that we and Christ are one so that He puts the greatest faith in God. I reply that the argument stands because if He had not been a man subject to human needs, He would have no need of such faith. Since He depends on the help of God, His condition is therefore the same as ours. We certainly do not trust God in vain or for nothing, but because, if we are destitute of His grace, we would be wretched and lost. Therefore the faith that we place in God is the token of our need. At the same time we differ from Christ, because the infirmity which is laid on us of necessity, was undergone by Him of His own accord. It ought to be no little encouragement to us to trust in God, that we have Christ as our Leader and Teacher. Who is afraid of going astray in following His footsteps? There is no danger, I say, that our faith which we have in common with Christ will be useless, when we know that He cannot be wrong.

Behold, I and my children. It is certain that Isaiah (8.18) is speaking of himself. When he was giving his people hope of freedom and found that they put no trust in his promise, so that he should not be broken by the obstinate unbelief of the people and lose hope, the Lord bids him to impress the teaching which he heralds among the few faithful people, as if he said, that even though he is rejected by the multitude, there will be a certain few who will receive it. Isaiah relies on this answer and takes heart, and testifies that he and the disciples who are given to him will always be ready to follow God.

Now we must see why the apostle applies this sentence to Christ. First, no one in his senses will deny that what is said in the same passage, namely that the Lord will be a rock of stumbling and a stone of offence to the kingdom of Israel and Judah, is fulfilled in Christ. Again, just as the release from the exile in Babylon was a kind of prelude to the glorious redemption which was brought to us and to the fathers at the hand of Christ, so also the fact that so few of the Jews used that loving-kindness of God that only a small remnant was saved was a prototype of their future blindness which brought it about that in rejecting Christ they themselves in turn were rejected by God and perished. We must observe that the promises about the renewal of the Church which are to be found in the prophets from the time when the Jews were brought back from exile refer to the kingdom of Christ, as the Lord, in bringing back the people, had in view the purpose of setting up the Church for the coming by His Son by whom at long last it would be established. This being so God addresses not only Isaiah whom He orders to seal the law and the testimony, but in his person all his ministers who in time to come will battle with people's unbelief, and above all Christ whom the Jews were to treat with greater insolence than all the prophets before Him. Now we see that those who are substituted in the place of Israel not only reject His Gospel, but attack Him Himself with fury. However much the teaching of the Gospel may be a stone of offence to the household of the Church, yet it is not God's will that it should fail; but rather He orders it to be sealed among His followers, and Christ in the name of all the doctors, as being their Head, indeed as the supreme Doctor who governs us by their teaching, proclaims that in spite of this lamentable ingratitude of the world, there will always be some who give themselves to God in obedience.

See then how this passage of Isaiah is rightly applied to Christ. From it the apostle concludes that we are one with Him because he joins Himself to us in offering Himself and us equally to God the Father. Those who obey God under the same rule of faith form one body. What could more fittingly be said in commendation of the faith than that in it we are the companions of the Son of God who encourages us by His example and shows us the way? If we follow the Word of God we know for sure that we have Christ as our Leader, just as those who turn away from obeying the Word have no part in Christ. What, I pray you, is more desirable than for us to agree with the Son of God. This agreement consists in faith: therefore we depart from it by unfaithfulness, than which there is nothing more abominable. The word 'children', which in many places means 'servants', is used here for 'disciple'.

Which God hath given. What is noted here is the first reason for obedience, namely because God has adopted us for Himself. Christ brings none to the Father unless they are given to Him by the Father. We know that this giving depends on eternal election because those whom the Father has elected to life, He gives into the care of His Son for Him to look after. This is what is said in John 6.37: 'All that which the Father giveth me shall come unto me.' Let us learn as we submit ourselves to God in the obedience of faith, that we do this because it pleases His mercy, because in no other way are we brought to Him at the hand of Christ. This teaching provides a unique support for our faith. Who will be afraid under the faith and guardianship of Christ? Who relying on such a protector will not boldly disregard all dangers? Indeed when Christ says, 'behold, I and the children', He is fulfilling in fact what elsewhere He promises (John 10.28) that He will not allow any of those He has received from the Father to perish.

Finally, let us note this, that although the world may reject the Gospel with violent disdain, yet the sheep will always recognize the voice of the Shepherd. Therefore let us not be disturbed by the ungodliness of almost all ranks and ages and nations, so long as Christ gathers His own together who are committed to His trust. If evil men hasten themselves to death by their own ungodliness the plants which God has not planted are thus rooted out (Matt. 15.13). Meantime let us know that His people are known to Him (II Tim. 2.1) and that the salvation of all of them is sealed by Him, so that none will be lost. Let us be content with this seal.

> *Since then the children are sharers in flesh and blood, he also himself in like manner partook of the same: that through death he might bring to nought him that had power of death, that is, the devil: and might deliver all them who through fear of death were all their lifetime subject to bondage.* (14-15)

14. *Since then the children.* This is the conclusion of what has gone before, and at the same time a fuller explanation than what has been shortly touched on above, of the reason why it was necessary for the Son of God to put on our flesh, so that He might share the same nature with us and by undergoing death redeem us from it. This passage is worth attention because it not only asserts the truth of the human nature of Christ, but because it also shows the fruits that come from it to us. The Son of God (he says) was made man to share the same state and nature as us. What could be said more fittingly to confirm our faith? Here is shown His priceless love towards us. The climax comes in the

fact that He put on our nature in order to submit Himself to the state of death: for God could not undergo death. Although he touches only briefly on the fruits of His death, yet this very brevity of words gives a particularly vivid and effective picture of the fact that He has freed us from a diabolical tyranny, so that we are safe from it, and in this way He has redeemed us from death, so that we need no longer be afraid of it.

Because each individual word has weight we must probe them a bit more carefully. First, the destruction of the devil about which he speaks means that he cannot have any power against us. Even if the devil still thrives, and works hard for our ruin, nevertheless his power to harm us is abolished or blunted. It is a great encouragement for us to know that we have to deal with an adversary who has no power against us. We may assume from the next phrase that this is said in respect of us: 'that he might bring to nought him that had the power of death'. The apostle means that the devil has been destroyed in so far as he had power to ruin us. His power is so called from its effect of being ruinous and deadly to us. He teaches us that not only has the tyranny of Satan been broken by the death of Christ, but that the devil himself has been so laid low as to be of no more account, as if he did not exist. He speaks of 'devil' in the singular in accordance with the usual custom of Scripture, not because there is only one, but because they all form one body which cannot be thought of without its head.

15. *All who through fear of death.* This passage expresses very well the misery of the life of those who are afraid of death, since it must of necessity be terrible to those who think of it without Christ: for in that case it appears to be nothing but a curse. Where does death come from but from God's anger against sin? Hence arises that state of servitude through the whole of life, that is the constant anxiety in which unhappy souls are imprisoned. The judgment of God always shows itself in consciousness of sin. It is from this fear that Christ has released us, by undergoing our curse, and thus taking away what was fearful in death. Although we must still meet death, let us nevertheless be calm and serene in living and dying, when we have Christ going before us. If anyone cannot set his mind at rest by disregarding death, that man should know that he has not yet gone far enough in the faith of Christ. As an overdose of fear comes from ignorance of the grace of Christ, so it is a sure sign of unfaithfulness. 'Death' here means not only the separation of soul from body, but the punishment which is imposed on us by an angry God to bring about our eternal damnation. Where a man stands accused before God, then the powers of darkness show themselves.

For verily not of angels doth he take hold, but he taketh hold of the seed of Abraham. Wherefore it behoved him in all things to be made like unto his brethren, that he might be a merciful and faithful high priest in things pertaining to God, to make propitiation for the sins of the people. For in that he himself suffered being tempted, he is able to succour them that are tempted. (16-18)

16. *For verily not of angels.* By making this comparison he extends the benefits and the honour which Christ has bestowed on us by putting on our flesh, because He never did so much for the angels. Since there was greater need for an outstanding remedy for such terrible human ruin, the Son of God willed that there be some incomparable pledge of His love towards us, such as was not shared even by the angels. The fact that He preferred us to the angels was not because of our excellence but because of our wretchedness. There is no reason for us to boast that we are superior to the angels, except in that the heavenly Father has bestowed on us greater loving-kindness because we needed it, so that the angels themselves might see from on high such great goodness shed abroad on the earth. I understand the present tense of the verb with reference to the testimony of Scripture, as though he placed before our eyes what had already been testified by the prophets.

This one passage is quite enough to confound Marcion, Manichaeus, and crazy fellows of that sort who deny that Christ was truly man begotten of human seed. If He only took the appearance of a man, having formerly appeared more often in the form of an angel, then there would have been no distinction. But because it cannot be said that Christ has ever really been an angel, clothed with the angels' nature, so it is said that He assumed the nature of man rather than that of angels. The apostle is speaking about nature, and shows that when Christ was clothed with flesh He was true man, so that there was unity of person in two natures. Further this passage gives no support to Nestorius, who invented a double Christ as if the Son of God had not been truly man, but had only lived in human flesh. We see that this is very different from the position of the apostle: his aim is to teach us that in the person of the Son of God we have found a Brother because of the fellowship of our common nature. He is therefore not content just to call Him a Man, but says that He is born of human seed. He expressly names 'the seed of Abraham', so that we may have more faith in what he says, because it is taken from Scripture.

17. *Wherefore it behoved him to be made like unto his brethren.* In the human nature of Christ there are two things to be considered, the essence of the flesh and the affections. Therefore the apostle teaches that He put on not only human flesh itself, but also all the affections

which belong to men. He shows also the fruits that come therefrom, and what is the true teaching of faith when we feel in ourselves why the Son of God took on Himself our infirmities. Without such fruits all our knowledge is cold and dead. He goes on to teach that Christ was made subject to our human passions 'that he might be a merciful and faithful high priest'. I take these words to mean 'that he might be merciful and therefore faithful'. In a priest, whose office it is to appease the anger of God, to help the unfortunate, to restore the fallen, to relieve the oppressed, the first and foremost requirement is mercy, such as a sense of fellowship creates in us. It is rare for those who are always fortunate to be touched by the struggles of others. Certainly this line of Virgil is taken from everyday human experience:

'Out of my experience of misfortune I learn to help the needy.'

It was not because the Son of God needed to experience it to become accustomed to the emotion of mercy, but because He could not persuade us that He is kind and ready to help us, unless He had been tested by our misfortunes: and this like other things He has given us. Whenever, therefore, all kinds of evils press upon us, let this be our immediate consolation, that nothing befalls us which the Son of God has not experienced Himself, so that He can sympathize with us; and let us not doubt that He is in it with us as if He were distressed along with us.

Faithful means true and just: it is the opposite of a pretender or one who does not do his duty. His experience of our misfortune turns Christ to such compassion that He is moved to implore the help of God for us. What more? To make atonement for our sins He has put on our nature so that we may have the price or our reconciliation in our own flesh, so that, indeed, He might lead us with Himself into God's holy of holies by virtue of our common nature. By the phrase *things pertaining to God* (τὰ πρὸς τὸν Θεόν) he means the things that have the purpose of reconciling men to God. Since freedom of faith is the first way of approach to God, we need a Mediator who will remove all doubt.

18. *In that he himself suffered.* He is tried, he says, by our evils, and is therefore ready to bring us help. *Temptation* here means simply experience or testing, and *to be able* means to be fit, or inclined, or suitable.

CHAPTER THREE

Wherefore, holy brethren, partakers of a heavenly calling, consider the Apostle and High Priest of our confession, even Jesus; who was faithful to him that appointed him, as also was Moses in all his house. For he hath been counted worthy of more glory than Moses, by so much as he that built the house hath more honour than the house. For every house is builded by some one: but he that built all things is God. And Moses indeed was faithful in all his house as a servant, for a testimony of those things which were afterward to be spoken: but Christ as a son, over his house: whose house are we, if we hold fast our boldness and the glorying of our hope firm unto the end. (1-6)

1. *Wherefore holy brethren.* He concludes the doctrine already discussed with the profitable exhortation that the Jews should give attention to recognizing the nature and the greatness of Christ. Because he has earlier briefly compared Him with Moses and Aaron by describing Him as Doctor and Priest, he now brings both descriptions together. He adorns Him with double honours as He sustains a double character (*duplicem sustinet personam*) in the Church of God. Moses performed the office of prophet and doctor, Aaron that of priest: but both duties are laid on Christ. If, then, we want to look up at Him properly, we must consider His nature: He must be endued with His own power, in case we catch hold of an empty shadow instead of Him. The verb 'consider' at the beginning is of importance. It means that He is to be given particular attention, because He cannot be disregarded with impunity, and at the same time it means that true knowledge of Christ is sufficient to dispel the darkness of every error. In order to give them greater encouragement for this study, he reminds them of their calling: as if he were saying—God has bestowed no ordinary grace on you when He called you into His kingdom. It now remains for you to have your eyes directed at Christ who is the Guide of your way. The calling of the saints can only be confirmed if they turn wholly to Christ. So we ought not to imagine that this is said about the Jews alone, but that what is here propounded is a general doctrine applicable to all who wish to attain to the kingdom of God, that they should look steadily at Christ, both because He is the only Master of our faith and because He has ratified it by His sacrifice. 'Confession' is taken here as meaning 'faith', as though he were saying that the faith which we profess is vain and empty unless it is directed to Christ.

2. *Who was faithful.* This is a commendation of the apostolate of Christ, so that the faithful may safely find rest in Him. He commends it in a twofold context, because the Father has set Him over us as our Teacher, and because Christ Himself has faithfully carried out the task imposed on Him. These two things are always necessary to provide a doctrine with authority. God only is to be heard, as all Scripture declares. So Christ bears witness (John 7.16) that the doctrine which He sets forth is not His own but the Father's. Elsewhere (Luke 9.48) He says, 'Whosoever shall receive me, receiveth him that sent me.' We are speaking of Christ in so far as He has put on our flesh, and is thus the Servant of the Father for the carrying out of His commands. To the calling of God there is added its faithful and unadulterated ministration in Christ, such as is required in all true ministers so that they may gain trust in the Church. If both these requirements are found in Christ, He cannot be disregarded without despising God in Him.

As also was Moses. So as not to seem to make Christ equal to Moses, he shows how much more excellent He is; and he demonstrates this by two arguments—that Moses presided over the Church, while being still a part and a member of it; but Christ is the architect and superior to the whole building: and secondly, in ruling others Moses was at the same time under authority, as a servant; but Christ because He is the Son holds supreme power. It is a frequent and familiar metaphor of Scripture to call the Church the house of God (I Tim. 3.15). Because it is made up of the faithful they are called individually living stones (I Pet. 2.5), or sometimes the vessels with which the house is equipped (II Tim. 2.20). There is no one person so eminent as not to be a member and to be included in the whole body. God alone as the architect is to be placed over His own work; and God lives in Christ so that whatever is said of God applies to Him.

If anyone objects that Christ is also part of the building, because He is the Foundation, because He is our Brother, because He holds fellowship with us, or that He is not the Architect because He Himself was made by God, there is a ready answer, namely that our faith is so founded on Him that He nonetheless governs us: that He is our Brother in such a way that He is also our Lord: that He was so made by God as to His humanity that as eternal God He gives life to all things and restores all things by His Spirit. Scripture uses various metaphors to express the grace of Christ towards us, but there is none which detracts from His honour of which the apostle is now speaking. The position here is that all men are to be put into their proper place, because they ought to be subject to the Head, and that Christ alone is exempt from this condition because He is the Head.

If a further objection is made that Moses is no less a master-builder than Paul who boasts of this title, I reply that this name is given to the prophets and teachers, but incorrectly, since they are merely instruments and dead ones at that, unless God inspires efficacy in them from heaven; and further, that they toil to build up the Church so that they themselves may enter the building. But the case of Christ is different, for He has always built the Church by the power of His own Spirit, and moreover He stands out above the common herd, seeing that He is the true Temple of God and at the same time the God who dwells in it.

4. *But he that built all things.* Although these words can be extended to the creation of the whole world, I restrict them to our present instance, that we are to understand that nothing is done in the Church that ought not to be taken as agreeable to the power of God. It is He alone who founded the Church by His own hand (Ps. 87.5). Speaking of Christ Paul says (Eph. 4.16) that He is the Head 'from whom all the body fitly framed and knit together through that which every joint supplieth, according to the working in due measure of each several part, maketh increase'. He often declares that the success of his ministry is the work of God. If we think accurately, whatever human works God uses for the building of His Church, He alone accomplishes everything. The instrument in no way detracts from the craftsman.

5. *And Moses indeed was faithful.* The second distinction is that there was given to Moses a teaching to which he along with everyone else was subject. But Christ, although He put on the form of a Servant, is the Master and Lord, to whom all men ought to be subject. He has been made the Heir of all things as we saw in chapter 1.2.

For a testimony of those things which were afterward to be spoken. This I explain simply, that while Moses is the herald of that doctrine which was to be proclaimed to the people of old as their time demanded, at the same time he bore testimony to the Gospel although it was not yet ripe for proclamation. It is certainly the case that the purpose and fulfilment of the Law is the perfection of wisdom which is contained in the Gospel. The future tense of the participle seems to demand this explanation. To sum up, Moses faithfully handed down to the people what God had commanded him; but a measure was laid down for him which he could not lawfully exceed. God of old spoke in many different ways through the prophets, so as to postpone the complete revelation of the Gospel until the fulness of the time.

6. *Whose house are we.* Just as when Paul introduced himself as the appointed apostle to the Gentiles he adds to their number the Romans to whom he is writing, so as to win their trust (Rom. 1.6), so now the author of this epistle exhorts the Jews, who had already given themselves to Christ to persevere in the faith so as to be numbered in

the household of God. He had earlier said that the house of God was subject to the rule of Christ. In accordance with this sentence he adds the reminder that they will have a place in the family of God if they obey Christ. Since they have now begun to embrace the Gospel, he adds the condition—*if they hold fast in their faith.* I take the word 'hope' as meaning 'faith'; indeed hope is reinforcing its power. Thus we adduce that those who assent to the Gospel in doubt like folk who are uncertain have little or no faith. There can be no faith without that settled peace of mind from which comes the carefree confidence of glorying. These are the two effects of faith that are ever present, namely, boldness and glorying. As we have said in the commentary on Rom. 5 and Eph. 3.

The whole teaching of the Papists is against this, and this very fact, even if it had no other evil content, destroys the Church of God rather than builds it. The certainty, by which alone, according to the apostle's teaching, we are consecrated as temples to God, is not only obscured by their fancies but is clearly destroyed by their presumption. What stability of confidence can there be when men do not know what they are to believe? That monstrosity of implicit faith which they invent is nothing but a licence to err. This passage reminds us that we must always go forward right to the day of death, because the whole of life is like a race.

Wherefore even as the Holy Ghost saith (Ps. 95.8-11), *Today if ye will hear his voice, Harden not your hearts, as in the provocation. Like as in the day of temptation in the wilderness, Wherewith your fathers tempted me by proving me, And saw my works forty years. Wherefore I was displeased with this generation, And said, They do always err in their heart: But they did not know my ways: As I swore in my wrath, They shall not enter into my rest. Take heed, brethren, lest haply there shall be in any one of you an evil heart of unbelief, in falling away from the living God: But exhort one another day by day, so long as it is called Today; lest any one of you be hardened by the deceitfulness of sin.*
(7-13)

He continues in his exhortation that they should obey Christ when he speaks, and to give this more weight, he supports it with the evidence of David. Since they were to be more sharply goaded, it was better for the sake of avoiding offence to introduce a different person. If he had simply reproached them with the unbelief of their fathers he would have been heard less willingly: but in introducing David the matter is less distasteful. The sum of it is this: just as from the beginning God willed that His voice should be obeyed, but could not bear obstinacy without inflicting severe punishment on it, so today, if we do not show ourselves amenable to Him, He will impose no lighter penalties on our stubbornness. The utterance is suspended until we come to the part where he says, 'Take heed, brethren, lest haply there shall be in any of you,' etc. To make the context run better, the rest should be regarded in parenthesis. We shall now follow the verses in order.

As the Holy Ghost saith. This is far more effective in touching the heart than to quote the name of David. It is useful to accustom oneself to this form of speaking, so that we remember that it is the words of God and not of men which are found in the books of the prophets. Moreover, since this verse, *Today if ye will hear his voice* is a part of the preceding verse, some have rendered it not inappropriately as *Would that ye heard.* It is certain that when David called the Jews God's people and sheep he immediately inferred that they would thereby hear the voice of God. In that passage he instructs those whom he calls on to sing praises to God and to celebrate His loving-kindness, that obedience is the especial worship that He requires, even in preference to all sacrifices. The first priority is to submit to the Word of God. Then follows *harden not your hearts* to indicate that our rebellion against God flows from no other source than from our wilful depravity in hindering the entrance of God's grace. We have by nature a heart of stone, and this hardness is inborn in us from birth, and only God can soften and correct it. If we reject the Voice of God, we do so by our own obstinacy and not by any outside influence: and everyone is his own witness to the truth of this fact. Thus the Spirit rightly accuses all unbelievers of resisting God, and of being masters and authors of stubbornness in themselves, so that they cannot put the blame on to anyone else. From this there is drawn the wrong conclusion that there is in us a power which is free to turn our own hearts to the service of God. Rather the opposite is true, that men must always of necessity harden their hearts, until another heart is given from heaven. As we are prone to evil, so we shall never cease to resist God, until we are tamed and subdued by His hand.

8. *As in the provocation.* It was useful for a double reason for them to be reminded of the disobedience of their fathers. When they were foolishly puffed up with the glory of their race, they often used to imitate the vices of their forefathers as if they were virtues, and defended themselves by their example. Then when they heard that their fathers had been so disobedient to God, they recognized more readily that this instruction was not superfluous. Although both reasons had force in the time of the apostle he readily puts what was earlier said by David to his own use, so that those to whom he speaks will not be too drawn to the fathers. From this one can adduce the general principle

of how far we are to defer to the authority of the fathers so as not to be
led away from the one God. If ever any fathers deserved honour, the
Jews certainly were chief among all others. Yet David specifically tells
their sons to take care not to be like them. I have no doubt that this
refers to the history that is related in Exod. 17. David uses two names
which Moses tells us were with advantage given to a place: מריבה
which means strife and imitation: and מסה which means temptation.
They tempted God by denying that He was in the midst of them,
because they were in trouble for want of water, and they provoked
Him by striving with Moses. Although they had given very many
examples of their unbelief, David chooses this one particularly because
it was memorable above all the others: further, because in order of
time it followed for the most part all the others, as is seen best in the
fourth book of Moses, where the continual series of their many
temptations is contained from chapter 10 and continued right up to
chapter 20. This circumstance makes for a great increase in the enor-
mity of their crimes. How great is their ingratitude in that they so
often experienced the power of God, and yet still so shamelessly
disputed with Him and renounced all faith in Him! He has quoted one
example to stand for many. The words *of temptation* are taken in a bad
sense as meaning to provoke arrogantly and by stubbornness, as we
say in French, *défier comme en dépitant*. Although God had often and
often brought them help, they forgot it all, and asked mockingly
where was His power.

9. *By proving me.* This phrase is to be explained as follows—When
they had proved me and seen my works. The fact that they had been
instructed by so many trials and had made so little progress increases
the charge of impiety. It was incredible stupidity and folly on their
part that they thought nothing of the power of God, though it had
been so fully established. The bit about *forty years* that follows is
connected in the psalm with the verses that follow. We know that
when they quote evidence the apostles pay more attention to the gist
of the matter than to the exact meaning of the words. Certainly God
is lamenting that the people were a burden to Him for forty years
because so many benefits were of no avail in teaching them. Although
God faithfully did good to the unworthy, they did not cease to rise up
against Him. Hence his continual indignation, as if He said—they
have not provoked Me just once or for a short time, but with constant
sinning through the course of forty years. *Generation* means age, or
the men of one span of years.

10. *And I said.* This is the sentence of God, by which He declares
that they have lost a sound mind, and He adds the reason—*because they
did not know my ways.* In short, He considers them without hope.

because they lack sense and reason. Here He assumes the character of a man who after a long series of trials says that he acknowledges persistent madness. He says that they are always winning because there appears to be no hope of recovery.

11. *As I sware.* It was the punishment of their madness that they were deprived of their promised rest. Further God calls the land where they ought to have fixed their settlement His rest. They were sojourners in Egypt: they wandered through the wilderness: but the land of Canaan was to be their perpetual inheritance according to the promise. It is in respect of the promise that God calls the rest His, because we have no fixed dwelling except when we are settled by His hand. Their right of undisputed possession was rooted in what God had said to Abraham. To thy seed I will give this land (Gen. 12.7). The fact of God's oath expresses the more clearly and forcefully the monstrosity of their evil: it is a sign of anger still further kindled.

If they shall enter. This is the form of oath in which some further clause is to be supplied, like an imprecation of something similar when men speak. When God Himself speaks it is as if He said—If this is not so, let me not be thought true, or let no faith be put in me hereafter. This defective form of speech encourages fear and awe, so that we shall not jump readily into swearing in the way that many people have the habit of uttering horrible curses. As far as the present passage is concerned we ought not to think that it was by God's oath that they were first dispossessed of entry into the Land when they tempted Him at Rephidim. They had been shut out much earlier from the time when they heard the report of the spies and declined to advance any further. God does not here attribute their dispossession of the Land to the temptation as a first cause. He indicates that they could not be brought back to a sound mind by any chastisement, but that they kept piling new offences on top of the earlier ones. He shows that they were most deserving of being severely punished, because they never ceased to increase His anger more and more by their various sins: as though He said: This is the generation to whom I have refused possession of the Promised Land, and which showed its obstinate madness by countless sins throughout all the succeeding forty years.

12. *Take heed, brethren, lest haply.* I have preferred to keep what the apostle literally says, rather than to derive a paraphrase about *an evil heart of unbelief*, by which he means that unbelief would be linked with crookedness and badness if they had experienced Christ, and then resiled from His faith. He is addressing those who were imbued with the rudiments of Christianity. He therefore immediately adds *in falling away*, for the charge of desertion includes that of treachery. He

also points out that the remedy for not falling into this wickedness is to exhort one another. As by nature we are prone to fall into evil, we have need of various helps to help us in the fear of God. Unless our faith is repeatedly encouraged, it lies dormant; unless it is warmed, it grows cold; unless it is aroused, it gets numb. He therefore wishes them to stimulate one another by mutual encouragement, so that Satan will not steal into their hearts and by his falsehoods lead them away from God. This sequence of thought should be noted. It is not at the first attack that we rush at once into this insanity of struggling against God, but Satan attacks us bit by bit with indirect guiles until he holds us entangled in his impostures. Then we are blinded and we break out into open rebellion. We must therefore meet this danger early. It is a danger which threatens everyone, because there is nothing easier than to be deceived: and from deception there grows at length hardness of heart. From this we see how necessary it is for us to be urged on by the continual stimulus of encouragement. The apostle does not just throw out a general instruction to everyone to take care of themselves: but he desires them to be so concerned for the safety of each member, that they do not allow any of those who have once been called to perish because of their negligence. He who feels that he must stand watch for the safety of the whole flock so that he neglects no single sheep thereby performs the office of the good shepherd.

13. *So long as it is called.* He now applies what David says more particularly to its own purpose. He tells us that the word *today* which is mentioned in the psalm ought not to be confined to the age of David, but that it embraces all time in which God accosts us. Therefore as often and as long as he opens his holy mouth to teach us, this sentence would come to mind, 'Today if ye will hear his voice'. In the same way Paul teaches us that, when the Gospel is preached to us, that is the accepted time in which God hears, and the day of salvation in which He helps us. Further, we should take advantage of this opportunity, because if we allow it to pass through our folly we shall afterwards deplore its loss in vain: as Christ says (John 12.35), 'Walk while ye have the light; the night will shortly come.' The particle *so long as* implies that the opportunity will not always be there if we have been slow to follow when God was calling us. God is now knocking at our door. If we do not open to Him, it will come about that in turn He will close the door of His kingdom to us. Then those who despise the grace offered today will find that their groans are too late. Therefore, since we do not know whether it is God's will to continue His call into tomorrow, let us not put off. He calls today: let us answer as soon as possible. There is no faith except where there is such quickness to obey.

*For we are become partakers of Christ, if we hold fast the beginning of
our confidence firm unto the end: while it is said (Ps. 98.5), Today if ye
shall hear his voice Harden not your hearts, as in the provocation.
For who, when they heard, did provoke? nay, did not all they that came
out of Egypt by Moses? And with whom was he displeased forty years?
was it not with them that sinned, whose carcases fell in the wilderness?
And to whom swore he that they should not enter into his rest, but to
them that were disobedient? And we see that they were not able to enter
in because of unbelief.* (14-19)

14. *We are become partakers.* He praises them for having begun well.
But in case they indulge themselves with the indifference of the flesh
on the pretext of the grace which they have obtained, he says that there
is need for perseverance. Most people only taste the Gospel, as though
they have reached the summit, and do not think of progress. Thus it
happens they not only desist in the middle of their race, or even at the
very start, but they turn their course in another direction. There is
indeed a superficial objection—What further do we want when we
have found Christ? But if He is possessed by faith, we must stand
firm in it, so that we may remain in perpetual possession of it. Christ
has given Himself to us to enjoy on this condition, that we preserve
to the moment of death this great blessing by the same faith by which
we were brought to partake of Him. Therefore he says 'beginning',
meaning that faith is only commencing. Since subsistence sometimes
means 'confidence', it can be taken here in that sense. I do not dislike
the noun *subsistence* which some others have read here, although I
expound it a little differently. They think that faith is thus spoken of,
because everything that man has without it is nothing but vanity: but
I accept it because we rest on faith as there is no other support on
which it is possible to reply. The adjective *firm* fits with this exposition.
We shall be stable and free from the danger of wavering provided we
are on the foundation of faith. The sum of it all is, therefore, this, that
faith whose beginnings only are fixed in us goes on firmly and constantly to the end.

15. *While it is said.* He indicates that as long as we live the opportunity of advancing never ceases, because God is calling us every day.
Since faith answers the proclamation of the Gospel, just as the practice
of preaching is continuous through the whole course of life, so it is to
be completed in the increase of faith. The phrase ἐν τῷ λέγεσθαι has
the force of saying, Since God never makes an end of speaking, it is
not enough for us to embrace His teaching with a ready mind, unless
we show that we are obedient to Him with the same teachableness
tomorrow, and every day.

16. *Who, when they heard.* David speaks of the fathers as though their whole generation were unbelievers; but it is clear that there were to be found among the wicked ones some who truly feared God. The apostle records this to tone down what David said too sharply, so that we may know that the Word is proclaimed to everyone to this end, that everyone may obey it with common consent, and that unbelief is deservedly condemned in the whole people when the body is torn and mutilated by a rebellion of the majority.

When he says that some *provoked*, when they were by far the greater majority, he does this not just to avoid giving offence, but to encourage the Jews to follow the example of those who believed. It is like saying, Just as God forbids you to follow the unbelief of the fathers, so He sets before you other fathers, whose faith should be an example. Thus he softens what could otherwise appear on the face of it to be too harsh, if they had been told to repudiate the fathers altogether.

To come out of Egypt by Moses means by the hand of Moses, because he was the agent of their liberation. There is an implied comparison of the benefit which God bestowed on them through Moses with that of participation in Christ, of which he has previously spoken.

17. *With whom he was displeased.* He indicates that God has never been angry with His people without just cause, as Paul says in I Corinthians 10.5 and 6. Whatever punishments we read of as inflicted on the ancient people, we shall find the same number of the most grievous sins which provoked the vengeance of God; yet we must always return to this point, that faithlessness is the chief of all the evils. Although he recounts this towards the end, he understands it to be the first cause of their being cursed. Certainly from the very moment of their first unbelief, they never stopped committing one sin after another, and so continually brought new scourges on themselves. Those same people who through their distrust rejected the possession of the land that was offered to them, continued in their stubbornness, sometimes by covetousness, sometimes by complaining, sometimes by prostitution, sometimes by defiling themselves with pagan superstitions, so that their wickedness became more clearly attested. That unbelief, therefore, which they had shown from the beginning, prevented them from enjoying the blessing of God, because their contempt for His Word was always inciting them to sin. Just as at first by their unbelief they earned God's deprivation of their promised rest, so whatever sins they later committed came from the same source.

The next question is whether Moses and Aaron and their like are included in this number. I reply that the apostle is speaking of the whole body rather than of individual members. Certainly there were very many good men who were either not involved in the general apostasy, or soon came to their senses. Indeed Moses' faith was once shaken, but only once and only momentarily. There is a synedoche in the words of the apostle, which is frequently used whenever the subject is about a multitude or a body of people.

CHAPTER FOUR

Let us fear therefore, lest haply, a promise being left of entering into his rest, any one of you should seem to have come short of it. For indeed we have had good tidings preached unto us, even as also they: but the word of hearing did not profit them, because they were not united by faith with them that heard. (1-2)

1. *Let us fear, therefore.* He concludes that it is to be feared that the Jews to whom he writes might be deprived of the blessing offered to them. He goes on to say further, *lest anyone*, indicating that he has it in mind to bring them all to the one God. As it is the duty of the Good Shepherd in caring for the whole flock to watch over the individual sheep in case any one is utterly lost, so likewise we ought also to be so disposed one towards another, that each of us fears for his neighbours as much as for himself. This fear is commended to us, not as something that drives away the assurance of faith, but as something that inspires us with concern that we do not grow slack with carelessness. We are to be afraid not because we ought to tremble or be in despair as if we were uncertain of the final outcome, but in case we desert the grace of God. When he says, *lest a promise being left we come short of it*, he means that no one comes short unless he has already renounced the promise by rejecting the grace. Indeed God is so far from repenting of His loving-kindness, that He continues to present us with His gifts except when we despise His calling. The inference therefore means that we are instructed in humility and watchfulness by the fall of others, as Paul says (Rom. 11.20), 'By their unbelief they were broken off: be not high-minded, but fear.'

2. *For we have.* He reminds us that it is the same doctrine by which God invites us to Himself today as that which He once delivered to our fathers. Why does he say this? So that we may know that the calling of God will no more profit us than it did them unless we make it firm by our faith. He makes this addition by way of concession, that the Gospel is proclaimed to us. But in case we make vain boasts, he quickly qualifies it by saying that the unbelievers whom God has formerly favoured by giving them a share in so many benefits will enjoy no fruit from them. Indeed we ourselves will have no share in His blessing unless we receive it by faith. He repeats the word 'hearing' a second time, so that we may know that hearing is useless, even if the word is directed to us, unless it is accompanied by faith.

Here note must be taken of the relation between the Word and faith. It is such that faith cannot be separated from the Word. On the other hand the Word separated from faith is ineffectual. It is not that the efficacy of the Word depends on us: for even if the whole world were false, He who cannot lie would not cease to be true. It is that the Word brings its power to bear on us only when faith gives it entrance. It is the power of God unto salvation, but only to those who believe (Rom. 1.16). There is revealed in it the righteousness of God, but it is from faith to faith. Thus it is that the Word of God is continually effective and saving to men if it is thought of in itself and by its own nature; but its fruit will only be enjoyed by those who believe.

With regard to my earlier statement, when I said that where the Word is lacking faith no more exists, and whoever tries to effect this divorce at once extinguishes faith and reduces it to nothing, this is something worth looking at. From this it appears that faith is not possible except in the sons of God to whom alone is offered the promise of adoption. What sort of faith do devils have, to whom no salvation is promised? What sort of faith do all the heathen have, who ignore the Word? Hearing must therefore always precede faith, and for this reason also that we know that it is God who speaks and not men.

For we which have believed do enter into that rest, even as he hath said (Ps. 95.11): As I sware in my wrath They shall not enter into my rest: although the works were finished from the foundation of the world. For he hath said somewhere (Gen. 2.2: Deut. 5.14) of the seventh day in this wise, And God rested on the seventh day from all his works: and in this place again (Ps. 95.11): They shall not enter into my rest. Seeing therefore it remaineth that some should enter thereinto, and they to whom the good tidings were before preached failed to enter in because of disobedience, he again defineth a certain day, saying in David, after so long a time (as it hath been said (above 3.7)): Today if ye shall hear his voice, Harden not your hearts. For if Joshua had given them rest, he would not have spoken afterward of another day. There remaineth therefore a sabbath rest for the people of God. For he that is entered into his rest hath himself also rested from his works, as God did from his. (3-10)

He now begins to ornament the passage which he had quoted from David. So far he has followed it according to the letter, as they say: that is, in its literal meaning. Now he amplifies it with embellishments. He now plays upon the words of David more than he expounds them. This kind of working over (ἐπεξεργασία) is found in St Paul in Rom. 10.6 in dealing with the testimony of Moses: 'Say not, who shall ascend into heaven?' It is not absurd either for Scripture to be accommodated to present use to illustrate (so to speak) typographically what is said there more simply. The gist of all this comes to the fact that what God threatens in the psalm about the loss of His rest applies to us also, just as He invites us also today to rest of some kind. The main difficulty of this passage comes from its being violently twisted by many commentators; whereas the apostle's sole purpose in claiming some sort of rest for us is to whet our desire for it and at the same time to move us with fear that we may be shut out from it by our unbelief. Meantime he teaches us that that rest to which an entrance now opens before us is of far more value than that of the land of Canaan. But let us come to the verses one by one.

3. *We which have believed do enter.* The argument is one from the opposite. It is unbelief alone that shuts us out; therefore the way in lies open to faith. We must keep in mind what has already been expounded, that in His wrath against the unbelievers God has sworn that they will not share in the promised blessing. Therefore those who are not shut out by unbelief enter in, provided God invites them. By speaking in the first person He draws them to Himself with greater sweetness, distinguishing them from strangers.

Although the works were finished. In order to define the nature of our rest, he now recalls us to the description given by Moses that immediately after the creation of the world God rested from His works. He infers from this that the true rest of the faithful which lasts to all eternity is to conform to that of God. As it is the highest human blessedness to be united with God, so that ought also to be man's ultimate purpose, to which all his plans and actions should be directed. He proves this from the fact that a long time after, God, who is said to have rested, denies His rest to those who do not believe; and there would be no purpose in His doing this unless it was His will for the faithful to have rest according to His own example. Hence he says, *it remaineth that some should enter thereinto.* If the punishment of the unbelievers is not to enter in, as has been said, the way in lies open to those who believe.

What follows immediately after this is a little more difficult, namely, that another today is appointed for us in the psalm, because those who lived in earlier days have been shut out. The words of David do not seem to bear any such meaning. They mean simply this, that God repaid the faithlessness of the people by removing from them the possession of the land. I reply that the inference is valid. What was taken away from them is offered to us, since the Holy Spirit warns us that we must not commit this sin by our own fault, so as to incur the same form of punishment. What follows then? If nothing is promised to us today, what is the point of the warning, 'See that what happened to your fathers does not happen to you'? The apostle rightly says that, because the unbelief of the fathers left them empty-handed and deprived of their possession, the promise is renewed to their sons, so that they may obtain what the others had lost.

8. *For if Joshua had given them rest.* He does not mean to deny that by rest David understands the land of Canaan, into which Joshua led the people. But he means that this is not the final rest to which the faithful aspire, and which is our common possession with the faithful of that age. It is certain that they looked higher than that earthly land; indeed the land of Canaan was only thought of as of value for the reason that it was the type and the symbol of our spiritual inheritance. Therefore when they had obtained possession of it, they ought not to have rested, as if they had arrived at the answer to all their prayers, but rather to have thought on the spiritual meaning it contained. Those to whom David addressed the psalm enjoyed possession of the land, but they were encouraged to look for a better rest.

We see, then, that the land of Canaan was a rest, but one of shadow, beyond which believers ought to progress. In this sense the apostle says that Joshua did not give them rest, because under his leadership the people entered the promised land in order to strive on towards heaven with greater zeal. From this one can readily infer the sort of difference there is between them and us. Although the same goal is set before both, they have in addition the outward type by which to be guided; we do not have it, nor do we need it, since the whole matter is set plainly before our eyes. Even if our salvation is so far placed in hope, yet, having regard to our doctrine, it leads us straight to heaven. Christ does not stretch out His hand to us to lead us round by figures, but to take us from the world and raise us to heaven. In separating the shadow from the truth, the apostle does it for this reason, that his concern was with the Jews, who stuck too much to the externals. He concludes by saying that there remains a rest for the people of God; that is, a spiritual rest to which God daily invites us.

10. *For he that is entered into his rest.* This is a definition of the perpetual Sabbath, in which the highest human happiness consists, where there is a likeness between men and God in which they are united with Him. Whatever the philosophers have argued about the *summum bonum* was stupid and fruitless, because they confined man within himself, when the need was for us to go outside of ourselves to find happiness. The highest human good is therefore simply union with God. We attain it when we are brought into conformity with His likeness.

The apostle further says that this conformation happens if we rest from our works: whence it follows that man is blessed by denying himself. What does ceasing from our works mean but the mortification of the flesh, when a man renounces himself in order to live to God? This is where we must always make a beginning when we speak of the rule of pious and holy living, that a man should be in a sense dead to allow God to live in him; that he should be cut off from his own works so as to give room for God to act. It must be admitted that a life is properly formed when and only when it is yielded to God. Yet because of our native wickedness this never happens until we cease from our own works. Such, I say, is the opposition between the rule of God and our disposition that He cannot work in us except when we are at rest. Because the completion of this rest is never attained in this life, we must always be striving towards it. Thus believers enter in, but on condition that they continuously run and press on.

I have no doubt that the apostle refers to the works particular to the Sabbath in order to recall the Jews from the purely external observance of it. The annulment of it cannot be understood except by the recognition of its spiritual purpose. He deals with two things at the same time: by commending the excellence of grace he encourages us to accept it by faith, and meantime incidentally shows us what the true pattern of the Sabbath is, in case the Jews in their perverseness stick to the external ceremonies. He does not expressly speak of its annulment, because this is not his specific subject: but in teaching them to look at its observance in another way, he thus gradually weans them away from their superstitious view. Whoever believes that the purpose of the commandment is something other than an external rest or an earthly worship soon and easily sees by looking at Christ that the ceremonial usage has been abolished by His coming. The shadows flee away at the sight of the substance. Therefore our first concern must always be to teach that Christ is the end of the Law.

Let us therefore give diligence to enter into that rest, that no man fall after the same example of disobedience. For the word of God is living and active, and sharper than any two-edged sword, and piercing even to the dividing of soul and spirit, of both joints and marrow, and quick to discern the thoughts and intents of the heart. And there is no creature that is not manifest in his sight: but all things are naked and laid open before the eyes of him with whom we have to do. (11-13)

Having shown the goal to which we ought to strive, he now exhorts us to follow along the way to it, which we do when we accustom ourselves to self-denial. As he compares entering into rest to the right course, he refers to falling as the opposite, and thus he carries on the metaphor in both clauses. At the same time he alludes to the story which he relates from Moses (Num. 26.65) about those who fell in the

wilderness because they rebelled against God. He says τῷ αὐτῷ ὑποδεί-
γματι (after the same example), meaning that the punishment of unbelief
and obstinacy is there set before us as if a picture, and there is no doubt
that the same fate awaits us if a similar lack of faith is found in us. Thus
he uses *fall* in the sense of *perish*, or, to put it more plainly, not in the
sense of sin, but of punishment. The metaphor applies to the earlier
word 'entering' as well as to the tragic overthrow of the fathers, by
whose example He intended to terrify the Jews.

12. *The word of God is living, etc.* Everything that he says here about
the efficacy of the Word is with the purpose that they should know
that they cannot disregard it with impunity. It is as though he were
saying—Whenever the Lord accosts us by His Word, He is dealing
seriously with us to affect all our inner senses. There is therefore no
part of our soul which should not be influenced. But now before we
go any further, we must consider whether the apostle is speaking
generally about the Word, or whether he is making particular reference
to those who believe. It is agreed that the Word of God is not equally
efficacious in everyone. It applies its power to the elect to humble
them by a true recognition of what they are so that they flee to the
grace of Christ. This can never happen unless the Word penetrates to
the depths of the heart. Hypocrisy, which has wondrous and infinitely
tortuous dens in human hearts, must be beaten out. We must not be
gently pricked or scratched, but we must be deeply wounded, so that
we are laid low by the sense of eternal death and learn to die to ourselves. We shall never be renewed in our whole mind (as Paul requires
—Eph. 4.23) until our old man has been slain by the edge of this sword
of the Spirit. That is why Paul says in another place (Phil. 2.17) that
those who believe are offered as a sacrifice to God, because they cannot
be brought back into obedience to God except by the death of their
own wills, and they cannot see the light of divine wisdom, except by
the destruction of their carnal wisdom. This sort of thing does not
apply in the case of unbelievers. Either they carelessly disregard God
when He speaks, and thus mock Him, or they clamour against His
teaching and rise up rebelliously against it. Just as the Word of God is
like a hammer, so their heart is like the anvil whose hardness withstands
all blows, however forceful. They are a far cry from having the Word
of God penetrate them *even to the dividing of soul and spirit.* Thus it
seems that this sentence is to be restricted to those who believe only,
since they alone are searched to the quick.

On the other hand the context of the apostle shows that this is a
general principle which applies also to the unbelievers. However little
they are softened but rather meet the Word of God with a heart of
iron or of steel, nevertheless they must of necessity be restrained by

their own feeling of guilt. They laugh, indeed, but it is a sardonic laugh, because they feel as if they were being inwardly choked, and they make all kinds of evasions to avoid coming before the judgment-seat of God; but unwilling though they are, they are dragged there by this very Word which they so vehemently deride, so that they may be fittingly compared to mad dogs which bite and claw at the chain to which they are attached, but to no avail, because they still remain bound fast. Further, although the effect of this Word may not show itself immediately on the first day, still one may take it that in the event it will not have been preached to anyone in vain. Christ certainly spoke in terms of general application when He said (John 16.8), 'When the Spirit comes, He will convict the world.' The Spirit exercises this judgment through the preaching of the Gospel.

Finally, even if the Word of God does not always exert this power on men, yet it has it in some measure contained in itself. The apostle is discoursing here about the nature and proper function of the Word for the sole purpose that as soon as it has sounded in our ears our consciences are cited in accusation before the judgment-seat of God. It is as though he were saying, If anyone thinks that the air echoes with an empty sound when the Word of God is sent forth, he is making a great mistake. This was something alive, and full of hidden power which leaves nothing in man untouched. The sum of all this is that as soon as God opened His sacred mouth all our senses ought to be opened to receive His Word, because it is not His will to scatter His words in vain either to fade away or to fall neglected to the ground, but effectively to challenge the consciences of men, so as to bring them under His rule. He has therefore endued His Word with this power, to search out every part of the soul, to scrutinize the thoughts, to decide between the affections, and indeed to show itself as the judge.

From this there arises a new question, whether this is to be taken as of the Law or as of the Gospel. Those who think that the apostle is speaking of the Law adduce these Pauline evidences: that it is a minis-tration of death; that it is the letter which kills (II Cor. 3.6–7); that it works nothing but wrath (Rom. 4.15), and others to the same effect. But here the apostle points out its differing effects. It is (as we have said) a kind of killing that makes alive that happens through the Gospel. We must know, therefore, that when the apostle says that it is living and efficacious he is speaking of the general teaching of God. Paul bears witness to this effect (II Cor. 2.16) that from his preaching there comes a savour of death to the death of those who do not believe, and of life to the life of the faithful, so that God never speaks in vain without bringing some to salvation and thrusting others to destruction. This is the power of binding and loosing which the Lord conferred on His apostles (Matt. 18.18). This is the power of the Spirit in which Paul glories (II Cor. 10.4). Indeed he never promises us salvation in Christ, without on the other hand pronouncing vengeance on the unbelievers who by rejecting Christ bring death on themselves.

Further we must notice that the apostle is here discussing the Word of God which is brought to us by the ministry of men. Those notions that though the internal Word is certainly efficacious that which comes from the lips of men is dead and lacking in any effect are crazy and even dangerous. I admit that efficacy certainly does not come from the human tongue, nor does it lie in the sound itself, but ought to be wholly ascribed to the Holy Spirit; but this does not prevent the Spirit bringing forth His power in the Word that is preached. Because God does not speak Himself, but through men, He takes great care that His teaching is not received with contempt because its ministers are men. Thus when Paul says that the Gospel is the power of God (Rom. 1.16), he deliberately garlands his own preaching with this description which he saw was approved by some and rejected by others. When he teaches us elsewhere (Rom. 10.8-10) that our salvation is conferred on us by the teaching of faith, he expressly says that it is that doctrine which is preached. We see that God always openly commends the teaching that is ministered to us by human effort, so that it may keep us in reverence of Him.

When he calls the Word *living*, we must take as understood 'in relation to men'. This is made clearer by the second adjective. He shows what kind of life it has when he goes on to call it *efficacious*. The apostle's object is to teach us the kind of use the Word has for us. Scripture makes use of the metaphor of the sword in other passages, but the apostle is not content with a simple comparison. He says that the Word of God is *sharper than any sword*, and indeed that it is *two-edged*, because in his time it was often the case that swords had one blunt side, and only cut with the other.

Piercing even . . . etc. The noun *soul* often means the same as *spirit*, but when they are both joined together the former includes all the affections, while the latter indicates the faculty which they call the intellectual. Thus in I Thess. 5.23, when Paul prays God to keep their spirit, soul and body blameless till the coming of Christ, he means simply that they should remain pure and holy in mind and will, and in their outward actions. Similarly when Isaiah says (26.9), 'My soul hath desired thee in the night, with my spirit have I sought thee', he certainly means that he is so intent on seeking God, that he applies his mind as well as his heart to it. I know that some give a different interpretation: but all sensible people will, I hope, readily agree with me.

Now let us come to the passage we are considering. God's Word pierces *to the dividing of soul and spirit.* That means that it tests the whole soul of a man. It inquires into his thoughts and it searches his will and all his desires. The same meaning is implied in the phrase *of both joints and marrow.* It means that there is nothing so hard or firm in a man, nothing so deeply hidden that the efficacy of the Word does not penetrate through to it. This is what Paul says in I Cor. 14.24, that prophecy has the power of convicting and judging men so that the secrets of the heart are made manifest. Since it is the function of Christ to uncover and to bring to light the thoughts that come from the innermost recesses of the heart, He does this in large measure through the Gospel.

The Word of God is therefore κριτικός (a discerner) because it brings the human mind to the light of knowledge as out of a labyrinth in which it has formerly been entangled. There is no thicker darkness than that of unbelief, and hypocrisy makes us blind in a terrifying way. The Word of God scatters this darkness, and puts hypocrisy to flight. From this comes the discernment and the judgment which the apostle mentions, since the vices which lay hidden beneath a false façade of virtues now begin to be recognized and to have their varnish rubbed off. Even if the reprobates stay for the time being in their hidden lairs, they find that the light of the Word has at last penetrated even there, so that they cannot escape the judgment of God. Hence arises their murmuring and indeed their rage, because if they had not been struck by the Word, they would not betray their madness. They would want to escape or to evade and avoid its power, or even to behave as if they had not noticed. God does not allow them to do this. Therefore as often as they slander or inveigh against the Word of God, they admit, however unwillingly or reluctantly, that they feel its power within themselves.

13. *And there is no creature . . . etc.* The conjunction here, in my opinion, has the force of a causal particle. To confirm the truth that whatever is hidden in men is judged by the Word of God, he adduces a proof from the nature of God. There is no creature, he says, which is hidden from the eyes of God. Therefore there will be nothing so deep in the soul of man that it is not brought out into the light by His Word, which carries in itself its Author. As it is the work of God to search hearts, He carries out this study by His Word.

In not considering that the Word of God is like a long pole with which He tries and tests what lies hidden in our hearts, expositors have violently twisted this whole passage, without helping themselves at all. Every difficulty is removed if it is reasoned out this way, that the Word of God must be obeyed sincerely and with the honest feeling of the heart, because God, who is the discerner of hearts, has given His word the task of penetrating to the most secret thoughts of the heart. What has confused the expositors is the ambiguous phrase πρὸς ὃν ἡμῖν ὁ λόγος ('with whom we have to do'). They render this, 'to whom we speak'; but it is rather to be rendered, 'with whom we are concerned'. The meaning of this phrase is that it is God who deals with us, or with whom we are concerned, and therefore we must not treat Him lightly as we do mortal men. Whenever His Word is set before us, we must tremble, because nothing is hid from Him.

Having then a great high priest, who hath passed through the heavens, Jesus the Son of God, let us hold fast our confession. For we have not a high priest that cannot be touched with the feeling of our infirmities: but one that hath been in all points tempted like as we are, yet without sin. Let us therefore draw near with boldness unto the throne of grace, that we may receive mercy, and may find grace to help us in time of need.
(14-16)

14. *Having then.* Thus far he has been speaking of the apostleship of Christ, and now he turns to His second office. We have said above that when the Son of God was sent to us, He was given a twofold character, that of Teacher and that of Priest. Now that he has exhorted the Jews to embrace the teaching of Christ and to obey it, the apostle shows the benefit that His priesthood has brought. This is the second of the two parts of the argument with which he is dealing. He connects His priesthood to His apostleship aptly when he says that the aim of both is to bring us to God. He uses the inferential word *then* because he has previously touched on this point that Christ is our Priest: but because the power of His priesthood can only be seen from His teaching, he had to open up this way to prepare our minds to listen to Christ. It now remains for those who acknowledge Him as Master and who give themselves to Him as willing disciples to learn from His lips or in His school what are the benefits and the use and the purpose of His priesthood. He begins by saying *Having then a great high priest, Jesus the Son of God, let us hold fast our confession.* Confession here, as above, is used by metonymy for faith. Because His priesthood must serve to confirm His teaching, the apostle concludes that we have no reason to doubt or to waver in the faith of the Gospel which the Son of God has approved and ratified. Anyone who regards this teaching as unconfirmed, dishonours the Son of God, and deprives Him of His honour as a Priest. A pledge of this kind and of this extent ought to increase our trust in putting our faith unhesitatingly in the Gospel.

15. *For we have not . . . etc.* In the name Son of God, which he has mentioned, there inheres that majesty which drives us to awe and to

obedience. But if we saw nothing else in Christ, our consciences would not yet be pacified. Who will not dread the sight of the Son of God, especially when we think of our own condition, and our sins come to our minds? Moreover there could have been another obstacle to the Jews, because they were accustomed to the Levitical priesthood. In it they saw a single mortal man chosen from all the others who went into the Holy of Holies to reconcile his brethren to God by his prayers. It is a great thing when the mediator who can mollify God's wrath against us is one of ourselves. This enticement could have trapped the Jews into perpetuating their attachment to the Levitical priesthood, if the apostle did not meet it, and show that the Son of God does not only excel in glory but is endowed with equal goodwill and kindness towards us.

He is concerned with this truth when he says that He was tried by our infirmities so as to sympathize with us. In regard to the word συμπάθεια (sympathy), I am unwilling to argue too closely. The question whether Christ is now subject to our sorrows is frivolous no less than inquisitive. The apostle had no intention of wearying us with such arguments and idle speculations, but only to teach us that since Christ holds out His hand to us we have no need to look for a mediator far off: that there is no reason for us to fear the majesty of Christ, since He is our Brother; and that we must not be afraid that He is unaware of our ills and not touched by any feeling of humanity to bring us help, since He has taken our infirmities on Himself so as to be better able to help us.

The whole tenor of the apostle's argument is to be taken in the context of the meaning of faith, because he does not discuss the nature of Christ in Himself, but His nature as He shows Himself to us. He takes *likeness* to be that of our nature, by which he means that Christ has put on our feelings along with our flesh, not only to show Himself to be truly man, but to be taught by that very experience how to help our miseries; and that, not because as Son of God He needed such instruction, but because only thus could we grasp the concern He has for our salvation. Whenever we are labouring under the infirmities of our flesh, let us bear in mind that the Son of God experienced them too, to encourage us by His power in case we are overwhelmed by them.

It may be asked what he means by *infirmities*. This word can be taken in various senses. Some take it to mean cold and heat, hunger and other bodily necessities, or else contempt, want and other things of that sort, as in many Pauline passages, and especially II Cor. 12.10. There is, however, a more accurate opinion which includes along with these external troubles the emotions of the soul, such as fear, sorrow,

dread of death and the like. Certainly it would have been unnecessary
to add the qualification *without sin*, had he not been speaking of feelings
which are always sinful in us because of our fallen nature. In Christ in
whom dwelt the highest righteousness and absolute purity these were
free from all sin. Surely poverty and death and these external troubles
are not to be included among the sins. So then when he speaks of
infirmities which are connected with sin, there is not the slightest doubt
that he refers to the emotions of the soul to which our human nature
is subject, and that on account of its infirmity. The condition of the
angels is preferable to ours in this respect, that they have no sorrow,
that they have no fear, that they are not tortured by all sorts of cares,
and that they are not afraid of death. Christ took on Himself these
infirmities and with them the intention to strive not only to obtain
victory for us over them, but also that whenever we are tempted by
them we should be assured that He is unfailingly present with us. He
was not only made man; He assumed the qualities of our human
nature. The qualification *without sin* is added because we must always
make this distinction between Christ's feelings and ours, that while
His always arose out of a strict principle of justice, ours on the other
hand flow from a disturbed fountain, and always savour of their
original nature, because they are boisterous and uncontrolled.

16. *Let us therefore draw near with boldness.* He concludes that the
way to God is open for all who trust the mediation of Christ and come
to Him. Indeed he encourages those who believe to be bold in presenting themselves before the sight of God without any hesitation.
This is the outstanding fruit of spiritual teaching, namely the sure
confidence of calling on God, just as on the other hand all religion
falls and perishes when this certainty is taken away from men's
consciences.

It is an easy step to deduce from this that the light of the Gospel has
been put out in the papacy, where men in their wretchedness are
bidden to have doubts whether God is propitious towards them or
hostile. They teach that God must be sought; but they show no way
by which it is possible to come to Him, and the door by which alone
entry may be obtained is barred. They admit in theory that Christ is
the Mediator, but in actual fact they destroy the power of His priesthood and deprive Him of His honour. This principle must be established, that Christ is not really known as Mediator unless the doubt is
removed whether men may approach God themselves or not. In any
other context the conclusion come to here would not stand, namely,
that we have a High Priest who is willing to help us, and therefore we
may come before the *throne of God* boldly and without any hesitation.
Indeed if we were so persuaded that Christ was holding out His hand

to us, who would not seize the full boldness of approaching? What I have said is therefore true, that the power is taken away from the priesthood of Christ as long as men hesitate and look anxiously for other mediators as though that one were not enough by whose protection all those who really trust Him (as the apostle has said) know for sure that their prayers are heard.

The basis of this confidence is that the throne of God is not marked by a naked majesty which overpowers us, but is adorned with a new name, that of *grace*. This is the name that we ought always to keep in mind when we avoid the sight of God. If we turn our minds to it alone, the glory of God cannot but fill us with despair, such is the awfulness of His throne. Therefore in order to help our lack of confidence, and to free our minds of all fears, the apostle clothes it with grace and gives it a name which will encourage us by its sweetness. It is as if he were saying, Since God has fixed on His throne as it were a banner of grace and of fatherly love towards us, there is no reason why His majesty should ward us off from approaching Him.

The sum of all this is that we may safely call on God, since we know that He is propitious to us. This happens because of the mercy of Christ, as is stated in Eph. 3.12, because when Christ accepts us into His faith and discipleship, He covers with His goodness the majesty of God which could otherwise be fearful, so that nothing appears except grace and fatherly goodwill.

That we may receive mercy . . . etc. This is added for the important reason of specifically confirming those who need mercy in case anyone is so cast down by the sense of his own affliction that he blocks the way by his own lack of faith. This phrase *That we may receive mercy* contains this most pleasing teaching, that all those who rely on the advocacy of Christ and pray to God will be certain of receiving mercy. By implication the apostle also warns all those who do not keep to this way, and indicates that God will not be moved by their prayers, because they have disregarded the only way of making peace with Him.

He adds *to help us in time of need*, that is, if we want to get what is necessary for our salvation. This time of need refers to the time of our calling according to the passage of Isaiah (49.8) which Paul applies to the preaching of the Gospel (II Cor. 6.2)—'Behold, now is the acceptable time,' etc. The apostle refers to that today when God speaks with us. If God speaks to us today and we put Him off until tomorrow, there will come the dead of night when what is possible now will no longer be possible and we shall knock in vain on the closed door.

CHAPTER FIVE

For every high priest, being taken from among men, is appointed for men in things pertaining to God, that he may offer both gifts and sacrifices for sins: who can bear gently with the ignorant and erring, for that he himself also is compassed with infirmity; and by reason thereof is bound, as for the people, so also for himself, to offer for sins. And no man taketh the honour unto himself, but when he is called of God, even as was Aaron. So Christ also glorified not himself to be made a high priest, but he that spake unto him. Thou art my Son, This day have I begotten thee (Ps. 2.7); as he saith also in another place, Thou art a priest for ever After the order of Melchizedek (Ps. 110.4). (1-6)

1. *For every high priest.* He compares Christ with the Levitical priests and shows where He is like them, and where unlike. The point of this whole discourse is the proper understanding of the office of Christ, and to show that everything that was instituted under the law was instituted for His sake. From this the apostle goes on to make the transition to the abolition of the old priesthood. He says first of all that the priests were *taken from among men*: secondly, that they did not act privately, but for the whole people; thirdly that they did not come to appease God empty-handed, but were provided with sacrifices: fourthly, that they did not need to be immune from our infirmities in order to be better able to help us in our troubles: and finally that they did not need to rush to take up this task rashly, but that it only brought its true honour when they were elected to it and approved by God. Now let us briefly deal with these points in turn.

Before doing so, however, we must expose the ignorance of those who apply these principles to our time as if the necessity for priests to offer sacrifices were the same today. This does not require any lengthy rebuttal. What is clearer than that the truth which is in Christ, is being compared with its types, which were prior to it in time and have now ceased? This will appear more plainly from the context. Those who want to found the sacrifice of the mass on this passage are more than ridiculous.

I return to the true sense of the apostle. He says that the priests are taken from among men. Hence it follows that Christ must have been truly man. Because we stand a long way off from God, we are in some way placed before Him in His priestly character. This could not be so if He were not one of us. The fact that the Son of God has a common nature with us does not detract from His dignity, but rather commends Him the more to us. He is fitted to reconcile God to us because He is Man. In order to prove that He is our Mediator Paul expressly calls Him Man, since if He had been chosen from among the angels or from anywhere else, we could not have been united with God through Him because He would not reach down to us.

For men. Now the second point that the priest does not minister for himself by himself, but is appointed for the common good of the people. This is well worth noticing, so that we know that the salvation of all of us is effected by and turns on the priesthood of Christ. The form of this benefit is expressed by the words *ordains things pertaining to God.* There is a possible double reading here, because the verb καθίσταται (ordain, appoint) may be taken in a passive or active sense. Those who take it as passive, render it as follows, 'He is appointed for these things,' thus understanding the preposition which governs the noun *things.* The alternative reading pleases me equally well: the priest cares for or ordains the things pertaining to God. The construction is smoother and the meaning is fuller. Whichever way it is taken the apostle's meaning is that we would have no dealings with God unless there is a priest present. Since we are unholy, what have we to do with holy things? We are stangers to God and to His worship until a priest comes in between us and undertakes our cause.

That he may offer gifts. The third point of the priesthood is the offering of gifts. There are two words here—gifts and victims. The former of these (in my opinion) covers the different forms of sacrifices, and is as it were a general term. The second defines specifically sacrifices of atonement. The gist of this is that the priest is only a peacemaker between God and men when a victim is sacrificed, because without sacrifice there is no remission of sins and the wrath of God is not appeased. Whenever there is a question of reconciliation between God and men, this pledge must always necessarily precede it. We see, therefore, that the angels are quite incapable of obtaining God's favour for us, because their way has not been prepared by any sacrifice. The same is true both of the prophets and the apostles. It is Christ alone who has taken away our sins by His sacrifice and who now prays for us to God.

2. *Who can . . . etc.* This fourth point bears some relation to the first. Nevertheless it ought to be distinguished from it. There the apostle was saying that mankind was united with God in the person of one man, because all men are made up of the same flesh and the same nature. Now he is making a different point. It is that the priest should be fair and of goodwill to sinners, because he is the companion of their infirmities. Both Greek and Latin commentators make varying

interpretations of the word μετριοπαθεῖν (to bear reasonably with) which the apostle uses here. I think that its force is simply the same as if he had said that he brings himself to συμπάθεια (sympathy). Not all the things that are attributed to Levitical priests are applicable to Christ. We know that Christ was free from every infection of sin. In this He differed from all others, in that He had no need to offer sacrifice for Himself. It is sufficient that He Himself bore our infirmities, although He was free from and undefiled by sin. As far as the old Levitical priests are concerned, the apostle says that they were subject to human infirmity, and so they atoned for their own sins as well, by their sacrifices, so that they were not only fairer to the transgressions of others, but they suffered with them. This office ought to be applied to Christ to the extent of inserting the qualification previously mentioned, that He shared our infirmities yet without sin. Although He was always free from sin, yet that feeling for infirmities which has been spoken of is alone sufficient to make Him disposed to help us, merciful and ready to forgive, and concerned for our ills. The sum of all this is that Christ is not only our Brother because of His oneness with our flesh and nature, but He is also led and as it were fashioned to kindness and goodwill by His fellow-feeling for our infirmities. The participle δυνάμενος has more force than *who can* in our common speech. It expressed suitability or fitness. He takes *the ignorant and erring* to mean sinners, following the Hebrew idiom. The Hebrews use שָׁגָה (*shegageh*) for every kind of offence, as there will be occasion to explain a little later.

4. *And no man taketh the honour.* In this verse there is partly a likeness and partly a distinction to be noted. The call of God makes for a lawful office so that no one performs it properly or validly unless he has been elected by God. Christ and Aaron have this in common, that each was called by God. On the other hand there is this difference between them, that when Christ succeeded according to a new and different form, and was made a High Priest for ever, it was clear that Aaron's priesthood had been temporary, and was due to cease. We see the direction of the apostle's argument. He wants to defend the right to Christ's priesthood. He does this by showing that it has God as its Author. But this would not be enough unless he established that the old order had been brought to an end to give place to the new. He proves this by looking back at the condition on which Aaron was appointed (for it is not for us to extend it further than God's decree allows). He will presently make clear how long God determined that earlier order to last. Christ is therefore a true High Priest, because He is appointed by God's authority. What then is to be said of Aaron and the rest of his successors? This, that they had as much right as was

given them by God, but not as much as men have given them according to their own thinking.

Although this has been said in the light of this present case, it is yet legitimate to draw from it this general principle, that no form of government is to be drawn up in the Church by human judgment, but that men must wait for the command of God: but further, that we must follow the established procedure of election so that no one forces himself in of his own desire. Both these points should be carefully noted. The apostle is speaking here not only of persons but also of the office. He denies, I say, that any office which men have invented for themselves without the authority of God is lawful and holy. As it is the promise of God to govern the Church, so He reserves to Himself alone the right to lay down the order and manner of its administration. On this I found the principle that the papal priesthood is a spurious one, because it was fabricated in a human workshop. God nowhere commands that a sacrifice should now be offered to Him for the forgiveness of sins. He nowhere ordains that priests should be appointed for this purpose. Therefore when the Pope instals his priests to make sacrifices, the apostle says that they are not to be considered lawful unless perchance by some new and special law they exalted themselves above Christ, who Himself did not dare to take this honour on Himself, but waited for the Word of the Father.

This should also hold good in the case of individual persons, that no one should grasp this honour for himself as an individual, but that public authority should come first. I refer to offices that are divinely ordained. It may sometimes be that someone who is not called by God is yet to be tolerated however little he may be approved, provided that the office is holy and approved by God. There are many who steal in either through ambition or by evil tricks, of whose calling there is little or no evidence. They are not to be summarily rejected, especially when they cannot happen by a public council of the Church. For two hundred years before the advent of Christ the most dreadful corruptions held sway in the priesthood in power: yet the right to honour remained with the office itself because it came from the calling of God, and the men themselves were tolerated, because the freedom of the Church was suppressed. From this it is clear that the greatest fault lies in the character of the office, when men invent for themselves something which God has never commanded. All the less to be tolerated are the Romish sacrificers who chatter about nothing but keeping their sacred titles, when they have chosen themselves without any reference to God.

5. *Thou art my Son.* This evidence may seem to be a bit far-fetched, for granted that Christ is born of God the Father, He is not thereby

ordained to be High Priest. But if we think of the purpose for which
Christ was revealed to the world, it will be readily apparent that that
quality necessarily attached to Him. It must be borne in mind first and
foremost, as we have said in chapter one, that this birth of Christ of
which the Psalm speaks was the testimony that the Father gave Him
among men. The point here is not the mutual relationship between
the Father and the Son. It is rather the regard for the men among
whom He was manifested. What kind of Son did God show forth to
us? One endowed with no honour and with no ability? Certainly
not. He was to be the Mediator between God and men. Therefore
His birth includes His priesthood.

6. *As he saith also in another place.* The apostle's purpose is more
clearly expressed here. The passage, and indeed the whole psalm from
which it is taken, is well known. There is scarcely any other clearer
prophecy both of the eternal priesthood of Christ and of His kingdom.
Yet the Jews busy themselves in making all kinds of captious objections
so as to obscure the glory of Christ: but to no avail. They apply it to
David, as if it were he whom God bids to sit at His right hand: but
that is so much sheer effrontery. We know that it was unlawful for
kings to exercise the priesthood. It was for this crime of meddling in
an office that was not his that Uzziah provoked the wrath of God and
was smitten with leprosy (II Chron. 26.18). It is therefore quite
certain that neither David nor any other of the kings is referred to here.

If people take exception on the grounds that *princes* [as well as priests]
are sometimes called כוהנים (*kohanim*), I admit that that is true, but
I maintain that that does not fit this present passage. The comparison
leaves no doubt. Melchizedek was the priest of God. The psalmist
declares that this king whose place is at the right hand of God will be a
כוהן (*kohen*) *according to the order of Melchizedek.* Is there anyone who
does not see that this is to be understood as referring to priesthood?
As it was a rare and almost unique occurrence for the same person to
be both king and priest, and indeed it was a quite unusual thing among
the people of God, Melchizedek therefore provides a pattern of the
Messiah, as if he were saying, that His royal dignity will not hinder
Him from performing the task of the priesthood as well, because the
type of this has already occurred in Melchizedek. Certainly all those
Jews who have any feelings of propriety will both allow that this
passage refers to the Messiah and will have no doubt that His priesthood
is here commended.

What is rendered in Greek κατὰ τάξιν (according to order) is in
Hebrew על־דבהתי (*al-dibrathi*) which means 'according to the likeness
of' or 'after the fashion of', and this confirms what I have said that as
it was a most unusual thing among the people for the same person to

hold the office of both king and priest, this ancient example is adduced which foreshadows the Messiah. The apostle will explain the rest in more detail in its context.

> *Who in the days of his flesh, having offered up prayers and supplication with strong crying and tears unto him that was able to save him from death, and having been heard for his godly fear, though he was a Son, yet learned obedience by the things which he suffered; and having been made perfect, he became unto all them that obey him the author of eternal salvation: named of God a high priest after the order of Melchizedek. Of whom we have many things to say, and hard of interpretation, seeing ye are become dull of hearing. (7-11)*

7. *Who in the days of his flesh.* Because the form of Christ is grossly disfigured by the Cross, and men do not consider the purpose of His humiliation, the apostle repeats the point that he has touched on above, that His wonderful loving-kindness shines forth in the fact that He submitted Himself to our infirmities for our good. From this it is clear that our faith is confirmed and His honour undiminished because He bore our ills. He distinguishes two reasons why Christ had to suffer— a superficial one and a fundamental one. The superficial one is that He should learn obedience; the fundamental one that in this way He should be consecrated a Priest for our salvation.

The days of his flesh. No one has any doubt that this is to be taken as referring to His life in this world. Hence it follows that the word 'flesh' does not signify the material substance, but the quality of His life, as in I Cor. 15.50—'flesh and blood cannot inherit the kingdom of God'. Those fanatics who imagine that Christ has now put off His flesh because the days of His flesh are said to have passed are talking nonsense. It is one thing to be truly man, even though endowed with a blessed immortality. It is a quite different thing to be subject to the human trials and infirmities which Christ underwent as long as He lived in the world but has laid aside now that He has been received into heaven.

Let us now look at the matter. Christ, who was the Son, who sought a remedy from the Father, and who was heard, yet suffered death to be instructed in this way of obedience. There is great weight here in every word.

By saying *the days of his flesh* he indicates that the time of our human miseries is limited, a fact which affords us no little relief. It would surely be a hard and almost intolerable state of affairs if we could point to no limit to our suffering. The three clauses which follow also add considerable comfort. Christ was the Son who was exempted from the common lot of men by His own dignity, and yet He subjected Himself to it for our sake. What mortal man will now dare to decline to undergo the same condition? There is in addition a further argument, that if we are oppressed by adversity we are not excluded from the number of God's children, when we see going before us Him who was by nature His only Son. The fact that we are reckoned as sons only happens by the grace of our adoption, inasmuch as He who alone claims this honour in His own right admits us to His fellowship.

Having offered up prayers. The second thing he refers to in Christ is that when the time came He sought a way of relief to be delivered from evil. He says this in case anyone thinks that Christ had an iron spirit which felt nothing. We must always look to see why anything is said. If Christ had been untouched by any sorrow, then no consolation would come to us from His sufferings. But when we hear that He too endured the bitterest agonies of spirit, the likeness to us is clear. Christ, he says, did not undergo death and all the other tribulations in such a way as to make little of them or not to be oppressed by any feeling of trouble. He prayed with tears, thus bearing witness to the supreme anguish of His spirit. By *tears* and *strong crying* the apostle's intention is to express the force of His grief, in accordance with the normal usage of marking something by signs. I have no doubt that he is speaking of the prayer contained in the Gospels (Matt. 26.39); *Father, if it be possible, let this cup pass away from me.* And also of the other prayer (Matt. 27.46), *My God, my God, why hast thou forsaken me?* In the second of these mention is made in the Gospels of a strong cry: while in the first it is incredible that His eyes were dry since in the immensity of His agony bloody drops of sweat flowed from His whole body. It is certain that He was reduced to utter extremity. He was oppressed by real sorrows, and prayed the Father in all earnestness to send help.

What is the point of all this? It is that whenever our troubles press us and torture us, we should cast our minds back to the Son of God who toiled under the same burdens. As long as He goes before us, we have no reason to fail. At the same time we are warned not to look for out salvation in time of trouble from any other than from God alone. What better rule for prayer can we have than the example of Christ? He went directly to the Father. The apostle shows us what ought to be done, when he says that He addressed His prayers to Him who was able to deliver Him from death. By that he means that He rightly prayed because He had recourse to God who is the only Deliverer. *Tears* and *crying* commend to us a zeal and a closer application in prayer. We must not pray to God perfunctorily, but with earnest desires.

And having been heard. Some have translated this *for his godly fear,* but I do not agree at all. Firstly, the apostle puts εὐλάβεια simply, without 'His'. Secondly, the preposition is ἀπό (from) and not ὑπέρ (on behalf of) or any other similar one which shows cause. Since in Greek εὐλάβεια generally means fear or anxiety, I have no doubt that the apostle means that Christ was heard out of that which He feared, so that He was not overwhelmed by and did not give way to these evils, nor was He overcome by death. The Son of God descended to this struggle, not because He laboured under unbelief, the source of all our fears, but because He underwent in mortal flesh the judgment of God, the terror of which cannot be overcome without laborious effort. Chrysostom expounds this as meaning the dignity of Christ which the Father in some way reverenced: but that is absurd. Others understand it as piety. But the exposition which I have given is much more fitting, and does not need any lengthy confirmation.

He goes on to add a third point, in case we should think that because He was not immediately delivered from His troubles Christ's prayer was rejected. At no time was He deprived of God's mercy and help. From this we can take it that God often answers our prayers, even when it is least apparent. Although it is not for us to lay down any hard and fast rule for Him, nor is it in keeping for Him to have to grant our petitions in whatever frame of mind or form of words they are expressed, yet in every way in which He takes care for our salvation He shows that He has answered our prayers. So when we seem on the face of it to be repulsed, we get far more than if He had given us all we asked.

In what way was Christ heard out of His fear, when He underwent the death which He shrank from? My answer is that we must look to the point of His fear. Why did He dread death except that He saw in it the curse of God, and that He had to wrestle with the total sum of human guilt, and with the very powers of darkness themselves. Hence His fear and anxiety, because the judgment of God is more than terrifying. He got what He wanted inasmuch as He emerged from the pains of death as Conqueror, was upheld by the saving hand of the Father, and after a brief encounter gained a glorious victory over Satan, sin and the powers of hell. It often happens that we ask for this or that or the next thing, but for a different purpose: and while God does not grant us what we ask, He finds a way to help us.

8. *He learned obedience.* The first purpose of the sufferings of Christ was that in this way He should be made accustomed to obedience: not that He was forcibly compelled to it, or had any need of such practices, in the way that the fierceness of oxen or horses is tamed. He was more than willing of His own accord to give the Father the

obedience due to Him. He did this for our benefit, to give us the
instance and the pattern of His own submission even to death itself,
although this can be said with truth, that it was in His death that Christ
fully learned what it meant to obey God, since that was the point at
which He reached His greatest self-denial. He renounced His own
will and gave Himself over to the Father to the extent of meeting
death, which He dreaded, freely and willingly. The meaning is, therefore, that by the experience of His sufferings Christ was taught how
far we ought to submit to and obey God. Therefore we also should be
instructed and guided into obedience by God by His example, by our
various tribulations, and finally by death itself. Indeed our need is
much greater because we have rebellious and untamed spirits unless
God has subdued us to bear His yoke by trials like these.

This benefit which comes from the Cross ought to allay the bitterness of it in our hearts. What is more to be desired than our return
to God in obedience? That cannot happen except by the Cross; for in
times of prosperity we run riot as though on a loose rein, and in most
cases when the yoke is thrown off the lust of our flesh breaks out. But
when our will is brought under restraint so that we will what is pleasing
to God, then our obedience really asserts itself. The clear proof of our
perfect submission, I say, is when we prefer death to which God calls
us, even though we shudder at it, rather than life which we naturally
desire.

9. *And having been made perfect.* The final and so-called remoter
purpose why Christ had to suffer was that in this way He was initiated
into His priesthood. It is as if the apostle were saying, that to endure
the Cross and to die were a solemn form of consecration for Christ
thus indicating that all His sufferings had regard to our salvation. From
this it follows that they in no way detract from His dignity, but indeed
rather are to His glory. If our salvation is precious to us, with how
much honour should we regard its Author? This passage not only
speaks of the example of Christ, but goes further and says that by His
obedience Christ has blotted out our transgressions. He became the
Author of our salvation because He made us just in the sight of God,
when He remedied the disobedience of Adam by a contrary act of
obedience.

'Sanctified' suits the context better than 'made perfect'. The Greek
word is τελειωθείς, which means either. But because the passage is
about priesthood the writer quite properly and fittingly mentions
sanctification. Christ Himself speaks thus in another place (John 17.19),
'For their sakes I sanctify myself.' It is clear from this that the reference
is properly to His human nature in which He performed the office of
Priest and in which He suffered.

Unto all them that obey Him. If we want the obedience of Christ to
be of advantage to us, we must copy it. The apostle indicates that the
fruits of it do not come to any but to those who are obedient. In saying
this he commends faith to us, for neither He nor His benefits become
ours unless, and in so far as, we accept them and Him by faith. At the
same time he has inserted the universal term 'to all' to show that no
one is excluded from this salvation who proves to be attentive and
obedient to the Gospel of Christ.

10. *Named of God.* Because it is worthwhile to pursue the comparison between Christ and Melchizedek further than he has reached, and
to stir up the minds of the Jews to give more attention, he now passes
on to a digression at the same time keeping hold of the main argument.
He prefaces it with the words that he has many things to say, but they
must prepare themselves so that they are not said in vain. He warns
them that what he has to say will be hard, not to frighten them off but
to sharpen their wits. Just as something that is easy usually makes us
lazy, so we are apt to listen more intently if we are faced with something
that is obscure. He assigns the cause of the difficulty to them and not to
the subject-matter. Indeed God deals with us so plainly and unambigu-
ously that His Word is truly called our light. Its brightness is dimmed
by our darkness. This happens partly through our dullness, and partly
through our folly. Though we are more than dull in our understanding
of the teaching of God, there is added to this vice the depravity of our
affections. We would rather apply our minds to vanity than to the
truth of God. We are continually hindered either by our rebellious-
ness, or by the cares of this world, or by the lusts of our flesh.

Of whom does not refer to Christ, but to Melchizedek: although he
is referred to not as a private individual, but in so far as he is a type of
Christ and in a way embraces His person.

*For when by reason of the time ye ought to be teachers ye have need again
that someone teach you the rudiments of the first principles of the oracle
of God: and are become such as have need of milk, and not of solid food.
For every one that partaketh of milk is without experience of the word of
righteousness: for he is a babe. But solid food is for full-grown men,
even those who by reason of use have their senses exercised to discern
good and evil.* (12-14)

12. *When ye ought to be teachers.* This reproof contains a goodly
measure of goads to prod the Hebrews out of their laziness. He says
that it is absurd, and they ought to be ashamed of it, that they are still
in the primary classes when they should be teachers. You are the
people, he says, who ought to be the masters of others, but in fact you

are not even pupils capable of grasping ordinary teaching. You do
not yet properly understand the first rudiments of Christianity. In
order to drive home the shame even more, he uses the words *first
principles*, just as one speaks of the alphabet. We must learn from the
whole of life, because the truly wise man is the one who knows how
far short he comes of any complete understanding. But we must
progress in our learning, so that we do not always stick at the first
beginnings. We must let it happen that Isaiah's prophecy becomes
fulfilled in us (28.10). 'It is precept upon precept, precept upon precept . . .' etc. but rather we must take care that our progress corresponds
to our time. Not only our years but our individual days are to be
called into the reckoning, so that everyone presses on to make progress;
but there are few who discipline themselves to a review of the time
past, or who concern themselves about time to come. So we justly pay
the penalty of our laziness in that most of us spend our lives in the
elementary stages like children. We are further reminded that it is the
duty of each one of us, the more understanding he has, to seek to pass
it on to his brethren, so that no one keeps his wisdom to himself, but
each one uses it for mutual edification.

Such as have need of milk. Paul uses the same metaphor in I Cor. 3.1,
when he reproaches the Corinthians with the same sin as this, or at
least with one not unlike it. He says that because they are carnal they
cannot bear solid food. Milk is the elementary teaching with which
the ignorant begin. Peter uses it in a different sense (I Pet. 2.2) when
he bids us desire milk without guile. There is a twofold childishness—
that of wickedness and that of sense. Thus Paul in another passage
(I Cor. 14.20) says: *Be not children in mind, but in malice.* Those who are
of such tender years that they cannot receive the more advanced
teaching are called children by way of reproach.

Hence the true purpose of teaching is to fit us together so that we
grow up to a perfect man, to the measure of full maturity, so that we
are not children tossed to and fro and carried about with every wind
of doctrine (in the words of Eph. 4.14). We must of course show
indulgence to those who have not yet tasted Christ, if they are incapable of taking solid food: but anyone who ought to grow with
time is inexcusable if he remains for ever a child. We see that Isaiah
brands the reprobates with this mark that they are like children newly
weaned from the breast (Isa. 29.8).

Certainly the teaching of Christ provides milk for children just as it
provides solid food for adults. But as an infant is nourished on the
milk of its nurse, not that it may always depend on the breast, but that
it may be gradually weaned on to stronger food, so we must suck milk
from Scripture at first, that we may later feed on its bread. The apostle

distinguishes between milk and solid food in such a way as to understand sound doctrine by both words; but the ignorant begin with the one, while those who have learned something are strengthened by the other.

13. *Every one that partaketh of milk.* He means those who still reject solid teaching on account of their tenderness, for in other respects an adult is not averse to milk. Here he is reproving a childishness of the mind which compels God continually to speak to us in riddles. He says therefore that such children are not capable of comprehending the *word of righteousness,* meaning by righteousness the perfection of which he will speak a little later on.

In my opinion the apostle is not referring here to the question of how we are justified before God. He takes the word in the simpler sense of the fulness of knowledge which leads us to perfection. This is the office which Paul ascribes to the Gospel in Colossians 1.28, saying in effect that those who indulge their ignorance are shut out from any genuine knowledge of Christ, and the teaching of the Gospel bears no fruit in them because they never reach the goal, nor indeed even come near to it.

14. *Solid food is for full-grown men, etc.* He calls adults full-grown, setting them in opposition to babes as in I Cor. 2.6, 14.20, and Eph. 4.13. Middle age, the age of manhood, is as it were the mature age of human life. Figuratively he calls those who are spiritual men in Christ. He wants all Christians to be like those who by continual practice have contracted the habit of *discerning good and evil.* We are only properly instructed in the truth if we are garrisoned by this protection against the falsehoods of Satan. That is the meaning of the sword of the Spirit. Paul is referring to this benefit of sound doctrine when he says (Eph. 4.14): *Be not carried about by every wind of doctrine, etc.* What kind of faith is it anyway that wavers in suspense between truth and falsehood? Is it not liable to collapse at any moment?

The writer is not content to leave this in the mind alone, but he mentions all the senses to show that we must never give up until we are furbished and armed on all sides for the battle, by the Word of God, in case Satan steals up on us with his deceits.

It is clear from this what kind of Christianity there is in popery, where not only is the grossest ignorance commended in the name of simplicity, but the people are rigidly prohibited from searching for real understanding. I maintain that it is easy to judge the spirit that actuates those who scarcely allow men to touch what the apostle bids them handle constantly; who pretend that the neglect which is here so severely reproved is in fact praiseworthy: who take away the Word of God, the only rule of true discernment, which is declared here to be a necessity for all Christians. Even among those who have been freed from that devilish prohibition and who enjoy the freedom to learn there is nonetheless an indifference both to hearing and to reading. When we neglect this discipline we are senseless and void of all discernment.

CHAPTER SIX

Wherefore let us cease to speak of the first principles of Christ and press on unto perfection: not laying again a foundation of repentance from dead works, and of faith toward God, of the teaching of baptisms, and of laying on of hands, and of resurrection of the dead, and of eternal judgment. (1-2)

1. *Wherefore let us cease.* To his reproof he appends this exhortation to leave the first principles and advance to the goal. By *first principles* is meant the first introductory training which is to be given to the uninstructed when they are being received into the Church. He bids them leave such elementary matters, not because believers should ever forget them, but because they are to remain at that stage for as short a time as possible. This appears more clearly in the simile of a *foundation* which immediately follows. In building a house one must never abandon the foundation, but at the same time it is ridiculous to spend all one's time in laying it. A foundation is laid for the sake of the building, and the man who spends time in building it but who never goes on to the superstructure only wearies himself with foolish and useless toil. In a word just as the work of an architect must begin with the foundation, so it must go on immediately to the erection of a house. It is the same with Christianity. We lay our foundations as it were in the first principles, but there must follow the more advanced teaching which completes the building. Those who settle down in the first principles behave ridiculously, because they have no set aim. They are like a builder who spends all his labour on the foundation and never bothers to build a house. The writer's desire for our faith is that it should be so founded at the beginning that it builds itself up, until at last by its daily progress it reaches completion.

Of repentance from dead works. This has reference to a commonly used catechetical formula. Hence it may be conjectured with some degree of probability that this epistle was not written immediately after the early proclamations of the Gospel, but when some pattern of polity had been established in the churches, such as that before the catechumen was admitted to baptism he should make confession of his faith. There were certain cardinal matters about which the pastor questioned the catechumen, as clearly appears from the various evidences of the fathers. This examination was concerned particularly with what is known as the Apostle's Creed. This was as it were the first door into the Church for those who as adults entered the service of Christ, when before they had been strangers to His faith. The apostle is referring to the practice whereby there was a short space of time given to catechumens in which they were initiated into the doctrine of their religion, just as a teacher instructs his pupils in the alphabet, so that he may take them on at once to something more advanced. Let us examine what he says.

He refers to *repentance* and *faith*, two things on which the whole perfection of the Gospel is rooted. What other command does Christ give to His apostles but to preach repentance and faith? So when Paul wants to testify that he has performed his duty faithfully, he adduces his care and diligence in inculcating these two things. It seems absurd, therefore, that the apostle should order the omission of repentance and faith in which one must continue throughout the whole course of life. But when he adds *from dead works*, he is indicating that he is speaking of the initial act of repentance. Although every sin is a dead work, either because it works death or because it arises from the spiritual death of the soul, yet believers, who are already born again by the Spirit of God, are not properly said to repent from dead works. Certainly regeneration is not complete in them, but however tender the seed of new life may be, it has at least this effect, that they are no longer reckoned dead before God.

The apostle is therefore not contemplating all repentance in general, the practice of which should continue actively to the very end, but he is concerned with the beginning of repentance, by which those who have been recently, and indeed only now for the first time, converted to faith begin their new life. In the same way the word *faith* means the short summary of religious teaching which is commonly called the Articles of Faith.

There is the same relevance in the phrase *the resurrection of the dead and eternal life*. These are some of the greatest mysteries of heavenly wisdom. Indeed this is the goal of all our religion, to which we ought to strive all through our lives. But since the same truth is taught in one way to the uninstructed, and in another way to those who have made some progress, the apostle refers to the common form of putting the question—Do you believe in the resurrection of the dead? Do you believe in eternal life? This was right and proper for children, and on one occasion. To go back to them again simply means to fall away.

2. *Of the teaching of baptisms.* Some read this separately as 'of baptisms and of teaching'. I prefer to take them together, although I explain them differently from others. I take them, as grammarians say, in apposition in the following sense—not laying again the foundation of repentance, faith toward God, and the resurrection of the dead,

which is the doctrine of baptism and of the laying on of hands. If these two phrases, 'of the teachings of baptisms' and 'of laying on of hands', had been put in brackets, the context would run better. If you do not read it in this appositive way, you are left with the absurdity of a double repetition. What is the doctrine of baptism but what is reviewed here, namely, faith toward God, repentance, judgment, and the like?

Chrysostom thinks that 'baptisms' in the plural are spoken of because those who return to their first beginnings in some measure destroy their earlier baptism. I cannot agree with this. This doctrine is not concerned with a plurality of baptisms, but by 'baptisms' is meant the solemn rites or the stated diets for baptizing. He joins *the imposition of hands* to baptism, because as there were two orders of catechumens, so there was a double rite. Those who were outside did not come forward for baptism until they had made profession of their faith. In their case, therefore, catechizing usually preceded baptism. But the children of believers were baptized as infants, since they were adopted from the womb, and belonged to the body of the Church by right of the promise. Then after their infancy was over, and they had been instructed in the faith, they too offered themselves for a catechumenate, which in their case came after their baptism. Another sign was then added in the laying on of hands.

This single passage is abundant evidence that the origin of this rite came from the apostles. Afterwards it was turned into a superstition, as the world almost always degenerates to corruptions even from the best institutions. They have invented the fiction that it is a sacrament by which the spirit of regeneration is conferred. By this invention they have mutilated baptism. What was proper to the latter they have transferred to the imposition of hands. We should know that it was instituted by its first authors to be a solemn ceremony of prayer, as indeed Augustine declares. They intended by this sign to confirm the profession of faith which adolescents make when they pass from their childhood, but they have planned nothing less than the destruction of the force of baptism. Today we must retain the institution in its purity, but we must correct the superstition.

This passage also tends towards the approval of paido-baptism. Why should the same doctrine be called baptism for some and the imposition of hands for others except because the latter were instructed in the faith after baptism, so that nothing remained but to lay hands on them?

And this will we do, if God permits, for as touching those who were once enlightened and tasted of the heavenly gift, and were made partakers of the Holy Ghost, and tasted the good word of God, and the powers of the age to come, and then fell away, it is impossible to renew them again unto repentance: seeing they crucify to themselves the Son of God afresh, and put him to an open shame. (3-6)

3. *This will we do.* There follows a fearsome denunciation; but the apostle makes these fulminations so that the Jews may not trifle with the grace of God in indulging themselves too much in their own idleness. It is as though he were saying that there must be no procrastination here, because there will not always be the opportunity of going on. It is not in a man's power to jump from the starting-point to the goal as often as he likes. The completion of our course is the gift of God alone.

4. *For it is impossible.* This passage has provided many with the opportunity of rejecting this epistle, especially since the Novatians find here ammunition for denying pardon to those who fall. The western fathers therefore preferred to deny the genuineness of the epistle because the Novatian sect were their enemies, and they were not strong enough in doctrine to be equal to refuting their arguments. But once the mind of the apostle is laid bare it will soon be quite clear that there is nothing here to support such a stupid mistake. There are others to whom the authority of the epistle is sacrosanct and who try to refute this absurdity, and all the time they are taking refuge in inanities. Some take *impossible* to mean 'unusual' or 'hard', which is wholly foreign to the meaning of the word. Others (the majority) restrict its meaning to the repentance by which catechumens in the early Church were accustomed to be prepared for baptism just as the apostles prescribed fasting or the like for those to be baptized. But what great thing would the apostle be saying in maintaining that the repentance which is the adjunct of baptism could not be repeated? He threatens the direct vengeance of God on all who throw away the grace they have once received. What force would this sentence have in instilling fear into the careless and the wavering if he were warning them that there was no further place for their first repentance? This would apply to every kind of offence. What is to be said, then? Since God gives the hope of mercy to all without exception, it is absurd that anyone at all should be excluded for any reason.

The hub of this problem is in the words *fell away.* Anyone who understands their force will easily extricate himself from all the difficulties. We must notice that there is a twofold fall: one is particular, the other is general. Anyone who offends in some way or indeed in many ways has fallen from his status as a Christian man. Therefore all sins are so many falls. But the apostle is not talking here about theft, or perjury, or murder, or drunkenness or adultery. He is referring to a complete falling away from the Gospel, not one in which the sinner has offended God in some one part only, but in which he has utterly renounced His grace.

To understand this more clearly, let us draw a contrast between this falling and the grace of God which he has described. The man who falls is the one who forsakes the Word of God, who extinguishes its light, who denies himself the taste of the heavenly gift, and who gives up partaking of the Spirit. This is complete renunciation of God. We can now see who are shut out from hope or pardon. They are the apostates who have estranged themselves from the Gospel of Christ which they previously embraced and from the grace of God. This does not happen to anyone unless he sins against the Holy Spirit. The man who violates the second table of the Law, or who in his ignorance transgresses the first is not guilty of this rebellion, and certainly God does not deprive any others of His grace except those who are wholly reprobate. There is nothing left for them.

If anyone asks why the apostle makes mention of this kind of apostasy when he is addressing believers who are far from such sinful treachery, my answer is that he is giving them early warning of the danger, so that they may be on their guard against it. This is worth noting. When we turn aside from the straight way, we not only make excuses for our vices to others, but also impose them on ourselves. Satan creeps up on us stealthily, and allures us gradually by subtly hidden devices, so that when we go astray we are not conscious of so straying. We slip down gradually, until at last we fall headlong. This can be seen every day in a multitude of cases. It is therefore not without cause that the apostle forewarns all followers of Christ to take care for themselves in time. A long continued inactivity leads almost always to a lethargy which is followed by mental alienation.

We must note in passing the terms by which he denotes knowledge of the Gospel. He calls it *enlightenment*, from which it follows that men are blind until Christ, who is the light of the world, shines upon them. He calls it *the taste of the heavenly gift*, by which he means that the gifts which are bestowed on us in Christ are above the natural world, and are tasted by faith. He calls it *partaking of the Holy Spirit*, because it is He who gives to every man according as He wills whatever light and understanding he has, without whom no man can call Jesus Lord (I Cor. 12.3), who opens the eyes of our mind and reveals the hidden things of God. He calls it *the taste of the good word of God*, meaning that the goodness of God is not revealed to us in any kind of way, but as that which agreeably pleases us. This description further denotes the difference between the Law and the Gospel. The former contains nothing beyond sternness and judgment, but the latter is a pleasing evidence of the divine love and fatherly kindness towards us. Finally he calls it the *taste of the powers of the age to come*, by which he means that by faith we are as it were given entrance to the kingdom of heaven so that we see in the Spirit that blessed immortality which is hidden from our senses. We must recognize, therefore, that the Gospel cannot be properly known except by the illumination of the Spirit, and thus knowing it we are drawn out of the world and raised up to heaven, and as we see the goodness of God we rest on His Word.

Now there arises from this a new question, as to how it can be that one who has once arrived at this point can afterwards fall away. The Lord calls only the elect effectively, and Paul bears witness (Rom. 8.14) that those who are led by His Spirit are truly His sons, and he teaches us that it is the sure pledge of adoption if Christ has made a man a partaker of His Spirit. Moreover the elect are outwith the danger of mortal lapse, for the Father who gave them to Christ the Son to be kept by Him is greater than all, and Christ promises (John 17.12) that He will care for them all, so that none perishes.

My answer is this, that God certainly bestows His Spirit of regeneration only on the elect, and that they are distinguished from the reprobate in the fact that they are re-made in His image, and they receive the earnest of the Spirit in the hope of an inheritance to come, and by the same Spirit the Gospel is sealed in their hearts. But I do not see that this is any reason why He should not touch the reprobate with a taste of His grace, or illumine their minds with some glimmerings of His light, or affect them with some sense of His goodness, or to some extent engrave His Word in their hearts. Otherwise where would be that passing faith which Mark mentions (4.17)? Therefore there is some knowledge in the reprobate, which later vanishes away either because it drives its roots less deep than it ought to, or because it is choked and withers away.

By this rein the Lord holds us in fear and humility, and we see clearly how prone human nature otherwise is to carelessness and foolish confidence. At the same time our concern ought to be such as does not disturb the peace of our conscience. The Lord at one and the same time encourages our faith and subdues our flesh. He wills our faith to remain quiet and at rest as if in a safe harbour. Our flesh He exercises with various testings, so that it is not wanton in idleness.

6. *To renew them again unto repentance.* Although this seems hard there is no reason for anyone who pays such a penalty for his rebellion to accuse God of cruelty. This is not inconsistent with other Scripture passages where the mercy of God is offered to sinners as soon as they sigh for it (Ezek. 18.27). In them a repentance is required by which he who has once fallen headlong away from the Gospel is never really touched. Such men are deprived, as they deserve, of the Spirit of God,

and are given over to a reprobate mind, so that they are delivered to the devil and go on rushing to their doom. Thus it comes about that they do not cease from adding one sin to another until they are so hardened that they despise God or rail at Him in furious hate like men in despair. All those who are apostate come to this end, that either they are smitten with insensibility and have no fear, or because they cannot escape they curse God who is their Judge.

In short, the apostle is telling us that repentance is not in men's hands. It is given by God only to those who have not wholly fallen away from faith. This is a very salutary warning for us not to keep putting off until tomorrow and thereby estranging ourselves more and more from God. The ungodly deceive themselves by such sentiments as that it will suffice if they repent of their wicked life with their last breath. But when they come to that point, tortured as they are with dreadful torments of conscience, they have it proved to them that a man's conversion is no ordinary task. Therefore when the Lord promises pardon to none except those who repent of their sin, it is no wonder if those perish who either through despair or through contempt have hastened on obstinately to their death. But if anyone rises again from a fall, we may conclude that however seriously he may otherwise have sinned he is not guilty of rebellion.

Seeing they crucify to themselves afresh. He adds this phrase to justify the severity of God against human attacks. It is unseemly for God to expose His Son to ridicule by pardoning those who rebel against Him. Therefore such people are unworthy to obtain mercy. His reason for saying that Christ is crucified afresh is that we die with Him for the very purpose of entering into a lasting new life. Therefore those who return to death need a second sacrifice, as we shall see in chapter ten. Crucifying to *themselves* means as far as it lies in them. It would be as if Christ were a prisoner in a triumphal procession if men were free to return to Him after they had rebelled.

For the land which hath drunk the rain that cometh oft upon it, and bringeth forth herbs meet for them for whose sake it is also tilled, receiveth blessing from God: but if it beareth thorns and thistles, it is rejected and nigh unto a curse; whose end is to be burned. But, beloved, we are persuaded better things of you, and things that accompany salvation, though we thus speak: for God is not unrighteous to forget your work and the love which ye showed toward his name, in that ye ministered unto the saints, and still do minister. (7-10)

7. *For the land.* This is a most apt comparison for arousing zeal for making due progress. Just as the earth cannot bring forth a good crop

at harvest time unless the seed begins to germinate almost as soon as it has been sown, so if we want to bring forth good fruit, as soon as the Lord has sown His Word, we must strike roots in us so that they begin to emerge without delay. We cannot expect that it will bear fruit if it either becomes choked or decays. As the comparison is highly appropriate, we must apply it carefully to the apostle's purpose.

The earth, he says, which by sucking in the rain immediately from the moment of sowing brings forth a fruitful stalk, in the end by the blessing of God is brought on to a full harvest. In the same way those who take in the seed of the Gospel in their hearts, and from it bring forth a genuine shoot will keep on increasing until they produce ripe fruit. On the other hand the earth which after culture and irrigation brings forth nothing but thorns gives no hope of a harvest. Indeed the more what is produced there grows, the more hopeless it is. The only cure is for the farmer to burn the harmful and useless weeds. Similarly those who corrupt the seed of the Gospel either by their indifference or by their depraved appetites so as to produce no sign of good progress in their life show that they are unfaithful and that therefore no harvest is to be looked for in them.

The apostle is referring here not only to the fruits of the Gospel. He is also following on his advice to us to embrace the Gospel promptly and with alacrity. Moreover he says that a blade must appear soon after the seed has been sown: and further that increases come from daily irrigation. Βοτάνην εὔθετον is rendered by some 'a seasonable herb', by others 'a herb meet for them'. Either meaning suits the context. The former rendering has reference to the season: the latter to the quality. I pass by the allegorical meanings which other expositors have played with here, because they are far from the mind of the writer.

9. *But we are persuaded.* Because the foregoing sentences have been like thunderbolts which could stun the readers, their sharpness must be tempered: and so he now says that he did not speak in this way as having such an opinion of them. Certainly anyone who wants to be a good teacher ought to treat his pupils in such a way as always to encourage rather than discourage them. There is nothing that has a greater effect in alienating us from listening to teaching than to see that we are thought of as hopeless. The apostle assures the Jews that he gives them this warning because he has good hopes of them and wants to bring them to salvation. From this we conclude that it is not only unbelievers who are to be chided sharply and forcibly, but even the elect themselves, the very ones whom we reckon among the sons of God.

10. *For God is not unrighteous.* These words mean that in effect he is saying that from good beginnings he hopes for a good end. But the

difficulty arises here, that it seems as if God is bound by human obligations. I am persuaded of your salvation, he says, because God cannot forget your works: and this seems to suggest that their salvation is founded on works and that God is put in the position of being their debtor. The sophists who oppose the merits of works to the grace of God lay great stress on this sentence that God is not unrighteous. From this they conclude that He would be unjust if He did not repay works with the reward of eternal salvation.

My reply to this quite shortly is that the apostle is not referring expressly here to the cause of our salvation, and therefore no conclusion should be drawn from this passage about the merits of works, nor is it possible to determine from this what works are due. It is clear everywhere in Scripture that there is no other fount of salvation but the free mercy of God. The fact that God here and there promises rewards for works depends on the free promise by which He adopts us as sons, and reconciles us to Himself by not imputing our sins to us. 'A reward is laid up for works not through merit but out of the sheer bounty of God, and even this gratuitous recognition of works has no place except after our reception into grace through the mercy of Christ.

From this we conclude that God is not paying us a debt that He owes but He is keeping the promise He has already made, and indeed keeps it in the act of pardoning us and our works. He looks not so much on our works as on His grace in our works. Thus it happens that He is not oblivious of our works, because He recognizes in them Himself and the work of His Spirit. This is justice as the apostle understands it, because He cannot deny Himself. This passage thus corresponds to the words of Paul (Phil. 1.6): 'He which began a good work in you will perfect it.' What else will God find in us to induce Him to love us except what He has already given us?

In short, the sophists are mistaken when they imagine that there is some mutual relation between God's justice and the merits of our works. The truth rather is that God considers Himself and His gifts so as to carry on to the end what He has begun in us of His own free will, and not because of any inducement or obligation on our side. I repeat that God's justice in rewarding works lies in the fact that He is faithful and true. He has made Himself our debtor not by receiving anything from us, but by fully promising us all things, as Augustine says.

The love which ye showed. Literally, the labour of love: by which he means that we are not to spare ourselves from labour if we want to do our duty to our neighbours. We are not to help them financially only, but with advice, and by our efforts and in all kinds of ways. We must show great zeal, and put up with many annoyances, and sometimes undergo many hazards. Whoever wants to engage in the tasks of loving must be prepared for a laborious way of life.

The apostle finds proof of their love in the fact that they *ministered unto the saints and still do minister*. This reminds us that we are not to refuse the service of our brethren. In expressly mentioning *the saints* he does not mean that we are debtors to them alone. Our love ought to be visibly extended to the whole human race. But because those of the household of faith are especially commended to us, they must be our particular care. As love, when moved to do good, acts partly out of regard to God and partly out of regard to our common nature, so it follows that the nearer anyone has come to God the more worthy he is of our help. Indeed whoever we recognize as a son of God ought to be surrounded with our fraternal love.

In saying *ye ministered and still do minister*, he commends their perseverance, which is most necessary in this connexion. There is nothing easier than to grow weary in well-doing. Although there are plenty of people to be found who are ready to help their brethren, yet the virtue of constancy is rare, and a good number of them soon begin to lose their enthusiasm as though their ardour had grown cold. Yet this single word ought to give us continual encouragement, when the apostle affirms that love shown to the saints is shown toward the name of the Lord. He means that God accepts as a gift from us whatever we do for our neighbours, according to the words of Matt. 25.40: 'Inasmuch as ye did it unto one of the least of these, ye did it unto me'; and likewise Prov. 19.17: 'He that hath pity upon the poor, lendeth unto the Lord.'

And we desire that each one of you may show the same diligence unto the fulness of hope even to the end: that ye be not sluggish, but imitators of them who through faith and patience inherit the promises. For when God made promise to Abraham, since he could swear by none greater, he sware by himself, saying, surely blessing I will bless thee, and multiplying I will multiply thee. And thus, having patiently endured, he obtained the promise. (11-15)

11. *And we desire.* Just as he mixed praise with admonition os as not to irritate their spirits unreasonably, so now he gives them full warning of what they still lack in case his civility should give any sign of flattery. You have given evidence of your love, he says, by many proofs and demonstrations. Now it remains for your faith to correspond to it. You have worked earnestly so as not to fail in your obligations to men; you must now apply yourself with no less zeal to progress in your faith, so as to show God its firm and full certainty. By saying this the apostle is showing that there are two parts of Christianity

corresponding to the two tables of the law. Anyone who separates the one from the other is left with something torn and mutilated. From this is it clear what sort of teachers they are who omit any mention of faith and simply urge honesty and integrity towards men. I maintain that this is a pagan philosophy lurking beneath the mask of a superficial justice, if indeed anything deserves the name of a philosophy which so misarranges its tenets that it robs God who has the pre-eminence of His rights. Therefore let us remember that the Christian life is complete in all its parts only if we direct our energies both to faith and to love.

Unto the fulness of hope. Because those who professed the Christian faith were being distracted by all kinds of opinions, or were still being entangled in many forms of superstition, he bids them be so established in a sure faith that they do not waver any more nor be driven this way and that before the alternating winds of doubts. This advice applies to everyone. As the truth of God is unwavering, so likewise the faith which relies on Him, if it is to be true, must be sure and above all doubt. This is πληροφορία, that is, an undoubting conviction by which the godly mind resolves in itself that it is not right to call in question what God who cannot deceive or lie has spoken.

The word *hope* is used here in the sense of faith because of their close association. The apostle seems to have used it on purpose because he is speaking about perseverance. From this we may conclude how far removed from faith is that general kind of understanding that is common both to unbelievers and to devils. They too believe that God is just and true: but they derive no good hope from that belief because they do not know His fatherly grace in Christ. We must therefore know that true faith always goes hand in hand with hope.

He says *even to the end*, or to perfection, so that they will know that they have not yet reached the goal and will therefore think of further progress. He mentions *diligence* so that they will know that they are not to subside into idleness but must strive with all earnestness. It is no small thing to ascend above the heavens, especially for those who can hardly crawl on the earth. There are innumerable obstacles in the way. There is nothing more difficult than to keep our minds raised to heavenly things when the whole force of our nature presses us to turn downwards and when Satan drags us earthwards with all his countless stratagems. For these reasons he instructs us to beware of spiritual laziness or softness.

12. *But imitators of them.* Against idleness he contrasts this call to imitation. It is exactly as though he were saying that we must have continual quickness of mind. This carries much more weight when he reminds us that the fathers were only made partakers in the promises

by the unconquered firmness of their faith. Examples show us better things. If the bare doctrine is propounded it does not have the same effect as when we see what is demanded of us actually fulfilled in the person of Abraham. The example of Abraham is taken, not because it is unique, but because it is more outstanding than the others. Abraham has this in common with all the saints, and yet he was deservedly made the father of the faithful. It is therefore no wonder that from them all the apostle chooses him especially on whom to direct the attention of his readers, when he is concerned to provide the clearest mirror of faith.

Faith and patience are used by hypallage for a patient faith, that is faith that has patience as its companion. Faith is required first. But, because many people, who at first show a wonderful faith, soon grow weary, endurance is the true proof of a faith that is not passing nor transient. In saying *through faith inherit the promises*, he takes away the notion of merit, and that becomes still clearer when he says that they obtained their inheritance. We are only heirs by right of adoption.

13. *For when God made promise to Abraham.* The writer's purpose here is to show that the grace of God is offered to us in vain unless we accept the promise by faith and patiently foster it in our heart of hearts. He does so by this argument that when God promised innumerable off-spring to Abraham, the thing seemed to be incredible. Sarah had been barren for the whole of her life; they had both reached senile old age: they were nearer the grave than the conjugal bed; they had no vigour to beget children, and Sarah's womb, which had been barren even in the prime of her life, was now lifeless. Who could believe that from them would come a race equalling the number of the stars and like the sand of the sea? It was against all reason. Nonetheless Abraham looked forward to this and had no fear of being disappointed because he relied on the Word spoken by God. To follow the apostle's reasoning we must note the temporal circumstances of all this. That is the point of what follows, that he was made partaker of this blessing after he had waited for what no one thought would ever happen. We must give glory to God in the way that we quietly hope for what He does not yet show to our senses, but hides away and postpones for a long time so as to exercise our patience.

Why God swears *by Himself* we shall see in a moment. The force of the oath, *surely blessing I will bless thee* has already been explained in chapter three. God's name is not expressly used here, but is to be understood, because unless He fulfils His promises, He is shown to be unfaithful.

For men swear by the greater: and in every dispute of theirs the oath is

final for confirmation. Wherein God, being minded to show more
abundantly unto the heirs of the promise the immutability of his counsel,
interposed with an oath: that by two immutable things, in which it is
impossible for God to lie, we may have a strong encouragement, who
have fled for refuge to lay hold of the hope set before us: which we have
as an anchor of the soul, a hope both sure and stedfast and entering into
that which is within the veil; whither as a forerunner Jesus entered for
us, having become a high priest for ever after the order of Melchizedek.

(16-20)

16. The writer argues from the less to the greater. If trust is placed
in the oath of a man (who is by his very nature a liar) because he invokes the name of God as a guarantee, how much more trust is due to
God Himself, who is eternal truth, when He swears by Himself? He
embroiders this sentence at some length.

First of all he says that *men swear by the greater*, meaning that because
they lack due authority in themselves, they borrow it from somewhere
else. He goes on to say that there is so much reverence given to an
oath, that it is sufficient confirmation and puts an end to all disputes
where there is no human testimony or other evidences of proof. Will
not he then be an adequate witness whom all parties call as a witness?
Will not he awaken confidence in what he says who removes all doubt
between others by his authority? If when the name of God is pronounced by a man it carries so much weight, how much more should
it have, when God Himself swears by His Name. So much for his
main point.

In passing, there are two things to be noted here. We must swear
by the Name of God when necessity demands that we swear, and
secondly that the use of an oath is permissible for Christians because
it is a lawful means of resolving controversies. God clearly orders us
to swear by His Name, and if other names are mixed in with His, He
warns us that that is a profanation of the oath.

There are three particular reasons for this. First, that when there is
no way of bringing truth to light, we may not have recourse to anyone
other than God for the purpose of declaring it: for He is Himself
eternal truth. Secondly, since He alone is the searcher of hearts (Jer.
17.10), we deprive Him of His proper function if we appeal to any
other judge in matters that are shrouded in mystery and hidden from
human investigation. Thirdly, when we swear we not only call on
Him to be our witness, but we also appeal to Him to be the avenger
of our perjury if we are false. It is therefore no wonder that He is
aroused to such anger against those who swear by another name. To
that extent He is robbed of His proper honour.

The fact that from time to time different forms are used in Scripture makes no difference to this doctrine. Men do not swear by heaven and earth as though they attribute some divine power to them, or ascribe to them the smallest particle of Godhead. By this (so to speak) indirect protestation they refer to God alone. There are various kinds of protestations. The chief one is when we call Him Judge, and appeal directly to His judgment-seat. Another is when we name things that are especially dear to us, such as our life or our head or the like. A third is when we set up creatures as witnesses before God. In all these ways we are properly swearing by none other than God. For this reason those who maintain that it is lawful to join dead saints along with God giving them also the right to punish show their depravity no less than their ignorance.

Moreover, as has been said, this passage teaches us that some form of oath is legitimate among Christians. We must have regard to this fact as against some extremists who completely repudiate the rule of solemn swearing which God has laid down in His Law. Certainly the apostle talks here about the practice of swearing as of something holy and approved by God. He does not say that it used to be the practice once upon a time, but declares that it is still in force. Let this therefore be our aid to lay hold of truth when other forms of proof are lacking.

17. *God being mindful to show more abundantly.* See how tenderly God indulges our slowness, as a good Father should. He sees that we will not be satisfied simply with His Word and therefore to impress it more fully on our hearts He adds His oath. This makes it clear how important it is for us for this certainty of His goodness towards us to be manifest, so that there is no further occasion for hesitation or fear. As God forbids His Name to be taken in vain or lightly, and proclaims merciless vengeance on all who rashly abuse it, insisting that due respect must be paid to His majesty, so He instructs us that it must be held in the highest regard and honour. Certainty of salvation is therefore a necessary thing and in order to secure it God who forbids rash swearing has deigned to take His oath. Hence we may conclude what great store He sets by our salvation for the interest of which He not only pardons our unbelief, but gives up His own right, yields to us far more than there is any need to, and in His kindness heals us.

Unto the heirs. He seems to designate the Jews in particular. Even though the inheritance has at last been given to the Gentiles also, yet the Jews were His first and lawful heirs. The Gentiles are outsiders and second heirs, so made against the law of nature. Thus Peter in Acts 2.39 addressing the Jews in his first sermon says: 'To you is the promise and to your children, and to all that are afar off, even as many as the Lord our God shall call unto Him.' Of course he leaves a place for extraordinary heirs but he places the Jews in the front rank, as again he says in chapter 3.25: 'Ye are the sons of the prophets and of the covenant...' etc. So in this passage, in order to make the Jews more ready to accept the covenant the apostle says that it was chiefly on their account that it was confirmed by the addition of an oath: although nowadays this sentence refers to us also because we have entered into the place which they left empty by their faithlessness.

Note that he calls the *counsel* of God what the Gospels bear witness to us, so that no one may doubt that this doctrine is the expression of the inmost feeling of God. Those who believe must be firmly persuaded that whenever they hear the Word of the Gospel, the secret counsel of God which was hidden in Him is being proclaimed to them, and that from this it is being revealed what He has decreed about our salvation before the creation of the world.

18. *By two immutable things.* Where God is concerned both what He says and what He swears are immutable. With men it is quite different. Their vanity results in their word being too unreliable, but the Word of God is described in terms such as that it is pure and undefiled like gold seven times refined (Ps. 12.7). Indeed, Balaam, even though he was an avowed enemy, was forced to make this testimony (Num. 23.19): 'God is not like a man, that he should lie: neither the son of man that he should repent. Hath he said and shall he not do it? Or hath he spoken, and shall he not make it good?' The Word of God is therefore certain truth, $\kappa a \grave{\iota} \ a\dot{\upsilon}\tau\acute{o}\pi\iota\sigma\tau os$. When to this there is added a sworn oath, what is already a full measure receives still further increase. From this we have strong encouragement in that God who cannot lie when He speaks is not content merely to promise but gives His sworn Word.

We who have fled for refuge. By this he means that we do not really trust God except when we are stripped of all other defence and take refuge in His firm promise, finding there our only asylum. The participle $\kappa a\tau a\phi\acute{\upsilon}\gamma o\nu\tau\epsilon s$ expresses our need and necessity, because we do not fly for refuge to God without being forced thereby. When he adds *to lay hold of the hope set before us* he indicates that we have not far to seek for the assistance that we need, because God meets us of His own accord, and as it were puts the stuff of faith (*fidendi materiam*) into our hands. Just as it was His will to encourage the Jews with this truth to embrace the Gospel in which salvation was offered them, so He has deprived those who do not believe of every excuse for rejecting the grace offered to them. Certainly this can be said more truly now that the Gospel has been revealed, than it could in the promulgation of the Law. There is now no cause for saying: 'Who shall ascend into heaven, or who shall descend into the abyss, or who shall cross over the sea?

The word is nigh thee, in thy mouth and in thy heart' (Deut. 30.12, Rom. 10.6).

The word *hope* is used by metonymy, the effect being taken for the cause. I understand it as referring to the promise on which our hope relies, and I do not agree with those who take hope as meaning the thing hoped for. Further this must also be added, that the apostle is not speaking of the promise in a vacuum or suspended in the air, but as received by us in faith, or if you prefer it in a word, hope here means the promise laid hold of by faith. The verb κρατῆσαι, like the noun *hope*, indicates the same immutability as before.

19. *As an anchor.* There is a graceful simile here in the comparison of faith leaning on the Word of God to an anchor. Certainly as long as we are pilgrims in this world we have no firm ground to stand on, but we are tossed about as if we were in the midst of the sea, and a stormy one at that. The devil never ceases from stirring up countless tempests which would at once capsize and submerge our ship if we do not cast our anchor far down in the depths. There is no haven anywhere apparent to our sight, but to whatever direction we turn our gaze, the only thing in view is water, and indeed waves which mount up and threaten us. But just as an anchor is let down through the midst of the water to a dark, hidden place, and while it remains there it holds the ship that is exposed to the waves safely in its station so that it is not swept away, so our hope is fixed on the unseen God. There is this difference, that an anchor is cast down on the sea because there is solid ground at the bottom, but our hope rises and flies aloft because it finds nothing to stand on in this world. It cannot rely on created things, but finds rest in God alone. Just as the cable on which the anchor hangs joins the ship itself to the ground through a long dark gulf, so the truth of God is a chain for binding us to Himself, so that no distance of place and no darkness may hinder us from cleaving to Him. When we are bound in this way to God, even though we have to contend with continual storms, we are safe from the danger of shipwreck. That is why he says that the anchor is *sure and stedfast.* It is possible for an anchor to be torn out or for a cable to break or a ship to be broken in pieces by the violence of the waves. That happens on the sea. But the power of God to support us is quite different, as is also the strength of hope and the firmness of His Word.

Entering into that. As we have said, until faith reaches to God, it finds only what is unstable and transient. It is therefore necessary for it to break through to heaven. But because the apostle is concerned with Hebrews, he refers to the old tabernacle, and says that they ought not to linger in the things which are seen, but go on to the holy of holies which lies behind the veil. It is as though he were saying that we must rise above all the old external forms, so as to put faith in Christ alone.

This line of reasoning is to be carefully noted, namely that because Christ has entered heaven our faith must also be directed there. This is the source of our knowledge that faith must not look anywhere else. It is useless for men to look for God in His majesty, because it is too remote and far from them: but Christ stretches out his hand to lead us to heaven, as was indeed foreshadowed earlier in the Law. The high priest used to enter the holy of holies not only in his own name, but in that of the people, as one who in a way carried all the twelve tribes on his breast and on his shoulders, because twelve stones were woven into his breastplate and their names were engraved on the two onyx stones on his shoulders to be a reminder of them, so that they all went into the sanctuary together in the person of the one man. The apostle is therefore right when he states that our High Priest has entered heaven, because He has done so not only for Himself, but also for us. There is therefore no cause to fear that the door of heaven may be shut to our faith, since it is never disjoined from Christ. Because it is for us to follow Christ who goes before us, He is called our Fore-runner.

CHAPTER SEVEN

For this Melchizedek, king of Salem, priest of God most High, who met Abraham returning from the slaughter of the kings and blessed him, to whom also Abraham divided a tenth part of all (being first, by interpretation, King of righteousness, and then also King of Salem, which is, King of peace: without father, without mother, without genealogy, having neither beginning of days nor end of life, but made like unto the Son of God), abideth a priest continually. (1-3)

1. *For this Melchizedek.* So far in his exhortations he has encouraged the Jews to give their attention to the force of the comparison between Christ and Melchizedek. At the end of the last chapter he has again quoted from the Psalms in order to return from that digression to his starting-point. Now he follows more fully the theme which he has lightly touched on, and He enumerates one by one the points to be noticed about Melchizedek which make him like Christ. It is no wonder that he marshals his argument so carefully. It was no ordinary occurrence that in a country possessed by so many pagan superstitions a man was found who held to the pure worship of God. He was the neighbour on the one hand of Sodom and Gomorrah, and on the other of the Canaanites, so that on every side he was hedged about by unholy men. Moreover the whole world had so fallen into godlessness that it was scarcely believable that God was truly worshipped anywhere but in the family of Abraham. His father and grandfather who ought to have been men of the highest integrity had already fallen into idolatry. It was therefore quite remarkable that there was still a king who not only preserved true religion, but himself performed the office of a priest. It was certainly necessary that everything excellent should be found in the one who was the type of the Son of God. It is clear from the Psalms that Christ was foreshadowed in this type. It was not without reason that David said: *Thou art a high priest for ever after the order of Melchizedek.* Rather on the contrary in this verse a sublime mystery is commended to the Church. Let us now look at the different ways in which the apostle draws a comparison between Christ and Melchizedek himself.

The first similarity is in the name. There is no lack of mystery in his being called king of righteousness, because, even though this compliment is given to kings who rule with moderation and justice, yet such a title properly belongs to Christ alone, since He not only exercises a just rule like others, but in addition He communicates to us the

88

justice of God. He does this partly by making it possible for us to be accounted righteous by a free act of reconciliation, and partly by renewing us by His Spirit so that we live holy and godly lives. He is therefore said to be king of righteousness because of what He does in imparting righteousness to all His people. From this it follows that outside His kingdom nothing but sin holds sway among men. Thus when Zechariah sends Him to take possession of His kingdom as it were by a solemn divine decree, he praises Him in this way (Zech. 9.9): *Rejoice, O daughter of Zion: behold thy king cometh unto thee: he is just.* He means by this that justice which we otherwise lack is brought by the advent of Christ.

The second likeness that the apostle notes is in the realm of *peace.* This peace is the fruit of justice about which he has been speaking. It follows from this that wherever the reign of Christ extends there must be peace, as is set forth in Isa. chapters 2 and 9, and in other similar places. But since to the Hebrews peace means a condition of prosperity and happiness, this passage could be so taken. I prefer, however, to understand it as the inner peace which gives us a calm and peaceful conscience in the sight of God. You cannot properly appreciate the real value of this blessing unless you think on the other hand how dreadful it is to be tortured by a continual dispeace, a thing which is the inevitable fate of us all until our consciences are set at peace by reconciliation with God through Christ.

3. *Without father.* I prefer this to reading 'of an unknown father'. The apostle wants to express something more emphatic than the mere fact that the family of Melchizedek was obscure or unknown. I am unimpressed by the objection that the reality does not correspond with the figure in that Christ has a Father in heaven and a mother on earth. The apostle quickly shows his meaning in adding the single phrase *without genealogy.* By this he exempts Melchizedek himself from the general law of descent by birth, and by this he shows that he was eternal, and that his recent birth among men is not to be looked for. It is certain that he was begotten by parents, but the apostle is not discussing him here as an individual man, but rather setting him forth as the type of Christ. Therefore he allows himself to see in him nothing but what Scripture teaches. In dealing with everything that has to do with Christ we must scrupulously observe that we do not accept anything that is not from the Word of God. Now, since the Holy Spirit in introducing this king as the most outstanding of his time makes no mention of his origin, nor later does He make any mention of his death, does this not have the force of ascribing to him eternity? What was foreshadowed in Melchizedek, was shown in reality in Christ. We ought therefore to be content with this moderate know-

ledge that in showing us Melchizedek as one who was never born and who never died, Scripture is setting forth as in a picture the truth that for Christ there is neither beginning nor end.

From this we learn how much reverence and restraint is called for in dealing with the spiritual mysteries of God. What he cannot find written anywhere in Scripture the apostle not only freely ignores, but wishes us also to ignore. Surely it is not legitimate for us to assume anything about Christ from our own senses. Melchizedek is not thought of here (as the phrase goes) in his private capacity, but as a sacred type of Christ. It must not be thought to be an omission either by accident or by lack of thought that he is given no family connexion, and that there is no word of his death. The truth is that the Spirit has done this purposely so as to elevate him for us above the common herd of men. It does not seem a likely conjecture of those who accept Melchizedek as Shem, the son of Noah. If we try to refer to some definite and known man, then this third likeness between Melchizedek and Christ will not hold good.

Made like unto. That is, as far as the mode of signification (*significandi ratio*) required: for the analogy between the reality and the sign (*analogia inter rem et signum*) must always be kept in mind. Those who invent the story that he came down from heaven so that they can assimilate him to the reality are merely stupid. It is enough that we see the lineaments of Christ in him, just as the form of a living man can be seen in a painting, and yet the man himself is different from his picture. It does not seem to be worth while to refute the fancies of those who dream that it was Christ who appears there, or the Holy Spirit, or an angel, unless anyone thought it to be the duty of a right-minded man to argue with Postellus and other such fanatics. That worthless imposter asserts that he is Melchizedek with no less arrogance than those mad spirits of old (of whom Jerome speaks) who imagined that they were Christ.

Now consider how great this man was, unto whom Abraham, the patriarch, gave a tenth out of the chief spoils. And they indeed of the sons of Levi that receive the priest's office have commandment to take tithes of the people according to the law, that is, of their brethren, though these have come out of the loins of Abraham: but he whose genealogy is not counted from them hath taken tithes of Abraham, and hath blessed him that hath the promises. But without any dispute the less is blessed of the better. And here men that die receive tithes: but there is one, or whom it is witnessed that he liveth. And so to say, through Abraham even Levi who receiveth tithes, hath paid tithes: for he was yet in the loins of his father when Melchizedek met him. (4-10)

4. *Now consider*. The fourth point in the comparison between Christ and Melchizedek is that Abraham paid him tithes. Although the institution of tithes arises from several causes, the apostle here refers to the one that serves his present purpose. One such reason why tithes were paid to the Levites was because they were the sons of Abraham to whose seed the land was promised. Thus by hereditary right a portion of the land was allotted to them. Since they were deprived of the possession of land, compensation was given in the form of tithes. There was also another reason, namely, that, since they were occupied with the worship of God and the public ministry of the Church, it was right that they should be supported at the cost of the whole people. The rest of the Israelites owed them their tithes as the proper recompense for their work. But those reasons are not relevant to the present argument, and so the apostle passed them by. The one which is germane to the present discussion is that the people offered tithes to God as a sacred tribute, and the Levites received them. From this it is clear that it was no light honour, because God was in some way using them as His substitutes in His place. Therefore when Abraham a foremost servant of God and a prophet offered tithes to Melchizedek the priest he thereby admitted that Melchizedek excelled him in honour. If *Abraham, the patriarch*, considered him to have precedence over himself, his rank must be one of unusual and outstanding dignity. The description *patriarch* is adduced to add weight. It is especially a mark of honour for Abraham to be called a father in the Church of God.

The argument thus is as follows. Abraham who excels all others is himself inferior to Melchizedek. Therefore Melchizedek has the highest place of honour and has precedence over all the Levites. This is proved by the fact that what Abraham owed to God he paid into the hand of Melchizedek: thus by the payment of tithes he admitted his inferiority.

5. *And they indeed, etc.* This is preferable to the rendering 'because they are the sons of Levi'. The apostle is not giving it as a reason, that the priests receive the tithes because they are of the sons of Levi, but he is comparing the whole tribe with Melchizedek in this way: when God gave the Levites the right to exact tithes from the people, he set them over all the Israelites, although they were all alike descended from the same parent. Yet Abraham, who is the father of them all, paid tithes to a priest of another race. Therefore all the descendants of Abraham are subject to this priest. Thus the right bestowed on the Levites was a particular one in regard to the rest of their brethren, but Melchizedek occupies the highest place without exception, so that all are subject to him. Some think that the apostle is speaking of the tenths of the tithes which the Levites paid to the higher priests, but there is no

reason why we should thus restrict the trend of his argument. The
more probable interpretation is the one I have expounded.

6. *He hath blessed.* This is the fifth thing that the apostle points out
in his comparison between Christ and Melchizedek. He assumes one
of the accepted axioms that what is less is blessed by the greater. He
goes on to say that Melchizedek blessed Abraham. Therefore it follows
that Abraham is the lesser. For the sake of adding weight he again gives
Abraham particular praise, since the more excellent Abraham is, the
higher is the dignity of Melchizedek himself. For this purpose he says
that Abraham had the promises, by which he means that he was the
first founder of the holy people with whom God made a covenant of
eternal life. It was no common mark of honour that God should
choose him alone out of all men on whom to bestow the right of
adoption and the testimony of His love. Yet all this did not prevent
him with all his excellence submitting himself to the priesthood of
Melchizedek. It can thus be seen how great is he to whom Abraham
deferred in two matters—that he allowed himself to be blessed by him,
and that he paid tithes to him as to God's representative.

7. *That which is less.* We must first ask what is meant here by the
word *blessing*. Blessing is a solemn act of prayer with which one who
is endowed with some outstanding public honour commends to God
private individuals who are under his care. There is another kind of
blessing which happens when we pray in turn for one another. This
is a common practice among all holy people. This blessing of which
the apostle speaks is the symbol of greater power. In this way Isaac
blessed his son Jacob (Gen. 27.27) and Jacob himself blessed his grand-
sons Ephraim and Manasseh (Gen. 48.15). This was not a mutual
blessing such as would make the son the equal of the father: but a
higher authority was needed for a valid blessing. Further evidence for
this can be found in the sixth chapter of Numbers (Num. 6.23), where,
after the command to bless the people is given to the priests, the promise
is immediately added that those to whom they gave their benediction
would be blessed. The priestly blessing, I repeat, depended on the principle that it was not so much of man but of God. As the priest took the
place of Christ in offering sacrifices, so in blessing the people he was
nothing but the servant and representative of God most High. We must
take it in this sense when Luke records (24.50) that Christ lifted up His
hands and blessed the apostles. Without doubt He borrowed the rite of
raising His hand from the priests to show that He is the One through
whom God the Father blesses us. Mention is also made of this benediction in Ps. 116.17 and 118.1.

Let us now apply this idea to the apostle's discussion. Since the
priestly blessing is a divine work it is at the same time evidence of

greater honour. Therefore in blessing Abraham Melchizedek arrogated to himself a higher status. He did not do this presumptuously, but in accordance with the rights of a priest. He is therefore more eminent than Abraham. Yet Abraham is the one with whom God was pleased to conclude a covenant of salvation. Therefore although he excelled all the others, he was surpassed only by Melchizedek.

8. *Of whom it is witnessed that he liveth.* He takes silence about death as evidence of life (as I have said above). Certainly this does not hold in other cases, but it is properly valid in the case of Melchizedek in so far as he is the type of Christ. Because he is here dealing with the spiritual kingdom and priesthood of Christ, there is no place for human conjectures, nor is it proper for us to look for any information apart from what we read in the Scriptures. At the same time you are not to conclude from this that the very man who met Abraham is still alive as some stupid people have naïvely thought. This truth is to be applied to the other figure whom he represented, that is, that of the Son of God. In this verse the apostle is arguing that the dignity of Melchizedek's priesthood is perpetual, while that of the Levites is temporal. He reasons thus—those to whom the Law assigns tithes are mortal men, thus indicating that the rights of the priesthood are to be annulled at some time, just as their life had an end. But Scripture has no record of the death of Melchizedek when it describes how tithes were paid to him. Therefore the right of his priesthood is not limited within any given length of time, but rather bears out that it is of eternal duration.

This addition is made so that it does not seem as if a later law (as is usual) had taken the place of an earlier. Otherwise it could have been objected that the right which Melchizedek once possessed was now no longer valid because God had brought in another law by Moses transferring that right to the Levites. The apostle meets this objection by saying that tithes were paid to the Levites for the time being, because they did not live on, whereas Melchizedek being immortal retained to the very end what was once given him by God.

9. *Even Levi hath paid tithes.* He goes on further to say that even Levi *who was then in the loins of Abraham* was not immune from the same subjection, because in paying tithes Abraham subjected both himself and those who came after him to the priesthood of Melchizedek. On the other hand it could be objected that in the same way Judah, from whose ancestry Christ was born, had also paid tithes. This problem can be easily resolved by bearing in mind two things which ought to be established as beyond dispute by Christians. Firstly, Christ is not to be thought of as any ordinary man among the sons of Abraham, but is exempted from the common herd by His particular privilege. This is what He Himself said (Matt. 22.45): 'If David then

calleth him Lord, how is he his son?' We see therefore that it is wrong to argue from Levi to Christ.

Secondly, since Melchizedek is the type of Christ we should not be guilty of any reasoning that puts the one in opposition to the other. We must keep in mind the common saying that what is subordinate is not in conflict. Therefore since the type comes short of its reality it ought not to be set in contrast to it, nor can it be: that would be a conflict of equals.

With these five points the apostle has completed his comparison between Christ and Melchizedek, and in so doing has repudiated the comment of those who look for the main likeness in the offering of bread and wine. We see that the apostle is here carefully and with proper attention examining each point. He takes up one by one the name of each man, the seat of his kingdom, the fact of his endless life, the law of tithes, and the blessing.

Some say that these matters are less important than the offering. Are we then to say that the Spirit of God lapsed into forgetfulness so that He took time over these little things and yet left out what was the chief thing and had the greatest relevance to the matter in hand? I am all the more surprised that so many ancient doctors of the Church were so taken up with this trend of thought that they confined their attention to the offering of bread and wine. They speak like this—Christ is a high priest according to the order of Melchizedek. Melchizedek offered bread and wine. Therefore the sacrifices of bread and wine are the symbols of the priesthood of Christ. After this the apostle goes on to speak at length about the old sacrifices, but he says nothing at all about this new sacrifice of bread and wine. Where then did the ecclesiastical writers get this idea from? Surely it was in this way, that as one error leads to another, having invented on their own a sacrifice in the Lord's Supper without any authority of Christ, and thus having debased the Supper by adding an idea of sacrifice, they then tried afterwards to find justification to give credence to their error. This offering of bread and wine seemed attractive, and they adopted it forthwith without thinking. Who will admit that these men were more intelligent than the Spirit of God? If we accept their tradition then the Spirit of God will be found guilty of ignorance in failing to take note of a fact of such importance, especially when it refers directly to the matter in hand.

I conclude from this that these fathers invented for themselves a sacrifice of which Moses never thought. He does not record that Melchizedek offered bread and wine to God, but in fact to Abraham and his companions (Gen. 14.18): 'And Melchizedek, king of Salem,' went out to meet him and 'brought forth bread and wine: and he was priest of God Most High. And he blessed him.' The first thing he records was a royal act, namely, the refreshment of those who were tired after their battle and their journey. The blessing referred to his office as a priest. If there is any mystery about the offering, it is only fulfilled in Christ inasmuch as He feeds us when we are hungry and tired out with weariness. The papists are doubly ridiculous, in that they first of all deny that there is bread and wine in the Mass, and then go on to prattle about the sacrifice of bread and wine.

Now if there was perfection through the Levitical priesthood (for under it hath the people received the law), what further need was there that another priest should arise after the order of Melchizedek, and not be reckoned after the order of Aaron? For the priesthood being changed, there is made of necessity a change also of the law. For he of whom these things are said belongeth to another tribe, from which no man hath given attendance at the altar. For it is evident that our Lord hath sprung out of Judah: as to which tribe Moses spake nothing concerning priests. (11-14)

11. *If there was perfection.* On the same evidence the apostle concludes that the Old Testament was repeated by the coming of Christ. So far he has been discussing the function and person of the priest. But because God instituted the priesthood in order to ratify the Law, it follows that when the one is abolished the other also ceases. To understand this better we must keep in mind the axiom that no covenant between God and men is confirmed and ratified unless it is supported by a priesthood. The apostle says that the Law was imposed on the people of old under the Levitical priesthood, implying thereby not only that that priesthood prevailed in the time of the Law, but that it was instituted in order to establish the Law, as we have said.

The argument now runs as follows—If the ministry of the Church was perfected under the order of Aaron, why was it necessary to go back to a different order? There is no change in perfection. It follows, therefore, that the ministry of the Law was not perfect, because a new order had to be set up, of which David speaks.

For under it hath the people received the law. This parenthesis is put in so that we may know that the Law was attached to the priesthood. The apostle's aim is to demonstrate that the law of Moses had no final goal at which one could stop. He demonstrates it by the abolition of the priesthood in this way: if the old priesthood had had the power fully to establish the Law on a firm foundation, God would never have replaced it with something new and different. But now because someone might doubt whether the abolition of the Law was the consequence of the end of the priesthood he says that the former was not only brought under the latter, but was established by it.

12. *For the priesthood being changed.* Since the circumstances of the Law and of the priesthood are the same, Christ is made not only Priest but Lawgiver. Thus there is transferred to Him not only the right of Aaron but also that of Moses. The main point of this is that the ministry of Moses was no less temporal than that of Aaron, and therefore by the coming of Christ both have been repealed, since the one could not stand without the other.

By the phrase *of the law,* we must understand what refers particularly to Moses. The Law contains both the rule for good living and the free covenant of life, and there run through it many outstanding passages which instruct us in the faith and in the fear of God. None of this has been abolished in Christ, but only that part which was involved in the old priesthood.

Christ is here being compared with Moses. What is common to both of them does not come into the argument, but only those points where they differ from each other. It is common to both to offer God's loving-kindness to us, to set down the rules for holy and godly living, to teach the true worship of God and to encourage us to faith and patience and all the practices of holiness. There is however this difference between Moses and Christ, that since the Gospel was not yet revealed in all its clearness, Moses kept the people under a veil: that since the reality was not yet shown forth he presented the foretaste of Christ in types and shadows: that he adapted himself to convince the ignorant people and did not rise above the childish elements. We must remember that the Law is spoken of as that part of his ministry which was peculiar to Moses, and different from that of Christ. Since it was subject to the ancient priesthood, when this was abolished, the other came to an end at the same time.

Since Christ is set up as Priest, and is also invested with the power of a Lawgiver in order to be the Servant and Interpreter of the New Testament the word Law is applied, somewhat inappropriately, to the Gospel. This impropriety, however, is not really absurd, but rather by its very antithesis adds grace to the argument as in Rom. 7.

The depravity of the Pope was utterly impudent in inserting in his decretals that he was now endowed with this same power that Aaron once had in that the Law with the priesthood has been transferred to him. We see what the apostle is saying. He maintains that the ceremonies have ceased from the time that Christ came forth with the command to proclaim the new covenant. It is nonsense to conclude from that that anything has passed to the ministers of Christ. It is the person of Christ alone that is contrasted with Moses and Aaron. On what pretext will Antichrist arrogate to himself any such right? I do not argue here simply for the sake of refuting such gross impertinence but it is worth while indicating to readers this sacrilegious impudence so that they see how unconcerned this good servant of the servants of Christ is about the honour of his Master, and how horribly he violates the Scriptures in order to give some kind of pretence to his tyranny.

13. *He of whom these things are said.* Because the apostle is writing to those who confess that Jesus the Son of Mary is the Christ, he shows that an end was put to the ancient priesthood because this new Priest who has taken the place of the old is from a different tribe than Levi. Now according to the Law the priestly dignity was to remain in possession of that tribe as a particular privilege. He says that it was *evident* that Christ was born of the tribe of Judah, because it was then a commonly known fact. There was especial certainty resting in the promise. When they recognized Him as Christ it was also necessary to be convinced that He was the Son of David; for He who was promised could not come from any other origin.

And what we say is yet more abundantly evident, if after the likeness of Melchizedek there ariseth another priest, who hath been made, not after the law of a carnal commandment, but after the power of an endless life: for it is witnessed of him, Thou art a high priest for ever after the order of Melchizedek. For there is a disannulling of a foregoing commandment because of its weakness and unprofitableness (for the law made nothing perfect), and a bringing in thereupon of a better hope, through which we draw nigh unto God. And inasmuch as it is not without the taking of an oath (for they indeed have been made priests without an oath; but he with an oath by him that saith of him, The Lord sware and will not repent himself, thou art a high priest for ever); by so much also hath Jesus become the surety of a better covenant. (15-22)

15. *Is yet more abundantly evident.* He adduces another argument to prove that the Law has been repealed. Up till now he has argued from the person of the Priest: now he argues from the nature of the priesthood and the reason for which it was set up. The old priesthood (he says) was set up by external rites, but the priesthood of Christ then is nothing but the spiritual. This makes it clear that the former was liable to change and transitory, and at the same time demonstrates the eternal nature of the latter.

Carnal commandment is taken in the sense of physical, that is, of external ceremonies. We know how Aaron and his sons were initiated. What was fulfilled in Christ by the hidden, heavenly power of the Spirit was in His case foreshadowed by oil, by various vestments, by the sprinkling of blood, and by other earthly rites. This kind of institution fitted the nature of the priesthood. It follows, therefore, that the priesthood itself was liable to change, although, as we shall see later, the priesthood was not so carnal as not to be at the same time spiritual. Here the apostle is only concerned with the difference of Aaron from Christ. However spiritual the meaning of these shadows may have been, they were nevertheless simply shadows, and are properly called earthly because they consist of elements of this world.

16. *After the power of an endless life.* Because Christ is the eternal Priest He ought to be distinguished from Aaron by the manner of His institution. This is done in that it was not Moses, a mortal man, who consecrated him but the Holy Spirit, and that not with oil, nor with the blood of goats, nor by the outward show of vestments, but by the heavenly power which the apostle contrasts with the weak elements. We see, therefore, how the eternity of the priesthood is shown in Christ.

17. *Thou art a high priest for ever.* In this passage the apostle lays stress on the single word *for ever*. It strengthens what he has said about *endless life*. He points out that Christ is different from the whole tribe of Levi, because He has been made a Priest for ever. It could be objected (as the Jews do) that לעולם (*le'olam*) does not always mean eternity, but rather the space of one age, or a long time. There is the fact that when Moses speaks of the oil sacrifices (Exod. 12.17 and 19.9) he often uses this kind of language, 'This will be an ordinance for ever.' My answer is that whenever the sacrifices of the Law are mentioned, the word 'for ever' is confined to the time of the Law. This should not be thought absurd, for the coming of Christ has in a sense brought about a renewing of the world. Whenever Moses speaks of the status of his own ministry, he extends the longest time no further than Christ.

At the same time, however, it must be noticed, that the duration 'for ever' is applied to the old sacrifices not in respect of the external rite so much as on account of its mystical significance. For the present, however, we should be content with this reasoning, that 'for ever' refers to Moses and his ministry, which was brought to an end by the kingdom of Christ, under whom the world was renewed. When Christ arises, and an everlasting priesthood is conferred on Him, we shall find no end to His age to allow of a termination in a given period of time. We must, therefore, take this word to mean nothing else than eternity. The force of the phrase לעולם must always be judged in this context.

18. *For there is a disannulling.* Since the apostle's argument turns on the point that the Law came to an end with the priesthood, he explains the reason why it had to be abolished, namely, because it was weak

and futile. He says this with regard to the ceremonies which had no substance in themselves, nor in themselves could have any saving power. The promise of grace that was attached to them (as Moses constantly testifies) that God would be appeased by sacrifices and that sins would be expiated, did not really belong organically to the sacrifices, but was fortuitous. As all the types had reference to Christ, so they all derived their power and effect from Him. They could do nothing or effect nothing by themselves, but all their power depended on Christ alone. Since the Jews in their stupidity set these in opposition to Christ, the apostle relates his argument to their way of thinking and draws the true contrast between them and Christ. The moment they are separated from Christ, they have nothing left but the weakness about which he is speaking. In short, no benefit will be found in the ancient ceremonies until they are related to Christ. He made the Jews more sure of the grace of God by keeping them in a measure waiting for it. Let us therefore bear in mind that the Law is said to be of no use when it is Christless. The fact that he calls it *the foregoing commandment* makes for the further confirmation of this teaching. It is common, everyday usage that earlier laws are repealed by later ones. The Law was promulgated long before David: he was on the throne of his kingdom when he made his prophecy about the creation of a new priest. This is, therefore, a new Law, that outdates the old.

19. *Made nothing perfect.* Since he has spoken rather sharply of the Law, he now qualifies his harshness and as it were corrects it. He allows it a measure of usefulness in that it pointed a way which leads at last to salvation. However, it was of such a kind as to be far from being perfect.

The apostle argues like this—The Law made a beginning for a while: therefore something more perfect had to follow it, because it is not right for the sons of God to remain for ever in the childish elements. By the word *bringing in* he means that some preparation was made by the Law, as children are taught the elementary things to pave the way for them to go on to more advanced teaching. Since the preposition ἐπί indicates result, when one thing is the result of another, I think the verse should be rendered 'but a bringing in'. As I see it he is mentioning two introductions: the first in the type of Melchizedek, and the second in the Law, which came later in time. Further, by the word *Law* he means the Levitical priesthood which was added over and above the priesthood of Melchizedek.

A better hope: By this is understood the condition of believers under the reign of Christ, but it also has regard to the fathers who could not rest content with their existing state, but had aspirations of better things. Thus Luke 10.24, 'Many kings and prophets desired to see the things which ye see.' They were led by the Law as a schoolmaster to strive higher.

Through which we draw nigh. There is an implicit contrast between us and the fathers. We excel them in privilege in the fact that God has made Himself known to us face to face, whereas He appeared to them only at a distance and in shadows. Allusion is made here to the form of the tabernacle or the temple. The people stood far off in the courtyard, and no one was allowed any closer approach to the sanctuary except the priests. Only the high priest went into the inner sanctuary. But now that the tabernacle has been abolished God admits us into His intimate presence, from which the fathers were prohibited. Anyone who still holds to, or wants to restore, the shadows of the Law not only obscures the glory of Christ, but also deprives us of a great blessing in that he puts a barrier of space between us and God, to approach whom freedom is given us by the Gospel. Whoever sticks to the Law, knowingly and voluntarily deprives himself of the nearness of God.

20. *Inasmuch as it is not without the taking of an oath.* A further argument for the Law giving place to the Gospel is that God gave precedence to the priesthood of Christ over that of Aaron when He swore an oath for the honour of the former. When He set up the priests of old, He interposed no oath: but it is said of Christ, 'The Lord sware', and that was without any doubt in order to honour Him. We can see the purpose for which he again quotes the psalm, namely that we may know that because of God's oath more dignity is to be attributed to the priesthood of Christ than to the others. This principle is to be continually kept in mind, that a priest is made to be the guarantor of a covenant. The apostle concludes from this that the covenant which God has made with us by the hand of Christ is far better than the old one whose interpreter was Moses.

And they indeed have been made priests many in number, because that by death they are hindered from continuing: but he, because he abideth for ever, hath his priesthood unchangeable. Wherefore also he is able to save to the uttermost them that draw near unto God through him, seeing he ever liveth to make intercession for them. For such a high priest became us, holy, guileless, undefiled, separated from sinners and made higher than the heavens: who needeth not daily, like those high priests, to offer up sacrifices, first for his own sins, and then for the sins of the people: for this he did once for all, when he offered himself. For the law appointeth men high priests, having infirmity: but the word of the oath, which was after the law, appointeth a Son, perfected for evermore. (23-28)

23. *And they indeed.* He had already touched on this comparison, but because the matter is worth greater attention, he expounds it again more fully, although the thread of his argument is different from that above. Previously he concluded that the old priesthood ought to come to an end because those who presided in it were mortal men, but now he simply points out why Christ remains a High Priest for ever. He does this by arguing from contrasts. The ancient priests were more in number because death put an end to their priesthood. There is no death that hinders Christ from performing His office. Therefore He is the only and the perpetual priest. Diversity of cause produces diversity of results.

25. *Wherefore also he is able to save, etc.* The fruit of eternal priesthood is our salvation, if we gather this fruit by faith, as we should. Where there is death or change, you will look in vain for salvation. Thus those who adhere to the old priesthood never attain to salvation.

When he says *them that draw near unto God,* he uses this circumlocution to describe the believers who alone enjoy the salvation imparted by Christ. At the same time he indicates what faith should look for in a mediator. The highest human good is to be united with God who is the fountain of life and of all good things. It is their own unworthiness that keeps everyone from approaching Him, and it is therefore the proper office of the Mediator to help us here, and to stretch out His hand to lead us to heaven.

He keeps alluding to the old shadows of the Law. Although the high priest carried the names of the twelve tribes on his shoulders and their symbols on his breast, yet he alone went into the sanctuary while the people stood in the courtyard. But now that we rely on Christ as Mediator, we enter by faith right into heaven, because there is no longer any veil to obstruct us. God appears to us openly, and invites us lovingly to meet Him face to face.

Seeing he ever liveth to make intercession. What is the nature and extent of the pledge of His love towards us? The fact that Christ lives for us and not for Himself, and that He was received into eternal bliss to reign in heaven—this happened, says the apostle, for our sakes. Thus the life and the kingdom and the glory of Christ aim at our salvation as their target, and Christ has nothing that is not to be put to our benefit, because He was given to us by the Father on this condition, that everything that was His should be ours. At the same time he shows us by what He does that Christ performs the office of Priest, it belongs to a priest to intercede, in order that the people may find favour with God. Christ is continually doing this because He rose from the dead for this purpose. He justifies His rightful Name of Priest by His continual task of intercession.

26. *For such a high priest.* He reasons from connexions. These are
the conditions or qualities (as they are commonly called) that are
necessarily required in a priest, namely, that he should be just, blameless, and pure from every stain. This honour fits Christ alone. What
was required for the proper discharge of the office was lacking in the
priests of the Law. It follows from this that there was no perfection in
the Levitical priesthood, and that it was not even legitimate in itself
except in so far as it served Christ. Indeed the external adornment of
the high priest showed this defect. What was the point of those
precious, splendid vestments which God ordered Aaron to wear when
performing sacred rites, except that they were symbols of holiness and a
more than human excellence in every kind of virtue? Those types were
employed, because the reality was absent. It therefore appears that
Christ is the only suitable Priest.

The phrase *separated from sinners* includes all the rest. There was some
holiness and blamelessness and purity in Aaron, but only in the smallest
degree. They were defiled by many stains. But Christ, in that He is
above the common herd of men, is alone free from sin. Thus true
holiness and blamelessness are found in Him alone. He is described as
separated from us, not because He rejects us from His society, but
because He has this exceptional attribute over us, that He is free from
all uncleanness. From this we conclude that all prayers which are not
supported by the intercession of Christ are rejected.

It could be asked whether the angels are also separated from sinners.
If so, what is to hinder them from performing the office of priesthood
and being our mediators before God? The answer is easy. No lawful
priest is ordained without the command of God; and God has never
delegated this honour to angels. It would be a blasphemous presumption for them to intrude on the office without being called to it.
Moreover, as we shall see at the beginning of the next chapter, it is
necessary for the one who is the mediator between God and men to be
a man, although this last condition, which the apostle refers to, is in
itself a sufficient answer to this question. No one can unite us with
God except someone who reaches to God. This is not given even to
the angels, because they are not said to have been carried up above all
heavens. It is the sole prerogative of Christ to reconcile us to God,
since He has ascended above all heavens. This description has the force
of saying that Christ has been set above all creaturely orders so that
He is pre-eminent over the angels.

27. *Who needeth not.* He follows out the contrast between Christ
and the Levitical priests in which he notes two especial defects (so to
speak) in the old priests from which it is plain that they were not
perfect in all respects. Here he is only touching briefly on the gist of

the matter. Later on he expounds the individual points at greater length, and especially the second point about the daily sacrifices, just as the main controversy was about them. I shall also touch briefly on the individual heads. One was the defect in the old priesthood that the high priest offered sacrifices for his own sins. How could he have appeased God for others when God was rightly wrath with him himself? They were quite unequal to the task of atoning for sins. The second defect is that they offered various sacrifices every day, and it therefore follows that there was no true atonement because when the cleansing is repeated the sins remain. The case of Christ is quite different. He needed no sacrifice inasmuch as He was not tainted by any stain of sin. His sacrifice was such that its once-for-all oblation sufficed to the end of the world. He offered Himself.

28. *For the law.* From the vices of men he deduces the weakness of the priesthood, as though he were saying, Since the Law did not set up true priests, this fault must be corrected in some other way. It is corrected by *the word of the oath*, for Christ is not created from the common herd of men, but was the Son of God, subject to no fault, but adorned and endowed with supreme perfection. He again reminds us that the oath was later than the Law, to show that God was not content with the priesthood of the Law, but that His will was to institute something better. In the institutions of God what comes later advances what is earlier to a better state, or else abolishes what was only meant to be valid for a limited period.

CHAPTER EIGHT

Now in the things which we are saying the chief point is this: We have such a high priest, who sat down on the right hand of the throne of the Majesty in the heavens, a minister of the sanctuary and of the true tabernacle, which the Lord pitched, not man. For every high priest is appointed to offer both gifts and sacrifices: wherefore it is necessary that this high priest also have somewhat to offer. Now if he were on earth, he would not be a priest at all, seeing there are those who offer the gifts according to the law; who serve that which is a copy and a shadow of the heavenly things, even as Moses is warned of God when he is about to make the tabernacle: for, See, saith he, that thou make all things according to the pattern that was showed thee in the mount. But now hath he obtained a ministry the more excellent, by how much also he is the mediator of a better covenant, which hath been enacted upon better promises. (1-6)

1. *Now in the things which we are saying the chief point is this.* In order that his readers may know the subject of his argument, he informs them that he is concerned to show that the priesthood of Christ by which that of the Law was abolished is a spiritual one. He proceeds with the same argument, but because he does so with various reasons he has put in this statement to keep his readers' minds on his aim.

He has already established that Christ is the High Priest. Now he argues that His priesthood is heavenly. It follows from this that by His coming what Moses had set up under the Law disappeared because it was earthly. Because Christ suffered in the humility of the flesh, and taking the form of a servant made Himself of no reputation in the world (Phil. 2.7), the apostle harks back to His ascension, by which not only the offence of the Cross was removed, but also that humbling and inglorious condition which He took on Himself along with our flesh. It is by the power of the Spirit which shone out in the resurrection and ascension of Christ that the dignity of His priesthood is to be reckoned. He argues as follows—Since Christ has ascended to the right hand of God to reign graciously in heaven, He is the Minister not of our earthly sanctuary but of a heavenly.

The genitive *sanctorum* is taken here as being of neuter gender, and the apostle explains himself by adding, of *the true tabernacle.* It could be asked whether the tabernacle as erected by Moses was built falsely or presumptuously. There is an implicit contradiction in these words. My answer is that this truth of which he speaks is not contrasted with falsehood but only with types, as in John 1.17, 'The law was given by Moses: grace and truth came by Jesus Christ.' The old tabernacle was not an empty contrivance of man, but the figure of a heavenly tabernacle. But since the shadow differs from the substance, and the sign from the thing signified, so the apostle says that that was not the true tabernacle, as though saying that it was merely shadowy.

2. *Which the Lord pitched.* What is the apostle's intention in saying that the priesthood of Christ is located in heaven? Certainly He suffered on earth, and atoned for our sins with earthly blood (because he had derived his origin from the seed of Abraham); the sacrifice of his death was a visible one; indeed to offer Himself to the Father, He had to descend from heaven to earth and be subject as a man to the troubles of mortal life and at the end to death. I reply that whatever appears superficially to be earthly Christ is to be looked at as spiritual with the eye of faith. Thus His flesh, which came from the seed of Abraham, was the temple of God and therefore life-giving. Indeed the death of Christ was life for the whole world, and that is surely supernatural. The apostle is referring not so much to the particular properties of human nature but rather to the hidden power of the Spirit. Hence the death of Christ has no earthly flavour. When we are dealing with Christ, let us learn to raise up all our thoughts to the level of the kingdom of God. In this way no doubt will remain.

Paul speaks to almost the same purpose in II Cor. 5.1. He calls God the Builder of this tabernacle in order to remark on its stability and durability, just as on the other hand those which are built by human hands are unstable, or at least liable to fall in ruins. He says this because the redemption wrought by the death of Christ was a truly divine work, and in it the power of Christ was shown in a wonderful way.

3. *For every high priest.* The apostle's intention is to show that the priesthood of Christ cannot exist along with the old Levitical priesthood. His method of proving it is as follows. The Law instituted priests to offer sacrifices to God; hence it is clear that the title of priesthood without sacrifice is empty. But Christ had no victims such as were offered under the Law. Hence it follows that His priesthood is not earthly or carnal, but of a more excellent kind.

Let us now examine the clauses one by one. In this first one it should be noticed that he says that no priest is appointed except to offer gifts. From this it is evident that men cannot find favour with God except by an intervening sacrifice. Therefore for our prayers to be heard they must be founded on sacrifice, with the result that those who pass by Christ and forget to remember His death, and who yet rush into the presence of God are guilty of fatal presumption. If we want to pray properly, we must learn always to set before us the death of Christ which sanctifies our prayers. God will never hear us unless He is favourably inclined, and therefore He must first be appeased since our sins have made Him angry with us; and so there must of necessity be a preceding sacrifice for our prayer to have any effect. From this we can further conclude that no one, either man or angel, is good enough to appease God, because they all lack any sacrifice of their own which they can offer to appease God. This fully refutes the impertinence of the papists in making the apostles and martyrs indiscriminately mediators of intercession along with Christ. It is of no use to give them tasks of this kind without supplying them with sacrifices.

4. *Now if he were on earth.* It is now beyond dispute that Christ is the High Priest. Just as the office of a judge cannot exist without laws and statutes, so the office of sacrificing must be joined in Christ with the name of priest. Yet He has no earthly or visible sacrifice, and therefore He cannot be an earthly priest. We must always hold on to the truth that, when the apostle is describing the death of Christ, he is not doing so in reference to its external action but to its spiritual fruit. He suffered death in the common way of men, but He made divine atonement for the sins of the world as a Priest. Outwardly He shed His blood, but inwardly and spiritually He brought cleansing. In short, He died on earth, but the power and efficacy of His death came from heaven.

Some render what immediately follows as, 'of the number of those who offer gifts according to the Law'. But the words of the apostle mean something different. I prefer to take them, 'as long as there are, or since there are, priests'. His meaning is to show one of these two things, either that Christ is not a Priest, if the priesthood of the Law still continues, because He has no sacrifices; or that the sacrifices of the Law cease as soon as Christ appears. The first of these is absurd, because it is impossible to deprive Christ of the honour of priesthood. It therefore remains for us to admit that the Levitical order is now abolished.

5. *Who serve that which is a copy.* I take λατρεύειν in the sense of doing holy things, with the particle ἐν or ἐπί being understood in the context in Greek. This fits much better than the rendering of some, 'who serve the shadow and example of heavenly things', and the Greek construction easily allows of this meaning. In short he is saying that the true worship of God does not consist in legal ceremony, and that hence the Levitical priests in exercising their function have only a shadow and a second-hand copy which is inferior to the original.

That is the meaning of the word ὑπόδειγμα. Thus he anticipates possible objection, for he says that the worship of God contained in the old sacrifices was not unnecessary, because it looked to what was higher, that is, to heavenly truth.

As Moses is warned. This passage is found in Exod. 25.40, and the apostle quotes it here in order to show that the whole of legal worship was nothing more than a picture which adumbrated the spiritual in Christ. God orders that all the parts of the tabernacle should correspond to the original pattern that had been shown to Moses on the mountain. If the form of the tabernacle referred to something else, the same must be true of the rites and of the whole priesthood. It follows from this that there is nothing permanent in them.

This is a noteworthy passage because it contains three points worth remarking. We learn first from it that the ancient rites were not brought about by chance for God to keep His people busy with them as if in a child's game, and that the building of the tabernacle was not an empty pursuit simply to entice and hold the attention of those who saw it by its outward splendour. There was a real spiritual meaning in everything, in that Moses was commanded to do everything according to the original pattern which was heavenly. The opinion of those, who think that the ceremonies were only enjoined, in order to be restraints to confine the lusts of the people, so that they would not hark after the foreign rites of the heathen, is utterly impious. This is part of the truth but not all. They omit what is much more important, that these practices were to hold the people to faith in the Mediator. There is no reason for us to be ultra-curious here and to look for some sublime mystery in every nail and other minutiae, as Hesychius and a good part of the ancient writers struggled anxiously to do. In their desire to philosophize subtly in things of which they were ignorant, they wove childish imaginations, and made themselves ridiculous by their stupidity. We must exercise moderation here, and this will happen if we do not try to know more than is revealed to us in Christ.

Secondly, we are here informed that all those forms of worship which men allow themselves to invent by their own ingenuity and contrary to the command of God are false and spurious. When God lays down that everything should be done according to His rule it is not permissible for us to do anything different. The two sentences mean the same thing, *See that thou make all things according to the pattern,* and, *See that you do nothing beyond the pattern.* By thus emphasizing the rule that He has laid down, He forbids us to depart from it in the very slightest. For this reason all the forms of worship produced by men fail, and also those things which are called sacraments and yet have not come from God.

In the third place we must learn from this that there are no true religious symbols except those which conform to Christ. We must beware that in wishing to fit our own inventions to Christ we do not so change Him (as the papists do) that He becomes unlike Himself. It is not permissible for us to invent anything we like, but it belongs to God alone to show us *according to the pattern that was showed thee.*

6. *But now hath he obtained a ministry the more excellent.* As he has previously deduced the excellency of the covenant from the worth of the priesthood, so he now maintains that the priesthood of Christ is more excellent because He is the Interpreter and Mediator of a better covenant. Both were necessary since the Jews had to be weaned away from the superstitious observance of ceremonies which prevented them from going on on the right way to the true, unadulterated truth of the Gospel. The apostle says that it is right for Moses and Aaron to give place to Christ, as to one who is more excellent, because the Gospel is a more excellent covenant than the Law, and the death of Christ is a much nobler sacrifice than the legal victims.

There is some difficulty in what he further says that the covenant of the Gospel was proclaimed on better promises. It is certain that the fathers who lived under the Law were given the same hope of eternal life in that the grace of adoption was common. Therefore their faith ought to have rested on the same promises. However the apostle's comparison refers more to the form than to the substance. Although God promised them the same salvation as he promises us today, yet neither the nature nor the form of the revelation was equal to what we have. If anyone wishes more information about this he should look at the fourth and fifth chapters of the epistle to the Galatians, and at my *Institutes.*

For if that first covenant had been faultless, then would no place have been sought for a second. For finding fault with them, he saith, Behold, the days come, saith the Lord, that I will make a new covenant with the house of Israel and with the house of Judah; nor according to the covenant that I made with their fathers in the day that I took them by the hand to lead them forth out of the land of Egypt; for they continued not in my covenant, and I regarded them not, saith the Lord. For this is the covenant that I will make with the house of Israel after those days, saith the Lord; I will put my laws into their mind, and on their heart also will I write them: and I will be to them a God, and they shall be to me a people and they shall not teach every man his fellow-citizen, and every man his brother, saying, Know the Lord: for all shall know me, from the least to the greatest of them. For I will be merciful to their iniquities, and their sins will I remember no more. In that he saith, A new covenant, he hath made the first old. But that which is becoming old and waxeth aged is nigh unto vanishing away. (7-13)

7. *For if that first covenant.* He adds confirmation of what he has said about the excellency of the covenant which God has made with us at the hand of Christ, and he does so on the ground that the covenant of the Law was neither stable nor lasting. If there was nothing wrong with it, why was another one substituted? This substitution was made, and therefore it is clear that the old one was not perfect in every respect. As evidence for this he cites the testimony of Jeremiah which we shall presently examine.

On the other hand it does not seem consistent that after saying that no place need be found for a second covenant if the first had been free from fault, he then says that the people are at fault and that for this reason the remedy of a new covenant was introduced. It is unfair for the blame to be laid on the covenant of God when the fault was in the people. The argument, therefore, does not seem to hold good, because however many hundreds of times God might blame the people, the covenant was not on that account defective. There is an easy answer to this objection. Even though the charge of breaking the covenant be justly made of the people, in that they had fallen away from God by their own faithlessness, yet at the same time the weakness of the covenant is shown because it had not been written in their hearts. Therefore to make it perfect and valid God says that it needs correction. It is therefore not without reason that the apostle says that a place must be found for a second.

8. *Behold the days come.* The prophet is speaking about the future. He charges the people with faithlessness because they received the Law but did not stand fast in their faith. Therefore the Law was the covenant which God complained was broken by the people. To remedy this evil, He promises a new covenant, different from this one, the fulfilment of which prophecy means the abrogation of the Old Testament. The apostle seems to do violence to this prophecy in order to suit it to his purpose. What is here at issue is the question of ceremony, but the prophet is speaking about the whole Law. What has it to do with ceremony when God writes on men's hearts a rule of holy and godly living handed down by the teaching and writings of men? I reply that the argument is from the whole to the part. There is no doubt that the prophet includes the whole Mosaic dispensation when he says, 'I have made a covenant with you which you have not kept.' Further the Law was, in a manner, clothed with ceremony. What is the use of garments after the death of the body? It is a common saying that what is accessory has the same character as its principle. It is

therefore no wonder that the ceremonies which are simply the accessories of the Old Testament come to an end with the whole dispensation of Moses. It is not unusual for the apostle in a controversy about ceremonies to take up the general question of the whole Law. Therefore although this prophecy of Jeremiah has a wider reference than simply that of ceremonies, yet because it includes them in the framework of the Old Testament it is properly applied to this present purpose.

The days, which the apostle mentions, are universally agreed as meaning the kingdom of Christ; from which it follows that the Old Testament was amended by the coming of Christ. He mentions by name *the house of Israel and the house of Judah* because the children of Abraham were divided into two kingdoms. The promise is given of the gathering of all the elect into one body again, although they have formerly been separated.

9. *Not according to the covenant.* This phrase expresses the difference between the covenant then in force, and the new one for which he bids them hope. Otherwise the prophet would only have said, 'I will renew the covenant which has failed by your fault.' Now he says expressly that it will be different. In saying that the covenant was made on the day that He took their hand to lead them out of slavery, He increases the charge of desertion by reminding them of this great blessing, although He does not accuse only one age of ingratitude, but since those who had been freed immediately fell away their descendants fell away also after the same example. Hence the whole nation was covenant-breaking. He says, that He *regarded them not*, or had no further concern for them, meaning that it would be no advantage to them to have been once adopted as His people if He had not come to their aid with a new kind of remedy. The prophet says something a little different in Hebrew, but it is of no concern with the present question.

10. *The covenant that I will make.* There are two main heads to this covenant; the first as regards the free remission of sins, and the second regarding the inward renewing of the heart. There is a third which is dependent on the second, about minds that are illumined in the knowledge of God. There are many points here very worthy of note. The first is that God calls us to Himself without effect, as long as He speaks only with a human voice. He certainly teaches and commands what is right but His words fall on deaf ears. If we seem to hear anything, our ears are struck merely by the outward sound but our hearts, being full of wickedness and stubbornness, reject all sound doctrine. In short the Word of God never reaches our hearts, since they are iron or stony until they are softened by Him. Indeed they have a contrary law

written on them and they are ruled by perverse passions which drive us to rebellion. Therefore God proclaims His law by human voice in vain unless He writes it in our hearts by His Spirit, that is, unless He forms and fits us for obedience. It is clear from this how much force free will has, and what rightness there is in our nature before God renews us. We will and we choose, and we do so of our own accord, but our will is carried away by an almost raging impulse to resist God and cannot in any way submit to His justice. So it comes about that the Law is fatal and deadly for us as long as it remains written on tablets of stone, as Paul says in II Cor. 3.3. In short, we accept God's command obediently when He changes and corrects the native wickedness of our hearts by His Spirit; otherwise He will find nothing in us but evil passions and a heart wholly given to wickedness. It is clearly laid down that a new covenant is to be made by which God will write His laws on our hearts, because otherwise it will be of no effect.

The second head is about the free pardon of sins. Even though they have sinned (says the Lord), I shall pardon them. It is more than necessary to say this, for God does not ever conform us to the obedience of His justice without there remaining many passions of our sinful flesh. Indeed the sinfulness of our nature is only partly corrected, and so evil lusts continue to break out. From this comes the struggle complained of by Paul (Rom. 7.19) that the faithful do not obey God as they should but offend in all kinds of ways. Whatever desire we have to live righteously, we shall still be guilty of eternal death before God because our life is always far removed from the perfection of the Law. There would therefore be no permanence in the covenant unless God freely pardoned our sins. It is the particular privilege of those who believe, who have accepted the covenant once offered to them in Christ, that they know for certain that God is favourable to them and that there is no sin to which they are subject for which they do not have the promise of pardon. It is to be noted that this promise is not given to them for one day only, but to the very end of life, so that they are daily reconciled with God. This grace extends to the whole kingdom of Christ, as Paul clearly shows in II Cor. 5. This is the sole refuge of our faith, and if we do not fly to it there remains for us only continual despair. We are all held in guilt, and we cannot be released except by taking refuge in the mercy of God which pardons us.

And they shall be to me. The fruit of the covenant is that God chooses us to be His people, and proclaims that He will be the guardian of our salvation. That is the meaning of the phrase *I will be to them a God*, because God is not a God of the dead, nor does He receive us into His patronage without giving us a share in righteousness and life, as David properly explains (Ps. 144.15), 'Happy is the people, whose God is the

Lord.' There is no doubt that this teaching applies to us. Although the Israelites hold first place, and are the proper, lawful heirs of the covenant, nevertheless their prerogative does not prevent us from having a place in it. In short, however far and wide the kingdom of Christ ranges, there this covenant of salvation is in force.

It may be asked if there was no sure and effective promise of salvation under the Law, if the fathers lacked the grace of the Spirit, if they have no trace of the fatherly favour of God in the remission of their sins? It is evident that they worship God with sincere hearts and pure consciences, and walk in His commandments. This could not have been, unless they had been inwardly taught by the Spirit. It is evident that whenever they thought of their sins they were raised up again by their trust in a free pardon. Yet the apostle seems to deprive them of both these blessings by referring the prophecy of Jeremiah to the coming of Christ. My answer is that he is not simply denying that God once wrote the Law in their hearts and pardoned their sins, but that he is making a comparison between the greater and the less. Because the Father has released the power of His Spirit much more abundantly in the reign of Christ, and has likewise poured out His mercy on mankind, this prominence brings it about that the small portion of grace which He bestowed on the fathers under the Law becomes of no account. We see that the promises made then were shadowy and confused, so that they shone only like the moon and the stars compared with the clearness of the Gospel which radiates on us.

If anyone objects that the faith and obedience of Abraham was so excellent that no equivalent example can be found today in the whole world, I reply that he is not discussing persons but the economy that must rule the Church. Moreover whatever spiritual gifts the fathers obtained were accidental to their age. It was necessary for them to direct their eyes to Christ to become partakers of them. It is therefore not unreasonable for the apostle in comparing the Gospel with the Law to take away from the latter what is the property of the former. At the same time there is no reason for God not extending the grace of the new covenant to the fathers. This is the true explanation.

11. *And they shall not teach.* We have said that this third head is as it were part of the second, where we read, I will put my laws into their *mind.* It is the work of the Spirit of God to illumine our minds so that we know the will of God and turn our hearts to obey it. The right knowledge of God is a wisdom which far exceeds what can be comprehended by human understanding, and therefore no one can attain it except by the secret revelation of the Spirit. It is for this reason that Isaiah (28.16, 26), in speaking of the renewal of the Church, says that all the children of God will be His disciples. Our prophet means the

same thing when he introduces God as saying, *They shall know me.* God does not promise what is in our power, but what He alone can do for us. In short, these words of the prophet have the force of saying that our minds are blind and empty of right understanding until they are illumined by the Spirit of God. God is therefore rightly known only by those whom He has thought worthy of having this revelation by His special favour.

In saying, *from the least to the greatest,* he means first of all that the grace of God will be poured out on all kinds, so that no class of men will be without it. He means further that common ordinary men are not shut off from heavenly wisdom, nor can great and noble men attain it by their own sharp wits or by the help of learning. God thus joins together the lowest and humblest with the highest, so that ignorance does not hinder the former, nor can the latter climb so high by their own acumen, but their one common Master is the Spirit equally.

Fanatics have taken occasion from this to do away with public preaching as though it were superfluous in the kingdom of Christ, but their madness is easily refuted. Their objection is as follows, that after the coming of Christ there is no need for anyone to teach his neighbour. Public preaching is then to be done away with so that its place may be given to the inward inspiration of God. They pass by what is especially worth noticing. The prophet does not wholly deny that they will teach one another, but he says this *They shall not teach saying, Know the Lord,* as though he were saying that ignorance will no longer possess the minds of men as heretofore, so that they do not know who God is. We know that teaching has a double purpose, first that those who are completely ignorant can begin from the first elements; and secondly that those who have made a start can make further progress. Therefore since Christians ought to make progress as long as they live, it is certain that no one is so wise that he does not need to be taught, with the result that willingness to learn is no small part of our wisdom. The way of making progress if we want to be the disciples of Christ is shown by Paul in Eph. 4.11, 'He gave some to be pastors and teachers', etc. From this it is clear that nothing was further from the mind of the prophet than to deprive the Church of such a necessary benefit. His sole desire was to show that God would reveal Himself both to small and to great as Joel also predicted in chapter 3.1, 2. We must also notice in passing that this light of sound understanding is particularly promised to the Church, and hence this passage refers only to the Household of Faith.

13. *In that he said, A new covenant.* He concludes that the one covenant has been overturned from the fact of the contrary establishment of the other, and he finds evidence from the name Old Testament,

that it was to be done away with, for age leads to decay. Because a new one is substituted it is necessary for the older to come to an end, because this second one, as has been said, is of a different nature. If the whole dispensation of Moses, in so far as it is contrary to the dispensation of Christ, has passed away, then the ceremonies have also ceased.

CHAPTER NINE

Now even the first covenant had ordinances of divine service, and its sanctuary, a sanctuary of this world. For there was a tabernacle prepared, the first, wherein were the candlestick, and the table, and the shew-bread; which is called the Holy place. And after the second veil the tabernacle which is called the Holy of holies; having a golden censer, and the ark of the covenant overlaid round about with gold, wherein was a golden pot holding the manna, and Aaron's rod that budded, and the tables of the covenant; and above it cherubim of glory overshadowing the mercy-seat; of which things we cannot now speak severally. (1-5)

1. *Even the first covenant.* Having spoken in general about the abrogation of the Old Testament, he now turns his consideration particularly to the ceremonies. His purpose is to show that there was no usage to which the coming of Christ did not put an end. First of all he says that there was in the Old Testament a fixed rule of divine worship and one which was peculiarly applicable to that time. It will appear later by comparison what all those rites were which were laid down in the Law. Some copies read πρώτη σκηνή, the first tabernacle: but I think there is an error in the noun tabernacle and I have no doubt that some ignorant reader who saw the adjective without a noun referred it in his lack of knowledge to the tabernacle instead of to the covenant and thus stupidly added σκηνή. I am indeed surprised that the mistake persisted so far that it appears in the great concensus of Greek manuscripts. However I am compelled of necessity to follow the old reading. As I have said, the apostle has been speaking about the Old Testament and he now comes to the ceremonies which were, as it were, appendages to it. He shows that all the rites of the law of Moses were part of the Old Testament and have the same antiquity so that they ought themselves to pass away. Λατρεία; many people take this as accusative plural. I tend to agree with those who read δικαιώματα λατρείας together; for the institutions or the rites which the Hebrews call חֻקִּים (*huqqim*) are described in Greek as δικαιώματα. The general sense is that the whole system of worshipping God which consisted in sacrifices and ablutions and other symbols along with the sanctuary was connected to the Old Testament. He calls it *a sanctuary of this world* because there was not yet in them any heavenly truth. Although it was the type of the original pattern which was shown to Moses nevertheless the type differs from the reality especially when they are compared with each other as

opposites, as is done here. The sanctuary was in itself earthly and is
rightly included among the elements of the world, and yet it was
heavenly in what it signified.

For there was a tabernacle. Because the apostle here touches only
lightly on the building of the tabernacle and does not spend more time
over it than is necessary for his argument I purposely abstain from any
more subtle exclamations. It is sufficient for our present purpose to
divide the tabernacle into three parts, the first of which is the court of
the people, the middle being that which is commonly called the
sanctuary, and the last the inner sanctuary which is called the *holy of
holies* κατ᾽ ἐξοχήν. As far as the first sanctuary is concerned which was
next to the court of the people, he says that there was there the *candlestick and table* on which the *shew-bread* was set. He calls this place in the
plural τὰ ἅγια. There came next the most secret place which they
called the holy of holies and which was yet more removed from the
sight of the people and even of the priests who ministered in the outer
sanctuary. Just as the outer sanctuary was shut off by a veil so a second
veil kept the priests out of the holy of holies. The apostle says that
there was there the θυμιατήριον, by which word I understand the altar
of incense or of fragrance rather than the *censer.* Then there was *the
ark of the covenant with its covering, the two cherubims, the golden pot
holding the manna, Aaron's rod and the two tables.* This is the extent of the
apostle's description of the tabernacle.

He says that the pot where Moses placed the manna and the rod of
Aaron which budded were in the ark along with the two tables but
this seems to be at variance with sacred history which in I Kings 8.9
says that there was nothing in the ark except the two tables. The
reconciliation of these passages is easy. God had commanded that the
urn and Aaron's rod were to be placed in front of the testimony; and
it is therefore probable that they were included in the ark along with
the tables. When the temple was built these items were arranged in a
different order. Certainly history records, as if it were something new,
that the ark had nothing except the two tables.

5. *Of which things we cannot now speak.* Since nothing is enough for
inquisitive men the apostle cuts out any opportunity for subtleties that
are not in keeping with his present purpose in case too much discussion
of these things might break the thread of his argument. If anyone
disregards the apostle's warning and dwells more minutely on this
matter he will do so inopportunely. There might be a place for doing
this elsewhere but for the present it is better to pay attention to the
matter in hand in the same way as philosophizing beyond reasonable
bounds (as some do) is not only futile but also dangerous. There are
some things which are not obscure and are suitable for the edification

of faith; but we must show discretion and moderation in case we desire
to know more than it has pleased God to reveal.

> *Now these things having been thus prepared, the priests go in continually
> into the first tabernacle, accomplishing the services; but into the second
> the high priest alone, once in the year, not without blood, which he
> offereth for himself, and for the errors of the people: the Holy Ghost
> signifying, that the way into the holy place hath not yet been made
> manifest, while as the first tabernacle is yet standing; which is a parable
> for the time now present; according to which are offered both gifts and
> sacrifices that cannot, as touching the conscience, make the worshipper
> perfect. Being only (with meats and drinks and divers washings) carnal
> ordinances, imposed until a time of reformation. (6-10)*

6. *Now these things having been thus prepared.* Leaving everything
else aside he turns to take up the matter of greatest controversy. He
says that the priests who perform the sacrifices were accustomed to go
into the first tabernacle every day, but that the high priest went into
the holy of holies only once a year with solemn sacrifices. From this
he concludes that while that legal tabernacle was standing the sanctuary
had been closed and that no road could be opened for us to the kingdom
of God unless it were destroyed. We see that the very form of the old
tabernacle warned the Jews that they must direct their aspirations elsewhere. Those who retain the shadows of the law and thereby obstruct
their own way of their own accord do so foolishly. Here he has used
πρώτην σκηνήν in a different sense from that above. Earlier he took it
to mean the common sanctuary but now he takes it in the sense of the
whole form of the tabernacle; this he does by setting it in opposition
to the spiritual sanctuary of Christ which he is going to mention at
once. He maintains that it was for our highest good that this was
destroyed because by its destruction there was given to us a more
intimate access to God.

7. *Which he offereth for himself, and for the errors of his people.* As שׁגג
means in Hebrew to err, the derivation is the noun שְׁגָגָה, which
properly denotes 'error', but is taken in general terms to mean any kind
of sin. Certainly we never sin unless we are deceived by the enticements
of Satan. By this the apostle does not mean just simple ignorance (as
they call it) but rather he includes all sins that are consciously committed.
As I have already said there is never any sin that is free from error.
However knowingly or willingly anyone sins he must needs nevertheless be blinded by his lust so that he does not judge rightly or rather
that he forgets himself and God. Men never purposely rush headlong
to their own ruin unless they are snared by the deceptions of Satan and
deviate from a right judgment.

9. *Which is a parable.* The Greek word is παραβολή, which in my opinion has here the force of saying ἀντίτυπος. He means that the second tabernacle was a pattern corresponding to the first; for the likeness of a man ought so to compare with the man himself that by looking at it our minds are immediately directed to the man. He further says that it was a parable for the time now present, that is as long as external observation was in force, in order to confine its use and duration to the period of the law. It has the same meaning as his further sentence a little later on that all the ceremonies were laid down up to the time of reformation. It is no objection that he uses the present tense when he says that *sacrifices are offered*, because since he is dealing with the Jews he speaks by way of concession as though he were one of those who offer sacrifice. Gifts and sacrifices differ in the sense that one is the genus and the other the species.

As touching the conscience. That is, they do not reach to the soul so as to give true holiness. Others read, 'to make perfect', which I do not reject, but the word 'sanctify' seems to me more fitting to the context. In order that his readers may better grasp the apostle's mind, the contrast between flesh and conscience should be noticed. He says that worshippers could not be cleansed spiritually or inwardly by the sacrifices of the law. He adds as a reason that all those rites were fleshly or carnal. What then does he leave for them? It is commonly supposed that they were a useful form of training for men to encourage honesty and propriety; but those who think this do not give sufficient weight to the promises which are added. This comment, therefore, is to be rejected. Those who understand the *carnal ordinances* as merely cleansing or sanctifying the body do so ignorantly and stupidly since the apostle understands by these works that they are earthly symbols which do not reach to the soul. Although they were true evidences of perfect holiness they contained nothing of it in themselves nor could they confer it on men. It is by such aids that the faithful are led to Christ to obtain from Him what the symbol lacked. If anyone asks why the apostle speaks with so little respect and even contempt about sacraments divinely instituted and depreciates their power, the answer is that he does so to differentiate them from Christ. We know that when they are viewed in themselves they are the weak elements of the world as Paul calls them (Gal. 4.9). When he speaks of the *time of reformation* he is referring to the prophecy of Jeremiah (31.37). The New Testament has succeeded the Old as the pattern of reformation. He mentions *meats and drinks* by name and other similar things which had no importance because out of such unimportant observations a more reliable judgment could be made as to how far the law is short of the perfection of the Gospel.

But Christ having come a high priest of the good things to come,
through the greater and more perfect Tabernacle, not made with hands,
that is to say, not of this creation, nor yet through the blood of goats
and calves, but through his own blood, entered in once for all into the
holy place, having obtained eternal redemption. (11-12)

11. *But Christ having come a high priest etc.* He now turns his attention
to the truth of those things which were under the Law in order to turn
our eyes from them to that truth. Whoever believes that the things
which were foreshadowed in it have been shown forth in Christ will
not remain any longer in the shadows but will embrace the substance
itself and the solid truth. We must carefully note the particulars in
which he compares Christ with the ancient high priest. He had said
that the high priest alone went into the sanctuary once a year with
blood to make atonement for sins. In this respect Christ is like that old
high priest because He alone has the dignity and the office of Priest.
There is, however, this difference that He brings with Him eternal
benefits which bring about perpetuity for His priesthood. There is
this second likeness between the old high priest and ours that both go
into the holy of holies through the sanctuary; but they differ in this
that Christ alone has entered heaven by the temple of His body. The
fact that the holy of holies was opened only once a year to the high
priest to make solemn atonement was a vague pre-figuring of the
unique sacrifice of Christ. That single entrance was common to both
but to the earthly it was every year but to the heavenly it is for ever
to the end of the world. The offering of blood is common to both
but there is a great difference in the blood because Christ did not offer
the blood of beasts but of Himself. Atonement is common to both
but the old legal atonement, because it was ineffective, was repeated
every year while the atonement made by Christ is valid for ever and
is the ground of our eternal salvation. So there is great importance in
almost every word. The phrase which some render with the help of
Christ does not properly express the mind of the apostle; for he means
that after the Levitical priests had performed their office for a fixed
time Christ came in their place as we have already seen in chapter
seven above.

Good things to come are to be taken as eternal things. Just as time to
come is set in contrast to the present so future blessings are contrasted
with present. The gist of it is that we are led to the heavenly kingdom
of God by the priesthood of Christ and that we are given a share of
spiritual righteousness and eternal life so that it is not right for us to
want anything better. Christ alone has the means of holding us to
Himself and confirming us.

Through the greater and more perfect tabernacle. Although this passage is given various explanations I have no doubt that he means the body of Christ. Just as there was once an access for the Levitical high priest into the holy of holies through the common sanctuary, so Christ has entered into the glory of heaven through His body; because when He put on our flesh and suffered in it He obtained for Himself the privilege of being our Mediator before God. In the first place the word sanctuary is properly and fittingly applied to the body of Christ because it is the temple in which the whole majesty of God dwelt. He is said to have made through His body a way to ascend into heaven because He consecrated Himself to God in that body: in it He was sanctified to be true righteousness and in it He prepared Himself to make His sacrifice. Further because in it He emptied Himself and endured the death of the cross so the Father has exalted Him and given Him a Name which is above every Name at which every knee shall bow etc. (Phil. 2.8-10). He has entered heaven through His own body because He now sits on the right hand of the Father. He intercedes for us in heaven because He has put on our flesh and consecrated it as a temple to God the Father and has sanctified Himself in it to make atonement for our sins and gain for us eternal righteousness.

It might seem strange that he denies that the body of Christ was *of this creation.* Certainly it was created of the seed of Abraham and subject to sufferings and death. I reply that he is not concerned here with the material body or its quality but with the spiritual power which comes to us from it. To the extent that the flesh of Christ gives life and is heavenly food to feed our souls, to the extent that His blood is spiritual drink and cleansing, to that extent we are not to think that there is anything earthly or elemental in them. Let us remember that this is said in respect of the old tabernacle which was made of wood, brass, skins, various coverings, gold and silver, that is of dead things. But the power of God breathes upon the flesh of Christ to make it a living and spiritual temple.

12. *Nor yet through the blood of goats.* All these things point to this that the qualities that are in Christ are of such excellence that they reduce all the shadows of the Law to nothing. What would be the value of the blood of Christ if it were valued on the level of the blood of beasts? What kind of atonement would be made by His death if the purifications of the Law retained their force? As soon as Christ is shown forth with the effectiveness of His death all the types must necessarily cease.

For if the blood of goats and bulls, and the ashes of a heifer sprinkling them that have been defiled, sanctify unto the cleanness of the flesh: how

*much more shall the blood of Christ, who through the eternal Spirit
offered himself without blemish unto God, cleanse your conscience from
dead works to serve the living God? And for this cause he is the mediator
of a new covenant, that a death having taken place for the redemption of
the transgressions that were under the first covenant, they that have been
called may receive the promise of the eternal inheritance. For where a
testament is, there must of necessity be the death of him that made it.
For a testament is of force where there hath been death: for doth it ever
avail while he that made it liveth?* (13-17)

13. *For if the blood of bulls.* This passage has been the occasion of
much misinterpretation because people did not see that it concerned
the sacraments which have a spiritual meaning. They explain the
cleansing of the flesh as that which is only valid among men just as
heathen men have their acts of penance by which they take away the
scandal of crime. This exposition is wholly unchristian, for it does
injury to the promises of God if we restrict their force merely to
earthly relationships. There occurs often in the writings of Moses this
kind of sentence—When a sacrifice has been duly performed iniquity
is taken away. This is surely the spiritual teaching of faith. It is so all
the more since all sacrifices have this aim in view that they lead to
Christ. As the eternal salvation of the soul is in Christ so these were
true evidences of this salvation. What therefore is in the apostle's mind
when he speaks of the cleansing of the flesh? He clearly understands it
symbolically or sacramentally in this sense—If the blood of beasts was
a true symbol of cleansing in that it did so in a sacramental way, all the
more will Christ Himself who is the truth declare a cleansing not only
by an external rite but one which will really reach men's consciences.
The argument is from the signs to the thing signified because the effect
preceded by a long way the reality of the signs.

14. *Through the eternal Spirit.* He now shows clearly how the death
of Christ is to be regarded; not from its external act but from the
power of the Spirit. Christ suffered as man, but in order that His death
might effect our salvation it came forth from the power of the Spirit.
The sacrifice of eternal atonement was a more than human work. He
calls the Spirit eternal so that we know that the reconciliation which
he effects is eternal. When he says *without blemish* although the allusion
is to the victims of the Law which were not allowed to be maimed or
defective, he means at the same time that Christ is the only lawful
victim capable of pleasing God. In all the others there was always
something that could justly be desired, and hence he has said above that
the covenant of the Law was not blameless. This latter sacrifice alone
is of complete perfection.

From dead works. Understand by this either those which end in death
or which are the fruits of death. As the life of the soul is our union
with God, those who are separated from Him by sin are properly
thought of as dead.

We must note the aim of atonement which is *to serve the living God.*
We are not cleansed by Christ so that we can immerse ourselves
continually in fresh dirt, but in order that our purity may serve the
glory of God. He goes on to say that nothing can proceed from us
which is pleasing to God until we are cleansed by the blood of Christ.
Since we are all enemies of God before our reconciliation all that we
do is likewise hateful to Him. The beginning to true worship is therefore reconciliation. Because no work is so pure or free from sin as to
be pleasing to God by itself, cleansing by the blood of Christ which
destroys all stains must necessarily intervene. This is the true contrast
between the living God and dead works.

15. *And for this cause etc.* He concludes that there is now no further
need for any other priest because Christ fulfils this office under the
New Testament. He does not claim for Christ the honour of a
Mediator so that others may at the same time share it with Him, but he
maintains that all the others were rejected when the office was placed
upon Christ. To confirm that more fully he recalls how He discharged
the office of Mediator even with the intervention of His death. If this
is found in Christ alone it is lacking in everyone else and it follows that
He is the only true Mediator.

He reminds us further of the force and efficacy of His death, which
he describes as the price paid for sin, which could not be taken away
by the blood of beasts under the Old Testament. By saying this his
aim has been to lead the Jews from the Law to Christ. If the Law is so
weak that whatever remedies it applies to atone for sin do not accom-
plish what they represent, who can find refuge in it as a safe harbour?
This one fact, I say, ought to have been enough to urge them to look
for something better than the Law, because they could not have been
other than continually anxious. On the other hand when we come to
Christ there is nothing that can disturb us any more because in Him
we obtain full redemption. By saying this he shows the weakness of
the Law so that the Jews may cease to rest in it, and he teaches them
how to stand in Christ because there is found in Him everything
necessary for setting their consciences at peace. If anyone asks whether
the sins of the fathers were remitted under the Law, we must hold to
the answer which I have given above, that they were remitted, but
remitted by the mercy of Christ. As far as their outward atonements
were concerned they were still held in bondage to their guilt. It is for
this reason that Paul says (Col. 2.14) that the Law was 'written in

ordinances against us'. When a sinner comes forward and openly confesses that he has sinned before God and acknowledges by sacrificing an innocent animal that he is worthy of eternal death, what followed from his sacrifice except that he sealed his own death as it were by his signature? It was only when they looked to Christ that they found satisfactory remission of sins. But if it is only looking to Christ that has taken away sin then those who remained in the Law were never set free. David proclaimed (Ps. 32.2), 'Blessed is the man unto whom the Lord imputeth not iniquity.' But in order to share in this blessedness it is necessary to forsake the Law and look to Christ. If a man holds to the Law he is never freed from guilt.

They that have been called may receive the promise. The divine covenant towards us aims at our adoption into sonship so that we may at the last be heirs of eternal life. The apostle says that we attain this by the mercy of Christ, and from this it is clear that the fulfilment of the covenant is in Him. The promise of inheritance is taken to mean the promised inheritance as though he had said, 'The promise of eternal life is given us to enjoy only through the death of Christ.' Certainly life was promised to the fathers and it has been from the beginning the inheritance of the sons of God, but we only enter into possession of it by the blood of Christ already given for us.

He speaks of *they that have been called* in order to make a greater impression on the Jews who were the partakers of this calling. This is a singular favour that the knowledge of Christ is bestowed on us. Therefore we must take all the more care that we do not neglect such a priceless treasure nor allow our minds to wander elsewhere. Some take *the called* in the sense of the elect; in my judgment wrongly. The apostle is saying here the same thing as in Rom. 3.25 that righteousness and salvation have been obtained by the blood of Christ and are laid hold of by us by faith.

16. *For where a testament is.* This single passage gives proof that the epistle was not written in Hebrew, because in Hebrew בְּרִית means a covenant but not a testament. In Greek διαθήκη includes both. The apostle refers to this second meaning and argues that the promise could only be ratified and valid if they had been sealed by the death of Christ. He proves this by reference to the common usage of testaments the effect of which is held over until the death of the testators. However, the apostle seems to rely on a rather weak argument so that what he says can be refuted without much trouble. God did not find a testament under the Law but he made a covenant with the people of old so that neither from the fact itself nor from the word can it be concluded that the death of Christ was necessary. If he infers that Christ had to die from the fact itself because a testament is only ratified

by the death of the testator, this is an immediate exception in that
ברית (a word which Moses continually uses) is a covenant which is
made between living people, and there is no other meaning of the fact
itself. As far as the word is concerned he has referred simply (as I have
said) to the ambiguous meaning that it has in Greek. Therefore he
builds his case principally on the fact itself. It is no objection that God
made the covenant with His people because the covenant was like a
testament in this regard that it was ratified by blood.

We must hold on to this truth that no symbols have ever been
introduced by God unnecessarily or without cause. Yet in establishing
the covenant of the Law God used blood. Therefore it was not a
contract between living people (as they say) but one which demanded
death. Moreover this is the proper condition of a testament that it
begins to take effect from the moment of death. If we think that the
apostle is arguing from the fact and not from the word, and moreover
if we allow that he takes it for granted (as I have already said) that
nothing has been set up by God without cause, there will not be much
difficulty. If anyone objects that the Gentiles honoured covenants by
sacrifices in another sense, I admit that that is true; but God has not
borrowed the right of sacrificing from the practice of the Gentiles
but rather all the sacrifices of the Gentiles were unworthy corruptions
which nevertheless derived their origin from those instituted by God.
We must continually return to this point that the covenant of God
which was sealed with blood can be fitly compared to a testament
because it has the same conditions and character.

*Wherefore even the first covenant hath not been dedicated without blood.
For when every commandment had been spoken by Moses unto all the
people according to the law, he took the blood of the calves and the goats,
with water and scarlet wool and hyssop, and sprinkled both the book
itself, and all the people, saying, This is the blood of the covenant which
God commanded to you-ward. Moreover the tabernacle and all the
vessels of the ministry he sprinkled in like manner with the blood. And
according to the law, I may almost say, all things are cleansed with blood,
and apart from shedding of blood there is no remission. It was necessary
therefore that the copies of the things in the heavens should be cleansed
with these; but the heavenly things themselves with better sacrifices
than these.* (18-23)

18. *Wherefore even the first covenant.* It is clear from this that the
apostle is referring chiefly to the fact, and that it is not a question of the
word although he has turned to his advantage a word offered to him
in the language in which he wrote, just as someone speaking about the
same covenant of God which is often called in Greek a μαρτυρία

(*testimony*), would commend it among other things by giving it this title. It is truly a μαρτυρία, to which the angels from heaven bear witness, of which there has been such a superfluity of witnesses on earth—all the holy prophets, apostles and the great company of martyrs—and of which at last the Son of God Himself made Himself the Guarantor. No one will find anything absurd in speaking like that. At the same time the particular meaning of the Hebrew word תעודה (*te'wudah*) does not bear it out, but since nothing is said that is inconsistent with the fact itself we need not be too scrupulous about the word.

The apostle says that the Old Testament was dedicated with blood and he deduces from this that men were then taught that it could not be valid or effective unless death intervened. He says that the fact that the blood of beasts was shed does not validate the confirmation of the eternal covenant. To make this clearer we must notice the rite of sprinkling which he puts here upon Moses. First of all he says that the covenant was dedicated not because it was profane in itself but because there is nothing so sacred that men will not profane it by their impurity unless God Himself prevents it by a renewal of everything. The dedication therefore was for the sake of men who alone need it.

He adds afterwards that *the tabernacle and all the vessels* and the very book of the Law were sprinkled. By this ceremony the people were then taught that God could only be sought or looked for for salvation or rightly worshipped if in every case faith looked to the mediation of blood. The majesty of God is rightly fearful for us and the way to it is a dangerous labyrinth until we know that He is appeased by the blood of Christ and until that same blood affords us an easy approach. All worship is faulty and impure unless Christ cleanses it by the sprinkling of His blood.

The tabernacle was a kind of visible image of God, and *the vessels of the ministry* were made for His worship and were thus the symbols of true worship. If none of them held salvation for the people without blood we may quickly conclude that where Christ does not appear with His blood we have nothing to do with God. However unchanging the loving-kindness of God may be, doctrine itself will be of no benefit to us unless it is dedicated by blood as is clearly expressed in this verse.

I know that others will interpret this differently. For them the tabernacle is the body of the Church, the vessels are individual believers whose ministry God uses; but what I have said is much more fitting. Whenever God was to be called upon they turned to the sanctuary, and it was a common way of speaking for them to say that when they appeared in the temple they stood before the face of the Lord.

20. *This is the blood of the covenant which God commanded.* If that was the blood of the testament then the testament is not ratified without blood nor does the blood avail for atonement without the testament. Both are necessarily joined together. We see that the symbol was added only when the Law had been expounded. What kind of a sacrament would it be unless the Word preceded it? Hence the symbol is a kind of addition to the Word. Notice that this Word is not whispered like a magic incantation but proclaimed in a loud voice. The words of the covenant *which God commanded to you-ward* agree with the fact that it is addressed to the people. It is therefore a perversion and abuse of the sacrament and a pagan corruption where no explanation of the command is heard which is as it were the soul of the sacrament. Therefore the papists who take away the true understanding of things from the signs retain only the dead elements.

This passage reminds us that all the promises of God are only profitable to us when confirmation of them comes from the blood of Christ. What Paul testifies (II Cor. 1.20), that all the promises of God are yea and amen in Christ, takes place when His blood is engraved in our hearts like a seal, or when we not only hear God speaking but discern Christ offering us Himself as a pledge of what is said. If only this thought came to our minds that what we read is written not so much with ink as with the blood of the Son of God, that when the Gospel is preached His sacred blood falls on us along with the words, both our attention and our reverence would be far greater. The symbol of this was the sprinkling mentioned by Moses, although there is more content here than the words of Moses contain. He does not record that either the book or the people were sprinkled nor does he name the goats or the scarlet wool or the hyssop. With regard to the book even though it cannot be clearly proved that it was sprinkled yet the probability of its so being is conjectured from the fact that Moses is said to have brought it out after he had sacrificed and that he did so in order to bind the people to God by a solemn agreement. As far as the other things are concerned the apostle seems to me to have mixed together the various kinds of expiations which have the same reference. There is nothing absurd in this since he is dealing in general with the question of cleansing in the Old Testament which was by blood. When there was a sprinkling of hyssop and scarlet wool there is no doubt that this represented the mystical sprinkling that comes by the Spirit. We know that hyssop has a particularly effective power of cleansing and refining, and in this way Christ uses His spirit in place of sprinkling to wash us with His blood when He gives us a true sense of penitence, when He refines the depraved lusts of our flesh and when He touches us with the precious beauty of His justice. God did not institute this for nothing. David also referred to this in Ps. 51.9, when he says, 'Purge me, Lord, with hyssop, and I shall be clean.' This will be enough for those who wish to think soberly.

22. *And almost all things.* When he says 'almost', he seems to indicate that some things were cleansed differently. Certainly they often used to wash themselves and other dirty things in water, but even water derived its power of cleansing from the sacrifices so that the apostle is right when he says at the end that there was no remission without blood. There was an imputation of uncleanness until it was expiated by sacrifice. Just as there is neither purity nor salvation apart from Christ so nothing could be either pure or saving without blood because Christ must never be separated from the sacrifice of His death. All that the apostle wanted to say was that this symbol was almost always made use of. But if at any time there was no cleansing the fault was not in the blood since all the rites derived their power in some way from the general atonement. The people were not sprinkled individually (how could a small portion of blood be sufficient for such a large number?) but nevertheless cleansing extended to all. The word almost has the force of saying that this ceremony was a very frequent usage and that they seldom omitted it in cases of cleansing. The view of Chrysostom that unfitness is denoted here because these were only figures is alien to the mind of the apostle.

There is no remission. Men are shut off from the sight of God because of the fact that since He is justly wroth with them all, there is no reason for them to promise themselves any favour from him until He has been pacified. The one way of pacifying is by the atonement of blood, and hence no pardon for sin can be hoped for unless we bring blood. This happens when we find refuge by faith in the death of Christ.

23. *The copies of the things.* In case anyone objects that the blood in which the Old Testament was dedicated was different from that of the testator, the apostle anticipates and says that it was no wonder that that tabernacle, being earthly, was consecrated by the sacrifice of beasts. There was an analogy and a likeness (*analogiam et similitudinem fuisse*) between the cleansing and the things that were cleansed. On the other hand the heavenly pattern about which he is speaking was consecrated in a very different way. There is no place here for goats or calves, and it follows from this that the death of the testator is necessary.

The meaning here is this: since under the law there were earthly types of spiritual things, so the rite of atonement was also carnal and (so to speak) figurative. But since the heavenly pattern does not allow of anything earthly it requires something other than the blood of beasts to conform to its excellence. The death of the testator is therefore necessary to bring about a true consecration of the testament.

He calls the kingdom of Christ heavenly because it is spiritual and has within it a firm revelation of the truth.

He speaks of *better sacrifices* in place of a victim because the latter is only one, but he uses the plural number more often on account of the contrast.

> *For Christ entered not into a holy place made with hands, like in pattern to the true; but into heaven itself, now to appear before the face of God for us: nor yet that he should offer himself often; as the high priest entereth into the holy place year by year with blood not his own; else must he often have suffered since the foundation of the world: but now once at the end of the ages hath he been manifested to put away sin by the sacrifice of himself. And inasmuch as it is appointed unto men once to die, and after this cometh judgment; so Christ also, having once offered to bear the sins of many, shall appear a second time, apart from sin, to them that wait for him, unto salvation. (24-28)*

24. *Not into a holy place made with hands.* This is a confirmation of the previous verse. He has spoken of the true sanctuary, that is, the heavenly one, and now he adds that Christ has entered into it. There must of necessity follow a suitable confirmation. He takes *holy place* to mean the sanctuary. He describes it as *not made with hands* because it is not to be included among created things which are liable to corruption. He does not mean here the heaven which we see with our eyes and where the stars shine, but the glory of the kingdom of God which is higher than all the heavens. He calls the old sanctuary a *pattern* of the true, that is a spiritual one, because all the external types show as in a mirror what is not otherwise experienced by our natural senses. Greek writers sometimes use the same word when they discuss our sacraments, and they do so intelligently and fittingly because every sacrament is the visible image of invisible things.

Now to appear. In olden days the Levitival priest stood before the face of God in the name of the people, but as a type; in Christ however there is the firm reality and the full fruition of the type. The ark was the symbol of the divine Presence, but it is Christ who truly offers Himself before God and stands there to seek His favour for us, so that there is now no reason why we should fly from the judgment-seat of God when we have such a good Advocate by whose faith and patronage we are made safe and secure. Certainly Christ was our Advocate when He lived on earth, but this is a further allowance for our weakness that He ascended into heaven to undertake the task of being our Patron. Whenever mention is made of His ascension into heaven, we must keep in mind that it has this advantage for us that He appears there before God to defend us by His advocacy. There is a stupid and out of place question raised by some as to whether He has not always appeared there, but here the apostle is speaking only of His intercession for the sake of which He entered the heavenly sanctuary.

25. *Nor yet that He should offer himself often.* How then, someone may ask, is He a Priest if He offers no sacrifices? I reply that the office or person of priest does not require a continual act of sacrifice. Under the Law there were statutory days every year for the principal sacrifices, and they had their prescribed times daily morning and evening. Since that one sacrifice which Christ offered once for all has eternal power, and is therefore perpetual in its efficacy, it is no wonder that the eternal priesthood of Christ is supported by its power which never fails. Here again he is showing how and where Christ is different from the Levitical priest. He has spoken above about the sanctuary, but he notes one difference in the nature of the sacrifice because Christ offered Himself and not a brute beast. He then adds a second difference in the fact that He does not repeat the sacrifice in the way that under the Law there was frequent and almost incessant repetition.

26. *Else must he often.* He shows now how absurd it is if we do not think that the one sacrifice of Christ effects sufficient atonement. If that is so he infers that He ought to have died more often because death is always joined to sacrifice. This last is quite absurd. It therefore follows that the power of the one sacrifice is eternal and extends to all ages.

He says *since the foundation of the world*, because in every age since the beginning there have been sins which needed atonement. Therefore unless the sacrifice of Christ was efficacious, none of the fathers would have obtained salvation. Since in themselves they were subject to the wrath of God, they had no remedy to deliver them had it not been that Christ by suffering once for all suffered what was necessary to reconcile men to the grace of God from the beginning of the world right to the end. Unless we look for more deaths let us be content with one sacrifice. From this it is clear how frivolous is the distinction the sharpness of which pleases the papist, when they say that the sacrifice of Christ on the Cross was a bloody one, but the sacrifice of the Mass which they pretend to offer every day to God is bloodless. If such a subtle evasion were valid, the Spirit of God must be charged with inadvertence for not having thought of this, since the apostle takes it for granted that there is no sacrifice without death. I do not care that ancient writers speak thus, because it is not within the power of men to invent sacrifices just as they please. The truth of the Holy Spirit that sins are not atoned for by sacrifice without the shedding of blood stands. It is an idea of the devil that Christ is offered more often.

But now at the end of the ages. What is called 'the fulness of time' in Gal. 4.4 he calls the end of the ages. It was the fulness of that time which God had determined by His eternal decrees. In this way no occasion is afforded for human curiosity to dare to ask why it was not sooner, or why not rather at this time or that. We must submit to the secret counsel of God the reason for which is plain to Him even though not to us. In short, the apostle is saying that the death of Christ was timely since He was sent into the world by the Father for this cause, in whose power is the rightful government both of all things and of all times, and who orders their progress by His consummate wisdom even though it is hid from us.

This end of the ages is set in opposition to the imperfection of time gone by. God held His people of old in suspense to facilitate the conclusion that they had not yet come to stability. Hence Paul declares in I Cor. 10.11 that the ends of the ages are come upon us, by which he means that the kingdom of Christ has brought fulfilment to everything. Since the fulness of the time was when Christ appeared to atone for sin, they do Him a terrible wrong who want to renew His sacrifice as if everything had not yet been fulfilled by His death. He appeared once for all because if He had come a second or a third time there would have been a defect in the first sacrifice which would deny this fulness.

To put away. This agrees with the prophecy of Daniel (9.24, 27) where, after the sealing up and the taking away of sins are promised, the end of the sacrifices is indicated. What is the purpose of expiation when sins have been destroyed? This destruction consists in the fact that sins are no longer imputed to those who take refuge in the sacrifice of Christ. Although we must daily seek for pardon just as we daily provoke the wrath of God yet because we are reconciled to God only by the pledge of the one death of Christ it is true to say that by it sin has been destroyed.

27. *Inasmuch as it is appointed.* The meaning is this that since after the death of a man, we wait patiently for the day of judgment, because this is the common law of nature against which there is no struggling, why should there be less patience in waiting for the second coming of Christ? If a long space of time does nothing to take away from the common herd of men the hope of a blessed resurrection, how absurd would it be to give less honour to Christ? We would show this lesser honour if we called on Him to undergo a second death when He has already undergone one for ever. If anyone objects that some did die twice, like Lazarus and the like, the answer is simply this that the apostle is speaking here of the ordinary condition of men but that he exempts from them those whom a sudden change has removed from

the influence of corruption because he includes only those who wait for a long time in dust for the redemption of their bodies.

A second time apart from sin. The apostle presses this one point that we should not be upset by senseless and misconceived desires for new kinds of expiation since the death of Christ alone is fully sufficient for us. He says that He appeared once for all and made sacrifice to take away sin; and by his second coming He will make clear the efficacy of His death so that sin will have no further power to hurt us.

To bear the sins means to free those who have sinned from their guilt by his satisfaction. He says many meaning all, as in Rom. 5.15. It is of course certain that not all enjoy the fruits of Christ's death, but this happens because their unbelief hinders them. That question is not dealt with here because the apostle is not discussing how few or how many benefit from the death of Christ, but means simply that He died for others, not for Himself. He therefore contrasts the many to the one.

What does he mean by saying that He will appear without sin? Some explain this as a sin-offering or a victim making atonement for sin, as in Rom. 8.3, and II Cor. 5.21, and in many passages in Moses. In my opinion his intention was to say something more specific, namely that Christ when He comes will make it clear how really He has taken away sins so that there is no need for any other sacrifice to appease God. It is as though he were saying that when we come to the judgment-seat of Christ we shall see that there was nothing lacking in His death. That is the point of the immediately following phrase, *to them that wait for him unto salvation.* Others render this differently, in this way—those who look to him for salvation. But the previous meaning is more apt, because he means that those who rely on it with quiet minds will find full salvation in the death of Christ. This kind of expectation fits the circumstances of this present subject. Elsewhere (I Thess. 1.10) Scripture has ascribed to believers a common expectation of the coming of the Lord in order to distinguish them from unbelievers for whom the mention of this is terrifying. As the apostle now maintains that we must find rest in the single sacrifice of Christ, he calls it the expectation of Christ since when we are satisfied with His redemption alone we shall not look for new remedies or support.

CHAPTER TEN

For the law having a shadow of the good things to come, not the very image of the things, they can never with the same sacrifices year by year, which they offer continually, make perfect them that draw nigh. Else would they not have ceased to be offered, because the worshippers, having been once cleansed, would have had no more conscience of sins? But in those sacrifices there is a remembrance made of sins year by year. For it is impossible that the blood of bulls and goats should take away sins.
(1-4)

1. *For the law having a shadow.* He has borrowed this metaphor from the art of painting. The word 'shadow' here means something different from Col. 2.17 where he thus describes the ancient ceremonies because they have no solid substance of the things which they represented. Now he says that they were like the rough outlines which are the foreshadowing of the living picture. Before they put on the true colours with paint artists usually draw an outline in pencil of the representation which they intend. This less distinct picture is called in Greek σκιαγραφία, just as you say in Latin shadowy, and just as for the Greek an εἰκών is the full likeness. Εἰκόνες are called in Latin likenesses which represent the true appearance of men or beasts or places. The apostle has established this difference between the Law and the Gospel, that the former has foreshadowed in elementary and sketchy outline what today has been expressed in living and graphically printed colour. In this way he again confirms what he has said above that the Law was not useless nor its ceremonies meaningless. Although it had in it no image of heavenly things like the final masterpiece (as they call it) from the artist's hand, yet it gave some sort of indication which was of some use to the fathers, even although our condition is much preferable. It is to be noticed that the things which were shown to them from a distance are the same as those which are now set before our eyes. Both are shown the same Christ, the same justice, sanctification, and salvation. Only in the manner of the painting is there difference.

Good things to come mean, I think, eternal things. I admit that the kingdom of Christ which is now a present fact for us was formerly announced as future, but the words of the apostle mean that we have a vivid image of good things to come. He is thinking of that spiritual pattern the full fruition of which is postponed to the resurrection and the age to come, although I admit again that these good things began to be revealed from the beginning of the kingdom of Christ. He is

132

concerned to say this that good things to come are spoken of not only in respect of the Old Testament but because we also still hope for them.

The same sacrifices year by year. He is speaking principally about the yearly sacrifice which is mentioned in Lev. 17, although the whole subject is included under this one kind. He argues as follows—Where there is no more consciousness of sin, there is no need of sacrifice. Yet under the Law the offering of the same sacrifice was continually repeated. Therefore God was not satisfied, guilt was not removed and consciences were not appeased; otherwise there would have been an end to sacrifice. It must be carefully noted that he gives the same name to sacrifices which had a similar purpose. They were thought of more in relation to God's institution than to the different beasts. This one thing is sufficient to refute the cleverness of the papists by which they seem to find an ingenious way round their absurdity in defending the sacrifice of the Mass. When they are faced with the objection that a repeated sacrifice is superfluous since the force of that which Christ offered once for all is eternal, they immediately make the excuse that it is not a different sacrifice that is made in the Mass but the same one. This is their answer, but what does the apostle say to the contrary? He says that the sacrifice which is offered a second time, even though it be the same, is not effective or suitable for atonement. Though the papists should shout a thousand times that the sacrifice which Christ made once for all on the cross and which they themselves make today is not different but one and the same, I shall still maintain from the apostle's own mouth that if the sacrifice of Christ availed to please God it not only put an end to other sacrifices but that it is impossible to repeat it. From this it is clear that the offering of Christ in the Mass is a sacrilege.

3. *A remembrance made year by year.* Although the Gospel is the message of our reconciliation with God we must remember every day our sins. The apostle means that our sins are set before us so that the guilt may be removed by the mediation of this present sacrifice. He does not mean any kind of remembrance, but one which brings such a confession of guilt before God that a sacrifice is needed to provide a remedy. The sacrifice of the Mass for the papists is that they imagine that in it the grace of the death of Christ is applied to us to take away our sins. But if the apostle is right in concluding that the sacrifices of the Law were weak because they were repeated yearly to obtain pardon, by the same token we may conclude that the sacrifice of the death of Christ was weak if it is to be offered daily for us to experience its power. Whatever be the pretences with which they colour their Mass, they can never escape the charge of dreadful blasphemy against Christ.

4. *For it is impossible.* He confirms the foregoing sentence on the

same ground as he has previously adduced, that the blood of beasts does not cleanse souls. The Jews had this symbol and pledge of real cleansing but in a different regard, namely in the way that the blood of a calf stood for the blood of Christ. Here the apostle is discussing the value of the blood of beasts in itself. He rightly takes away from it the power to cleanse. There is here an unexpressed contrast to be understood as though he had said that it is no wonder that the old sacrifices were weak so that they had to be offered continually. They had nothing in them but the blood of beasts which does not reach to the soul, whereas the power of the blood of Christ is something quite different. It is therefore not right to measure the sacrifice made by him by those former ones.

Wherefore when he cometh into the world, he saith, Sacrifice and offering thou wouldest not, but a body didst thou prepare for me; in whole burnt offerings and sacrifices for sin thou hadst no pleasure: then said I, Lo, I am come (in the roll of the book it is written of me) to do thy will, O God. Saying above, Sacrifices and offerings and whole burnt offerings and sacrifices for sin thou wouldest not, neither hadst pleasure therein (the which are offered according to the law), then hath he said, Lo, I am come to do thy will. He taketh away the first, that he may establish the second. By which will we have been sanctified through the offering of the body of Jesus Christ once for all. (5-10)

5. *Wherefore when he cometh.* This coming into the world was the manifestation of Christ in the flesh. When He put on the nature of man to show Himself as Redeemer to the world, and appeared to men, He is said to have come into the world, just as elsewhere (John 6.41) He is said to have descended from heaven. The fortieth psalm, which he quotes, seems difficult to apply to Christ, for the sentence 'my iniquities have laid hold on me' does not seem to fit His person, unless Christ of His own accord took on Himself the sins of His members. Certainly the whole argument properly fits David, but as it is well known that David was the type of Christ there is no absurdity in transferring to Christ what David declared in respect of himself, especially when mention is made, as in this passage, of abolishing the sacrifices of the Law. Not everyone agrees that the words contain this meaning. They think that it is not simply sacrifices that are rejected here, but that the superstitious opinion which was commonly current that the whole worship of God was contained in them is condemned. If that is so this evidence has little value for the present purpose.

It is therefore worthwhile to examine this passage more closely to see whether the apostle has introduced it relevantly. Sentences of this kind run right through the prophets that sacrifices do not please God, are not required by Him, and have no value, indeed that they are an abomination to Him. What is noted there however is not the vice which is inherent in the nature of the sacrifices but that which is accidental. When hypocrites were obstinate in their godlessness and yet wished to please God with sacrifices they were rebuked in this way. The prophets reject sacrifices not in being instituted by God but because they were defiled by wicked men and desecrated by impure consciences. The reasoning here is different. He is not condemning sacrifices brought in hypocrisy nor those that are otherwise improperly performed on account of the wickedness and sinfulness of men, but he is saying that they are not required from godly and honest worshippers of God. He is speaking of himself, that he offered them with a pure heart and with clean hands, and yet he says that they did not please God. If anyone makes the exception that they were not accepted of themselves or for their own worthiness but for some other purpose, I repeat that an argument of this kind is not suitable to this passage. Men are there being recalled to spiritual worship if they give the external ceremonies more than is right. The Holy Spirit is there declaring that the ceremonies had no value before God since they are exalted beyond measure by the error of men.

Since he was under the Law David should certainly not have neglected the custom of sacrificing. He ought, I admit, to have worshipped God with inner sincerity of heart, but he was not allowed to pass by what God had commanded him. In common with all the rest he was commanded to sacrifice. From this we conclude that he looked further than the pattern of his own age when he said 'sacrifice thou wouldest not'. Even in the time of David it was proved to some extent that God cared nothing for sacrifices, but, because they were still held under the yoke of the schoolmaster, David could not perform the worship of God completely except when it was (so to speak) clothed in this form. We must come to the kingdom of Christ for it to be completely true that God does not wish sacrifice.

There is a similar passage in Ps. 16.10, 'neither wilt thou suffer thine holy one to see corruption'. Although God saved David for a time from corruption, yet this was not truly completed until Christ. This is very important that in professing to do the will of God he gives no place to sacrifices. From this we conclude that they are contrary to that perfect obedience of God, a fact which would not be true unless the law were abolished. I do not deny that David both here and in Ps. 51.18 so disparaged external sacrifices as to prefer what is the chief thing. There is no doubt that in both places he looked forward to the kingdom of Christ. The apostle is witness that Christ is rightly introduced as speaking in this psalm when not even the lowest place among the commandments of God is left for the sacrifices which God strictly requires under the Law.

A body didst thou prepare. The words of David run differently, 'mine ears hast thou opened'. Some think that this phrase has been borrowed from an ancient legal ritual (Exod. 21.6). If anyone refused the freedom of the jubilee and wanted to pledge himself to perpetual slavery, his ear was bored with an awl. They want the sense to be, 'Lord, thou shalt have me as a servant bound to thee for ever.' I take this otherwise as an expression that he is attentive and obedient. We are deaf until God opens our ears, that is, corrects the stubbornness which is inherent in us. There is an implied contrast between the mixed vulgar mob (for whom the sacrifices were only a spectacle without power) and David to whom God had shown more exactly their spiritual and lawful usage. The apostle follows the Greek and says, *thou hast prepared a body.* They were not over-scrupulous in quoting words provided that they did not misuse Scripture for their convenience. We must always look at the purpose for which quotations are made because they have careful regard for the main object so as not to turn Scripture to a false meaning, but as far as words are concerned, as in other things which are not relevant to the present purpose, they allow themselves some indulgence.

7. *In the roll of the book.* The proper meaning of the Hebrew word is 'volume'. We know that in olden times books were rolled up in the form of cylinders. It is not out of place to take the word 'book' to mean the Law which lays down the rule of holy living for all the sons of God, although it seems to me to be a more natural exposition to say that he is including himself in the roll of those who give themselves in obedience to God. The Law bids us all obey God, but David means that he was among the number of those who are called to obey God. He indicates that he is obeying his call when he adds, *I am come to do Thy will.* This has a particular relevance to Christ. Although all the saints aspire after the righteousness of God, it is Christ alone who is fully fitted to do the will of God.

Nevertheless this passage ought to urge us all to a ready obedience. Christ is the example of perfect obedience in order that those who are His should eagerly endeavour to imitate Him so as to respond together to the call of God and confirm their calling with their whole life, with the words, 'lo, I come'. What follows has the same purpose; *it is written in the book,* that is, that we should do the will of God, as it is said elsewhere (Col. 1.22), that the purpose of our election is to be holy and blameless in his sight.

9. *He taketh away the first.* Notice the reason and the purpose of this quotation, namely for us to know that full and firm righteousness in the kingdom of Christ does not need legal sacrifices. When they are

taken away, the will of God is established as the rule of perfection. It follows therefore that the sacrifices of beasts were removed by the priesthood of Christ because they had no place in it. As we have said, there was no reason to reject sacrifices on account of accidental blame, because he is not dealing with hypocrites nor is he condemning the superstition of a distorted worship, but he is saying that the accustomed sacrifices are not demanded of any man who is holy and properly instructed, and he bears witness that God is perfectly obeyed even when sacrifices are omitted.

10. *By which will.* Having related the testimony of David to his subject he now takes occasion to turn some of the words to his own advantage, more for the sake of ornament than of explanation. David professes not so much in his own person as in that of Christ that he is prepared to do the will of God. That is extended to include all the members of Christ. This is the general teaching of Paul when he says (I Thess. 4.3), 'This is the will of Christ, even your sanctification, that ye abstain from fornication.' Because it was Christ's example of obedience pre-eminently above all others to give Himself to die on the Cross, and because for this particular purpose He took on Himself the form of a servant, the apostle says that by offering Himself Christ fulfilled the command of the Father, and thus we have been sanctified.

In adding *through the offering of the body* he refers to the sentence in the psalm, 'A body didst thou prepare.' At least so it is in Greek. He means that Christ found that in Himself He could please God so that He had no need of outside aids. If the Levitical priests had had a fit body the sacrifice of beasts would have been superfluous; but Christ alone is sufficient and is by Himself capable of performing whatever God requires.

And every priest indeed standeth day by day ministering and offering oftentimes the same sacrifices, the which can never take away sins: but he, when he had offered one sacrifice for sins for ever, sat down on the right hand of God; from henceforth expecting till his enemies he made the footstool of his feet. For by one offering he hath perfected for ever them that are sanctified. And the Holy Ghost also beareth witness to us: for after he hath said, This is the covenant that I will make with them after those days, saith the Lord: I will put my laws on their heart, and upon their mind also will I write them; then saith he, And their sins and their iniquities will I remember no more. Now where remission of these is, there is no more offering for sin. (11-18)

11. *And every priest.* This is the conclusion of the whole argument, namely that the practice of daily sacrifice is wholly inconsistent with and foreign to the priesthood of Christ, and therefore after His coming

the Levitical priests were deprived of their office since their place and purpose was to sacrifice daily. It is the nature of contrary things that when one is established the other falls. So far he has laboured adequately and more than adequately, in asserting the priesthood of Christ, and it therefore remains to say that that old priesthood ceases since it does not accord with Him. All the saints find a full consecration in the one sacrifice of Christ. The word τετελείωκε, which I have rendered 'consecrated', can be rendered 'made perfect', but I prefer the former meaning because he is now dealing with sacred things. When he says *them that are sanctified*, he includes in this phrase all the sons of God and reminds us that we shall only seek in vain if we look elsewhere for the grace of sanctification. In case men imagine that Christ is now lying at ease in heaven, he again repeats that He *sat down on the right hand of God*, by which phrase (as we have seen elsewhere) he denotes His kingdom and His power. There is therefore no reason to fear that He allows His power to be destroyed by death or to lie buried in the tomb, but He lives for the very purpose of filling heaven and earth with His power. He shows from the words of this psalm how long this state of affairs is to last, namely until Christ has conquered all His enemies. If therefore our faith looks for Christ sitting on the right hand of God, and rests quietly in that truth, we shall at the end enjoy the fruits of this victory along with Him who is our Head, and, when our foes are vanquished along with Satan and sin and death and the whole world and when we have put off the corruption of our flesh, we shall triumph.

15. *The Holy Ghost also beareth witness.* The fact that this evidence from Jeremiah is brought forward a second time is neither irrelevant nor superfluous. He quoted it before for another purpose, namely to show that the old Testament must be repealed since a new and a different one was promised in order to correct the weakness of the old. Now he has a different aim in view. He founds his contention on the single phrase *their iniquities will I remember no more*, and concludes from it that there is no further use for sacrifice since sins are blotted out.

It could be that this conclusion is not sound enough. Although there were in the Law and prophets innumerable promises about the remission of sins, nevertheless the Church did not cease to offer sacrifices for them. Therefore the remission of sins does not exclude sacrifices. But if you consider the individual points more closely, the fathers had under the Law the same promises about the remission of sins which we have today. They called on God in reliance on them and gloried in the pardon which they obtained. Yet the prophet promises that under the new covenant there will be no remembrance of sins before God as if he were introducing something new and previously unheard of. From this we may conclude that sins are now remitted in a different way from before. The difference lies not in the word or in faith but in the actual price of remission. God does not now remember sins because atonement has been made once for all. Otherwise the prophet would be speaking in vain when he says that this will be the benefit of the new Testament that God will not remember sin.

Now that we have come to the end of the discussion which has been taking place about the priesthood of Christ, readers must be briefly reminded that the sacrifices of the Law are repealed here not more completely than the invention of the papists about the sacrifice of the Mass is refuted. They maintain that their Mass is a sacrifice for the atonement of the sins of the living and the dead. The apostle says that there is now no place for sacrifice from the time that the prophecy of Jeremiah was fulfilled. The papists make the rejoinder that this is not something new or different from the sacrifice of Christ but the same thing. The apostle on the other hand maintains that the same sacrifice should not be repeated and he says that the sacrifice of Christ was not only unique but offered once for all. Add to that the fact that he very often claims the honour of priesthood for Christ alone so that no one but He alone is suitable to offer it.

The papists have another evasion in calling their sacrifice bloodless; but the apostle maintains without exception that death is necessary to make a sacrifice. The papists make excuses by saying that the Mass is the application of the one sacrifice which Christ made, but the apostle on the other hand teaches that the sacrifices of the Law were abolished by the death of Christ because there was remembrance of sins in them. It is clear from this that this kind of application which they invent has disappeared.

In short let the papists turn to any formula they like, they cannot escape the fact that this present argument of the apostle's makes it clear that their Mass abounds in all kinds of sacrilege. In the first place, by the testimony of the apostle, Christ alone was suitable to offer Himself; in the Mass He is offered by other hands. Secondly the apostle maintains that the sacrifice of Christ is not only unique but offered once for all so that it may not be repeated; in the Mass however they may chatter about the sacrifice being the same, yet it appears to be made every day and they themselves admit it. The apostle acknowledges that there is no sacrifice without blood and death; they talk nonsense when they say that the sacrifice which they offer is bloodless. When the apostle is dealing with obtaining pardon for sins he bids us take refuge in that one sacrifice which Christ offered on the Cross and he distinguishes us from the fathers by this mark, that the rite of continual sacrifice was done away with by the coming of Christ; they on the other hand require daily applications through sacrifice for the death of Christ to be efficacious for us, so that there is no difference between Christians and Jews except in the outward sign.

> *Having therefore, brethren, boldness to enter into the holy place by the blood of Jesus, by the way which he dedicated for us, a new and living way, through the veil, that is to say, his flesh; And having a great priest over the house of God; Let us draw near with a true heart in fulness of faith, having our hearts sprinkled from an evil conscience and our body washed with pure water: Let us hold fast the confession of our hope that it waver not; for he is faithful that promised.* (19-23)

19. *Having therefore, brethren.* He now draws together the conclusion or the sum of the foregoing teaching to which he adds a timely and weighty exhortation and severely threatens those who reject the grace of Christ. The sum of it is this, that all the ceremonies by which access to the sanctuary of God was gained under the Law find their solid reality in Christ, so that to anyone who has Christ the use of them is unnecessary and unprofitable. To put this more clearly he describes allegorically the way of access which Christ has opened for us. He compares heaven with the old sanctuary and he puts forward what is spiritually fulfilled in Christ in the form of metaphors. Allegories certainly sometimes obscure the point rather than illustrate it. But these ones have much grace and afford much light when the apostle relates the old figures of the Law to Christ so that we may recognize that what the Law foreshadowed is now truly shown in Him. As there is great importance in almost every word let us remember that there is an understood contrast so that the truth which is seen in Christ does away with the old types.

He says first that we have *boldness to enter into the holy place.* This privilege was never given to the fathers under the Law. The people were forbidden to approach the visible sanctuary except that the high priest wore on his shoulders the names of the tribes and on his breast the twelve stones as a memorial of them. The case now is very different. The way into heaven is open for us not only in symbol but in very truth by the mercy of Christ because He has made us a royal priesthood. He says *by the blood of Jesus* because the door of the sanctuary was not opened for the solemn entrance of the high priest except by the intervention of blood. He goes on to note a difference between this blood and that of beasts. The blood of beasts did not long retain its power because it immediately began to decay, whereas, since the blood of Christ is not corrupted by any decay but flows continually in unadulterated purity, it will suffice for us to the end of the world. It is no wonder that beasts slain in sacrifice had no power to give life because they were dead, but Christ who rose from the dead to give us life pours His own life into us. This is the continual consecration of His life that the blood of Christ is continually being shed before the face of the Father to spread over heaven and earth.

20. *Through the veil.* Just as the veil covered the recesses of the sanctuary and yet opened a door to it, so, though His Godhead was hidden in the flesh of Christ, He yet leads us to heaven, and no one will find God unless the Man Christ is his way and his door. We are thus reminded that the glory of Christ is not to be thought of from the outward aspect of His flesh nor is His flesh to be despised because it conceals like a veil the majesty of God and since it is that which directs us to the enjoyment of all God's benefits.

21. *And having a great priest.* All the things that he has previously said about the abolition of the old priesthood are now to be brought back to mind. Christ could not be a high priest unless the former priests were divested of their office since theirs was a different order. He means therefore that all those things which Christ changed at His coming are to be let go. He sets Him over the whole house of God so that whoever wishes to have a place in the Church must submit to Christ and choose Him and no other as his leader and ruler.

22. *Let us draw near with a true heart.* As he shows that there is nothing in Christ and His sacrifice which is not spiritual or heavenly, so he wants what we bring for our part to correspond. In days of old the Jews cleansed themselves by various washings in order to be prepared for the worship of God. It is no wonder that the ritual of cleansing was carnal since the worship of God itself was wrapped in shadows and had to some extent the taste of the flesh. A mortal priest was chosen from among sinners to perform sacred offices for the time being. He was adorned with precious vestments but with worldly ones in order to stand in the sight of God. He approached only the ark of the covenant in order to sanctify his entrance, and he borrowed the sacrifice of a beast from the herd or the flock. In Christ everything is far superior. He Himself is not only pure and blameless but is the fountain of all holiness and justice and is made a High Priest by a heavenly oracle not for the short space of mortal life but for ever. To ratify this an oath is interposed. He appears adorned with all the gifts of the Holy Spirit to the highest perfection. He appeases God by His own blood and reconciles Him with men. He ascends above the heavens to appear as our Mediator before God.

Because of all this we in our turn are to bring nothing which does not correspond since there must be a mutual concord between Priest and people. Outward washings of the flesh must therefore be done away with and the whole apparatus of ceremonies must cease. The apostle contrasts these outward figures with a true heart and the certainty of faith and the wiping away of all evil. From this we conclude how we must bear ourselves to enjoy the benefits of Christ. We cannot come to Him except with an upright or true heart, a sure faith, and a pure conscience. An honest or true heart is set against one which is simulated or deceitful. By the word πληροφορία (full assurance) the apostle describes the nature of faith, and at the same time tells us that the grace of Christ can only be received by those who bring a sure and unhesitating conviction. He calls the sprinkling of the heart from an evil conscience, either when we are looked on as pure before God by obtaining pardon for our sins, or when our heart is cleansed from all unholy affection and is not moved by the goads of the flesh. I include both of these.

What follows about the body washed with pure water is taken by most people as referring to baptism, but to me it seems more likely that the apostle is alluding to the old ceremonies of the Law and by the word 'water' means the Spirit of God, as Ezekiel says (36.25), 'I will sprinkle clean water upon you.' The sum of this is that we are made partakers of Christ if we come to Him sanctified in body and soul. This sanctification is not that which consists in the visible pomp of ceremonies, but is the sure faith and pure conscience and cleanness of body and soul which flows from and is effected by the Spirit of God. Thus Paul exhorts the faithful in II Cor. 7.1 to cleanse themselves from all defilement of flesh and spirit since they are adopted by God as sons.

23. *Let us hold fast the confession of our hope.* Since he is here urging the Jews to perseverance he speaks of hope rather than faith. Just as hope is the child of faith so it is fed and sustained by faith to the end. Moreover he demands confession because there is no true faith that does not show itself to men. He seems to be obliquely touching on the pretence of those who kept too scrupulously to the legal rites to please their own race. He therefore bids them not only to believe with their hearts but also to show by their profession the real extent of their obedience to Christ.

We must take careful note of the condition which follows that God *is faithful that promised.* This tells us first of all that our faith rests on the foundation that God is true. Further this truth is contained in His promise, because the Voice of God must come first so that we may believe. It is not any kind of voice that is suitable for producing faith, but it is on a promise alone that faith rests. From this passage therefore we can deduce the mutual relationship between the faith of men and the promise of God. If God makes no promises, no one can believe.

*And let us consider one another to provoke unto love and good works;
not forsaking the assembling of ourselves together, as the custom of some is,
but exhorting one another; and so much the more, as ye see the day draw-
ing nigh. For if we sin wilfully after that we have received the knowledge
of the truth, there remaineth no more sacrifice for sins, but a certain
fearful expectation of judgment, and a fierceness of fire which shall
devour the adversaries. (24-27)*

24. *Let us consider one another.* I am quite sure that this exhortation
is particularly addressed to the Jews. The extent of the pride of that
race is well known. Because they were the children of Abraham they
boasted that they alone to the exclusion of all others were chosen by
the Lord to share the covenant of eternal life. They were so puffed up
by this privilege and they so despised all other peoples that they were
in the habit of including only themselves in the Church of God. They
arrogated to themselves with the utmost pride the title of Church.
The apostle had to take great pains to correct this pride, and that in
my judgment is what he is now doing, so that the Jews will not take
it badly to associate with the Gentiles and to come together with them
in the same body of the Church.

First of all he says, *let us consider one another,* because God was then
gathering together His Church from Gentiles and Jews between whom
there had always been a great division, so that this union was like a
mixture of fire and water. The Jews recoiled from this because they
thought that it was beneath them to be on the same footing as the
Gentiles. To this goad of unholy emulation which pricked them the
apostle sets up another in opposition, namely that of love. The word
which he uses, παροξυσμός, means the fierceness of strife. In case the
Jews are roused by envy and led to strife, he encourages them to a holy
emulation, namely to urge each other in turn to love.

He strengthens this exposition by what immediately follows, when
he says, *not forsaking the assembling of ourselves together.* The etymology
of the Greek word should be noted. 'Eπί signifies an addition, and
therefore ἐπισυναγωγή has the force of a congregation increased by
new additions. By pulling down the barrier (Eph. 2.14) God added to
His children those who had been aliens from the Church; thus the
Gentiles were a new and unaccustomed addition to the Church. The
Jews thought that this was an insult to them, with the result that many
seceded from the Church thinking that they had a just pretext as a
result of this mixture. They could not be easily persuaded to give up
their right. They thought that the right of adoption was particularly
and exclusively theirs. The apostle therefore warns them not to allow
this equality to incite them to desert the Church and in case it seems

that he is doing so in vain, he reminds them that this vice was common
to many.

We can now grasp the apostle's purpose and the necessity which
forced him to this exhortation, and at the same time we may infer for
ourselves a doctrine of general reference. This is a disease which reigns
throughout the human race, that everyone prefers himself to others
and especially that those who seem to excel in anything do not easily
allow their inferiors to be equal to them. There is so much peevishness
in almost everyone that individuals, if they could, would gladly make
their own churches for themselves, because it is difficult to accommodate oneself to the ways of other people. Rich men are jealous of each
other and scarcely one rich man in a hundred will be found who thinks
that the poor are worthy of being called and included among his
brethren. Unless a similarity of habits or some other allurements or
advantages bind us together, it will be most difficult to foster a lasting
fellowship among us. This warning is therefore more than needed by
all of us that we should be encouraged to love rather than hatred and
that we should not separate ourselves from those whom God hath
joined with us. Rather we are to embrace with brotherly kindness
those who are joined to us by a common faith. Surely the more
keenly Satan watches us, the more intent we should be to achieve unity
so that he cannot in any way either tear us away from the Church or
wean us away by stealth. This will happen if no one pleases himself
more than is right, but if we all have this one aim, to encourage one
another to love and to allow no emulation to flourish except that of
doing good. Surely contempt of one's brethren, peevishness, envy,
over-estimation of ourselves, and other evil impulses bear witness
either that our love is cold or that it is non-existent.

Having said, *not forsaking the assembling of ourselves together*, he adds,
but exhorting one another, meaning that all believers ought to strive to
bring together the Church on every side by whatever ways they can.
It is on this condition that we are called by the Law that everyone
should seek to bring others, should strive to lead the wanderers back
to the road, should stretch forth a hand to the fallen and should win
over the outsiders. If we are to put out so much trouble on those who
are still strangers from the flock of Christ how much more earnestness
is required of us in encouraging the brethren whom God hath joined
to us.

25. *As the custom of some is.* It is clear from this that the first beginnings of all schisms was when proud men despised others and pleased
themselves more than was right. When we hear that even in the time
of the apostles there were faithless men who seceded from the Church
we ought to be less shattered and disturbed by similar instances of

desertion which can be seen today. It is of course no light offence when men who had given some sign of holiness and had professed the same faith as us fall away from the living God, but because this is nothing new we ought as I have said to be less disturbed. The apostle inserted this clause to show that he was not speaking without cause but was applying a necessary remedy to a disease that was gaining ground.

And so much the more. Some think that this passage is parallel to that of Paul (Rom. 13.11), 'It is high time for you to awake out of sleep: for now is salvation nearer to us than when we first believed.' I think rather that the reference here is to the final coming of Christ the expectation of which ought to arouse us most urgently to the contemplation of a holy life as well as to careful and zealous attempts to gather together the Church. What is the purpose of the coming of Christ but to gather us all together in one from this dispersion in which we are now wandering? Therefore the nearer His coming is the more we must bend our efforts that the scattered may be brought together and united and that there may be one fold and one Shepherd (John 10.16).

If anyone asks how the apostle can say that those who were still far off from the revelation of Christ saw the day at hand and almost upon them, I reply that the Church was so constituted from the beginning of the kingdom of Christ that the faithful ought to imagine the coming of the Judge as imminent. They were not deceived by any false imagination when they were prepared to receive Christ at almost any moment, for the condition of the Church from the time of the promulgation of the Gospel was such that that whole period was truly and properly called the last days. Those who have been dead for many generations lived in the last days no less than we do. Artful and sarcastic men, to whom it is ridiculous that we have any faith in the resurrection of the flesh and the last judgment, laugh at our simplicity in this direction; but in case they shake our faith by their mockery, the Holy Spirit teaches us (II Peter 3.8) that with God a thousand years are as one day, so that whenever we think of the eternity of the heavenly kingdom no period of time should seem long to us. Further since the time that Christ completed all the work of our salvation and ascended into heaven it is right and proper that we should continually expect His second revelation and think of each day as though it were the last.

26. *For if we sin wilfully.* He points out the heavy vengeance of God that awaits all those who fall away from the grace of Christ because they are deprived of their only salvation and as it were were given up to certain doom. It was with this evidence that Novatus and his sect armed themselves in their attempt to take away from all those who lapsed after baptism any hope of pardon quite indiscriminately. Those

who could not refute this falsity preferred to impugn the trustworthiness of this epistle rather than to support such absurdity. The proper meaning of this passage is enough in itself without the aid of any outside support to refute the impertinence of Novatus.

The apostle describes as sinners not those who fall in any kind of way but those who forsake the Church and separate themselves from Christ. He is not dealing here with this or that kind of sin but he is exposing by name those who withdraw themselves of their own accord from the fellowship of the Church. There is a great difference between individual lapses and a universal desertion of this kind which makes for a total falling away from the grace of Christ. Because this cannot happen to anyone who has not already been enlightened, he says *if we sin wilfully after we have received the knowledge of the truth*, as though he were saying, 'If anyone knowingly and willingly throws away the grace which he had received'. It can now be seen how this doctrine differs from the error of Novatus.

It is clear from the context that the apostle is referring here only to apostates. He does this so that those who have once been received into the Church will not desert it as some have the habit of doing. He declares that for such there is no longer any offering for sin because they have sinned wilfully after receiving knowledge of the truth. At the same time Christ daily offers Himself for sinners who have fallen in any other way so that they need look for no other offering to atone for their sins. He says that there is no offering left for those who reject the death of Christ because such rejection does not come from some particular offence, but from a total rejection of faith.

This severity of God is certainly terrible, but it is set out to inspire fear. At the same time he cannot be accused of savagery. Since the death of Christ is the only remedy to free us from eternal death, is it not right that those who destroy as far as they can its power and benefit should have nothing left but despair? Those who hold to Christ are called by God daily to reconciliation, are daily refreshed by the blood of Christ, and find daily atonement for their sins by His eternal sacrifice. If no salvation is to be found apart from Him, we should not be surprised that those who let go of Him of their own accord are deprived of every hope of pardon. This is the meaning of the adverb ἔτι, or no more. The sacrifice of Christ is efficacious for believers right to the time of death even if they repeatedly sin. Moreover it always retains its power because they cannot be wholly free from sin as long as they live in the flesh. The apostle is therefore directing his attention only on those who desert Christ in their unbelief and so deprive themselves of the benefit of His death.

The phrase *after we have received the knowledge of the truth* is inserted to heighten their ingratitude, for anyone who of his own accord and with deliberate wickedness quenches the light of God when it has once been kindled in his heart has no excuse to allege before God. Let us learn from this not only to accept the truth that is given us with reverence and a ready meekness of mind, but to persevere continually in the knowledge of it so that we do not pay such dreadful penalties for contempt of it.

27. *But a certain fearful expectation.* He means by this the torture of a bad conscience which is felt by the ungodly who not only have no taste of grace but once they have tasted it know that they have lost it for ever by their own fault. Such people must not only be pricked and bitten but tortured and cut to pieces in a most terrible way. This brings them to struggle rebelliously against God since they cannot bear a Judge so severe. They certainly try all manner of things to get rid of the sense of God's anger, but they do so in vain. As soon as God allows them a brief relief He soon drags them back to His judgment-seat and harasses them with torment which they try at all costs to escape.

He adds *a fierceness of fire* meaning by this last word a forceful impulse or a violent passion—or so I think. There is a common metaphor in the word fire. Just as unbelievers are now inflamed by the fear of divine wrath, so they will then burn with the same feeling. It does not escape me that philosophers have speculated with some sharpness on the nature of this fire but I pay no attention to their remarks since it is clear that it is the same way of speaking as when Scripture connects fire with worm (Eccles. 7.19). No one is in doubt that he uses worm metaphorically for the terrible torment of conscience which gnaws at unbelievers.

Which shall devour the adversaries. It will so devour them as to destroy but not consume them because it will be inextinguishable. In this he reminds us that all those who reject the place which is given them among the faithful are included among the enemies of Christ. There is no middle course. Those who secede from the Church give themselves over to Satan.

A man that hath set at nought Moses' law dieth without compassion on the word of two or three witnesses: of how much sorer punishment, think ye, shall he be judged worthy, who hath trodden under foot the Son of God, and hath counted the blood of the covenant, wherewith he was sanctified, an unholy thing, and hath done despite unto the Spirit of grace? For we know him that said, Vengeance belongeth unto me, I will recompense. And again, The Lord shall judge his people. It is a fearful thing to fall into the hands of the living God. (28-31)

28. *A man that hath set at nought.* This is an argument from the less

to the greater. For if it was a capital offence to break the law of Moses,
how much greater is the penalty due for the rejection of the Gospel,
surrounded as it is by so many and such terrible acts of profanation?
This form of argument was most suitable to move the Jews. That kind
of severe censure against those who fell from the Law could not have
been new to them nor have seemed less than just. They ought to
recognize it as a just punishment, however severe, by which today God
validates the majesty of His Gospel.

This confirms what I have said above that the apostle is not arguing
about specific sins but about a general denial of Christ. The Law did
not punish any kind of transgression by death but only apostasy when
a man departed completely from his religion. The apostle has referred
to the passage in Deut. 17.2-5, which says that if anyone transgresses
the covenant of your God to serve other gods you shall take him out
of the gate and stone him to death.

Although the Law was given by God and Moses was not its author
but its servant, the apostle calls it the Law of Moses because it was
handed down by him and in order to heighten the value of the Gospel
which has been given us by the Son of God.

On the word of two or three witnesses. This has no relevance to the
present passage but is part of the polity of Moses because two or three
witnesses were required to convict an accused. We may conclude from
this more certainly the kind of crime the apostle wanted to draw
attention to, for if this addition had not been made there would have
been a loophole for many false conjectures. It is now beyond dispute
that he is speaking of apostasy. At the same time we must keep in mind
the sense of justice which almost all politicians have observed that no
one is to be convicted without the testimony of two witnesses.

29. *Who hath trodden under foot the son of God.* There is this likeness
between the apostates from the Law and the Gospel that both perish
without mercy; but the kind of death is different. For those who
despise Christ the apostle threatens not only bodily death but eternal
destruction. He therefore says that for these matters there remains a
worse punishment. He expresses this desertion of Christianity under
three forms of speech. He says that in this way the Son of God is
trodden under foot, that His blood is profaned and the Spirit of grace
is despised. It is a worse thing to tread down than to throw away and
the dignity of Christ is something far different from that of Moses.
Add to that that he does not simply contrast Gospel with Law but the
person of Christ and the Holy Spirit to the person of Moses.

The blood of the covenant. He heightens the ingratitude by comparing
the benefits. It is most unworthy to profane the blood of Christ which
is the agent of our sanctification; and that is what those who depart

from faith do. Our faith is not a matter simply of doctrine but of blood by which our salvation has been ratified. He calls it the blood of the covenant because the promises were made valid for us when this pledge was added. He calls attention to the manner of this confirmation by saying that we were sanctified because the blood which was shed would be of no advantage unless we were sprinkled with it through the Holy Spirit. Hence come our atonement and sanctification. The apostle is at the same time referring to the old rite of sprinkling which did not avail for true sanctification but was its shadow or type.

The spirit of grace. He calls it the Spirit of grace from its effects, in that through it and by its power we receive the grace that is offered in Christ. It is He who enlightens our minds with faith, who seals in our hearts the adoption of God, who regenerates us to newness of life, and who grafts us into the body of Christ so that He lives in us and we in Him. The Spirit of grace is therefore rightly so called because through Him Christ with all His benefits becomes ours. To treat with contempt Him by whom we are endowed with so many great benefits is the most criminal wickedness. Learn from this that all those who of their own accord render His grace useless when they had enjoyed its favour are contemptible of the Spirit of God. It is therefore no wonder that God revenges blasphemies of this kind so severely, and no wonder that He shows Himself inexorable to those who tread under their feet Christ the Mediator who alone entreats Him on our behalf, and no wonder that He precludes from the way of salvation those who reject the Holy Spirit as their one true Guide.

30. *For we know him that said.* Both passages are taken from Deut. 23.35. When Moses there promises that God will revenge the wrongs brought upon His people, it seems that what he says here about vengeance is improperly and violently twisted. With what is the apostle concerned, if not that the unbelief of those who despise God will not be unpunished? In Rom. 12.19 Paul follows the true meaning of the passage and gives it a different reference. In his desire to exhort us to have patience he says that we should give a place for God to take vengeance because that is His province; and he supports that by this evidence of Moses. There is certainly no reason why we should not apply particular sentences to universal teaching. Although the purpose of Moses is to encourage the faithful by the fact that they will have God as the avenger of their injuries, it is nevertheless always permissible to conclude from his words that it is the proper office of God to avenge Himself on the ungodly. It is no abuse of this evidence to prove from it that contempt for God will not go unpunished because He is Himself the righteous Judge who claims the right to take vengeance. It could

be that the apostle is arguing here from the less to the greater in this
way: God says that He will not allow His people to be injured with
impunity and promises that He will certainly be their avenger. If He
does not allow injuries done to men to go unpunished, will He not
avenge those done to Himself? Will He have so little care or thought
for His own glory, or none at all, that He ignores or neglects insults
that are offered to Him? But it is simpler and less forced to take the
view that the apostle is merely showing that God will not be ridiculed
with impunity since it is His peculiar office to render to the ungodly
what they deserve.

The Lord will judge his people. The same or a greater difficulty arises
here because the meaning of Moses does not seem to agree with what
is here intended. The apostle seems to quote this passage as if Moses
had written 'judge' in the sense of 'punish'. When he adds immediately
afterwards by way of explanation, 'He will be merciful to his saints',
it is clear that the word 'judge' is taken in the sense of 'governor', which
is a frequent use in Hebrew. This seems to have little to do with the
present purpose. Nevertheless anyone who examines all this properly
will recognize that this passage is fittingly and suitably quoted here.
God cannot govern His Church without purifying it and restoring to
order the confusion that is in it. Further this government will be
deservedly dreadful for the hypocrites who will pay the penalty of
usurping their place among the faithful and of treacherously abusing
the sacred Name of God when the Master of the house Himself takes
care to set His house in order. God is said to rise to judge His people
in the sense that He separates the godly from the hypocrites (Ps. 145.20).
Similarly Ps. 125.3, where the prophet is speaking about the extermina-
tion of hypocrites so that they do not boast any more that they belong
to the Church, because God indulges them, promises that there will be
peace for Israel when this judgment is completed.

The apostle is therefore not out of place in reminding them that God
is the Head of His Church and leaves out nothing that makes for lawful
government so that they may all learn to keep themselves carefully
under His sway and remember that they must give account to their
Judge.

He concludes from this that *it is a fearful thing to fall into the hands of
the living God*, because mortal man, however inimical he may be,
cannot carry his enmity beyond death, but the power of God is not
confined to such narrow limits. We often escape from men, we cannot
escape the judgment of God. Everyone who ponders the fact that he
has to do with God must of necessity (unless he is very stupid) seriously
tremble and be afraid. Indeed it cannot be other than that such a sense
of God absorbs the whole man that no sorrows or tortures can be

compared with it. However many delights our flesh provides for us or in whatever way we deceive ourselves in our sins, this warning ought to be enough to arouse us, that it is a fearful thing to fall into the hands of the living God whose wrath is armed with so many dreadful punishments for eternal death.

The sentiments of David (II Sam. 24.14) seem to be contrary to this sentence when he explains that it is better to fall into the hands of God than into those of men. The answer to this question is simple when we consider that David in his reliance on the faithfulness of God's mercy was choosing to have Him as Judge rather than men. Although he knew that God was rightly angry with him he trusted that he would be reconciled because although he was prostrate on the ground he was nonetheless raised up by the promise of grace. Since he considers that God is placable it is no wonder that he dreads His wrath less than that of men. The apostle is here declaring that the wrath of God is dreadful to the reprobate who are deprived of any hope of pardon and look for nothing but extreme severity because they have shut themselves off from approach to the grace of God. We know that God is described in various ways in accordance with the character of the men to whom He speaks. This is what David means in Ps. 18.27, 'With the merciful thou wilt show thyself merciful, and with the perverse thou wilt show thyself froward.'

But call to remembrance the former days, in which, after ye were enlightened, ye endured a great conflict of sufferings; partly, being made a gazingstock both by reproaches and afflictions; and partly, becoming partakers with them that were so used. For ye both had compassion on them that were in bonds, and took joyfully the spoiling of your possessions, knowing that ye yourselves have a better possession and an abiding one. Cast not away therefore your boldness, which hath great recompense of reward. (32-35)

32. *But call to remembrance.* To add additional stimulus to them and to urge them to speed of action he recalls to their minds the example of piety they had previously shown. It is a shameful thing when you have started well to grow tired half way, and even more shameful to go back when you have made considerable progress. For this purpose it is useful to remember past warfare if we have waged it faithfully and energetically under Christ, not by way of looking for a pretext for laziness as though we were now finished but by way of making us more ready to finish the course which lies before us. Christ has not enlisted us on such terms that we should look for discharge after so many years as if we were time-served soldiers, but in order that we should continue our service to the very end.

He strengthens his exhortation by saying that they themselves carried out notable acts of warfare at a time when they were still new recruits. All the more shame therefore if they now desert after such long experience. The word *enlightened* is restricted to the time when they first began to serve Christ, as though he were saying—as soon as you were initiated into the faith of Christ you underwent hard and arduous struggles, and now your experience ought to have strengthened you to become more courageous. At the same time he reminds them that they achieve this by the goodness of God so that they should have faith by His efforts and not by their own. The enlightened are those who were formerly surrounded by darkness and were without eyes with which to see had not light shone on them from elsewhere. Whenever the things we have done or suffered for Christ come to mind they should urge us on and incite us to higher attainment.

33. *Partly, being made a gazingstock both by reproaches.* We see that those whom he addresses are those whose faith had been tested by no ordinary trial, and yet he does not cease from exhorting them to greater effort. Let no one deceive himself by a false self-flattery as if he had reached the target or had no need of incentives from others. He says that they were *made a gazingstock both by reproaches and by afflictions* as though they had been displayed as a public spectacle, whence we conclude that the persecutions which they underwent were especially notable. The last clause is to be carefully noted where he says that they were the companions of believers in their persecution. For since the cause for which all believers strive and which is common to them is the cause of Christ, whatever one of them suffers ought to be taken by all the others personally to themselves and this is to be done universally if we do not wish to disjoin ourselves from Christ Himself.

34. *And took joyfully.* There is no doubt that as they were men subject to human feelings the loss of their goods brought them sorrow, but their sadness was such as not to deprive them of this joy of which the apostle speaks. Poverty is included among the disadvantages of life and the deprivation of their goods considered by itself brought them sorrow, but when they looked higher they found cause for joy which softened whatever sorrow they had. It is right that our feelings should be thus led away from this world by the prospect of heavenly reward. I do not say anything but what all believers have experienced. Surely we joyfully accept what we are persuaded will lead to our salvation, and the sons of God have without any doubt this feeling about the struggle which they endure for the glory of Christ, so that the feelings of our flesh are never so strong in overwhelming them with sorrow that they do not emerge into spiritual joy when they raise their minds to heaven.

This is the meaning of what follows: *knowing* (he says) *that ye your-selves have a better profession and an abiding one.* They accepted with joy the deprivation of their goods not because they liked to see themselves plundered but because their minds were looking for the promised compensation and they easily forgot the sorrow brought by their present sense of trouble. Indeed wherever the feeling of heavenly good things is strong, there is no taste for the world with its allurements, so that no sense either of poverty or of shame can overwhelm our minds with sorrow. If then we wish to bear anything for Christ with patience and equanimity let us grow accustomed to frequent meditation on that happiness in comparison with which all the goods of this world are but rubbish. We must not pass by the words *knowing that ye yourselves have.* Unless a person is convinced that the inheritance which God promises His children belongs to him all his knowledge will freeze.

35. *Cast not away therefore.* He shows that what especially strengthens us to persevere is for us to hold on to our faith, for whenever we throw that away we deprive ourselves of the promised reward. It is clear from this that that reward is the basis of holy and godly living. In using the word reward he does not detract from the free promise of salvation. Believers know that their labour is not in vain in the Lord in such a way that they rely solely on the mercy of God. In this connexion it has often been said elsewhere that the idea of reward is not at variance with the free imputation of righteousness.

For ye have need of patience, that, having done the will of God, ye may receive the promise. For yet a very little while, He that cometh shall come, and shall not tarry. But my righteous one shall live by faith: and if he shrink back, my soul hath no pleasure in him. But we are not of them that shrink back unto perdition; but of them that have faith unto the saving of the soul. (36-39)

36. *For ye have need of patience.* He says that patience is necessary not only because we must endure to the end but because Satan has countless devices with which he harasses us. Unless we are furnished with a wonderful patience we shall be broken a thousand times before we are half way through our course. The inheritance of eternal life is already sure for us, but because this life is like a racecourse we must strive on towards the goal. In this course many obstacles and difficulties come in our way not only to delay us but also to divert us from our course unless we have great courage of spirit to stand against them. Satan in his subtlety hurls all kinds of annoyances at us to discourage us, and indeed no Christian will ever take two steps without being tired unless he is upheld by his patience. This then is the only way by which we can constantly advance, and we shall only thus obey God and ever

attain the promised inheritance which is called here the promise by metonymy.

37. *For yet a very little while.* In case it is difficult for us to be patient he says that the time will not be long. Indeed there is nothing more able to lift up our spirits whenever they become faint than the hope of a quick and speedy relief. Just as a general proclaims to his soldiers that the end of the war is not far off if only they hold on for a little, so the apostle declares that the Lord will soon come to deliver us from all evil if only our spirits do not give up by becoming weak. In order that this encouragement might have more credibility and authority he adduces the evidence of the prophet Habakkuk from chapter 2.4. Since he follows the Greek translation thereby departing somewhat from the words of the prophet, I shall first of all briefly explain what the prophet says, and then we shall compare it with what the apostle says here.

When the apostle had spoken about the terrible destruction of his people he was so terrified by his prophecy that there was nothing left for him but to leave the world and to retreat to his watch-tower. Our watch-tower is the Word of God by which we are raised to heaven. Standing as he is in this place he is bidden to write a new prophecy which will bring hope of salvation to the godly. Since men are by nature importunate and are so hasty in their wishes that they always think that God is delaying however much He hastens, he says that the promise will come without delay though with this addition, 'If it tarries wait for it.' He means by this that what God promises will never come so quickly that it does not seem to us to come late, as the old proverb says, 'Speed itself is delay to desire.' Then follow these words, 'Behold his soul is puffed up, it is not upright in him: but the just shall live by his faith.' In these words he is saying that whatever be the defences by which the ungodly are fortified or in which they trust they will not stand because firm life consists only in faith. Let the unbelievers fortify themselves how they please, they will find nothing in all the world that is not ready to fall so that they must always be afraid; but believers will never be frustrated in their faith because it rests in God. This is the meaning of the prophet.

The apostle applies to God what Habakkuk says of the promise since by fulfilling His promises God in some way reveals Himself. There is not much difference as far as the main point is concerned. The Lord comes, I maintain, whenever He puts out His hand to help us. The apostle, following the prophet, says that this will be soon because God does not postpone His help longer than is necessary. He does not deceive us as men often do by dragging out the time, but He knows His own good time which He will not allow to pass by without intervening at the critical moment. He says, *he that cometh shall come, and shall not tarry.* There are two clauses in this sentence: the first says that God will come to us because He has promised; the second that He will do so timeously and not later than He ought.

38. *But my righteous one.* He means that patience is born of faith, which is true. We shall not be equal to carrying on the struggle unless we are supported by faith. Likewise on the other hand John says (I John 5.4) that this is the victory which overcomes the world. It is by faith that we ascend on high; by faith that we surmount all the hazards of this present life, all its sorrows and troubles; by faith that we find a quiet place in the midst of storm and tempest. The apostle's purpose is to show that those who are reckoned just before God can only live by faith. The future tense of the word live shows the continuity of life. Readers should look for further comment in Rom. 1.17 and Gal. 3.11, where this passage is quoted.

And if he shrink back. This stands for the prophet's word עפלה ('*upplah*), that is where a man is puffed up or over confident his spirit is not upright in him. The Greek version, to which the apostle here refers, partly agrees with the mind of the prophet and is partly foreign to it. This shrinking back differs little or nothing from the pride with which the ungodly are filled, since the fact that they presumptuously rise up against God happens because they are drunk with false confidence so that they renounce His authority and promise themselves peace and quiet from all evil. They are said to shrink back when they set up false defences of this kind by which they drive away all fear and respect for God. This word therefore expresses the power of faith no less than the character of unbelief. Unbelief is proud because it does not give God His due honour by making man subject to Him. It is the result of indifference, pride and contempt that as long as things go well with the wicked they dare, as someone says, to insult the clouds. Since there is nothing more contrary to faith than shrinking back, it is the nature of faith to bring man back to obedience to God when he has been drawn away by his own nature.

The clause, 'He will not please my soul', or (as I have rendered it more fully), *my soul hath no pleasure in him,* is to be taken as though the apostle put down this sentence as his own feeling. It was not his purpose to quote exactly the words of the prophet but to call attention to the passage and to invite readers to examine it more closely.

39. *We are not of them that shrink back.* The apostle made free use of the Greek translation because it fits most aptly the above doctrine which he has been discussing just as now he applies it neatly. He has warned them already not to deprive themselves of the faith and grace of Christ by deserting the Church, and now he teaches them that they

have been called not to shrink back. Again he contrasts faith and shrinking back against one another just as he contrasts the preservation of the soul with its death. Notice that this sentence refers to us also, because we whom God hath once favoured with the light of His Gospel, ought to see this purpose in our calling that we should advance more and more in obedience to God and earnestly try to draw nearer to Him. This is the real preservation of our soul because by so doing we escape eternal death.

CHAPTER ELEVEN

Now faith is the assurance of things hoped for, the proving of things not seen. (v. 1)

1. *Now faith is.* Whoever made this the beginning of the eleventh chapter broke up the sequence wrongly. The purpose of the apostle is to support what he has said, that there is need for patience. He has quoted the testimony of Habakkuk who says that the just shall live by his faith. He now shows what remained that faith can no more be separated from patience than from itself. The sequence of his thoughts is this: we shall never arrive at the goal of salvation unless we are furnished with patience. The prophet declares that the just shall live by faith, but faith calls us to far off things which we have not yet attained; and therefore it necessarily includes patience in itself. The minor proposition in the syllogism is: *faith is the substance, etc.* It is clear from this that those who think that an exact definition of faith is being given here are greatly mistaken. The apostle is not discussing the nature of faith as a whole but he selects that part which fits his purpose, namely that it is always joined to patience.

Let us now consider the words. He calls it the substance of things hoped for. We know that what is hoped for is not what is in our hand but what is so far hidden from us or at least the enjoyment of which is put off to another time. The apostle is saying the same thing as Paul in Rom. 8.24, where after he has said that what is hoped for is not seen, he draws the conclusion that it is waited for in patience. Thus our apostle teaches us that we do not have faith in God from things present but from the expectation of things still to come. The appearance of this contradiction is not without its charm. He says that faith is the substance, that is, the prop or the foundation on which we place our feet; but of what? Of things absent which are so far from being under our feet that they far exceed the power of our understanding to capture.

The same idea runs through the second clause where he calls faith the evidence, that is, the demonstration of things not seen. A demonstration makes things appear, and commonly refers only to what is subject to our senses. These two things apparently contradict each other, but yet they agree perfectly when we are concerned with faith. The Spirit of God shows us hidden things, the knowledge of which cannot reach our senses. Eternal life is promised to us, but it is promised to the dead; we are told of the resurrection of the blessed, but meantime we are involved in corruption; we are declared to be just, and sin dwells within us; we hear that we are blessed, but meantime we are overwhelmed by untold miseries; we are promised an abundance of all good things, but we are often hungry and thirsty; God proclaims that He will come to us immediately, but seems to be deaf to our cries. What would happen to us if we did not rely on our hope, and if our minds did not emerge above the world out of the midst of darkness through the shining Word of God and by His Spirit? Faith is therefore rightly called the substance of things which are still the objects of hope and the evidence of things not seen. Augustine sometimes interchanges evidence and conviction, and I do not disagree, for that faithfully expresses the mind of the apostle. I prefer the noun 'demonstration' or 'evidence', because it is less forced.

For therein the elders had witness borne to them. By faith we under-stand that the worlds have been framed by the word of God, so that what is seen hath not been made out of things which do appear. By faith Abel offered unto God a more excellent sacrifice than Cain, through which he had witness borne to him that he was righteous, God bearing witness in respect of his gifts: and through it he being dead yet speaketh. (2-4)

2. *For therein.* The argument will continue to the very end of the chapter that the fathers obtained salvation and were acceptable to God only by faith. There was some reason for the Jews to show much deference to the fathers, but there was also among them a somewhat irrational admiration which proved a great hindrance to their allowing themselves to be completely ruled by Christ. This happened either out of ambition or superstition or both. When they heard that they were the blessed and holy seed of Abraham they were so puffed up by this description that they turned their eyes to men rather than to God. From this there arose a distorted spirit of emulation because they did not think of what was most worth imitating in the fathers. So it came about that they held to the old ceremonies as if the whole of religion and perfect holiness consisted in them. The apostle refutes this error and shows what the main feature of the fathers was, so that their descendants can understand how they will be truly like them. We must remember that this is the foundation or, if you like, the hinge on which the apostle's argument turns, that the fathers who were approved by God from the beginning of the world were joined to Him only by faith, so that the Jews may know that it is only by faith that they are bound together with the father into a holy unity, and that as soon as they reject faith they resile from the Church and are no longer true sons of Abraham but false and unworthy.

3. *By faith we understand.* This is the best possible proof of the last sentence. We are no different from brutish beasts if we do not under-

stand that the world was made by God. Why are men endowed with reason and intellect except for the purpose of recognizing their Creator? It is by faith alone that we understand that the world was created by God, and it is therefore no wonder that among the fathers faith took pre-eminence over all other virtues.

It may here be asked why the apostle maintains that what un-believers themselves know is understood by faith. The appearance of heaven and earth compels even ungodly men to recognize some Creator. It is on this ground that Paul (Rom. 1.21) accuses them all of ingratitude because knowing God they did not give Him the honour due to Him. Certainly religion would not always have flourished among all peoples if the minds of men had not been persuaded that God is the Creator of the world. It would seem therefore that this knowledge which the apostle includes in faith exists outside of faith.

I reply that there has always been a certain supposition that the world was created by God among the heathen, but a vague one. Whenever they imagined some sort of God they quickly became vague in their thinking so that they groped uncertainly at a shadow of deity in the darkness rather than grasping the true God. Furthermore since it was only a fleeting conjecture that flitted through their minds, it was far from any understanding. Add to that the fact that they gave the power of government in the world to chance, and made no mention of the providence of God which is the sole governor. The minds of men are blind to this light of nature which shines in all created things until they are enlightened by the Spirit of God and begin to understand by faith what they can never grasp otherwise. The apostle is therefore quite right in ascribing such understanding to faith, because those who believe do not just think that God is the Architect of the world, but they have a firm conviction deep in their hearts and they behold the true God. Moreover they understand the power of His Word not only as shown at the moment of creating the world but as continually displayed in its preservation; and they have this sense not only of power but of goodness and wisdom and justice which encourages them to the worship, love and reverence of God.

Out of things which do not appear. I believe that all commentators have been misled in this clause. Their mistake has arisen from the fact that they separate the preposition ἐκ from the participle φαινομένων, so that they translate, 'so that visible things are made from those which are not seen'. Scarcely any sense can be taken from these words or at least only very meagre, and moreover the context does not allow this meaning, for then the words would have been ἐκ μὴ φαινομένων. The apostle's sequence is different. If we translate word for word, this clause can only be rendered thus, 'So that they became the visibles of things not seen, that is the spectacles', so that the preposition ἐκ is joined with the participle. These words contain the very important teaching that in this world we have a clear image of God, and in this passage our apostle is saying the same thing as Paul in Rom. 1.20 where he says that the invisible things of God are made known to us by the creation of the world, since they are seen in His works. In the whole architecture of His world God has given us clear evidence of His eternal wisdom, goodness and power and though He is invisible in Himself He shows Himself to us in some measure in His work. The world is therefore rightly called the mirror of divinity not because there is enough clarity for men to know God by looking at the world but because He makes Himself clear to unbelievers in such a way that they are without excuse for their ignorance. On the other hand believers to whom He has given eyes to see discern the sparks of His glory as it were shining out in every individual creature. The world was founded for this purpose, that it should be the sphere of divine glory.

4. *By faith Abel.* The apostle is now going to show that however excellent were the works of the saints they derived their value, their worth and whatever excellence they had from faith. From this it follows, as he has already said, that the fathers pleased God by faith alone. He is here speaking of faith in a double sense, first because of its obedience, because it attempts or undertakes nothing except by the express Word of God; and then because it relies on the promises of God and thus procures value and worthiness for its works by the sheer grace of God. Whenever the word 'faith' is found in this chapter we must remember that the apostle's purpose is that the Jews should have no other rule of faith than the Word of God and that they should depend on His promises alone.

He says first of all that the sacrifice of Abel was more acceptable than that of his brother only because it was sanctified by faith; certainly the fat of brute beasts did not smell so pleasantly that it was able to please God by its odour. Scripture shows plainly why God was pleased with his sacrifice. The words of Moses are, 'God had respect to Abel and to his gifts' from which we may readily conclude that his sacrifice pleased God because he himself was pleasing to God. Where did his pleasing come from other than that he had a heart purified by faith?

God bearing witness. He confirms what I have just said that no works pleasing to God proceed from us until we ourselves are received into favour or (to speak more briefly) no works are reckoned just before God except those of a just man. His reasoning is as follows: God bore witness to the gifts of Abel, and therefore he obtains the praise of being just before God. This teaching was profitable and should be carefully noted because we are not easily persuaded of it. Whenever something glorious appears in any work we are immediately captured with admiration and we do not think that it can be disapproved of by God with justice. But God who looks only at the inner purity of the heart takes no regard of the outward façade of works. We must learn therefore that no right work can proceed from us until we are justified before God.

He being dead. It is also a matter of faith that God bore witness of his concern for Abel no less after his death than in his life. In saying that although he is dead he still speaks he means what Moses says that God was moved by his unworthy death to avenge him. The fact that either Abel or his blood is said to speak is figurative. It was an especial evidence of God's love towards him that God was concerned for him in death; and from this it is clear that he was thought of as one of the saints of God whose death is precious to Him.

> *By faith Enoch was translated that he should not see death; and he was not found because God translated him: for before his translation he hath had witness borne to him that he had been well-pleasing unto God: and without faith it is impossible to be well-pleasing unto him: for he that cometh to God must believe that he is, and that he is a rewarder of them that seek after him.* (5-6)

5. *By faith Enoch.* He chooses a few of the oldest to make the transition from Abraham to his posterity. He says that it happened as a benefit of his faith that Enoch was translated. We must notice especially the reason why God took him from the earth in this unusual way. It was an outstanding sign by which all might see how dear he was to God. Unbelief and all kinds of corruption were then rife everywhere. If he had died in the ordinary way of men it would never have occurred to anyone that he had been kept by the providence of God from being infected by the contagion, but his being snatched away without death showed clearly the hand of God from heaven removing him as if from a fire. This therefore was no ordinary honour with which God favoured him. The apostle maintains that it was the result of faith. Moses says that he was a just man and that he walked with God, but since justice begins with faith the fact that he pleased God is properly attributed to his faith.

It is better to pass over the subtle questions with which curious men harass themselves. They ask what became of these two men, Enoch and Elijah. In case they seem to ask empty questions they prophesy that they are kept to the final day of the Church so as to be displayed to the world suddenly then. The Apocalypse of John is cited in support of this. Let us leave this airy philosophy to those with small intellects which cannot find a firm foundation. It should be enough for us that their rapture was a kind of extraordinary death, and we should not doubt that they put off mortal and corruptible flesh to be renewed with the other members of Christ in blessed immortality.

6. *And without faith.* This premiss is common to all the examples which the apostle cites in this chapter, but since there is some obscurity about it it is worth while examining the meaning more closely.

There is no better interpreter than the speaker himself, and therefore the proof which he subjoins immediately afterwards can provide for us an explanation. The reason, I say, why no one can please God without faith is because no one ever approaches God if he does not believe that God is and is convinced that He is the Rewarder of all who seek Him. If the way to God is only open to faith it follows that all those who are outside of faith are displeasing to God. From this the apostle shows first how faith procures favour for us because it is our teacher in worshipping the true God; and secondly because it makes us more sure of His goodness so that we do not seem to seek Him in vain. These two clauses must not be passed over lightly, namely that we should believe that God is and secondly that we be persuaded that we do not seek Him in vain.

The fact that the apostle demands that we should believe that God is does not seem to be a great demand, but if you consider it more closely you will find that it contains a rich and profound and sublime doctrine. Although it is agreed by almost all without dispute that God is, nevertheless unless the Lord holds us to a firm knowledge of Himself all kinds of doubts creep in to crowd out every sense of divinity. The human intellect is particularly prone to this kind of vanity so that it is easy to forget God. The apostle does not just mean that men should be persuaded that there is some God, but he is speaking of the true God. It will not be enough, I say, if you think of some kind of God unless you discern who is the true God. What advantage will it be to invent an idol and to ascribe to it the glory of God?

We now see what the apostle means in this clause. He says that we have no access to God unless we are convinced in the depth of our souls that God is so as not to be carried around hither and thither by all kinds of opinions. It is clear from this that men weary themselves purposelessly in worshipping God if they do not follow the right way and that all religions which do not contain a sure knowledge of God are not only vain but also vicious, since all those who do not differentiate Him from idols are barred from approaching God. There is no religion where truth does not reign. If a true knowledge of God dwells in our hearts it will inevitably follow that we are brought to reverence and fear. God is not truly known apart from His majesty. From this comes the desire to worship Him and from this it comes about that the whole life is directed towards Him as towards its goal.

The second clause is that we should be convinced that God is not sought in vain, a conviction which includes the hope of salvation and of eternal life. No one will be disposed in spirit to seek Him in the hope of salvation from Him except by a conscious sense of the divine goodness. Where no salvation is apparent we shall either flee from or disregard God. We must remember that this must be believed and not merely thought, because even unbelievers may sometimes have such a notion, but they do not approach God because they do not rely on a sure and firm faith. This is the second part of faith, by which we obtain favour before God, that we are certain that our salvation rests in Him.

There are many who falsely pervert this clause and induce from it the merits of work and trust in what they deserve. They reason this way: if we please God by faith because we believe Him to be the Rewarder it follows that faith has regard to the merit of work. This error cannot be better refuted than by considering the way to seek Him, for if anyone wanders from that way he cannot be thought to seek God. Scripture lays down that the right way to seek God is that a man prostrate, smitten with the accusation of eternal death, and despairing of himself, should fly to Christ as the only refuge for salvation. We shall certainly never find that any merit of work is to be brought to God in order to put us in favour with Him. Those who honestly hold to this principle in seeking God will find no difficulty because reward refers not to the worth or the price of works but to faith.

This disposes of those cold glosses of the sophists who say, that we please God through faith because in deserving we have the intention of pleasing. The intention of the apostle is to carry us much higher so that every man's conscience is firmly convinced that seeking God is no empty pursuit. This certainty far surmounts anything that we can grasp for ourselves especially when anyone applies it personally. It is not to be thought of in abstraction that God is the Rewarder of those who seek Him, but everyone ought to apply to himself in person the advantage and benefit of this doctrine so that we may know that we are the concern of God, that He is so concerned for our salvation that He will never desert us, that our prayers are heard by Him and that He will be our unfailing Deliverer. Since none of these things come to us without Christ it is necessary that our faith should always have regard to Him and rely on Him alone.

From these two clauses we may now conclude how and why it is impossible for a man without faith to please God. Since by nature we

are under His curse He rightly regards us with wrath, and the remedy
is not in our power. It is therefore necessary for God to anticipate us
with His grace, a thing which happens when we know that God is, so
that no corrupt superstition may lead us elsewhere; and further when
we are assured of salvation from Him.

If anyone wishes a fuller development of this argument he should
take as his starting-point the fact that we attempt and try everything
in vain unless we look to God. The sole purpose of a true life is to
serve His glory, and that will never happen unless knowledge of Him
comes first. But this is only half of faith and it is of little profit unless
trust is added to it. Faith will only be complete in all its parts to secure
for us favour before God when we confidently trust that we do not
seek Him in vain and thus assure ourselves of salvation from Him. No
one will have confidence that God will be the Rewarder of his merits
unless he is blinded by pride and bewitched by depraved self-love.
This trust that we speak of lies therefore not in works, nor in man's own
worthiness, but in the favour of God alone. Since the grace of God is
found only in Christ He is the only one to whom faith should have
regard.

*By faith Noah, being warned of God concerning things not seen as yet,
moved with godly fear, prepared an ark to the saving of his house;
through which he condemned the world, and became heir of the righteousness which is according to faith.* (7)

7. *By faith Noah.* It was a wonderful example of virtue that when
the whole world was indulging its pleasures without care or restraint
and promising itself impunity, Noah alone had regard to the vengeance
of God which was already long overdue; that he tired himself out for
a hundred and twenty years in building an ark; that he stood unbending
among so many mockeries of unbelievers; and that in the midst of the
ruin of the whole world he had no doubt that he would be saved and
committed his life to the grave, that is, to the ark. I shall touch on this
matter briefly, for everyone can better consider the circumstances for
himself.

The apostle gives the credit for this outstanding virtue to faith. So
far he has spoken of the faith of the fathers who lived in the first days
of the world, but it was a kind of regeneration when Noah and his
family emerged from the flood. It is evident from this that in all the
ages men were never approved by God and nothing was done that was
worthy of praise except by faith.

Let us now see what we think must be considered in the case of
Noah—that he was warned of things to come but not yet visible and
was afraid; then that he built the ark; thirdly that by building it he

condemned the world; fourthly that he was the heir of righteousness which is by faith.

What I have put first in the list is the greatest expression of the power of faith, for the apostle is always recalling us to the principle that faith is the evidence of things not seen. It is surely the task of faith to see in the Word of God what is hidden and removed from our senses. When he was told that there would be a flood after a hundred and twenty years the length of time could have removed his fear. That is the first point. Secondly the thing in itself was incredible; thirdly he saw unbelievers indulging themselves without a care; and finally the terrifying announcement of the flood could have seemed merely a threat. Yet Noah paid such respect to the Word of God that he turned his eyes from the contemporary view of things and went in fear of the destruction which God threatened as though it were present to him. Therefore the faith which he had in the Word of God prepared him for obedience to God, proof of which he afterwards gave by building the ark.

The question is raised here as to why the apostle makes faith the cause of fear since it has reference to the promises of favour rather than to threats. In this sense Paul (Rom. 10.8) calls the Gospel by which God's justice is offered to us for our salvation the Word of faith. It seems therefore to be inappropriately said that Noah was led by faith to fear. I reply that faith properly comes from promises, that it is founded on them, and rests on them. Hence we say that Christ is the true goal of faith, that in Him our heavenly Father is reconciled to us, and in Him all the promises of salvation are sealed and ratified. Yet there is nothing to hinder faith having regard to God and reverently accepting whatever He says, or, if you prefer it more shortly, it is the office of faith to hear God when He speaks and to accept without hesitation whatever comes from His sacred mouth. Faith is therefore subject to His commands and warnings no less than to His free promises. Since no one is ever moved sufficiently to obey the commands of God, nor impelled by warnings to avert His wrath unless he has already grasped the promises of grace and acknowledges Him as the loving Father and the Author of salvation, so the Gospel is called, by synecdoche from its principal part, the Word of faith and a mutual relationship is established between the one and the other. Although faith has reference directly to the promises of God it nonetheless has regard to His warnings so far as it is necessary for us to be brought up in the fear and obedience of God.

Prepared an ark. There is noted here an obedience which flows from faith like water from a fountain. The work of building the ark was long and laborious, was hindered by the daily scoffings of unbelievers

and could have been broken off a thousand times, for there is no doubt
that they insulted the holy man on every side. The fact that he bore
their shameless insults with an unbroken spirit shows that he had no
ordinary resolution to obey. How was it that he obeyed God so
constantly except that he had already found rest in the promise which
gave him hope of salvation and that he stood firm in this trust to the
very end? He could not have had the courage by himself to undergo
so many troubles, nor could he have been equal to overcoming so
many obstacles, nor could he have held so firmly to his purpose except
by a prevenient faith. Faith is therefore the only teacher of obedience,
from which we may draw this conclusion on the other hand that it is
lack of faith which hinders us from obeying God. Today lack of faith
shows itself in a terrible way in this part of the world because so few
people obey God.

Through which he condemned the world. It would be hard to say of the
salvation of Noah that it condemned the world and the context
scarcely allows us to understand this of faith. We must therefore
understand this to refer to the ark. He says that the world was condemned by the ark in a double sense. The fact that he was taken up
so long in building it removes all excuse from the wicked and the
event which followed proved that the destruction of the world was
just. Why was the ark the custodian of the safety of a single family
except in virtue of the fact that the wrath of God spared a righteous
man from perishing with the ungodly? If he had not survived, the
condemnation of the world would not have been so clear. The fact
that Noah obeyed the command of God condemns by his example the
obstinacy of the world, and the fact that he was miraculously saved
from the midst of death is proof that the whole world, which God
would doubtless have preserved had it not been unworthy of salvation,
justly perished.

Of the righteousness which is according to faith. This is the last thing
which the apostle says we must notice in the person of Noah. Moses
says that he was a just man. History does not say that faith was the
cause and root of this justice but the apostle says that this is shown by
the facts. This is not only true because no one ever really gives himself
in obedience to God unless he relies on the promises of His paternal
loving-kindness and has faith that his life will be accepted by Him, but
also because the life of no man however holy when it is measured by
the standard of God can please Him without pardon. Justice must
therefore of necessity rest on faith.

*By faith Abraham, when he was called, obeyed to go out unto a place
which he was to receive for an inheritance; and he went out, not knowing*

whither he went. By faith he became a sojourner in the land of promise, as in a land not his own, dwelling in tents, with Isaac and Jacob, the heirs with him of the same promise: for he looked for the city which hath the foundations, whose builder and maker is God. By faith even Sarah herself received power to conceive seed when she was past age, since she counted him faithful who had promised: wherefore also there sprang of one, and him as good as dead, so many as the stars of heaven in multitude, and as the sand, which is by the sea shore, innumerable. (8-12)

8. *By faith Abraham.* He now comes to Abraham himself who is the principal father of the Church of God on earth and in whose name the Jews gloried as though they were removed from the common rank and file of men by this sole distinction of being the holy seed of Abraham. He shows what they ought to consider the main reason for being thought the sons of Abraham, and thus he calls them back to faith because Abraham himself had no excellence which did not come from faith. He says to begin with that faith was the reason why he immediately obeyed God when he was ordered to emigrate from his fatherland, and then that it was due to the same faith that he held steadily to his calling to the very end. The faith of Abraham was clearly confirmed by this double evidence of his readiness to obey and his perseverance in action.

When he was called. The old commentator and Erasmus take this to refer to his name, but this is too weak and ineffective. I rather take it as referring to the oracle by which he was called to leave his country. He submitted himself to this voluntary exile of his own accord because he did nothing that was not by the command of God. This is surely one of the principles of faith that we do not move a step unless the Word of God shows us the way and shines before us like a lantern, as David says (Ps. 119.105). We must learn that this is a thing to be observed through the whole of life, to attempt nothing unless God calls.

To go out into a place. To the command there was added the promise that God would give him a land to inherit. He accepted this promise at once and hastened on as one who was sent to take possession. It is a rare trial of faith to leave what is in one's hand to go seeking for what is far off and unknown to us. When God orders him to go out He does not show him the place where He wants him to go but leaves him in suspesne and perplexity of spirit. Go (he says—Gen. 12.1) to the place which I shall show thee. Why does He put off telling him the place except to provide more and more testing for his faith? The love of his native land could not only retard the speed of Abraham but could keep his spirit in bonds so that he did not leave home. This was

no ordinary faith which broke through all the hindrances and carried
him along where the Lord called him.

9. *By faith he became a sojourner.* The second point is this, that having
entered the land he is only just received as a stranger and an incomer.
Where is that inheritance for which he hoped? It must surely have
occurred to him that he had been deceived by God, and there is an
even greater appearance of frustration, which the apostle omits, in that
a little later on he was driven by famine from the country and was
compelled to fly a second time to the land of Gerar. The apostle considered it sufficient to commend his perseverance by the single fact of
saying that he was a sojourner in the promised land; for the condition
of a sojourner was contrary to the promise. It was the outstanding
virtue of Abraham that he withstood this temptation bravely, a fact
which comes from faith alone.

With Isaac and Jacob. He does not mean that they lived in the same
tents or at the same time, but he joins Abraham's son and grandson to
him as companions because they were sojourners in the promised
inheritance with him, and they did not resile although God delayed
them for a long time. The longer the delay the greater the temptation
grew if they had not repelled all the assaults of doubt by setting up the
shield of faith.

10. *For he looked.* He gives it as the reason for ascribing their patience
to faith that they looked to heaven; that was to see things invisible.
Although it was a great thing for them to cherish in their hearts the
faith that God had given them that they would possess the land, until
the reality materialized after some ages, nevertheless since they did not
even rest there but looked further to heaven itself they showed more
clearly thereby their faith. He calls heaven *the city which hath foundations*
because it is fixed for all eternity and there is nothing in the world
except what is transient and falling. It may appear absurd that he
makes God the Creator of heaven as though He had not also created
the earth. I reply that as the hands of men are put to the materials of
earthly building so the workmanship of God is not unfittingly compared with them. Whatever is built by men reflects its creators in its
impermanence, just as the eternity of heavenly life fits the nature of
God as its Creator. Further the apostle points out that all weariness is
relieved by this expectation, so that we should never grow tired in
following God.

11. *By faith even Sarah herself.* So that women may know that this
truth applies to them no less than to men, he adduces the example of
Sarah whom he names before all others because she is the mother of
all the faithful. It is strange that her faith is commended when she was
clearly exposed as an unbeliever because she laughed at the word of

the angel as if it were a fable. It was not the laugh of admiration, otherwise she would not have been so sharply rebuked by the angel. It must be confessed that her faith was mixed with distrust but, since she corrected her distrust when warned, her faith was recognized and praised by God. What she at first rejected as incredible, she obediently accepted as soon as she heard that it came from the mouth of God. From this we deduce a useful piece of teaching that even when our faith wavers or halts a bit, it does not cease to be approved by God, provided we do not give way to our distrust. The point is that the miracle which God performed when Isaac was born was the fruit of the faith of Abraham and his wife by which they grasped the power of God.

Since she counted him faithful. These reasons which express the power and nature of faith are to be carefully noted. If anyone heard only that Sarah had given birth by faith he would not comprehend what is meant here, but this exposition which the apostle has added removes every difficulty. He says that the faith of Sarah lay in this that she judged God to be true, and to be so in His promises. There are two clauses in this sentence. We learn from this first that there is no faith without the Word of God because we will not be persuaded of His truth until He has spoken. This single fact is quite sufficient to refute the comment of the sophists about implicit faith, for we must always hold to the interconnexion between the Word of God and our faith. Because faith is chiefly founded on the loving-kindness of God (as has already been said), not every Word is sufficient even though it comes from His mouth, but a promise is necessary as evidence of His favour. It is therefore said that Sarah judged God to be true because He had promises. This then, I say, is true faith, namely that which both hears God speaking and relies on His promise.

12. *There sprang of one.* He now points out to the Jews that it is by faith that they are the offspring of Abraham. Abraham was almost half dead, and Sarah his wife who had been barren in the flower of her life was now sterile with old age. Oil would therefore sooner flow from a stone than any nation come forth from them, and yet a countless multitude was born. If the Jews are now proud of their origin, they must look to its cause. Whatever they are is to be attributed to the faith of Abraham and Sarah. It follows from this that they cannot hold or defend the position which they have attained except on the basis of faith.

These all died in faith, not having received the promises, but having seen them and greeted them from afar, and having confessed that they were strangers and pilgrims on the earth. For they that say such things

make it manifest that they are seeking after a country of their own. And
if indeed they had been mindful of that country from which they went
out, they would have had opportunity to return. But now they desire a
better country, that is, a heavenly: wherefore God is not ashamed of
them, to be called their God: for he hath prepared for them a city. (13-16)

13. *These all died in faith.* He magnifies the faith of the patriarchs by
comparison, because although they had only tasted the promises of
God they were satisfied with their sweetness and spurned everything
in the world; nor did they ever forget the taste of them, although it was
slight, either in life or in death. The phrase, *in faith*, is explained in two
ways. Some simply understand it as meaning that they died in faith
because in this life they never obtained the promised good things, just
as today also our salvation is hidden from us in hope. On the other
hand I rather agree with those who think that a difference is here noted
between us and the fathers, and I expound it thus: Though God gave
to the fathers only a foretaste of His favour which is poured out
generously upon us, and though He showed them only a vague image
of Christ at a distance who is now set before our very eyes to see, yet
they were satisfied and never fell from their faith. How much more
cause is given to us today to persevere? If we fail we are doubly
without excuse. This is the more emphasized by the circumstance that
the fathers saw from afar the spiritual kingdom of Christ the view of
which is so near us today, and that they hailed from afar the promises
which are so familiar to us. If they nonetheless were stedfast to death,
how great will be our idleness if we grow tired of believing when the
Lord supports us with so many helps? If anyone objects that they
could not have believed without accepting the promises on which
faith is necessarily founded, I reply that this is to be taken comparatively. They were far removed from the state to which God has raised
us. Though the same salvation was promised to them they did not
have the clarity of the promises which we enjoy under the reign of
Christ, but were content to regard them from afar.

And having confessed that they were strangers. It was Jacob who confessed this when he answered Pharaoh that the time of his pilgrimage
was short compared with the time of the pilgrimage of his fathers, and
full of many hardships (Gen. 47.9). If Jacob saw that he was a pilgrim
in the land which had been promised to him for a perpetual inheritance,
it is clear that his mind was not fixed on this world but was raised above
the heavens. The apostle infers that in so speaking the fathers have
plainly shown that they had a better country in heaven, for if they were
pilgrims here their fatherland and their permanent home is elsewhere.
If they in spirit took flight through the clouds of darkness to a heavenly

country, what must we do today when Christ stretches forth His hand to us clearly from heaven to draw us to Himself? If the land of Canaan did not hold them back how much more ought we to be unhindered when no firm resting-place in the world is shown to us?

15. *If indeed they had been mindful of that country.* He anticipates the objection that could have been raised that they were strangers because they had left their native land. The apostle replies that when they called themselves strangers they did not think of Mesopotamia because if they had any desire they were at liberty to return there. Yet they voluntarily banished themselves from it and indeed disowned it as if it had nothing to do with them. They looked for another country which was beyond this world.

16. *Wherefore God is not ashamed.* He refers to the sentence (Exod. 3.6), 'I am the God of Abraham, the God of Isaac, and the God of Jacob.' It is a signal honour when God makes Himself known by the names of men and wishes to be distinguished by this mark from idols. The apostle says that this privilege also relies on faith because when the holy fathers reached out for their heavenly country God in His turn included them among the ranks of His citizens. From this we are to conclude that there will be no place for us among the sons of God unless we renounce the world and that there will be no inheritance for us in heaven unless we are pilgrims on earth. From the words, 'I am the God of Abraham, Isaac and Jacob,' the apostle rightly concludes that they were the heirs of heaven since God who speaks is God not of the dead but of the living.

By faith Abraham, being tried, offered up Isaac; yea, he that had gladly received the promises was offering up his only-begotten son; even he to whom it was said, In Isaac shall thy seed be called: accounting that God is able to raise up, even from the dead; from whence he did also in a parable receive him back. By faith Isaac blessed Jacob and Esau, even concerning things to come. By faith Jacob, when he was a dying, blessed each of the sons of Joseph; and worshipped, leaning upon the top of his staff. By faith Joseph, when his end was nigh, made mention of the departure of the children of Israel; and gave commandment concerning his bones. (17-22)

17. *By faith Abraham.* He continues with the rest of the story of Abraham and refers to the sacrifice of his son. This is such an outstanding example of virtue that scarcely anything like it can be found. For the sake of amplification he adds, *being tried.* Abraham had already shown by many trials what sort of a person he was, but just as this trial far exceeds all the others the apostle wishes it to be regarded as preeminent. It has the force of saying that the height of Abraham's virtue

was the sacrifice of his son because God is then said to have subjected
him to the greatest trial. Moreover this act originated in faith and
therefore Abraham had nothing more excellent than his faith which
produced such an outstanding result.

The word temptation simply means proving. When James (1.13)
says that we are not tempted by God, he uses it in another sense,
namely that we are not incited to evil. He says that this happens by
the individual's lust, but at the same time he does not deny that God
makes trial of our uprightness and obedience. God does not test us as
though He were otherwise ignorant of what lies in our heart. I maintain that God needs no trial to begin to know us but when He brings
us into the light so that we may show openly by our works what was
previously hidden He is said to try or to test us. That which is made
manifest openly is said to be made known to God. It is the usual and
constant scriptural way of speaking for God to transfer to Himself what
is peculiar to men. The value of the sacrifice of Isaac rests in the effect
on the spirit because it was not due to Abraham that he did not carry
out what he was commanded. His willingness had the effect of
obediencē as if he had in fact sacrificed his son.

Offering up his only-begotten son. His purpose is to remark in these
circumstances the extent and the severity of Abraham's trial although
there are other things to be seen in the history of Moses which have the
same purpose. Abraham is commanded to take his son, his only-
begotten and beloved son Isaac, to lead him to a place which was to be
shown to him later, and there to sacrifice him by his own hand. God
has taken pains to pile up such tender descriptions in order to pierce
the depth of the heart of the holy man with as many wounds as
possible, and then to add further to the torture He commands him to
go a three days' journey. How piercing must we think his torture was
when he had constantly to look at his son whom he was taking to a
cruel death? When they came to the place Isaac pierced his breast with
yet a new wound by asking where was the sacrifice? However bitter
might have been the death of his son, and a bloody death would have
brought still greater grief, to be ordered to kill him with his own hand
is more terrible than any father's spirit can bear. He must have been
stunned a thousand times had not faith raised his heart beyond this
world. It is therefore not without reason that the apostle remarks that
Abraham was tried.

It may be asked why Isaac is called his only-begotten when Ishmael,
who still survived, was born before him. The answer is that when he
was driven out of the family by God's command he was considered as
dead so that there was no place for him at least among the sons of
Abraham.

He that had gladly received the promises. However deeply the things that we have already related wounded the spirit of Abraham, they were all as pin-pricks compared with this temptation when after he had received the promises he was ordered to kill his son Isaac. All the promises had their foundation in this, 'In Isaac shall thy seed be called' (Gen. 21.12), since when this was taken away no hope of blessing or favour remained. There was nothing earthly at issue here, but the eternal salvation of Abraham and indeed of the whole world. To what straits must we imagine the holy man to have been brought, when it occurred to him that the hope of eternal life would be extinguished in the person of his son, and yet by faith he emerged above these thoughts and did what he was commanded? If it was a wonderful virtue to strive through so many steep obstacles then faith deserves the greatest praise that it alone made Abraham stand unconquered.

At this point some difficulty arises as to how Abraham's faith is praised when it departs from the promise. Just as obedience has its origin in faith, so faith arises from the promise. Therefore when Abraham was deprived of the promise, his faith must of necessity fall. The death of Isaac as has been said already was like the destruction of all the promises; and Isaac is not to be thought of as simply one of the common company of men, but as one who contained Christ in himself. The apostle explains this question which could otherwise have been difficult to resolve, by adding immediately that Abraham ascribed to God the honour of being able to raise his son from the dead. Therefore he did not reject the promise given to him, but extended its power and truth beyond the life of his son by refusing to limit the power of God to such narrow limits that it could either be confined or extinguished by the death of Isaac. In this way he retained the promise because he did not bind the power of God to the life of Isaac but was persuaded that it would be effective in his ashes when he was dead no less than when he was alive and breathing.

19. *From whence also.* This is as though he were saying, that this hope did not deceive Abraham because it was something like a resurrection when suddenly his son was released from the midst of death. The word parable which is used here is explained by different commentators. I take it to be simply a mark of likeness. Although Isaac did not in fact rise from the dead, yet it seemed to be a kind of resurrection when he was snatched back suddenly and miraculously by the unexpected grace of God. However I am not averse to the view of those who think that our flesh which is subject to death is signified by the ram which is substituted for Isaac. I admit that it is true, what some say, that an image of Christ is depicted in this sacrifice. But I am now discussing what the apostle meant and not what could be said

with truth. In my judgment the real meaning here is that Abraham received his son as one who had been restored to him from death to new life.

20. *By faith Isaac.* It was the work of faith to give blessing to the future because when the reality has not appeared but only the bare word, faith alone must of necessity hold sway. We must first of all note the force of the blessing about which he speaks, for the word *to bless* is often taken as meaning 'to ask for a boon'. The blessing of Isaac was something quite different. It was like a sending forth to take possession of the land which God had promised to him and his posterity, and yet he had no right in that land except that of burial. Those glorious titles seem therefore quite absurd, that 'the people will serve thee and tribes bow down to thee' (Gen. 27.29). What kingdom could he hand on when he himself was scarcely a free man? We see therefore that this blessing depended on faith because apart from the Word of God Isaac had nothing to bestow on his sons.

It may, however, be doubted whether there was any faith in the blessing of Esau since he was rejected and cast away by God. The answer is simply because faith shone forth most clearly when he differentiated between the twins born to him and in doing so gave priority to the younger. He followed the command of God and took away from his firstborn his ordinary and natural right. The condition of the whole nation depended on the fact that Jacob was chosen by God and that his choice was ratified by the blessing of his father.

21. *By faith Jacob.* It is the purpose of the apostle to attribute to faith everything worth remembering that happened to his people, but since it would take too long to set down everything, he chooses a few examples out of many, such as this one. The tribe of Ephraim was so superior to the others that in a sense they lay in its shade, and Scripture often includes all ten tribes under this name. Yet Ephraim was the younger of the two sons of Joseph and at the time that Jacob blessed him and his brother they were both children. What did Jacob see in the younger that he preferred him to the firstborn? Certainly when he did so his eyes were clouded and dim with old age, but it was not by chance that he placed his right hand on the head of Ephraim, because he arranged them crossways so as to move his right hand over to the left. Furthermore he assigned to him two portions as though he were already the lord of the land from which famine had driven him away. If faith is not the lord here, there is no sense in all this. Therefore if the Jews wish to be anything they must glory in faith.

And worshipped, leaning upon the top. This is one of the places where we can conjecture that originally the Hebrews made no use of pointing, because if they had had the same way of writing as today the Greek translators would not have made the mistake of rendering 'staff' instead of 'bed'. There is no doubt that when he said עַל־רֹאשׁ הַמִּטָּה Moses refers to the top of his bed, but the Greeks translated 'on the top of his staff', as if the word written were הַמַּטֶּה. The apostle does not hesitate to use what was commonly accepted for his purpose. He was writing to Jews, but to Jews, who because of their dispersal among different countries had changed their native language for Greek. We know that the apostles were not too particular in the matter of adjusting themselves to the ignorant who still had need of milk. There is no danger in this provided always that the readers are brought back to the pure, original sense of Scripture. In reality there is little difference because the fact that Jacob worshipped was the symbolic action of grace, and from this he was led by faith to submit himself to his son.

22. *By faith Joseph.* This is the last point that Moses relates of the doings of the patriarchs, and it is surely worth noticing. The fact that wealth, luxuries, and honours did not lead the holy man to forget the promise nor hold him back in Egypt, is a strong argument for faith. Where did he get such greatness of mind as to despise everything worth while in the world, and to think nothing of everything valuable, except that he had ascended into heaven? When he ordered his bones to be carried away he was not thinking of himself as if he would prefer to have his grave in the land of Canaan rather than in Egypt, but he wanted to sharpen the desire of his people so that they would look more earnestly for their redemption. He wanted also to strengthen their faith so that they could hope with certainty that they would at length be liberated.

By faith Moses, when he was born, was hid three months by his parents, because they saw he was a goodly child; and they were not afraid of the king's commandment. By faith Moses, when he was grown up, refused to be called the son of Pharaoh's daughter; choosing rather to be evil entreated with the people of God, than to enjoy the pleasures of sin for a season; accounting the reproach of Christ greater riches than the treasures of Egypt: for he looked unto the recompense of reward. By faith he forsook Egypt, not fearing the wrath of the king: for he endured as seeing him who is invisible. (23-27)

23. *By faith Moses.* There have been others, and some of them unbelievers, who have preserved their sons at some risk not out of fear of God but simply in their anxiety to continue their posterity. The apostle says that the parents of Moses were moved to save him for a different reason, namely that God had promised when they were oppressed by slavery that there would some day be an avenger. In this confidence they preferred their infant's safety to their own. It

seems contrary to the nature of faith that he says that they were induced to do this by the beauty of his form. We know that Jesse was rebuked when he brought his sons to Samuel in the order of their physical excellence, and certainly God does not hold us to external appearances. I reply that the parents of Moses were not induced by his beauty to be touched with pity and save him as men are commonly affected, but there was some sort of mark of excellence to come, engraved on the boy which gave promise of something out of the ordinary for him. There is no doubt that they were inspired by his appearance with hope of an approaching liberation and in that they were confident that the child was destined to do great things.

Further it should have had great weight with the Jews to hear that Moses who was the minister of their redemption had been snatched from death miraculously thanks to faith. Yet it must be remarked that the faith which is praised here was very weak, for after they had got over their fear of his death they should have brought up Moses instead of casting him away. It is therefore clear that their faith not only soon wavered but completely collapsed, and that they neglected at least part of their duty when they cast the baby on the bank of the river. On the other hand it encourages us the more when we hear that their faith although weak was so accepted by God as to secure the life of Moses on which depended the liberation of the Church.

24. *By faith Moses, when he was grown up.* The example of Moses ought to be remembered by the Jews above all others, because by his hand they were freed from slavery, the covenant of God with them was renewed and the foundation of the Church was laid with the promulgation of the Law. If faith is to be thought of as the chief feature of Moses it would be absurd if he led them away from it elsewhere. It follows from this that all those who are not guided by the Law to faith make little progress in it.

We must now see what are the things for which he commends the faith of Moses. First in order he places this virtue that when he was grown up he rejected his adoption by Pharaoh's daughter. He refers to his age because if he had done this as a boy it could have been put down to rashness or ignorance since understanding and reason are not strong in children and they rush rashly wherever they please; adolescents too are often carried hither and thither by unthinking enthusiasm. Therefore so that we may know that this was not done without due consideration and after a long period of thought, the apostle says that he was then grown up, a fact which history makes clear. Further he is said to have scorned his adoption because his visits to his brethren, his concern to help them, and his avenging of their wrongs, all showed that he would rather return to his own people than remain in the royal palace. This is just the same as if he had specifically rejected it. The apostle attributes this to faith, because it would have been much better for him to stay in Egypt had he not been persuaded that the tribe of Abraham had been blessed, of which blessing the promise of God was the sole witness, for nothing of the kind was visible to the sight. From this it is clear that he saw by faith what was far removed from sight.

26. *Accounting the reproach of Christ greater riches.* We must carefully notice this manner of speaking because it shows us that anything that we cannot obtain without offending God is to be avoided like deadly poison. All the enticements of the world which wean us away from our vocation to God he calls the *pleasures of sin.* They are not reckoned among those blessings of earthly life which we can enjoy with a pure conscience and by God's permission. We must always remember to distinguish what God allows us. There are some things lawful in themselves but whose use by us is forbidden because of the circumstances of time or place or other things. In enjoying all the blessings of this present life we must always have regard to the fact that they should be aids to our following of God and not hindrances. He calls the pleasures of sin *for a season,* because they quickly vanish away along with life.

Against these he contrasts the reproach of Christ, which all believers ought to accept willingly. Those whom God hath chosen He has foreordained to be conformed to the image of His Son, not because He tests them all in the same way with reproaches or some other kind of cross but because they ought all to be ready to submit to the fellowship of the Cross along with Christ. Therefore let everyone think within himself that as he is called to this fellowship so he is to throw off all hindrances. The fact must not be overlooked that among the reproaches of Christ he reckons all the ignominies which believers have endured from the beginning of the world. Just as they were members of the same body, so they are no different from us. All sorrows, being the rewards of sin, are the fruits of the curse which was laid on the first man, but whatever wrongs we suffer from the ungodly in the Name of Christ He takes upon Himself. For this reason Paul glories that he supplies what was lacking in the sufferings of Christ. If we think of this rightly it would not be so hard for us or so bitter to suffer for Christ.

In this clause he also explains more clearly what he means by the reproach of Christ when he says, *choosing rather to be evil entreated with the people of God.* Moses could only have professed that he was one of the people of God by joining himself as their companion in the sorrows of his people. Therefore since this is the end, let us not fall away from the body of the Church, and whatever we suffer let us know that it is consecrated in the name of our Head. On the opposite side, what nobody can possess without forsaking the Church he calls *the treasures of Egypt.*

He looked unto the recompense. He shows that this greatness of mind was due to faith by the description which he gives of how Moses fixed his eyes on the promise of God. He could not have hoped to be better off with the people of Israel rather than with the Egyptians unless he had trusted in the promise alone. If anyone infers that his faith did not rest solely on the mercy of God because he looked to a reward, I reply that the argument here is not about righteousness or the ground of salvation but that the apostle is including generally everything that applies to faith. Therefore in so far as righteousness before God is to be sought, faith looks not to the reward but to the free goodness of God, not to our works but to Christ alone. On the other hand outside the purpose of justification faith has regard to the reward that is promised because it extends generally to every Word of God. By faith, I maintain, we accept whatever God promises, and He promises reward for works; therefore faith lays hold on this. Yet all this has no place in the case of free justification because no reward for works can be hoped for unless the imputation of free righteousness comes first.

27. *By faith he forsook Egypt.* This could be referred as much to his first departure as to the second when he led the people out with him. He certainly left Egypt at the time when he fled from the house of Pharaoh. There is the additional fact that this departure is recorded by the apostle before the celebration of the passover. He seems therefore to be speaking of the flight of Moses, and there is no obstacle to this view in the addition that *he feared not the wrath of the king,* although Moses himself says that he was moved by fear. If we look at the beginning, he was not afraid when he professed himself as the avenger of his people. Everything considered, however, I prefer to refer this to the second exodus. It was then that he bravely disregarded the fierceness of the king and armed himself with such power of the Spirit of God that he persistently harassed that fierce beast. It was certainly a wonderful power of faith that he dragged along with him an unwarlike multitude, burdened with many encumbrances, in the hope that a way would be opened up by the hand of God through the countless difficulties. He saw the most powerful kings raging impotently, and he knew that there would be no end until he had tried his utmost. Because he knew that God was the Author of his journey, he commended its outcome to Him, and had no doubt that in due time He would hold back all the attacks of the Egyptians.

As seeing him who is invisible. He had seen God in the midst of the burning bush, and therefore this seems to come inappropriately and unfittingly to the present subject. I certainly admit that Moses was already strengthened by that vision before he began his outstanding task of liberating the people, but I do not think that it was such a sight of God as to deprive him of his fleshly sense and lead him beyond the dangers of this world. At that time God showed him only a kind of sign of His presence and he was far from seeing God as He is. The apostle means that Moses endured only because it was as if he was taken up into heaven and had God alone in sight, had no dealings with men, was not subject to the dangers of this life, and had no struggle with Pharaoh. It is certain that he was overwhelmed with so many difficulties that he must have sometimes thought that God was far away, or at least that the insolence of the king, fortified as it was with so many powers of resistance, would at length overcome him.

In short God showed Himself to Moses in such a way as to leave room for faith, and Moses beset on all sides by many terrors turned all his attention to God. He was certainly helped to do so by that vision of which we have spoken, but he saw more in God than that visible sign contained. He understood His power, a fact which took away all his fears and all hazards. In reliance on the promise he held it for certain that the people were lords already of the promised land, even though oppressed by the Egyptian tyranny. From this we conclude that it is the true nature of faith to have God always before the eyes; secondly that faith sees things in God higher and more hidden than our senses can perceive; and thirdly that the sight of God alone is sufficient corrective for our weakness so that we become stronger than rocks against all the attacks of Satan. Hence it follows that the weaker and the less courageous anyone is the less faith he has.

By faith he kept the passover, and the sprinkling of the blood, that the destroyer of the firstborn should not touch them. By faith they passed through the Red Sea as by dry land: which the Egyptians assaying to do were swallowed up. By faith the walls of Jericho fell down, after they had been compassed about for seven days. By faith Rahab the harlot perished not with them that were disobedient, having received the spies with peace. (28-31)

28. *By faith he kept the passover.* This ought to have great value in commending faith to the Jews because for them the passover was the chief sacrifice and one of the highest regard. He says that it was celebrated by faith not because the lamb was a type of Christ but because when he sprinkled blood on the doorposts there was no sign of its advantages. Where truth itself is not apparent, it must of necessity be looked for in faith. It could seem absurd that Moses set up a few drops of blood as a remedy for the vengeance of God, but he was

content with the Word of God alone and had no doubt that the people would be exempt from the plague which was coming upon the Egyptians. Hence the apostle justly praises his faith in this regard. Those who explain that the Passover was celebrated by faith because Moses had Christ in mind indeed say what is true, but the apostle here is simply referring to faith in so far as it rests in the Word of God alone, where the reality is not apparent. It is therefore out of place to indulge in a too sharp reasoning here. The fact that he mentions Moses alone as celebrating the Passover is because God instituted the Passover at his hand.

29. *By faith they passed through.* It is certain that many in that multitude were unbelievers, but God granted it to the faith of the few that the whole multitude should cross the sea dry-shod. In this same action there was a great difference between the Israelites and the Egyptians in that the former crossed over in safety, while the latter were drowned a little later. How did this difference come except in the fact that the Israelites had accepted the Word of God which the Egyptians lacked? He is arguing, therefore, from contraries in saying *the Egyptians were swallowed up.* That unhappy event was the punishment for their rashness, just as on the other hand the Israelites reached safety because they relied on the Word of God and did not refuse to make their way through the middle of the mass of waters.

30. *By faith the walls of Jericho fell down.* Just as he has described above how the yoke of slavery was broken by faith, so he now relates how by the same faith the people gained possession of their promised inheritance. The first obstacle to their entrance to the land was the city of Jericho, fortified and all but impregnable, which prevented any further advance and for which they had no means of attack. The Lord commanded all the men of war to go round the walls once every day cnd seven times on the seventh day. Such a perambulation was ahildish and full of nonsense, but nevertheless they obeyed the command of God and took it seriously so that success followed as they had been promised. It is certain that the walls did not fall because of the shouts of men or their noise or by the sound of the trumpet, but because the people hoped that God would do what He had promised. We can turn this to our own use because it is only by faith that we are set free from the tyranny of the devil and by the same faith that we overcome our enemies and all the strongholds of hell fall.

31. *By faith Rahab perished not.* Although at first sight this example seems less outstanding on account of the low character of the person, and almost not worthy of being included in this catalogue, it is nevertheless quoted by the apostle fittingly and relevantly. So far he has shown that the patriarch to whom the Jews gave the greatest honour

and respect did nothing praiseworthy except by faith and that all God's benefits towards us that are worth remembering are the fruits of the same faith. He now tells us that a foreign woman, who was not only of the humblest condition among her people but was also a harlot, was brought by faith into the body of the Church. It follows from this that those who have the highest excellence are of no value before God except by the estimation of faith; and that on the other hand those who earlier scarcely had a place among the unbelievers and the heathen are adopted into the fellowship of the angels.

James also bears testimony to the faith of Rahab (2.25) and it is easy to see from sacred history that this woman was endowed with true faith. She professed that she was fully persuaded of what God had promised to the Israelites, and as if those whom fear had kept from entering the land were already the conquerors she asked for pardon for herself and her people. In so doing she looked not to men but to God Himself. The evidence of this faith is that she received the spies with hospitality at the risk of her own life. Therefore it was thanks to faith that she escaped safely from the general ruin of her city. The name *harlot* is added to heighten the grace of God. There are some who translate זוֹנָה as 'hostess', as though she made her living from keeping an inn, but since this word all through Scripture means harlot there is no reason to translate it differently here. It was the rabbis who thought up this forced meaning because they thought that it was ridiculous and a disgrace to their nation that it should be said that the spies accepted the hospitality of a harlot. Such a fear was stupid, because in the story of Joshua the word הזוֹנָה is specifically added here so that we may know that the spies came secretly into the city of Jericho, and there lay low in the harlot's house. It is also certain that this refers to her past life for her faith is the evidence of her repentance.

> *And what shall I more say? for the time will fail me if I tell of Gideon, Barak, Samson, Jephthah; of David and Samuel and the prophets: who through faith subdued kingdoms, wrought righteousness, obtained promises, stopped the mouths of lions, quenched the power of fire, escaped the edge of the sword, from weakness were made strong, waxed mighty in war, turned to flight armies of aliens. (32-34)*

32. *And what shall I say more?* He anticipates the fear that by referring to individual examples he might restrict the praise of faith to a few men and he says that there would be no end if he dwelt on every instance since what he has described in the case of a few refers to the whole church of God. He speaks first of the middle period between Joshua and David when the Lord raised up judges to govern the people such as the four whom he mentions, *Gideon, Barak, Samson, and*

Jephthah. It was certainly nonsense for Gideon with three hundred men to attack the huge army of his enemies, and to smash the pitchers with their hands was a more than futile alarm. Barak was far from being equal to his enemies and was governed by the counsel of a single woman. Samson was a countryman who was not trained to use any arms except farm tools and what could he do against such proud victors whose power had subdued a whole people? Who would not at first have condemned the deed of Jephthah as rashness when he professed that he would be the avenger of his people when they were already hopeless? Since all these followed God as their Guide, and encouraged by His promise undertook the task that they were commanded, they were honoured with the evidence of the Holy Spirit. Everything praiseworthy that they did the apostle has attributed to faith, although there was none of them whose faith did not falter. Gideon was slower than he need have been to take up arms, and it was only with difficulty that he ventured to commit himself to God. Barak hesitated at the beginning so that he had almost to be compelled by the reproaches of Deborah. Samson was the victim of the enticements of his mistress and thoughtlessly betrayed the safety of himself and of all his people. Jephthah rushed headlong into making a foolish vow and was over-obstinate in performing it, and thereby marred a fine victory by the cruel death of his daughter. In every saint there is always to be found something reprehensible. Nevertheless although faith may be imperfect and incomplete it does not cease to be approved by God. There is no reason, therefore, why the fault from which we labour should break us or discourage us provided we go on by faith in the race of our calling.

Of David. With David he includes all the good kings and to them he adds Samuel and the prophets. His purpose in short is to show that the kingdom of Judah was founded on faith and that it stood by faith to the last. The many victories which David gained over his enemies are well known. The uprightness of Samuel and his supreme wisdom in governing the people was well known. The mercies of God which He showed to the holy prophets and kings were also well known. The apostle maintains that there is none of these which ought not to be thought of as due to faith.

He refers only to some of the innumerable benefits of God so that the Jews may conclude from this in general terms how the church under God has always been kept by faith and thus that there is no other way today by which we may know His loving-kindness toward us. David returned home many times victorious, Hezekiah recovered from his illness, Daniel emerged safe and sound from the lion's den, his friends walked joyfully in the burning furnace as if in a dewy meadow.

If all these things were due to faith the fact is established that it is only by faith that a place is given for the goodness of God to reach out to us. We must especially notice the clause that says that the promises were received by faith. Although God remains faithful even if we all disbelieve, yet our faithfulness makes the promises invalid, that is, ineffectual.

34. *From weakness were made strong.* Chrysostom takes this as referring to the return of the Jews from exile in which they had been without hope. I am not averse to taking it as referring to Hezekiah, although we could broaden the application to mean that the Lord stretched out His hand to raise up the saints whenever they were laid low and brought help to their weakness so that they recovered their full strength.

> *Women received their dead by a resurrection: and others were tortured, not accepting their deliverance; that they might obtain a better resurrection: and others had trial of mockings and scourgings, yea, moreover of bonds and imprisonment: they were stoned, they were sawn asunder, they were tempted, they were slain with the sword: they went about in sheepskins, in goatskins; being destitute, afflicted, evil entreated (of whom the world was not worthy), wandering in deserts and mountains and caves, and the holes of the earth. And these all, having had witness borne to them through their faith, received not the promise, God having provided some better thing concerning us, that apart from us they should not be made perfect. (35-40)*

35. *Women received.* Up till now he has been describing the successful results with which God has rewarded the faith of His people, and now he turns to a different argument, to the effect that when saints are reduced to the extremity of misery they have struggled by faith to continue unconquered to death. At first sight these examples seem to differ greatly among themselves because some triumph wonderfully in overcoming their enemies, are saved by the Lord by all kinds of miracles and are snatched from the midst of death in new and unaccustomed ways, while others are shamefully treated, despised by almost the whole world, overcome by necessity, and universally hated so that they have to hide in the dens of beasts, and finally are dragged out to cruel, savage torture. These latter seem to be completely deprived of the help of God since He exposes them to the pride and the cruelty of the godless, and therefore their case seems greatly different from that of the former. Yet in both faith holds sway and in both it is efficacious; indeed its force shines out more clearly in the second group. The victory of faith is more outstanding in the contempt of death than if life is continued to the fifth generation. It is a more

excellent result of faith and more praiseworthy to endure reproaches, necessity, and the extremities of trouble with patience and equanimity than to recover health by a miracle or to obtain some similar benefit from God. To sum up, the fortitude of the saints which has shone clearly in all the ages is the work of faith because our weakness is such that we are not able to overcome our ills unless faith sustains us. From this we conclude that all those who trust in God are furnished with the power which they need to resist Satan in whatever way he attacks them, and especially that we shall never lack the patience to bear our ills if faith is present; and further that we are not guilty of unbelief when we fail under persecutions or the cross. The nature of faith is the same today as it appeared of old in the holy fathers whom the apostle mentions here. Therefore if we imitate their faith we shall never fall into disgrace because of our cowardice.

In the word ἐτυμπανίσθησαν I have followed Erasmus, although others have taken it to mean 'imprisoned'. In my opinion it simply means that they were stretched on a rack as a skin is stretched over a drum. The words 'they were tempted' seem superfluous, and I have no doubt that the likeness of the two words ἐπρίσθησαν and ἐπειράσθησαν was the reason why the second gradually crept into the text being added erroneously by some ignorant scribe, as Erasmus conjectures. I do not think that sheepskins and goatskins mean tents which were made from skins so much as the common rough clothing of the saints with which they were clothed when they fled into the desert.

Although there is a tradition that Jeremiah was stoned and Isaiah sawn asunder, and sacred history relates that Elijah, Elisha, and other prophets wandered on mountains and in caves, I have no doubt that he is referring to the fierce persecution which Antiochus launched against the people of God, and others which followed later.

Not accepting their deliverance. This is a most apt phrase, for they would have bought themselves only a short lease of life by denying God, and the price would have been most shameful. To gain eternal life in heaven they rejected a life on earth which would have consisted, as we have said, in their denial of God and the desertion of their calling. We hear Christ saying that if we wish to preserve our lives in this world we shall lose them for eternity. If therefore there is any real love of a future resurrection occupying a place in our hearts, it will easily lead us to contempt of death. We must only live so as to live to God, and whenever we cannot live to God we must gladly and willingly meet death. In this sentence the apostle is confirming what he has said that the saints overcame all their torments by faith, for unless their spirits had been kept firm by the hope of a blessed resurrection they would have immediately collapsed. From this we may take an en-

couragement which will be useful to fortify us in adversity. We must
not refuse it when God brings us together with so many holy men
whom we know have been tried and troubled by so many sufferings.
This is the story not of the sufferings of a few men but of the universal
persecution of the Church, and that not for one or two years but which
has raged periodically from grandfathers to grandchildren. It is therefore no wonder if God is pleased to try our faith today by the same
testing and we must not think that we are deserted by Him when we
know that He cared for the holy fathers who underwent the same
sufferings before us.

38. *Of whom the world was not worthy.* Since the holy prophets
wandered about as refugees among the wild beasts they could have
seemed unworthy of being sustained by the earth. How is it that they
find no place among men? The apostle turns this round the opposite
way that it was the world that was not worthy of them. Wherever
God's servants come they bring His benediction with them like the
fragrance of a sweet scent. Thus the house of Potiphar was blessed for
the sake of Joseph (Gen. 39.5), and Sodom would have been saved if
ten righteous men had been found in it (Gen. 18.32). Although the
world may reject the servants of God as rubbish, the fact that it cannot
bear them is to be thought of as its penalty because along with them
there goes some blessing of God. Therefore whenever righteous men
are taken away from us we should know that this presages evil for us
since we are unworthy of their companionship and they are not to
perish with us.

At the same time the godly have ample ground for consolation if
the world casts them off like refuse, when they see that the same thing
happened to the prophets who found more mercy among wild beasts
than among men themselves. With this thought Hilary cheered himself when he saw the Church occupied by tyrants with blood on their
hands who used the Roman emperor as their executioner. At that
time, I say, the holy man called to mind what the apostle here says
about the prophets. 'Mountains and woods', he said, 'and lakes and
prisons are safer for me than the splendour of great temples, for when
the prophets dwelt or were buried in them they still prophesied by the
Spirit of God.' We ought therefore to have the courage to despise the
world bravely and if it spurns us to know that we make our exit from
a fatal flood, and that God is taking care of our salvation so that we
are not swallowed up in the same destruction.

39. *And these all.* This is an argument from the less to the greater.
If those on whom the great life of grace had not yet shone showed such
patience in bearing their ills, what effect ought the full light of the
Gospel to have on us? A tiny spark of light led them to heaven, but

now that the sun of righteousness shines on us what excuse shall we offer if we still hold to the earth? This is the real meaning of the apostle. I know that Chrysostom and some others have expounded this differently, but the context clearly shows that the reference here is to the difference in the grace which God bestowed on the faithful under the Law and which he bestows on us today. Since the grace bestowed on us is more abundant it would be absurd for us to have less faith. He says, therefore, that those fathers who were endowed with such a little faith did not have such strong grounds for belief as we have. He goes on immediately to give the reason, namely that God wished to bring us all together into one body, and therefore He bestowed a small portion of grace on them so as to put off its complete perfection to our time, that is, to the advent of Christ. It is a singular evidence of God's loving-kindness toward us that although He showed His bounty to His children from the beginning of the world, He has so arranged His grace as to take regard for the salvation of the whole body. What more could any of us desire than that we should have a share in all the benefits which God bestowed on Abraham, Moses, David and all the patriarchs, prophets and good kings, so as to be united with them in the body of Christ? We should know that we are ungrateful to God two or three times over if less faith appears in us under the reign of Christ than the fathers showed that they had under the Law by such outstanding examples of constancy. The phrase that they had not yet received the promise is to be understood in reference to its final fulfilment which has been announced to us in Christ, and about which something has already been said above.

CHAPTER TWELVE

Therefore let us also, seeing we are compassed about with so great a cloud of witnesses, lay aside every weight, and the sin which doth so easily beset us, and let us run with patience the race that is set before us, looking unto Jesus the author and perfecter of our faith, who for the joy that was set before him endured the cross, despising shame, and hath sat down at the right hand of the throne of God. For consider him that hath endured such gainsaying of sinners against themselves, that ye wax not weary, fainting in your souls. (1-3)

1. *Therefore let us also.* This conclusion is a kind of epilogue to the last chapter to show that his purpose in setting down this catalogue of the saints whose faith excelled under the Law is that everyone should be prepared to imitate them. He calls the great multitude metaphorically a *cloud*, setting what is thick in contrast to what is thin. If they had been few in number they ought none the less to have encouraged us by their example, but where there is a great crowd we ought to take encouragement. He says that we are surrounded by this throng or multitude so that wherever we turn our eyes they immediately light upon many examples of faith. The word *witnesses* I take not in a general sense as if he were calling them masters of God, but as referring to the subject in hand as though he were saying that faith is sufficiently proved by their testimony so as to give us no hesitation. The virtues of the saints are as evidences to confirm us in our reliance on them as our guides and companions in going on more keenly towards God.

Lay aside every weight. Since he uses the metaphor of a race he bids us be unhindered, for there is no greater hindrance to haste than for us to be burdened with luggage. There are all kinds of burdens which delay and impede our spiritual race, such as the love of this present life, the pleasures of the world, the desires of the flesh, earthly cares, riches and honours, and everything else of this kind. Anyone who wants to run in the race of Christ, must first relieve himself of all hindrances because we are already slow enough to start and we should admit no other causes of delay. He does not command us simply to throw away riches and the other benefits of life, but only in so far as they hold back our race because Satan binds us and entangles us with them as by troubles. The metaphor of a race is a frequent one in Scripture, but here he describes not any kind of race but a running contest which usually calls for greater exertions. The summing up of it all is therefore that we have entered on a contest, and one in the most famous stadium round which stand many spectators and where the Son of God presides to urge us to gain the prize. It would therefore be the highest disgrace to grow tired or lazy in the middle of the course. Although the holy men to whom he refers are not only spectators but also our companions in the same race who show us the way, he prefers to call them witnesses rather than runners to show that they are not competitors to snatch the prize from us, but rather supporters to cheer and applaud our victory, just as Christ is not only the umpire but stretches forth His hands to us and supplies us with strength and energy, and in short prepares us and trains us to start the race and leads us by His strength to the goal.

The sin which doth so easily beset us. This is the heaviest burden that hinders us. He says that we are thus entangled in order to know that no one is fit to run unless he has laid aside these snares. He is not speaking of the external or (as they call them) the actual sins, but of the fount of sin itself, that is the lust which so possesses all of us that we feel that we are held by its snares on every side.

With patience. This word continually reminds us that what the apostle wants us principally to consider in faith is that we should seek in spirit the kingdom of God which is invisible to the flesh and surpasses all our experience. Those who are taken up with this kind of meditation easily disregard earthly things. He could not better draw the Jews away from their ceremonies than by recalling them to the true practices of faith from which they might learn that the kingdom of Christ is spiritual and far above the elements of this world.

2. *For the joy that was set before him.* Although the Latin translation is a bit ambiguous, the meaning of the apostle is shown clearly in the Greek. He means that although Christ was free to exempt Himself from all trouble and to lead a life of happiness full of all good things, nevertheless He submitted Himself voluntarily to a bitter and disgraceful death. *For the joy* has the same meaning as in place of the joy, and joy includes every kind of advantage. He says that it was set before Him because Christ had the power to use it if He had wanted. If anyone thinks that the preposition ἀντί denotes the final cause I do not greatly object, since the meaning would be that Christ did not refuse the death of the Cross because He saw its happy issue. However I hold to my earlier exposition.

He commends the patience of Christ to us for two reasons, first because He endured a bitter death and secondly because He despised the shame. He goes on to say that the end of His death was glorious so that believers might know that all the evils which they endure will end in salvation and glory, provided they follow Christ. Thus James (5.11), 'Ye have heard of the patience of Job, and have seen the end.' The apostle means that the end of our sufferings will be the same as we see in Christ, in this following Paul (Rom. 8.17), 'If we suffer with him, we shall also reign with him.'

3. *Consider him.* He extends his exhortation by comparing Christ with us, for if the Son of God who ought to be adored by everyone willingly submitted Himself to such hard struggles, who of us would dare to refuse to undergo the same with him? This thought alone ought to be sufficient to conquer all temptation, when we realize that we are the companions of the Son of God and that He who was so far above us was willing to come down to our condition to encourage us by His example. Thus, I say, we gain new heart when otherwise we would melt away and dissolve into despair.

Ye have not yet resisted unto blood, striving against sin: and ye have forgotten the exhortation, which reasoneth with you as with sons, My son, regard not lightly the chastening of the Lord, nor faint when thou art reproved of him; for whom the Lord loveth he chasteneth, and scourgeth every son whom he receiveth. It is for chastening that ye endure; God dealeth with you as with sons; for what son is there whom his father chasteneth not? But if ye are without chastening, whereof all have been made partakers, then are ye bastards, and not sons. (4-8)

4. *Ye have not yet resisted unto blood.* He now goes a step further and says that when unbelievers persecute us in the Name of Christ we are striving against sin. Christ was not able to enter this strife because He was pure and free from all sin. We are unlike Him in this regard because sin always dwells in us and our afflictions serve to tame and overcome it.

Firstly we know that all the evil in the world, and particularly death itself, comes from sin, but the apostle is not dealing with that here. He is only saying that the persecutions which we undergo for the Gospel benefit us in this other direction also, that they are remedies to destroy sin. In this way God holds us under the yoke of His discipline so that our flesh does not grow licentious; sometimes He checks the impetuous, and sometimes He punishes our sins to make us more careful in future. Therefore whether He is healing our vices or whether He is preventing us before we sin, He is exercising us in the struggle against sin which the apostle mentions. Indeed the Son of God pays us this honour that He does not reckon the things that we suffer for His Gospel as the penalties of sin. Yet we must understand what we hear here from the apostle that we concern ourselves with and defend the cause of Christ against the ungodly in such a way as to wage war with sin which is our inward enemy. The grace of God toward us is twofold in that He turns the remedies which He applies to cure our vices to defend His Gospel.

We must bear in mind that those whom he is addressing here have gladly suffered the loss of their goods and have endured many reproaches. Yet he accuses them of laziness because they have grown tired half-way through the contest and have not gone on energetically right to the death. There is no reason for us to seek our discharge from the Lord, whatever service we have performed, because Christ does not have any discharged soldiers except those who have conquered death itself.

5. *And we have forgotten.* I read this as a question. He is asking whether they have forgotten, meaning that it is not yet time to forget. He is entering here on the part of the doctrine that it is necessary for us to be taught by the Cross. For this purpose he refers to the evidence of Solomon which falls into two parts; the first that we are not to reject the correction of the Lord, and in the second the reason is given, because whom the Lord loves He chastens. Since Solomon prefaces the words, 'my son', the apostle says that we should be allured by this kind and sweet description to allow this exhortation to find its way to the depths of our hearts. The argument of Solomon is as follows, that if the scourges of God bear witness of His love towards us, it is not right for us to dislike or to hate them. Those who do not bear the chastising of God for their salvation, and indeed who reject this sign of His fatherly kindness, are yet more ungrateful.

6. *Whom the Lord loveth.* This reason seems to be ill-founded. God takes measures indiscriminately against both unbelievers and the elect, and His scourges declare His wrath more often than His love. Even Scripture speaks thus, and experience confirms it. Yet when he addresses the godly, it is no wonder that he touches on the effect of the chastisement in so far as they feel it. However severe and wrathful a judge God shows Himself to be towards unbelievers whenever He punishes them, in the case of His elect He has no other purpose than to take counsel for their salvation. This is the demonstration of His fatherly love. Moreover since unbelievers are ignorant of the fact that they are governed by the hand of God, they think for the most part that they are afflicted by chance. Just as a stubborn boy who leaves his father's house and wanders far away until he is exhausted by hunger and cold and other ills will pay the just penalty for his foolishness and will learn from his sufferings the lesson of submission and obedience to his father, but yet will not see that this is a paternal chastisement, so when unbelievers have taken themselves off from God and His family they do not understand that the hand of God reaches to them.

Let us therefore remember that no trace of divine love can be seen

by us in chastisements unless we are persuaded that the rods with which
He punishes our sins are those of the father. No such thought can
occur to unbelievers because their minds are fugitive. There is the
further fact that judgment must begin at the house of God. Even if He
strikes foreigners and family alike, yet He stretches forth His hand
towards the latter to show that He has a particular concern for them.
The true answer is that everyone who knows and is persuaded that he
is chastised by God ought at once to advance to this realization that it
happens because he is loved by God. When believers find God in the
midst of their punishments, they have a sure pledge of His loving-
kindness because if He did not love them He would not be concerned
for their salvation. Thus the apostle concludes that God offers Himself
as a Father to all who endure His correction. Those who kick against
it as wild horses do, or who obstinately resist it have no place in this
order. In short he says that the corrections of God are only those of a
Father when we submit obediently to Him.

7. *For what son is there.* From the common practice of men he
reasons that it is not fitting for the sons of God to be free from the
discipline of the Cross. If no man, at least of prudence and sound
judgment, can be found who does not correct his children, since they
cannot be led to real virtue without discipline, how much less will God,
who is the best and wisest father, neglect so necessary a remedy? If
anyone objects that this kind of correction stops among men as soon as
children leave adolescence, I reply that as long as we live we are no
more than children in regard to God, and that this is the reason why
the rod should always be applied to our backs. The apostle rightly
draws the conclusion that anyone who seeks to be free from the Cross
is withdrawing himself from the number of the children of God. It
follows from this that we do not value the blessing of adoption as we
ought and that we reject all the grace of God when we want to avoid
His chastisement. That is what all those who do not bear affliction
with equanimity do. Why does he call those who avoid correction
bastards rather than foreigners? It is because he is addressing those who
were enrolled into the Church, and thus sons of God. He is indicating
that if they withdrew themselves from the discipline of the Father their
profession of Christ would be false and untrue so that they were
bastards rather than legitimate children.

*Furthermore, we had the fathers of our flesh to chasten us, and we gave
them reverence: shall we not much rather be in subjection unto the
Father of spirits, and live? For they verily for a few days chastened us
as seemed good to them; but he for our profit, that we may be partakers
of his holiness. All chastening seemeth for the present to be not joyous,*

*but grievous; yet afterward it yieldeth peaceable fruit unto them that
have been exercised thereby, even the fruit of righteousness.* (9-11)

9. *We had the fathers of our flesh.* This comparison is made in several
parts. The first is that if we give so much reverence to the fathers of
whom we are born after the flesh that we submit to their discipline,
much more honour is due to God who is our spiritual Father. The
second is that the discipline by which fathers bring up their children is
only useful for this present life, but God looks further to sanctify us
for eternal life. Thirdly, mortal men chastise their children as they
think good, but God applies His discipline with the wisest purpose and
the highest wisdom so that there is nothing in it that is out of control.
In the first place he lays down this difference between God and men,
that the latter are fathers of the flesh, and the former of spirits, and he
amplifies that by comparing flesh with spirit. It might be asked whether
God is not the father of flesh, because Job in his history does not include
the creation of men among the chief miracles of God without purpose,
and thus in this regard deservedly justify His Name as Father. If we
say that He is called the Father of spirits because He alone creates and
re-creates souls without the help of man, the exception can again be
made that Paul does not vainly boast that he is the spiritual father of
those whom he has begotten in Christ through the Gospel. I reply that
God is the Father both of soul and body, and properly speaking the
only one, and that this name is given to men by way of concession
whether in regard to the body or the soul. Since He does not use the
help of men in creating souls and renews them miraculously by the
power of His spirit, He is called particularly the Father of spirits *par
excellence.*

In saying, *we give them reverence*, he refers to the natural affection in
us by which fathers are given respect even when they treat us harshly.
The words, *shall we not be in subjection to the father of spirits*, mean that
it is right for us to give God the authority which He had over us by
virtue of His fatherhood. The phrase, *and live*, denotes the cause or the
end, and the conjunction is to be taken with the force of the participle,
'in order to'. We are reminded by this that nothing is more fatal to us
than to refuse to give ourselves in obedience to God.

10. *And they verily for a few days.* The second amplification, as I have
said, is that the chastisements of God have the purpose of taming and
mortifying the flesh, so that we are renewed to a heavenly life. From
this it is clear that the benefit is eternal, but should not be hoped for
from men since the discipline of men is part of the civil order (*pars
ordinis politici*), and therefore properly refers to this present life. It
follows from this that the chastisements of God bring far greater

benefit to the extent that the spiritual holiness of God excels the advantages of the body.

If anyone objects that it is the duty of fathers to bring up their children in the fear and worship of God and that therefore their discipline does not seem to be restricted to so short a time, I reply that that is true, but the apostle is speaking here of home life in the way that we are accustomed to speak of the state. Even if it is the duty of magistrates to care for religion, we must say that their duty is limited to the bounds of this life because otherwise there could be no distinction between the civil government of this earth and the spiritual kingdom of Christ. Moreover the fact that the chastisements of God are said to be profitable for participation in His holiness, is not to be taken as though they made us properly holy, but in the sense that they are aids to prepare us because by them the Lord exercises us in the mortification of the flesh.

11. *All chastening.* He adds this to prevent us from measuring the chastenings of God by our present feelings. He says that we are like children who are afraid of and avoid the cane as far as possible, because they are not old enough to judge how useful it is for them. The purpose of this admonition is that chastisements cannot be properly valued by the present feelings of our flesh, but that we must turn our eyes to the end, and thus we shall understand the *peaceable fruit of righteousness.* The fruit of righteousness means the fear of the Lord, and a godly and holy life of which the Cross is the teacher. He calls it *peaceable* because we are afraid and disturbed by our adversity. We are tempted by our impatience which is always restless, but when we are chastened our minds are quieted and we see how useful that was for us which previously seemed to be bitter and troublous.

Wherefore lift up the hands that hang down, and the palsied knees; and make straight paths for your feet that that which is lame be not turned out of the way, but rather be healed. Follow after peace with all men, and the sanctification without which no man shall see the Lord: looking carefully lest there be any man that falleth short of the grace of God; lest any root of bitterness springing up trouble you, and thereby the many be defiled; lest there be any fornicator, or profane person, as Esau, who for one mess of meat sold his own birthright. For ye know that even when he afterward desired to inherit the blessing, he was rejected (for he found no place of repentance), though he sought it diligently with tears. (12-17)

12. *Wherefore lift up the hands that hang down.* Having said that God even while He chastises us is concerned for our salvation he goes on to encourage us to new enthusiasm, for there is nothing that weakens and

indeed exhausts us more than to be taken up with such a false notion
and to have no trace of the grace of God in adversity. There is nothing
more effective in encouraging us than the realization that God is with
us and is concerned for us even when He afflicts us. In saying this he is
not only encouraging us to bear our afflictions with courage but he is
advising us that there is no reason for us to be backward or lazy in
doing our duty. We have more than enough evidence of the extent to
which the fear of a cross hinders us from serving God as we ought.
Many people gladly profess their faith, but because they fear persecution they refrain from giving hands and feet to that pious intention of
their minds. Many people would gladly contend for the glory of God,
and would privately and publicly take up good and just causes, and do
their duty to God and their brethren; but because there is danger of
the hatred of wicked men, and because they see all kinds of troubles in
store for them, they sit back quietly with their hands folded. If that
overwhelming fear of a cross in us could be set right and we could be
prepared to endure it, there would be no part of us that was not ready
and fitted to do its duty to God. This is what the apostle means. He
says that you have hands that hang down and that your knees are weak
because you do not see the true encouragement in your adversity;
therefore you are slow to do your duty. Now that I have shown you
the benefit of the discipline of a cross, this teaching ought to encourage
you to a new vigour in all your members so that you are quick and
ready to follow the calling of God with your hands and your feet. He
seems to refer to a passage in Isaiah at chapter 35.3, where the prophet
is telling the holy teachers to confirm the feeble knees and the weak
hands by setting before them the hope of grace. The apostle bids all
the faithful to do this, for if this is the benefit of the consolations which
the Lord bestows upon us, just as it is the task of the teacher to strengthen
the whole Church so it is the task of each individual to strengthen and
encourage himself by applying this teaching particularly to himself.

13. *Make straight paths.* Up to now he has said that we must rely on
the consolations of God to be strong and active in doing good and that
this is our support. He now adds a second point, that we should walk
carefully and hold to the right course. An irrational enthusiasm is no
less vicious than laziness and slackness. This right way, which he
commends, starts from the point where a man's mind overcomes all
fear and has regard only to what is approved by God, for fear has an
abundant ingenuity in seeking out by-ways. Just as, when we are
entangled by a perverse fear, we seek out tortuous ways, so on the
other hand the person who is ready to endure evil goes directly
wherever the Lord calls and does not turn either to the right hand or
to the left. In short he sets down this rule of right action, that we are to

guide our steps according to the will of God so that neither fear nor the enticements of the world nor anything else may draw us away.

He adds, *that that which is lame be not turned out of the way*, i.e. so that you do not depart too far from the way by halting. By halting he means when men's minds waver and they do not give themselves sincerely to God. Elijah spoke thus to those double-minded persons who mixed up the worship of God with their own superstitions (I Kings 18.21), 'How long halt ye between two opinions?' This is a fitting way of speaking, for it is much worse to go astray than to halt. Those who begin to halt do not immediately turn aside from the way, but gradually they depart from it more and more until they are snatched away into error, are bound up in the middle of Satan's labyrinth and stick there. The apostle therefore warns us to take pains early to remedy any halting, because, if we indulge it, it will turn us at last far from God.

The words may be rendered, 'lest halting should grow worse, or turn aside', but the meaning remains the same since the apostle is saying that those who do not hold to the right course but who gradually allow themselves by their carelessness to be deviated hither and thither will eventually be wholly alienated from God.

14. *Follow after peace.* Men are so born that they all seem to shun peace, for they all look to their own interests, want to follow their own ways, and do not care to accommodate themselves to the ways of others. Unless we follow peace energetically we shall never hold on to it, for many things happen every day which give rise to discords. This is the reason why the apostle bids us follow peace, as though he were saying that it is not to be cultivated now and again when it is convenient for us, but it is to be striven for with the utmost zeal so that it is kept among us. This cannot happen unless we forget many injuries and show each other mutual forgiveness in many things.

Because peace cannot be obtained with the ungodly except on the condition of agreeing with their vices and crimes, the apostle immediately adds that sanctification is to be followed along with peace, as though commending peace to us with this exception that we do not defile or pollute ourselves by friendship with the wicked. Sanctification has especial regard to God. Even though the whole world blazes with war, we must not let go of sanctification because it is the chain which binds us in union with God. In short let us calmly foster peace with men but only as far as conscience allows, as the proverb says. He says that no one can see God without sanctification since we shall only see God with eyes which have been renewed according to his image.

15. *Looking carefully lest there be any man*, or, taking care etc. These words show that it is easy to fall away from the grace of God, and that

constant attention is needed in this regard, because as soon as Satan sees us free from care or relaxed, at that moment he surrounds us. In short there is need for exertion and vigilance if we want to persevere in the grace of God.

In the word *grace* he includes our whole vocation. If anyone infers from this that the grace of God is ineffective unless we co-operate of our own volition, the argument is childish. We know how much laziness there is in our flesh, and therefore it needs constant encouragements. When God encourages us with warnings and exhortations at the same time He stirs up our hearts so that the exhortations are not in vain and do not pass away without effect. Therefore we cannot gather from precepts and exhortations the power a man has of himself or the capacity of his free will, for the attention which the apostle here requires is the gift of God.

Lest any root. I have no doubt that he is referring to the passage of Moses in Deut. 29. After he had proclaimed the Law Moses told the people to take care that no root or seed of wormwood should sprout among the people of God. He then explained what he meant, namely that nobody should indulge his soul in sin, or excite his sinful desires as drunk men are accustomed to excite their thirst, and so bring the judgment of God by being lured on with the hope of impunity. The apostle is doing the same thing now, for he says that it will happen that many are corrupted and depraved if we allow any such root to grow further. He not only bids them individually to root out any such pest from their hearts, but also forbids them to allow it to grow among them. It must happen that those roots inhere in the Church of God, because hypocrites and unbelievers are always mixed in with the good, but whenever they break out they ought to be cut back so that their growth does not choke the good seed. He puts bitterness in place of what Moses calls gall and wormwood, but the purpose of both is to indicate a poisonous and fatal root. Since this is such a deadly form of evil we ought to check it with greater care so that it does not rise up and creep further.

16. *Lest there be any fornicator or profane person.* Just as he has already exhorted them to sanctification so now he mentions a particular example to call them back from the opposite kind of pollution, and says that there must be no fornicator. He immediately goes on to the more general remark, 'nor any profane person', a word which is appropriately contrasted with holiness. The Lord calls us for the purpose of making us holy in His obedience. He does this when we renounce the world. Anyone who is so pleased with his own filthiness that he wallows in it profanes himself, and at the same time we can define the profane in general terms as those who do not value the grace of God

highly enough to seek after it and reject the world. Since men become profane in various ways, greater care must be taken that there is no opening given to Satan to defile us by his corruption, and as there is no true religion without consecration we must always progress in the fear of God, in the mortification of the flesh, and in the whole practice of piety. Just as we are profane until we separate ourselves from the world, so we resile from the grace of sanctification if we wallow in the world's filth.

As Esau. This example can sever for us as an exposition of the meaning of the word profane, for when Esau put more value on a single meal than on his birthright, he deprived himself of his blessing. The profane, therefore, are those in whom the love of the world so holds sway and prevails, that they forget heaven as men who are carried away by ambition, addicted to money and riches, given over to gluttony, and entangled with other kinds of pleasures, and give the spiritual kingdom of Christ either no place or the last place in their concerns. Moreover this example is most appropriate, because when the Lord wants to show the force of the love with which He follows His people, He calls all those whom He has called to the hope of eternal life His firstborn. This is a priceless honour which He bestows on us, compared with which all the wealth of the world, all its advantages, honours, pleasures, and everything else that is commonly thought of as leading to a happy life will be like a cheap meal. To set a high value on those things which are almost worthless happens because a depraved lust blinds our eyes and covers them over. Therefore if we want to have a place in the sanctuary of God we must learn to despise such meals by which Satan habitually lures the reprobate.

17. *Even when he afterward desired to inherit the blessing.* He thought to begin with that the act by which he sold his birthright was a playful thing as though it had been a childish game, but he found too late the loss he had suffered when the blessing was taken from him and given by his father to Jacob. In the same way those who are captivated by the enticement of this world and who alienate themselves from God and sell their salvation to feed themselves with earthly meals do not think that they are losing anything but rather are pleased with and congratulate themselves as though they were the most happy. Too late the Lord opens their eyes, with the result that they are confronted with the sight of their own wickedness and feel the sense of the loss which they have neglected.

As long as Esau was hungry he cared for nothing except to have a well-filled stomach, and when he was satisfied he laughed at his brother and thought him a fool because he voluntarily deprived himself of a meal. Such is the stupidity of the unbelievers, I say, as long as

they are excited by their depraved desires or immerse themselves
without control in their pleasures. Afterwards they understand how
fatal were all the things that they so eagerly sought after. The word
'rejected' has the force of repudiated or that he suffered a repulse.

He found no place of repentance. This means that he gained or obtained
nothing by his too late repentance even though he sought with fear
the blessing which he had lost through his own fault. Because he warns
that all those who reject the grace of God are in the same danger, it
could be asked whether there is no hope of pardon if the grace of God
has been received with contempt and His kingdom rejected in favour
of the world? I reply that pardon is not absolutely refused to such
people, but they are warned to take care that the same thing does not
happen to them. One can see daily many examples of the wrath of
God by which He avenges the mockery and the scornings of profane
men. When they promise themselves that there is always tomorrow,
He suddenly removes them often with a new and unexpected form of
death; when they say that what they hear about the judgment of God
is fairy tales, He so pursues them that they are forced to see Him as
their Judge; when their consciences are dead, they afterwards feel
terrible agonies as the reward of this deadness. Although this does not
happen to everybody, yet there is a danger that it may happen, and the
apostle properly warns everyone to take care.

A second question arises, whether the sinner who is granted repentance gains nothing by it? The apostle seems to suggest this when he
says that Esau gained nothing by his repentance. I reply that here
repentance is not taken in the sense of a true conversion to God, but
only in the sense of the terror with which God strikes unbelievers after
they have indulged themselves for a long time in their iniquities. It is
no wonder if this terror is said to be useless, because they do not come
to themselves again nor hate their vices but are merely tortured by the
sense of their punishment. The same thing is to be said of tears.
Whenever a sinner sighs the Lord is prepared to pardon him, and
God's mercy is never sought in vain since to him that knocks it is
opened (Matt. 7.8). Because the tears of Esau were those of a man
without hope, they were not directed to God; for however the ungodly may deplore their lot, complain, and lament, they do not knock
at God's door because this can only be done by faith. Indeed the more
grievously their conscience pricks them, the more they rage against
God and show their anger to Him. They want access to be given to
them to God, but because they find nothing but His wrath they flee
from his sight. Thus we often see those who jokingly say that they
will have sufficient chance for repentance when they come near death,
when in fact they get there, shouting out in the throes of fierce agony

that there is no time now to obtain mercy. They are doomed to destruction because they have sought God too late. Sometimes they break out in words like, 'If only! If only!' But soon hopelessness cuts away all their vows and shuts up their lips so that they go no further.

For ye are not come unto a mount that might be touched, and that burned with fire, and unto blackness, and darkness, and tempest, and the sound of a trumpet, and the voice of words; which voice they that heard entreated that no word more should be spoken unto them: for they could not endure that which was enjoined, If even a beast touch the mountain, it shall be stoned; and so fearful was the appearance, that Moses said, I exceedingly fear and quake: but ye are come unto mount Zion, and unto the city of the living God, the heavenly Jerusalem, and to innumerable hosts of angels, to the general assembly and church of the firstborn who are enrolled in heaven, and to God the Judge of all, and to the spirits of just men made perfect, and to Jesus the mediator of a new covenant, and to the blood of sprinkling that speaketh better than that of Abel. (18-24)

18. *For ye are not come.* He now makes his point with a different argument. He shows the greatness of the grace which is opened to us by the gospels so that we may learn to receive it with reverence; and secondly he commends to us its sweetness so as to entice us to Love and desire it. He emphasizes both of these by comparing Law and Gospel. The more the kingdom of Christ excels the dispensation of Moses, and the more glorious our calling is than that of the people of old, the baser and more inexcusable is our ingratitude if we do not accept the blessing that is offered to us with proper piety, and humbly receive the majesty of Christ which is here evident. Further since God does not show Himself to us as terrible, as He did to the Jews, but invites us to come to Him in friendship and fellowship, so we are doubly guilty of ingratitude if we do not accept His gracious invitation with the utmost earnestness. Let us remember therefore that Gospel is here compared with Law, and secondly, that this comparison has two parts: the first that the glory of God shows itself more clearly in the Gospel than in the Law, and the second that the calling of God today is in friendship when previously it held nothing but sheer terror.

Unto a mount that might be touched. There are various expositions of this sentence, but I think that an earthly mountain is contrasted with a spiritual; and the words which follow, *burned with fire, and unto blackness and darkness,* and the rest, have this intent. These signs which God manifested to provide trustworthiness and reverence for His Law are, considered by themselves, wonderful and indeed heavenly, but when we come to the kingdom of Christ, what God shows us there is far above all heavens. It follows from this that the whole majesty of the

Law begins to be something earthly. Mount Sinai can be touched with hands, but Mount Zion can only be known by the spirit. The things which we read about in the nineteenth chapter of Exodus were visible figures; but what we have in the kingdom of Christ is hidden from fleshly experience. If anyone objects that there was a spiritual meaning in all the former things, and that today there are external exercises of holiness by which we are carried up to heaven, I reply that the apostle is speaking comparatively about the greater and the lesser. There is no doubt that when Law and Gospel are contrasted what is spiritual preponderates in the latter while earthly symbols are more prominent in the former.

19. *They that heard entreated.* In this second clause he shows that the Law was very different from the Gospel because it was full of all kinds of terrors when it was proclaimed. Everything that we read about in the nineteenth chapter of Exodus had in view that the people should know that God was ascending His judgment-seat where He showed Himself as a severe Judge. If a harmless animal had accidentally come near, the order was that it should be killed. How much heavier punishment hung over sinners who were conscious of their guilt, and indeed who knew that they were condemned to eternal death through the Law? Provided the Gospel is received by faith it contains only love. For the rest you are referred to II Cor. 3.

In saying that the people entreated, he is not to be taken as saying that the people refused to hear the Word of God, but that they prayed not to be compelled to hear God Himself speaking. The intervention of the person of Moses went some way to lessen their dread. It puzzles commentators that the apostle has attributed these words to Moses, *I exceedingly fear and quake*, since we do not read anywhere that Moses used them. The answer is not difficult if you consider that Moses spoke in this way in the name of the people whose requests he was bringing to God as their intermediary. This, then, was the common complaint of the whole people, but Moses is included because he was the spokesman of them all.

22. *Unto Mount Zion.* He refers to those prophecies in which God had promised that His Gospel would go forth from there, as in Isa. 2, and similar passages. He compares Mount Zion with Mount Sinai, and he calls it the *heavenly Jerusalem*, using the word heavenly so that the Jews will not stick to that earthly mountain where the Law had flourished. When they sought stubbornly to remain under the servile yoke of the Law, it was turned to Mount Sinai, as Paul says in Gal. 4. He understands the heavenly Jerusalem as that which was to be built throughout the whole world, as the angel in Zechariah stretched his line from the east to the west.

23. *To innumerable hosts of angels.* This means that when Christ calls us to Himself by the Gospel we have fellowship with the angels, are included in the ranks of the patriarchs, and are given a place in heaven among the spirits of the blessed. It is indeed a priceless honour which the heavenly Father bestows on us to include us with angels and the holy fathers. The expression, myriads of angels is taken from Daniel, although I have followed Erasmus in rendering it *innumerable.* The description *firstborn* is not given here to the children of God indiscriminately, as Scripture sometimes does, but he gives this distinction to honour particularly the patriarchs and the other prominent men of the old Church. He says *enrolled in heaven,* because God is said to have all the elect written in His book or in His secret catalogue, according to Ezekiel.

To the judge of all. This seems to be said to inspire fear, as if he were saying that grace is offered to us in such a way as to remind us that we have to do with our Judge to whom we must render account if we have rashly invaded His sanctuary with pollution or profanity. He adds *the spirits of just men,* meaning that we are included among the holy souls who have put off their bodies, and left behind all the filth of the world. Therefore he calls them consecrated or *made perfect,* because now that they have laid aside their flesh they are no longer subject to the infirmities of it. From this we may conclude with certainty that after they are separated from their bodies holy souls live with God, because otherwise we could not be joined to their fellowship.

Finally he adds *Jesus the mediator,* because it is through Him alone that we are reconciled with the Father and He alone who makes His face clear and loving towards us so that we do not fear to approach Him. At the same time he describes how Christ is our Mediator, namely by His blood, which after the Hebrew idiom he calls the *blood of sprinkling,* meaning sprinkled blood, because since it was once shed to make atonement for us, so our souls must now be cleansed by it through faith. In doing so the apostle refers to the old legal rite of which mention has already been made.

24. *That speaketh better.* There is nothing to prevent us turning this adverbially and taking better things to mean a better way, in this sense —the blood of Christ cries more effectively and is better heard by God than the blood of Abel. I prefer however to take this literally in the sense that the voice itself speaks and is said to say better things, since it is efficacious in gaining pardon for our sins. The blood of Abel did not properly cry out, but it was his murder that demanded vengeance before God. The blood of Christ does cry out because the atonement made by it is heard daily.

See that ye refuse not him that speaketh. For if they escaped not, when they refused him that warned them on earth, much more shall not we escape, who turn away from him that warneth from heaven: whose voice then shook the earth: but now he hath promised, saying, Yet once more will I make to tremble not the earth only, but also the heaven. And this word, Yet once more, signifieth the removing of those things that are shaken, as of things that have been made, that those things which are not shaken may remain. Wherefore, receiving a kingdom that cannot be shaken, let us have grace, whereby we may offer service well-pleasing to God with reverence and awe: for our God is a consuming fire. (25-29)

25. *See that ye refuse not.* He uses the same word as he did before when he said that the people made excuses that God should not speak to them. But now he means, as I think, something different, namely that we should not reject the Word that is directed to us. He further points out (as he had in mind in the immediately preceding comparison) that the heaviest penalty awaits those who despise the Gospel, when men of old did not escape with impunity when they despised the Law. He continues his argument from the less to the greater by saying that God or Moses then spoke on earth, but now the same God or Christ speaks from heaven. I prefer to take both references to be to God. He says that God spoke on the earth because He spoke on a lower level. We must always remember that he is dealing with the external administration of the Law, which was of such a kind, compared with the Gospel, as to smack of the earthly, and not yet to lead men's minds above the heavens to perfect wisdom. At the same time the Law contained the same teaching, but because it was only a schoolmaster it always lacked perfection.

26. *Whose voice then shook the earth.* Since God shook the earth in proclaiming the Law, he now declares that He speaks more gloriously because He shakes both earth and heaven. In this connexion he quotes the evidence of the prophet Haggai. He does not give the quotation verbatim, but because the prophet foretells a future shaking of earth and heaven, the apostle draws on this to show that the sound of the Gospel echoes not only on earth but penetrates above the heavens. It should be beyond dispute that the prophet is speaking of the kingdom of Christ, for in the same context there follow these words, 'I will shake all nations, and the desire of all nations shall come and I will fill this house with glory.' It is certain that all the nations have only been brought together into one body under the guidance of Christ, and there is no other desire with which we are all satisfied than Christ Himself. Further the temple of Solomon was not surpassed in glory until the greatness of Christ was spread through the whole city.

Without doubt therefore the prophet refers to the time of Christ. If from the rise of the kingdom of Christ not only the lower parts of the world are to be shaken but its power is to penetrate right up to heaven, the apostle rightly concludes that the teaching of the Gospel is more excellent and ought to be heard more clearly by every creature.

27. *And this word, Yet once more.* The words of the prophet are, 'Yet once a little while'. He means that the troubles of the people will not be of long duration but that God will help them. The apostle does not lay stress on this sentence, but simply infers from the shaking of heaven and earth that the coming of Christ is to change the state of the whole world. Created things are subject to decay, but the kingdom of Christ is eternal. It is therefore necessary for all creatures to be re-formed for the better.

From this he passes to a different exhortation, that we should lay hold on the kingdom which cannot be shaken, since the Lord moves us to find our true and lasting foundation in him. I prefer rather the variant reading which the old commentator gives, 'Receiving a kingdom we have grace.' If you read this as an affirmation the sense runs better—when we embrace the Gospel we are given the Spirit of Christ to worship God with reverence and holiness. If you read this as an exhortation, 'Let us have', the sentence is forced and puzzling. In short I think that the purpose of the apostle is to say that provided we enter the kingdom of Christ by faith we shall obtain a firm grace which will effectively hold us to the service of God, because just as the kingdom of Christ is higher than the world so also is the gift of regeneration.

In saying that God is to be served εὐαρέστως, *with reverence and awe*, he means that although readiness and joy are demanded in our service, at the same time no worship is pleasing to Him that is not allied to humility and due reverence. He condemns both the perverse trust in the flesh and the idleness which usually comes from it.

29. *For our God is a fire.* Just as he has set forth already the grace of God in its sweetness, so now he declares its severity. He seems to have borrowed this sentence from Deut. 4. We thus see that God has left out nothing that may draw us to Himself because He begins with kindness so that we may follow Him more gladly, but if He makes no progress by allurement, He frightens us. It is right and proper that the grace of God should never be promised to us without an accompaniment of threats, for (as we are all too prone to indulge ourselves) if we are not moved by such spurs, the milder teaching will freeze in us. Therefore as the Lord is favourable and merciful to those who fear Him to a thousand generations, so He is a jealous and just avenger to the third and fourth generation, when He is rejected.

CHAPTER THIRTEEN

Let love of the brethren continue. Forget not to show love unto strangers: for thereby some have entertained angels unawares. Remember them that are in bonds, as bound with them; them that are evil entreated, as being yourselves also in the body. Let marriage be had in honour among all, and let the bed be undefiled: for fornicators and adulterers God will judge. Be ye free from the love of money; content with such things as ye have: for himself hath said, I will in no wise fail thee, neither will I in any wise forsake thee. So that with good courage we say, The Lord is my helper; I will not fear: what shall man do unto me? (1-6)

1. *Let love of the brethren continue.* He lays down this command to brotherly love perhaps because there was a possibility that a secret feud arising from the pride of the Jews might disrupt the churches. At the same time this command is very necessary in this generation, because nothing evaporates more easily than love when everyone looks after himself more than his wife and gives less consideration to others. Moreover many offences occur every day to separate us. He calls it *brotherly*, not only to say that we ought to be joined together by the particular and intimate feelings of love, but to remind us that we can only be Christians if we are brethren. He speaks of the love which the household of faith ought to cultivate towards one another, in the same way as the Lord has bound them together more closely by the common bonds of adoption. It was a good habit in the early Church for the Christians to call each other brethren, but now the name has fallen into disuse along with the practice except that the monks have grabbed for themselves the usage that has been neglected by others, but showing by their discords and their internal differences that they are all the children of their father, the devil.

2. *To show love unto strangers.* This humane duty has also ceased to be properly observed among men, because the old hospitality, celebrated in history, is unknown to us, and inns have today taken the place of private hospitality. He is not only speaking of the right of hospitality which used to be practised among the rich, but rather he is giving orders that the poor and the needy are to be received since at that time many were refugees from their homes for the Name of Christ. To add additional commendation for this kind of duty, he says that angels have sometimes been entertained by those who thought that they were receiving men. I have no doubt that he is thinking of

Abraham and Lot. In showing hospitality as an everyday custom they came upon the angels unknowingly and without any such thoughts, and in this way their home was given no ordinary honour. God surely made it clear that hospitality was especially near His heart when He gave such a repayment to Abraham and Lot. If anyone objects that this was an unusual occurrence, I have a ready answer in the fact that we receive not only angels but Christ Himself when we receive the poor in His Name. There is a fine alliteration in the Greek words which cannot be expressed in Latin.

3. *Remember them that are in bonds.* There is nothing that can give us a deeper feeling of compassion than to put ourselves in the place of those who are afflicted. So he says that we ought to think of those in bonds as if we were in their position. What follows in the second clause, *as being yourselves also in the body*, is explained in various ways. Some take it generally as, 'You are liable to the same troubles in accordance with the common lot of human nature.' Others restrict the sense, 'As though you were in their shoes'. I do not like either, but I take this as referring to the body of the Church, with this meaning, 'Since you are members of the same body, you ought to have a common feeling for one another's troubles, so that you are not divided amongst yourselves.'

4. *Let marriage be had in honour.* Some think that this is an exhortation to spouses to conduct their matrimonial relationships modestly and with proper honesty so that the man lives temperately and chastely with his wife and does not defile the marriage bed with unworthy wantonness. A word indicating exhortation is to be understood, 'Let marriage be honourable', although the indicative mood is not unsuitable. When we are told that marriage is honourable it ought immediately to occur to us to behave honourably and reverently in it. Others take what is said by way of concession, thus, 'Although marriage is honourable, it is not lawful to commit fornication.' This sense is obviously a barren one. I think rather that the apostle is here contrasting marriage with fornication as a remedy against a disease, and the context clearly shows that this was his intention. Before threatening that the Lord will punish fornicators he lays down the true way of avoiding this punishment, namely to live honourably in marriage. This therefore must be the main point, that fornication will not go unpunished because God will avenge it. Since God has blessed the union of man and wife which He has instituted, it follows that any divergence from this will be condemned and cursed by Him. He promises punishment not only to adulterers but to all kinds of fornicators because both depart from the holy ordinance of God, and indeed violate and overturn it by their promiscuity, since there is only one

205

lawful union which is approved by the Name and the Authority of God. Since promiscuous and unsettled lusts cannot be controlled without the remedy of marriage he commends it to us and calls it honourable.

The addition about the undefiled bed I take to mean that those joined in marriage should know that they cannot do what they please but that their use of the lawful marriage bed ought to be moderate so as to admit nothing that is contrary to the modesty and chastity of marriage.

By saying *among all*, I understand him to mean that there is no order of men prohibited from marriage. What God has allowed to the human race universally is fitting for all without exception. By this I understand all who are fit for marriage and have need of it. It was necessary to express this distinctly to meet the superstition, the seeds of which Satan was already secretly sowing, that marriage is a profane thing, or certainly far removed from Christian perfection. Those false spirits, of which Paul had prophesied, soon made their appearance and prohibited marriage. Therefore in case anyone foolishly imagines that marriage is allowed to the commonalty of men but that those who are prominent in the Church ought to abstain from it, the apostle removes every exception, and so far from teaching that it is allowed us by way of indulgence (as Jerome sophistically says) he asserts that it is worthy of honour. It is more than remarkable that those who introduced into the world the prohibition of marriage were not frightened by this express declaration except that it was necessary to give rein to Satan in order to punish the ingratitude of those who refused to hear God.

5. *Be ye free from the love of money.* With the purpose of correcting greed he rightly and wisely bids us be content with what we have. It is the true contempt of money or at least right-mindedness in the proper and moderate use of it, when we are content with what the Lord has given us whether it be much or little. It certainly rarely happens that anything will satisfy a greedy man, but rather that those who are dissatisfied with moderation, even though they enjoy the greatest riches, are always looking for more. This is the teaching which Paul says he had learned, in that he knew how to abound and how to suffer need. The man who has set a limit to his desire in order to rest contentedly with his lot, has banished from his heart the love of money.

For himself hath said. He quotes two pieces of evidence. The first people think has been taken from Joshua 1, but I think rather that this sentence has been adduced from the common teaching of Scripture, though he had said that the Lord promises everywhere that He will never fail us. From this promise he infers what is said in Ps. 118, that we have a ground to overcome fear when we are certain of the help of God. Here he pulls out the disease root and branch, as is necessary if we wish the minds of men to be truly cleansed of it. It is quite certain that lack of faith is the source of greed. Anyone who has the firm conviction that he will never be forsaken by the Lord will not be unduly anxious because he will depend on His providence. Therefore when the apostle wants to cure us of the disease of greed he properly recalls us to the promises of God by which he bears witness that He will always be present to us. From this he concludes that as long as we have such a helper there is no cause for fear. It will thus come about that no depraved desires will worry us because it is faith alone which can set the minds of men at rest when otherwise disquiet is only too noticeable.

Remember them that had the rule over you, which spake unto you the word of God; and considering the issue of their life, imitate their faith. Jesus Christ is the same yesterday and today, yea and for ever. Be not carried away by divers and strange teachings: for it is good that the heart be stablished by grace; not by meats, wherein they that occupied themselves were not profited. (7-9)

7. *Remember them.* What follows refers not so much to morals as to doctrine. In the first place he sets before the Jews the example of those who have been their teachers, and he seems particularly to be speaking about those who had sealed with their own blood the teachings handed on by them. He is pointing out something to be remembered when he says, *considering the issue of their life.* There is no reason, however, why we should not take this generally as referring to those who persisted in a true faith to the very end, and who both in death and in their whole life bore faithful testimony to sound doctrine. It has no little effect to set before them the example of their teachers to imitate, for those who have begotten us in Christ ought to be like fathers to us. When they had seen them faithful and unyielding sometimes among savage persecution and sometimes among all kinds of struggles, they ought with reason to be moved the more.

8. *Jesus Christ is the same yesterday.* The only way by which we persist in a true faith is to hold on to the foundation and not to depart from it in the slightest. Anyone who does not hold to Christ, even though he may comprehend heaven and earth, has no knowledge that is not sheer vanity. All the treasures of heavenly wisdom are included in Christ. This is a notable passage from which we learn that there is no other rule of true wisdom than to fix all our thoughts on Christ alone.

Because he is dealing with the Jews he says that Christ had always held the same position of sovereignty as He holds today, and that He will always be the same to the end of the world. He says, *yesterday and today, yea and for ever*, meaning by these words that Christ, who has now been shown forth to the world, has reigned from the beginning of the world, and that we cannot advance further when we have come to Him. Yesterday embraces the whole period of the Old Testament, and in case anyone expects a sudden change after a little while, because the promulgation of the Gospel was still a recent event, he declares that Christ has been lately revealed so that the knowledge of Him might continue the same for ever.

It is clear from this that the apostle is not discussing the eternal being of Christ but the knowledge of Him which flourished among believers in every age and which was the lasting foundation of the Church. It is certain that Christ existed before He put forth His power. It may now be asked what the apostle is dealing with. I say that this verse refers to quality (so to speak) and not to essence, because there is no discussion of whether He was eternally with the Father, but what was the knowledge that men had of Him. The manifestation of Christ, as far as its external form and mould is concerned, was different under the Law from that which we have today, but that is no reason why the apostle should not say with truth and propriety that Christ, to whom the faithful look, is always the same.

9. *By divers and strange teachings*. He concludes that we are not to waver, since the truth of Christ in which we ought to stand, is firm. Certainly all kinds of opinions, every sort of superstition, every monstrous error, and in short all deviations of religion arise from the fact of not standing in Christ alone. Paul does not teach us in vain that Christ is given to us by God to be our wisdom. The gist of this passage is that we are to rest on Christ alone in order that the truth of God might be firm in us. From this we conclude that all those who are ignorant of Christ are exposed to all the deceits of Satan because apart from Him there is no stable faith but only innumerable commotions. The subtlety of the papists who have devised a contrary remedy for driving away errors, namely by extinguishing or burying the knowledge of Christ, is remarkable; but this warning of the Holy Spirit must possess our hearts, that we shall never be free from peril unless we adhere to Christ. He calls the teachings which lead us away from Christ *diverse*, since there is no other simple and pure truth than the knowledge of Christ. He calls them *strange*, since God does not regard as His anything that is outside Christ. By this we are warned how we should proceed if we want to attain due proficiency in Scripture, for anyone who does not take a straight course to Christ is a wanderer. The apostle also means that there will always be a struggle in the Church of God with strange doctrine, and there is no other means of

guarding against them than to be fortified by a pure knowledge of Christ.

For it is good. He now moves from a general principle to a particular case. As is well known there was a familiar superstition among the Jews in regard to the choice of food, which gave occasion for many disputes and quarrels. This was one of the strange doctrines which arose out of ignorance of Christ, so that having laid the foundation of our faith on Christ, he says that the observance of meats has no connexion with our final salvation and true holiness. When he contrasts grace with meats, I have no doubt that by grace he means the spiritual worship of God and regeneration. He lays down *that the heart be stablished,* looking back on the verb *carried away,* as though he were saying that the spiritual grace of God and not the observance of meats will truly establish us.

In the following clause, *not by meats wherein they that occupied themselves were not profited,* it is uncertain to whom he refers. Certainly the fathers who lived under the Law had a useful training, part of which was distinction of foods. This seems rather to be understood as referring to the superstitious who after the revelation of the Gospel still adhere stubbornly to the old ceremonies. If however you explain this carefully as referring to the fathers, there is nothing absurd about it. It was a good thing for them to submit to the yoke imposed on them by the Lord, and to abide obediently the common discipline of believers and the whole Church. The apostle means that abstinence from foods of itself has no value. Certainly it is to be thought nothing of, except as a piece of elementary teaching at a time when, as far as their outward government was concerned, the sons of God were still like children. To be *occupied in meats* is to be taken in regard to them, in making a distinction between clean and unclean. What he says of meats can be applied to the other rites of the Law.

We have an altar, whereof they have no right to eat which serve the tabernacle. For the bodies of those beasts, whose blood is brought into the holy place by the high priest as an offering for sin, are burned without the camp. Wherefore Jesus also, that he might sanctify the people through his own blood, suffered without the gate. Let us therefore go forth unto him without the camp, bearing his reproach. For we have not here an abiding city, but we seek after the city which is to come. Through him then let us offer up a sacrifice of praise to God continually, that is, the fruit of lips which make confession to his name. (10-15)

10. *We have an altar.* This is a fine analogy (*anagoge*) from the old rite of the Law to the present state of the Church. There was a solemn kind of sacrifice, which is mentioned in Lev. 16, of which no part was

given back to the priests and Levites. He says, using a neat allusion, that this has now been fulfilled in Christ, since He was sacrificed on the condition that those who serve the tabernacle should not feed on Him. By the ministers of the tabernacle he understands all those who performed the ceremonies. He therefore means that we must renounce the tabernacle in order to have a share in Christ. Just as the word altar includes a sacrifice and a victim, so the tabernacle includes all the outward types which were joined to it. The sense is this that it is no wonder that the rites of the Law have ceased today, for what was prefigured in the sacrifice, which the Levites carried outside the camps to burn it there, was that just as the ministers of the tabernacle tasted nothing of it, so if we serve the tabernacle, that is, if we retain its ceremonies, we shall not participate in the sacrifice which Christ once for all offered nor in the atonement which He performed once for all in His own blood. He brought His own blood into the heavenly sanctuary in order to atone for the sins of the world.

13. *Let us therefore go forth unto him.* In case this allegory and its spiritual comparison becomes lifeless he joins to it the earnest duty which is required of all Christians. Paul is also in the habit of using this mode of teaching to show to believers what God wishes them to be engaged in in his anxiety to lead them away from vain ceremonies. It is as if he were saying, 'This is what God demands of you, and not that by which you tire yourself in vain.' That is what the apostle is now doing. In calling us to leave the tabernacle and follow Christ he is advising us that something is demanded of us very different from the service of God in the shade beneath the wonderful glory of the temple, because it is to be performed through exiles, flights, reproaches, and all kinds of trials. He contrasts this warfare, in which we are to labour to the point of blood, with the shadowy practices in which alone the masters of the ceremonies engaged.

14. *For we have not here.* He continues the idea of the going forth which he has mentioned to make us realize that we are strangers and pilgrims in this world and that we have no fixed abode except in heaven. Therefore whenever we are driven out of any place or any change happens to us we must think, as the apostle says here, that we have no sure place on earth because heaven is our inheritance; and when we are tried more and more we should prepare ourselves for our final end. Those whose life is too quiet imagine that they have a nest for themselves in this world, and therefore it is good for us who are prone to this kind of sloth to be continually tossed about hither and thither, so that we, who are inclined to look downwards, may learn to turn our eyes to heaven.

15. *Let us offer up a sacrifice of praise.* He returns to that particular

doctrine which he had touched on of the abrogation of the old ceremonies. He anticipates an objection that could be raised. Since the
sacrifices were attached to the tabernacle as appendages, it follows that
when it was abolished they too must cease. Yet the apostle had taught
that since Christ suffered outside the gate we were also called thither
and therefore that the tabernacle was deserted by those who wished to
follow Him. Hence arose the question whether any sacrifices remained
for Christians, for this would be absurd since they were ordained to
serve the worship of God. The apostle meets this timeously, and says
that another form of sacrifice is left for us which is no less pleasing to
God, namely the offering to Him of the calves of our lips, as the
prophet Hosea says (14.3). The sacrifice of praise is not only equally
pleasing to God but more so than all the outward things that were used
under the Law, as clearly appears from Ps. 50. There God rejects all
these things as of no account, and orders the sacrifice of praise to be
offered to Him. We see therefore that it is the finest worship of God,
and the one which is to be preferred to all other exercises, that we
should celebrate the goodness of God by the giving of thanks. This, I
say, is the rite of sacrifice which God commends to us today. At the
same time there is no doubt that the whole act of calling on the Name
of God is included in this single part, for we cannot give thanks to
Him unless we are purged by Him, and no one obtains anything unless
he prays. In short he means that without brute beasts we have something to offer God and that in this way He is rightly and perfectly
worshipped by us.

As it is the apostle's plan to tell us what is the proper way of worshipping God under the New Testament he reminds us in passing that we
cannot honestly call on God and glorify His name except through
Christ as our Mediator. It is He alone who hallows our lips which are
otherwise defiled to sing the praises of God, who opens the way for
our prayers, who in short performs the office of Priest by standing
before God in our name.

But to do good and to communicate forget not: for with such sacrifices
God is well pleased. Obey them that have the rule over you, and submit
to them: for they watch in behalf of your souls, as they that shall give
account; that they may do this with joy, and not with grief: for this were
unprofitable for you. Pray for us: for we are persuaded that we have a
good conscience, desiring to live honestly in all things. And I exhort
you the more exceedingly to do this, that I may be restored to you the
sooner. (16-19)

16. But to do good. He is here pointing out another way of offering
due and proper sacrifices, in the fact that all the duties of love are

equivalent of so many sacrifices. In this he shows that those who think that something is lacking if they do not offer beasts to God according to the Law are stupidly and perversely avaricious, since God supplies us with frequent and manifold materials for sacrifice. Although He can derive no benefit from us, yet He looks on our calling on His Name as a sacrifice, and indeed as the principal one which suffices for all the others. Moreover whatever benefits we show to men He regards as done to Himself, and gives them the name of sacrifice, so that it is clear that the elements of the Law are now not only superfluous but harmful since they draw us away from the true way of sacrificing.

In short the meaning is that if we want to sacrifice to God, we must call upon His Name, make known His goodness by giving thanks, and do good to our brethren. These are the true sacrifices with which true Christians should be engaged, and there is neither time nor place for any other.

In the words, *with such sacrifices God is well pleased*, there is an implied contrast in that He no longer demands the old sacrifices which He had commanded up until the abrogation of the Law. An exhortation is added to this teaching with the effect of stirring us up more keenly to show kindness towards our neighbours. It is no common honour that God regards what we do for men as sacrifices offered to Himself, and that He so values our works which are worth nothing that He calls them holy. Therefore where there is no love among us, we not only deprive men of their right, but God Himself who has solemnly dedicated to Himself what He commanded to be done to men.

The word *communicate* has a wider reference than *to do good*. It includes all the duties by which men help one another, and it is the true mark of love that those who are joined together by the Spirit of God communicate amongst themselves.

17. *Obey.* I have no doubt that he is speaking of the pastors and other governors of the Church. There were then no Christian magistrates, and when he says that *they watch in behalf of your souls*, he is referring properly to spiritual rule. He orders that first obedience and then honour are to be given to them. These two things are necessarily required for the people to have both faith in and reverence for their pastors. At the same time it must be noticed that the apostle is only concerned with those who faithfully exercise their office. Those who have nothing except the title, and indeed those who abuse the title of pastor to destroy the Church, deserve little reverence and even less faith. The apostle says this expressly in saying that they watch for your souls, because this does not apply to any except those who are true rulers, and who are in fact what they are called. The papists who use this as a foundation for the tyranny of their idol are doubly foolish.

The Spirit commands us to receive obediently the teaching of holy and faithful bishops, and to obey their wise counsels; He commends us to give them honour. How does this support pretending bishops? Not only are all those who are called bishops under the papacy pretenders, but they are savage murderers of souls, and ravening wolves. I shall say no more to describe them, but for the present I make this one comment that while we are bidden to obey our pastors we must carefully and shrewdly distinguish those who are true and faithful rulers, because if we give this honour indiscriminately to anyone we like, wrong will be done to the good, and moreover the reason added here that they are worthy of honour because they watch for our souls will have no force. For the Pope and his like to draw support from this evidence it is necessary first of all for all of them to prove that they are among those who watch for our salvation. If this is established there will be no question of their being held in reverence by all believers.

For they watch. He means that the heavier burden they bear the more honour they deserve, for the more trouble anyone takes for our sakes, and the greater difficulty and danger he incurs for us, the more are we obliged to him. The office of bishop is such that it includes the greatest labours as well as the utmost danger so that if we want to be thankful it is scarcely possible to repay what we owe to them. Moreover since they must give account of us to God it would be a disgrace if they were held in no account by us. He goes on to remind us how much their concern benefits us. If the salvation of our souls is precious to us those who watch over it will be by no means worthless. So he commands us to be willing and ready to obey so that our pastors may also gladly and joyfully do what is necessary for their duties. If their spirits are depressed with grief or weariness, even if otherwise they are sincere and faithful, they will become disheartened because their drive will fail at the same time as their cheerfulness. The apostle therefore says that it will be unprofitable for people to bring grief and sorrow to their pastors by their ingratitude, so as to show that we shall be troublesome or disobedient to our pastors only at the risk of our own salvation. Since scarcely one person in ten thinks of this it is clear how generally neglectful we are of our salvation. It is no wonder if today only a few are found who watch zealously for the Church of God. Moreover there are very few like Paul who open their mouths when the ears of the people are closed and who enlarge their own hearts when the heart of the people is straitened. The Lord punishes ingratitude which prevails almost everywhere. Let us therefore remember that we are paying the penalty of our own obstinacy whenever our pastors grow lax in their duties or are less diligent than they ought to be.

213

18. *For we are persuaded.* After he has commended himself to their prayers, in order to encourage them to pray he says that he has a good conscience. Although our prayers, like the love from which they flow, ought to embrace the whole world, it is yet right for us to be particularly concerned for good and holy men, whose integrity or other marks of virtue are known to us. He mentions the honesty of his conscience for the purpose of encouraging them to have a greater concern for him. In saying, I am persuaded, or, I trust, he is showing partly his modesty and partly his faith. The phrase in all, can refer to things as well as to men, and therefore I leave it undecided. He adds the further argument that the prayers which they will make for him will be useful not only to him himself, but to them all, as though he were saying, 'I am not concerned so much for myself as for you because it would be for the common good of all for me to be restored to you.' From this it can be conjectured as a probability that the author of this epistle was either beset by troubles or held back by the fear of persecution from being able to appear in person before those to whom he was writing. On the other hand it could be that he speaks in this way as a free man and unconfined because he regards the ways of men as being in the hand of God. This appears more likely from the end of the epistle.

Now the God of peace, who brought again from the dead the great shepherd of the sheep with the blood of the eternal covenant, even our Lord Jesus, make you perfect in every good thing to do his will, working in us that which is well-pleasing in his sight, through Jesus Christ; to whom be the glory for ever and ever. Amen. But I exhort you, brethren, bear with the word of exhortation: for I have written unto you in few words. Know ye that our brother Timothy hath been set at liberty; with whom, if he come shortly, I shall see you. Salute all them that have the rule over you, and all the saints. They of Italy salute you. Grace be with you all. Amen. (20-25)

Written to the Hebrews from Italy by Timothy.

20. *The God of peace.* To make what he wants them to do mutual, he closes his epistle with a prayer. He asks God to confirm, or to fit, or to perfect them in every good work; that is the force of καταρτίσαι. From this we conclude that we will not be fit to do good until we are formed by God, and that we will not long persist in doing good unless He confirms us. Perseverance is His particular gift. There is no doubt that since it seems that they already shone with unusual gifts of the Spirit, what is desired is not the initial form with which they began but the embellishments which will make them perfect. In laying down the will of God as a rule he gives a definition of good works. He means by

this that works are only thought to be good when they are done according to the will of God, just as Paul says in Rom. 12.2, and in many other passages. Let us therefore remember that the perfection of good and holy living is a life that is set out in obedience to Him. The clause which immediately follows is a development of this. He says, *working in us that which is well-pleasing in his sight.* He had spoken of the will shown forth in the Law, and he now shows that what God has not commanded is thrust upon Him in vain, because He values His own decree more highly than all the inventions of the world.

The words, *through Jesus Christ,* can be explained in two ways; either, 'working through Jesus Christ', or, 'what pleases him through Jesus Christ', and both senses fit very well. We know that the Spirit of regeneration and all graces are conferred on us by the blessing of Christ. It is certain that since we can protect nothing that is perfect in every way, so nothing can be pleasing to God without the pardon which we receive through Christ. Thus it comes about that when our works are suffused with the scent of the grace of Christ, they emit a sweet fragrance before God, whereas otherwise they smell badly. I am inclined to accept both meanings together. The last clause of the prayer, *to whom be glory,* I take as referring to Christ. In attributing to Christ here what belongs to God alone, he gives clear proof of his divinity. On the other hand if anyone prefers to refer this to the Father, I do not disagree, although I would rather take the other sense because it is less strained.

Who brought again from the dead. This description is added in confirmation. He means that we rightly pray God to lead us to perfection when we recognize His power in the resurrection of Christ, and recognize Christ Himself as our Pastor. In short he wants us to look to Christ to have good hope of the help of God. Christ was raised from death so that we might be renewed to eternal life by the same power of God, and is the great Shepherd of all in order to watch over the sheep given to Him by the Father.

What I have translated, 'in the blood', others have rendered, 'through the blood'. Since ⊐ is most often taken as meaning *with,* I prefer to take it here in that sense. The apostle seems to me to mean this, that Christ so rose from the dead that His death was not abolished but keeps its eternal power, as if he had said, that God raised up His Son in such a way that His blood once shed in death has power to ratify the eternal covenant after His resurrection, and brings forth its fruit as though it were always flowing.

22. *But I exhort you.* Some take this as though he were asking them to give him a hearing, but I take it differently. In my opinion he is saying that he had written to them *in a few words* or briefly so as not to

seem as if he wished in any way to lessen their daily practice of teaching. He speaks especially in the form of exhortation which he made more briefly. We must learn from this that Scripture is not given us to silence the voice of the pastors among us, and that we are not to be impatient when the same exhortations keep sounding in our ears. The Spirit of God has so controlled the writings which He dictated to the prophets and apostles as to detract nothing of His instituted ordinance. This ordinance is that exhortations should be constantly heard in the church from the lips of the pastors. Possibly he commends *the word of exhortation* for this reason that since men are by nature anxious to learn, they always prefer to learn something new rather than to hear what is already well known and often heard. There is the further fact that since they indulge their laziness they take badly with being stimulated and reproved.

23. *Know ye that our brother.* Since the ending of the Greek word γινώσκετε can be taken in either sense, it is possible to read either, 'You know', or, 'Know ye'. This latter rendering I prefer, although I do not reject the former. It is probable that he was telling the Jews across the sea what they did not yet know. If this Timothy is the noble companion of Paul (as I am inclined to think) it is probable that Luke or Clement is the writer of this epistle. Paul is more accustomed to call him his son, and further, what immediately follows, does not fit Paul. It is clear that the writer was free and able to do what he liked, and further that he was more likely elsewhere than in Rome, indeed that he was making a tour through various cities and was then preparing to cross the sea. All these points could suit either Luke or Clement after the death of Paul.

24. *Salute.* Since he writes this epistle to all the Hebrews in general, it is surprising that he bids some be greeted, as though they were chosen from the rest. In my opinion he is sending this greeting particularly to the rulers as a mark of honour to win them to himself and to lead them to a more favourable agreement with his teaching. When he adds *all the saints*, he either means that the faithful, both Jews and Gentiles, who were of the circumcision, are to learn to cultivate unity among themselves, or he intends that those who received this letter first are to share it with the others.

The First and Second Epistle of
PETER

DEDICATION

JOHN CALVIN
TO HIS MOST SERENE HIGHNESS
EDWARD THE SIXTH
THE KING OF ENGLAND, THE LORD OF IRELAND,
AND A MOST CHRISTIAN PRINCE

I RETURN to you again, most excellent king, for though I did not expect that the commentaries on Isaiah, which I lately dedicated to your Majesty would be a worthy gift, yet it was offered with the good wishes of my heart. I have, therefore, thought to add the Catholic Epistles* (as it is the accepted usage to call them) as it were to make up a full measure, so that both might come to your hands at the same time. Since they were written either to Gentiles far distant, or to Jews who lived in various far scattered countries, it is no new thing for them to cross the sea today, and make many a long detour to come to your Majesty. Thus as a private individual I offer my labours to you, most illustrious King, so that they may be published under your name, and bring profit to all.

Indeed, if there has ever been a time when the truth of God needed to be freely and boldly maintained, it has never been more necessary than in the present day, as all can see. Leaving out the atrocious cruelty shown everywhere towards its professors, and omitting also all those machinations by which Satan fights against it, here in hidden traps, there with open force of arms, there are places in which the pure doctrine of religion lately prevailed, but where now the satellites of the Roman Antichrist by their spurious maltreatment mock Christ as though they again gave a reed into His hand instead of a sceptre, and placed a crown of thorns on His head. When these crafty corrupters hope that the purity of the Gospel will be gradually extinguished, how cowardly are those who connive at these mockeries offered to Christ, when they ought rather to have hazarded their life a hundred times than to redeem it for a very short time by their perfidious silence?

In the meantime, to complete the last tragedy of crucifying the Son of God, the Pope himself is said to have summoned again his own masked council. Though he marches with his savage band of robbers to obliterate the name of Christ and to strangle His Church, yet every kind of council is to him as a sacred sword, forged for the solemn ritual

* i.e. the First and Second Epistle of Peter, the First Epistle of John and the Epistles of James and Jude.

of sacrifice. Thus, when Paul III had resolved to kill and destroy all who preferred to defend the truth to their own life, he made a show at Trent of that odious spectre, though disguised in fine colours, so that he might put an end to the Gospel as it were by crack of doom. But, when the good fathers had begun to dazzle the eyes of the simple by the gleams of the various sessions, all that preparation vanished in smoke by a secret and sudden blast from the holy seat, except that for the purpose of continuing the terror, a little cloud rested for a time on Bologna.

Julius, his successor, who had performed his part for the first time at Trent, is said to be girding himself now for this stratagem (as though this only thing that remains as a means of obliterating the Gospel from the memory of men is to fulminate against us with the horrible and terrifying decrees of the council) though there are many who think that he is only pretending. It does not matter much whether he is pretending or really means to call a council. The thing is clear and well proved, that since the Papacy began to decline from the time of Luther, whoever occupied that citadel of tyranny, though they might hope to obtain some support from a council (such as they would have) they yet have shunned this kind of remedy in way similar to a sick man who dreads the touch of even the most tender physician because he has sores all over his body. Therefore the saying is common even among children that a council can only help the Papacy by cauterizing or amputation.

I see no cause why the Popes are so afraid of councils, except that fear is an inseparable companion of a bad conscience. For what, I pray, was that recent rabble at Trent (to which they nevertheless gave the name of a holy, general, and ecumenical synod) but a sort of empty apparition, which did not disturb the pleasures of the Pope any more than the sound of the trumpets, or the beating of the drums, with which he daily amuses himself? If a synod from all parts really were assembled, there might be some cause for fear, in case a disturbance might arise in so great a multitude, and occasion a greater tumult. Who can believe that a Pope could be terrified by such fictitious councils as that of Trent, any more than by children's rattles, but that on the contrary he would slumber sweetly on through the blandish-ments of still quieter sleep? Two or three cardinals will be chosen by the Pope from among his bosom friends, who will wield all the authority. The same tyrant will hire from among his courtiers some greedy fellow for a few ducats a month, who will put on the mask of a patriarch, and servilely declare as his own opinion what has been dictated to him. Such was that blind Robert at Trent, whom I saw some time ago at Ratisbon, busying himself as much foolishly as wickedly on behalf of the Pope, when he tried by his inveiglements to draw me into debate with Contarenus. The three-halfpenny bishops, of whom there will be a vast abundance will fly together from all Italy. From France and Spain too, there will come some of the light-headed and fatuitous men, and others infamous for the vices of their former life, who will later return home boasting that they had rendered a good and faithful service to the Catholic Church. From all the caves of monks there will come forth a great conflux of frogs to that marsh, who by their eager croaking will banish far away every truth. What! do I imagine here a new thing, or do I not rather correctly describe the assembly which was lately seen at Trent?

Why is it then that the Pope is afraid of these guardians of his own throne, who are all, in the first place his own servants and slaves, and who in the second place seek nothing but to gain by any means his favour?

Our Julius especially, who is a veteran in this kind of business, can in mockery compose such a council as this whenever he likes, so as to leave the thing undone as usual. Indeed, the fact that he has given the red hat to many of the Dominicans seems to be a public prelude of such an event. This order (so they say) has always been in favour with him, but this profusion is caused for a higher reason. He knows well, that none are more shameless than these beggarly men, as he has often employed at his nod their mean and sordid services. When he raised them again to this dignity, he knew that whatever he might bid them to do wrongly and illegally, none would be more audacious or more cruel than they. He is not unaware of the fact that most of these hungry dogs will rush into any fight he wants with the incentive of the same rewards. I do not say that those who declare that he does not desire a council are mistaken, but when he has arranged his own theatre, some sudden storm will be raised with no great trouble, which will disturb the whole action. Hence, at the very beginning, if his advantage requires it, he will ring down the curtain. He thinks that a council of this kind however empty is like a Hercules' club to lay Christ prostrate, and to break in pieces the remnant of the Church.

When this prince of impiety so wickedly tramples upon the glory of our God and the salvation of men, does it become us by our silence to betray this sacred cause? Certainly not; we ought to undergo a hundred deaths, if that were possible, rather than suffer such unworthy, wicked, and barbarous oppression of sound doctrine to continue unknown through our cowardice.

But let us grant, what is hardly credible, that the Pope and his band do seriously intend to call a council. In that case Christ will not at first sight be assailed by such crude mockery. Indeed the greater the fame of the seriousness and splendour of the Papal council, the more harmful will it be to the Church, and the more dreadful pest it will prove. It cannot possibly be hoped, that an assembly which is assembled under the authority of Antichrist, will be governed by the Spirit, or that the slaves of Satan will exercise any moderation. In the first place the Pope, who is the professed and sworn enemy of Christ, would occupy the chief place of authority. Though he would be careful to pretend to ask the opinions of the Fathers sitting there, yet because they are terrified by his presence they would all follow what would please him alone. In an assembly fully agreeing in every impiety, what need would there be of dissimulation? I have no doubt that every one of the cardinals is like that. In that very college which purports to be a holier senate, there clearly prevails an Epicurean contempt of God, an obstinate hatred of truth, and a rabid fury against all believers. As for the order of bishops, does it not consist nearly of the same monsters, except that many among them are lazy asses, who neither openly despise God, nor hostilely oppose sound doctrine, but are so enamoured with their own depraved state, that they cannot bear any reformation? Add to this the fact that authority will rest almost wholly with the few who are far removed from any concern for true religion, and who will show themselves the keenest supporters of the Roman See; others will make up the number. As every one of these will speak the most terrible things against us, there will be many not only of the lesser ranks, but also of the princes, who will give their agreement either willingly and gladly according to their own inclinations, or from ambition, or from fear.

However, I am not so unjust as not to concede that some of these have a sounder judgment, and are not otherwise ill disposed, but they do not possess enough courage to dare to resist the wickedness of the whole body. Among a thousand there will be, perhaps, two or three wise ones who may dare to give a half-uttered word for Christ (as Peter Paul Vergerius at Trent) but the holy council of the Fathers will have a remedy at hand to prevent them making any further trouble. They will be cast into prison, they will presently be driven to a recantation, they will have to pay the penalty of death for too much freedom of speech, or they will have to drink the cup of perpetual silence.

Such is the justice with which we are treated, that we are untameable and hopelessly perverse heretics, unless we seek from the holy council the rule for proper reformation, and unless we accept without delay its decrees, whatever they may be. We have already given sufficient evidence by clear proofs that we do not shun the authority of a legitimate council (if such could be had), but when they require that we are to bow to the judgment of the chief adversary of Christ without any appeal, and indeed on condition that they should define religion at their will and pleasure, and not by the Word of God, what sense is there in submission, unless we are prepared willingly and knowingly to deny Christ? There is no reason for any one to object that we distrust them before the time. Let them give us a council in which we shall be given free liberty to speak in defence of the cause of truth, and if we refuse to come to that and to give a reason for all that we have done, then they will justly charge us with contumacy. But so far from permission being given us to speak, and express our feelings clearly, there is no doubt that we shall be prevented from making even a suitable defence. How can they listen to the clear-sounding thunders of truth, when their ears cannot bear warnings however mild and conveyed in soft whispers? They publicly do this—they invite us; is it so that they may grant us some place on the lowest seats? Nay, they declare that it is not lawful to admit any one to their sittings except the anointed and the mitred. Then let them sit while we stand, provided we are heard declaring the truth. They answer that they freely promise a hearing; that is, that where we have presented a suppliant petition, and are then ordered to depart at once, after some days of turbulent clamours, we shall be recalled for the purpose of being condemned. I say clamours, not that there will be any altercation of dissidents in that assembly, but that the sacred ears of bishops will be so irreverently offended by us that the indignity will appear to them intolerable. It is well known how tumultuous their violence is. Surely a reasonable determination of a cause can never be obtained from them, when not even a slight hearing can be hoped for.

We shall endeavour to restore God's worship to its purity, and to purge it from the innumerable superstitions by which it has been corrupted. Here the profane orators will chatter about nothing but the institutions and the old rites and ceremonies of the Fathers, as though the Church which has been taught by the celestial ministry of the prophets and of Christ knew no other way of worshipping God than by adopting, with animal stupidity, the dregs of Romulus, made fascinating by the old wives' tales of Numa Pompilius. Where is that simplicity of obedience which the Lord everywhere demands and so distinctly requires?

If the controversy be concerning the depravity of human nature, the miserable and lost state of mankind, the grace and power of Christ, or the free ground of our salvation, they will immediately bring forward the rotten axioms of the schools as mandatory and as things that ought to be received without dispute. The Holy Spirit teaches us in Scripture that our mind is smitten with so much blindness, that the affections of our heart are so depraved and perverted, that our whole nature is so vitiated, that we can do nothing but sin, until he forms a new will within us. He constrains us, who are condemned to eternal death, to renounce all confidence in our own works, and to flee to the mercy of God as our only asylum, and to trust in it for all our righteousness. By inviting us to God, He also testifies that God is reconciled to us only through the merits of the blood of Christ, and bids us to rely on Christ's intercession, and to come boldly to the heavenly judgment seat. Those endless decrees are passed, so that none of these things may be heard, and to violate them is deemed more unlawful than to deny God and all His angels.

They do not permit a word to be said about the sacraments that differs from the notions they entertain. What is this but to preclude the possibility of any reformation? It is easy to show how preposterous and perverted is the administration of the sacraments under the Papacy, so that hardly anything bears any resemblance to the genuine doctrine of Christ. What spurious corruptions have crept in, nay, what disgraceful sacrileges have entered! It is not lawful to move a question on this subject, and hence it is a common saying with theologians, which they have made everywhere in the books they have published, that for the Church to remain safe, special care must be taken that the council should not admit any doubt about the chief controversies of the present day. That feeble book of a certain Mutius has lately been produced in Italian, which in its ignorance breathes nothing but carnage and in which he dwells profusely on this point, that nothing remains to be done by the reverend Fathers, when they meet in council but to pronounce what is already clear to them on the whole subject, and to compel us to subscribe to their sanguinary edicts. I should not indeed have thought it necessary to mention the hoarse chatterings of this unfortunate owl, had not Pope Julius added his brief imprimatur to the work. Readers may judge from this that the sort of council Mutius recommends is to be expected from Julius the approver.

Since we see that these Antichrists rush on with desperate pertinacity in order to destroy sound doctrine, and with equal insolence boldly boast that they will set up a masked council for no other purpose than that they may put the Gospel to flight, and then sing songs of triumph for their own victory, let us also in our turn gather courage to put on the armour of truth and to follow the banner of our leader. If only the pure and simple doctrine of Scripture were to shine forth as it ought, every one who does not refuse to open his eyes would acknowledge the Papacy to be a savage and an execrable monster, made up through Satan's arts of an innumerable mass of errors. We make it evident by the most solid proofs that the glory of God is so scattered by sacrilegious rending among fictitious idols, that hardly a hundredth portion of His right remains to Him. Further, if they do reserve for Him some portion of worship, we can show that no part of it is sincere, but that it is all full of the superstitious inventions of men, and that the law of God is also overwhelmed with similar devices. We bear testimony that miserable consciences are held bound under the yoke of men, rather than ruled by God's commandments, and that they groan and toil under the unjust burden of so many traditions, and are oppressed with a cruel tyranny. We declare that prevaricating obedience can be of no avail except to lead men to a deeper labyrinth. We show clearly from Scripture, that Christ's power under the Papacy is almost abolished, that His grace is in a great measure made void, that unhappy souls are torn away from Him, and inflated with fatal confidence in their own power and works. We prove that prayer to God such as is prescribed by His Word (which is the only true refuge for salvation) is wholly subverted. We show plainly that the sacraments are adulterated partly by extraneous inventions, and partly also are transferred to a foreign purpose, in that the power of the Spirit is impiously tied to them, and what is peculiar to Christ is ascribed to them. Then we disown the number seven, which they have presumptuously adopted. We prove that the Mass, which they imagine to be a sacrifice, is a disgraceful denial of the sacrifice of Christ, and we make it clear that they are guilty of many other sacrifices besides.

If only Scripture were allowed its own authority, there is none of these things about which our adversaries would not be compelled to be silent. This is what they in fact admit, when they contend that owing to the ambiguous meaning of Scripture we ought to stand solely on the judgment of the Church. Who, I pray, does not see, that by laying aside the Word of God the whole right of defining things is thus transferred to them? Though they may kiss the closed copies of the Scripture as a kind of worship, yet when they charge it with being obscure and ambiguous they allow it no more authority than if not a single word of it existed in writing. Let them assume specious titles as they please, so that they do not appear to introduce anything apart from the dictates of the Spirit (as they are accustomed to boast), yet they are firm and settled in their view, their will alone is αὐτόπιστος, and all other reasons are bidden goodbye.

In case the faithful are carried about by every wind of imposture, in case they should be exposed to the crafty scoffings of the ungodly, let them be taught by the sure experience of faith, and know that nothing is more firm or certain than the teaching of Scripture, and on that support let them confidently rest. Since we see that it is shamefully deformed by the false comments of the Sophists, and that today the hired rabble of the Pope are bent on this stratagem, in order to obscure the light by their smoke, it is right for us to be more intent on restoring its brightness.

In an especial manner I have resolved to devote myself to this work as long as I live, if time and opportunity are afforded me. In the first place, the Church to which I belong shall thus receive the fruit of this labour, so that it may hereafter continue longer, for even if only a small portion of time remains to me from the duties of my office, yet that, however small it may be, I have determined to devote to this kind of writing.

To return to you, most illustrious king, you have here a small pledge, my Commentaries on the Catholic Epistles, in which many things which have been thought obscure and recondite, I have tried so to explain that easy access to the true meaning may be open to a reader who is not wholly lazy. As interpreters of Scripture according to their ability supply weapons to fight against Antichrist, so you also must bear in mind that it is a duty which belongs to your Majesty, to vindicate from unworthy calumnies the true and genuine interpretation of Scripture, so that true religion may flourish. It was not without reason that God commanded by Moses, that as soon as a king was appointed over his people, he was to take care to have a copy of the Law written out for himself. Why so, if as a private individual he had already exercised himself diligently in reading it? In order that kings might know that they themselves need this remarkable doctrine, and that it is their special duty to defend and maintain it, the Lord assigns to His Law a sacred habitation in their palaces. Moreover, since the heroic greatness of your mind far surpasses the measure of your age, there is no reason why I should add more words to stimulate you.

Farewell, most noble king. May the Lord continue to preserve your Majesty in His faith as He has already begun, govern you and your counsellors with the Spirit of wisdom and fortitude, and keep your whole kingdom in safety and peace.

Geneva, 24th January, 1551

THE THEME OF THE
FIRST EPISTLE OF PETER

PETER's purpose in this Epistle is to exhort the faithful to a denial and contempt of the world, so that they may be free from carnal affections and all earthly hindrances, and aspire with their whole soul after the celestial kingdom of Christ, and so that being lifted up by hope, supported by patience, and fortified by courage and perseverance, they may overcome all kinds of temptations, and pursue this course and practice throughout life.

Hence at the very beginning he proclaims as fully as he can the grace of God made known to us in Christ, and at the same time he adds that it is received by faith and possessed by hope, so that the godly may lift up their minds and hearts above the world. Then he exhorts them to holiness, in case they render void the price by which they were redeemed, and in case they allow the incorruptible seed of the Word, by which they have been regenerated to eternal life, to be destroyed or to die. Because he had said that they had been born again by God's Word, he makes mention of their spiritual infancy. Moreover, in order that their faith may not vacillate or falter, because they see that Christ is despised and rejected almost by the whole world, he reminds them that this was only the fulfilment of what had been written of Him, that He would be the stone of stumbling. He goes on to teach them that He would be a firm foundation to those who believe in Him. From this he again refers to the great honour to which God has raised them, so that they may be enlivened by the contemplation of their former state, and by the sense of their present benefits, to devote themselves to a godly life.

He afterwards comes to particular exhortations—that they are to conduct themselves humbly and obediently under the government of princes, that servants are to be subject to their masters, that wives are to obey their husbands and behave themselves modestly and with chastity, and that in their turn husbands are to treat their wives with kindness. He then commands them to follow what is just and right towards one another, and so that they will do this more willingly he sets before them what will be the fruit, a peaceful and happy life.

Because it is the lot of Christians that, however much they seek peace, they are often harassed by many injuries and face a world that is hostile to them for no just cause, he exhorts them to bear their persecutions with equanimity, which they know will promote their salvation. For this purpose he adduces the example of Christ. On the other hand, he reminds them what an unhappy end awaits the ungodly, whilst in the meantime God wonderfully delivers His Church from death by death. He further refers to the example of Christ to illustrate the mortification of the flesh. To this exhortation he adds various brief sentences, but shortly after he returns to the doctrine of patience, so that the faithful may temper the evils that they suffer by recalling in consolation that it is good for them to be chastised by the fatherly hand of God.

At the beginning of the fifth chapter he reminds the elders (*seniores*) of their duty, that they are not to tyrannize over the Church, but to preside humbly under Christ. He recommends to the young modesty and teachableness. Finally, after adding a short exhortation, he closes the Epistle with a prayer.

There is no agreement about the place from which he wrote, but I see no reason why we should doubt that he was then at Babylon, as he expressly declares. As the conviction had prevailed that he had moved from Antioch to Rome, and that he died at Rome, the ancients on this argument alone imagined that Rome is here allegorically called Babylon. As they have rashly believed what they have said of the Roman episcopate of Peter without any likelihood in the conjecture, this allegorical figment ought to be disregarded. It is much more probable that consistently with the character of his apostleship Peter travelled over those parts in which most of the Jews resided, and we know that a great number of them were in Babylon and in the surrounding countries.

CHAPTER ONE

Peter, an apostle of Jesus Christ, to the elect who are sojourners of the Dispersion in Pontus, Galatia, Cappadocia, Asia, and Bithynia, according to the foreknowledge of God the Father, in sanctification of the Spirit, unto obedience and sprinkling of the blood of Jesus Christ: Grace to you and peace be multiplied. (1-2)

1. *Peter, an apostle.* What this salutation has in common with those of Paul needs no new explanation. When Paul prays for *grace* and *peace*, the verb is left out, but Peter adds it, in the words *be multiplied*, but the meaning is the same. Paul did not desire the beginning of grace and peace for believers but the increase of them until God completes what He has begun.

To the elect. It may be asked, how this could be found out, as the election of God is a mystery and cannot be known except by special revelation of the Spirit. As everyone is made sure of his own election by the testimony of the Spirit, so he can know nothing certain about that of others. I reply that we are not to inquire anxiously about the election of our brethren, but ought rather to have regard to their calling, so that all who are admitted by faith into the Church are to be thought of as the elect. God separates them from the rest of the world, which is the sign of election. It is no objection to say that many fall away, having nothing but the appearance of election, for it is the judgment of charity and not of faith to consider as elect all those in whom the mark of divine adoption appears. It is clear from the context that he does not find their election in the hidden counsel of God, but deduces it from the effect, for soon afterwards he connects it with the *santification of the Spirit.* As far, then, as they showed that they were regenerate by the Spirit of God, he numbers them among the elect of God, because God does not sanctify any but those whom He has previously elected.

At the same time, however, he reminds us of the source of that election, by which we are separated for salvation, so that we do not perish with the world, for he says, *according to the foreknowledge of God.* This, I say, is the fountain and the first cause. God knew before the world was created those whom He had elected for salvation.

We must consider carefully the nature of this foreknowledge. In order to obscure the grace of God the sophists imagine that the merits of each are foreseen by God, and that thus the reprobate are distinguished from the elect, as each one proves himself worthy of this or that fate; but everywhere Scripture sets the counsel of God, on which our salvation is founded, in opposition to our merits. Hence, when Peter calls them elect *according to the foreknowledge of God*, he is showing that the cause of it depends simply on God alone, because He of His own free will has chosen us. Thus the foreknowledge of God excludes every worthiness on the part of man. We have treated this subject more fully in the first chapter of the Epistle to the Ephesians, and in other places.

Although he assigns an election in the first place to the gratuitous favour of God, at the same time he would have us know it by the effects, for there is nothing more dangerous or more absurd than to overlook our calling and to seek for the certainty of our election in the hidden foreknowledge of God, which is a very deep labyrinth. Therefore to obviate this danger, Peter supplies the best correction. Although in the first place he would have us consider the counsel of God, the cause of which is solely in Himself, yet he recalls to us the effect, by which he sets forth and bears witness to our election. That effect is the sanctification of the Spirit, that is, effectual calling, when faith which is born of the inward operation of the Spirit is added to the outward preaching of the Gospel.

To the sojourners. Those who think that all the godly are so called, because they are strangers in the world, and are going on metaphorically towards the celestial country, are greatly mistaken, and this mistake can be refuted by the word *dispersion* which immediately follows. This can apply only to the Jews, not only because they were banished from their own country and scattered here and there, but also because they had been driven out of that land which had been promised to them by the Lord as a perpetual inheritance. Indeed he later calls all the faithful sojourners, because they are pilgrims on the earth; but the reason here is different. They were sojourners, because they had been dispersed, some in Pontus, some in Galatia, and some in Bithynia. It is no wonder that he designed this Epistle especially for the Jews, because he knew that he was appointed to be their apostle, as Paul teaches in Gal. 2.8. In the countries which he enumerates he includes the whole of Asia Minor, from the Euxine Sea to Cappadocia.

Unto obedience. He adds two things to sanctification, and seems by *obedience* to understand newness of life, and by the *sprinkling* of the blood of Christ the remission of sins. If these are parts or effects of santification, then sanctification is to be taken here somewhat differently from what it often means when used by Paul, that is, more generally. God, then, sanctifies us by an effectual calling, and this happens when we are renewed to an obedience to His righteousness, and when we are sprinkled by the blood of Christ, and thus cleansed from our sins. There seems to be an implied allusion to the ancient rite of sprinkling used under the Law. As it was not then sufficient for the victim to be slain and the blood sprinkled, so now the blood of Christ which has been shed will avail us nothing, unless our consciences are cleansed by it. There is therefore a contrast to be understood here; that, as formerly under the Law the sprinkling of blood was done by the hand of the priest, so now the Holy Spirit sprinkles our souls with the blood of Christ for the expiation of our sins.

Let us now sum up. Our salvation flows from the gratuitous election of God, but it is to be regarded by our experience of faith, because He sanctifies us by His Spirit. There are two effects or ends for our calling, namely, renewal into obedience of God and ablution by the blood of Christ; and further, both are the work of the Holy Spirit. Hence we conclude that election is not to be separated from calling, nor the gratuitious righteousness of faith from newness of life.

Blessed be the God and Father of our Lord Jesus Christ, who according to his great mercy begat us again unto a living hope by the resurrection of Jesus Christ from the dead, unto an inheritance incorruptible, and undefiled, and that fadeth not away, reserved in heaven for you, who by the power of God are guarded through faith unto a salvation ready to be revealed in the last time. (3-5)

3. *Blessed be God.* We have said that it is the main object of this epistle to raise us above the world, in order that we may be prepared and encouraged for the battle of our spiritual warfare. For this purpose the knowledge of God's benefits is of great help, for, when we appreciate their value, all other things will become worthless, and especially, when we consider what Christ and His blessings are, everything without Him will seem but dross. It is for this reason that he highly extols the wonderful grace of God in Christ, so that we may not think it hard to give up the world in order to enjoy the priceless treasure of future life; and also so that we may not be broken by our present troubles, but patiently endure them, being satisfied with eternal happiness. Further, when he gives thanks to God, he invites the faithful to spiritual joy, which swallows up all contrary feelings of the flesh.

And Father of our Lord Jesus Christ. We must understand the words thus—'God, who is the Father of Jesus Christ.' As formerly He marked the difference between Him and all fictitious gods by calling Himself the God of Abraham, so now after He has manifested Himself in His own Son, He wills to be known only in Him. Hence those who conceive of God in His naked majesty apart from Christ have an idol instead of the true God, as the case is with the Jews and the Turks.

Whoever then seeks really to know the true God must regard Him
as the Father of Christ, for, whenever our mind seeks God, unless it
meets Christ it will wander and be confused, until it is wholly lost.
Peter meant at the same time to show how God is so bountiful and
kind towards us, for, unless Christ stands in between as Mediator, His
goodness could never be really known by us.

Who hath begotten us again. He means that supernatural life is a gift,
because we are born the children of wrath. If we had been born to the
hope of life according to the flesh, there would have been no necessity
of our being born again by God. Therefore Peter teaches us that we,
who are by nature destined to eternal death, are restored to life by
God's mercy. This is, as it were, our second creation, as it is put in the
first chapter of the Epistle to the Ephesians. *Lively hope* means 'the
hope of life', although there seems to be an implied contrast between
the hope fixed on the incorruptible kingdom of God, and the fading
and transient hopes of man.

According to his abundant mercy. He first mentions the efficient cause,
and then he points out the mediating cause (as they put it). He shows
that God was not induced by any merits of ours to regenerate us to a
living hope because he attributes this wholly to His mercy. In order
more completely to reduce the merits of works to nothing he says,
great mercy. All, indeed, confess that God is the sole Author of our
salvation, but afterwards they invent extraneous causes, which detract
to that extent from His mercy. Peter commends mercy alone; and he
immediately adds the means, namely, *by the resurrection of Christ.* God
does not show His mercy in any other way or elsewhere; hence
Scripture always directs our attention to this point. The fact that
Christ's death is not mentioned, but only His resurrection, involves no
inconsistency. It is included, because a thing cannot be finished without having a beginning, and he has especially adduced the resurrection,
because he was speaking of a new life.

4. *To an inheritance.* The three adjectives which follow are intended
to amplify God's grace. Peter (as I have already said) is endeavouring
to impress our minds well and truly with its excellency. Moreover,
these two clauses, 'to an inheritance incorruptible', and 'to salvation
ready to be revealed', I take as being in apposition, the latter being explanatory of the former; for he expresses the same thing in two ways.

Every word which follows has due weight. The inheritance is said
to be reserved in heaven so that we may know that it is beyond the
reach of danger. If it were not in God's hand, it would be exposed to
endless dangers. If it were in this world, how could we regard it
without qualms amidst so many changes? In order, therefore, to free
us from all fear, he maintains that our salvation is placed in safety

beyond the harms which Satan can do. Since the certainty of salvation can bring us little comfort, unless each one of us knows that it belongs to himself, Peter adds, *for you*. Our consciences will rest calmly when the Lord cries to them from heaven, 'Behold, your salvation is in My hand and is kept for you.' Since salvation is not indiscriminately for all, he calls our attention back to faith, so that all who are endued with faith may be distinguished from the rest, and may have no doubt that they are the true and legitimate heirs of the kingdom of God. As faith penetrates right to the heavens, so also it appropriates to us the blessings which are in heaven.

5. *Who are kept by the power of God*. We must note the connexion in his saying that we are kept while in the world, and at the same time our inheritance is reserved in heaven. Otherwise the thought would immediately creep in, 'What help is it to us that our salvation is laid up in heaven, when we are tossed here and there in this world as in a stormy sea? What help is it to us that our salvation is secured in a quiet harbour, when we are driven to and fro among a thousand ship-wrecks?' The apostle, therefore, anticipates objections of this kind, when he shows that though we are exposed to dangers in the world we are yet kept by faith, and that though we are thus near to death we are yet safe under the guardianship of faith. As faith itself through the infirmity of the flesh often quails, we would always be anxious about the morrow, if the Lord did not help us.

We see indeed that under the Papacy a diabolical opinion prevails that our final perseverance is doubtful because we are uncertain whether tomorrow we shall be in the same state of grace. But Peter does not leave us in suspense like this. He maintains that we stand by the power of God, in case any doubt arising from a consciousness of our own infirmity should disquiet us. However weak we may be, our salvation is not uncertain, because it is sustained by God's power. As, then, we are sustained by faith, so faith itself receives its stability from God's power. Hence its security is not only for the present, but also for the future.

Unto salvation. As we are by nature impatient of delay, and soon succumb to weariness, he reminds us that salvation is not deferred because it is not yet prepared, but because the proper time of its revelation is not yet come. This doctrine is intended to nourish and sustain our hope. Moreover, he calls the day of judgment *the last time*, because the restoration of all things is not to be expected before then, for the intervening time is still in progress. What is elsewhere called the last time, that is the whole period from the coming of Christ, is so called by comparison with the preceding ages. Peter however had a regard to the whole cycle of the world.

Wherein ye greatly rejoice, though now for a little while, if need be, ye have been put to grief in manifold temptations, that the proof of your faith, being more precious than gold that perisheth though it is proved by fire, might be found unto praise and glory and honour at the revelation of Jesus Christ: whom not having seen ye love; on whom, though now ye see him not, yet believing, ye rejoice greatly with joy unspeakable and full of glory: receiving the end of your faith, even the salvation of your souls. (6-9)

6. *Wherein ye greatly rejoice.* Although the ending of the Greek verb is doubtful, yet the meaning requires that we read, 'ye exult', rather than 'exult ye'. *In which* refers to the whole subject of the hope of salvation laid up in heaven. He rather exhorts than praises them, for his purpose is to show what fruit was to come from the hope of salvation, to wit, spiritual joy, by which not only the bitterness of all evil is mitigated, but also all sorrow overcome. The word exult is more expressive than 'rejoice'.

It seems somewhat inconsistent when he says that the faithful, who exult with joy, are at the same time sorrowful, for these are contrary feelings, but the faithful know by experience that these things can exist together much better than can be expressed in words. However, to explain the matter in a few words, it may be put thus: the faithful are not logs of wood, nor have they so divested themselves of human feelings as to be unaffected by sorrow, unafraid of danger, unhurt by poverty, and untouched by hard and unbearable persecutions. Hence they experience sorrow because of evils, but it is so mitigated by faith that they never cease at the same time to rejoice. Thus sorrow does not prevent their joy, but rather gives place to it.

Again, though joy overcomes sorrow, yet it does not put an end to it, because it does not divest us of humanity. Hence it is clear what true patience is. Its beginning, and, as it were, its root, is the recognition of God's blessings, especially when we think of that gratuitous adoption with which He has favoured us. All those who put their minds to this find it an easy thing to bear all evils calmly. How does it come about that our minds are pressed down with grief, unless because it is that we have no taste for spiritual things? All those who regard their troubles as necessary trials for their salvation, not only rise above them, but also turn them to an occasion for joy.

Ye are in heaviness. Is not sorrow also the common lot of the reprobate, for are they not free from evils? But Peter meant that the faithful endure sorrow willingly, while the ungodly murmur and perversely strive with God. Hence the godly bear sorrow as a tamed ox submits to the yoke, or as a broken-in horse to the bridle, even when held by a child. God afflicts the reprobate with sorrow, as a bridle is put in the mouth of a ferocious and refractory horse by force. He kicks and offers resistance, but all in vain. Then Peter commends the faithful, because they undergo sorrow willingly, and not as being forced by necessity.

The words *though now for a season* give consolation, for however hard evils may be, the shortness of time does little to lessen them, and the duration of the present life is like a moment of time. *If need be.* The condition is to be taken for a cause, for his purpose was to show that God does not thus try His people without reason, for if God afflicted us without a cause, it would be grievous to bear. Hence Peter has taken an argument for consolation from the design of God, not because the purpose always appears to us, but because we ought to be fully persuaded that it ought to be so, because it is God's will.

We must notice that he does not mention one temptation, but many; and not temptations of one kind, but *manifold temptations*. It is better, however, to look for the exposition of this passage in the first chapter of James.

7. *Much more precious than of gold*. The argument is from the less to the greater. If we think so much of gold, a corruptible metal, that we prove it by fire, so that it may acquire its real value, what wonder is it that God should require a similar trial in our faith, since faith has such excellence in His eyes? Though the words seem to have a different meaning, he yet compares faith to gold, and makes it more precious than gold, in order to draw the conclusion that it is worth being fully proved. It is moreover uncertain how far he extends the meaning of the verb δοκιμάζεσθαι and the noun δοκίμιον. Gold is, indeed, tried twice over by fire; first when it is separated from its dross, and then, when a judgment is to be formed of its purity. Both methods of trial may very suitably be applied to faith, for when there are many dregs of unbelief remaining in us, and when by various afflictions we are refined as it were in God's furnace, the dross of our faith is removed, so that it becomes pure and clean before God. At the same time a trial of it is made as to whether it is true or fictitious. I am inclined to take both these views, and what immediately follows seems to favour this explanation. As silver has no value before it is refined, so he means that our faith is not to be honoured and crowned by God until it is duly proved.

At the appearing of Jesus Christ. This is added so that the faithful may learn to hold on courageously to the last day, for our life is now hidden in Christ, and will remain hidden, as if it were buried, until Christ shall appear from heaven, and the whole course of our life leads to the destruction of the external man, and all the things we suffer are, as it were, the preludes of death. It is hence necessary that we should turn our eyes to Christ if we wish to see glory and praise in our afflictions. Our trials are full of reproach and shame for us but they become glorious in Christ. That glory in Christ is not yet plainly seen, for the day of consolation has not yet come.

8. *Whom having not seen.* He lays down two things; that they love Christ whom they have not seen, and that they believe on Him whom they do not behold. The first arises from the second. The cause of love is faith, not only because the knowledge of those blessings which Christ bestows on us moves us to love Him in return but because by offering us perfect happiness He draws us to Himself. He therefore commends the Jews, because they believe in Christ whom they did not see, that they might know that it is the nature of faith to be satisfied with blessings which are hid from our eyes. They had indeed some proof of this very thing, though he teaches them rather by exhortation.

The first clause in his sequence of thought is that faith is not to be measured by sight for since the life of Christians is to all appearances miserable, they would at once fail, unless their happiness depended on hope. Faith, indeed, has also its eyes, but they are such as penetrate into the invisible kingdom of God, and are contented with the mirror of the Word, for it is the demonstration of invisible things, as it is put in Heb. 11.1. Hence the truth of the expression of Paul that we are absent from the Lord while we are in the flesh, for we walk by faith and not by sight (II Cor. 5.6, 7).

The second clause is, that faith is not a cold notion, but one that kindles in our hearts love to Christ. Faith does not (as the sophists say) lay hold on God in a confused and complicated manner (for this would be to wander through devious paths); but it has Christ as its goal. Moreover, it does not lay hold on the bare name or essence of Christ, but thinks of what He is to us, and what blessings He brings, because it must be the case that human affliction is led to where a man's happiness is, according to the text 'Where your treasure is, there is also your heart' (Matt. 6.21).

Ye rejoice. He again refers to the fruit of faith which he had mentioned, and not without reason. It is an incomparable benefit not only that our consciences are at peace before God, but that we confidently rejoice in the hope of eternal life. He calls it *joy unspeakable* because the peace of God surpasses all comprehension. The addition *full of glory* admits of two explanations. It means either what is magnificent and glorious, or what is contrary to that which is empty and fading, of which men will soon be ashamed. Thus 'glorified' has the same meaning as that which is solid and permanent, beyond the danger of being brought to nothing. Those who are not carried up above the heavens by this joy, so that they are content with Christ alone and despise the world, boast in vain that they have faith.

9. *Receiving the end of your faith.* He reminds the faithful where they ought to direct all their thoughts, namely to eternal salvation. This world holds all our affections ensnared by its allurements. This life and everything belonging to the body are great hindrances preventing us from applying our minds to the contemplation of the future and spiritual life. Hence the Apostle sets before us this future life as a subject of deep meditation, and he indicates by implication that the loss of all other things is to be reckoned unimportant, provided our souls be saved. By saying *receiving*, he takes away all doubt, in order that they may go on more cheerfully in the certainty of obtaining salvation. In the meantime, however, he shows what the end of faith is, so that they should not be over-anxious, because it is as yet deferred. Our adoption ought to satisfy us at present, and we ought not to ask to be given the possession of our inheritance before the time. We may also take *the end* as meaning reward in the same sense. We learn from the Apostle's words that salvation is obtained only by faith, and we know that faith relies on the promise of gratuitous adoption alone. If it be so, then doubtless salvation is not on account of the merits of works, nor is it to be hoped for from that source.

Why then does he mention *souls* only, when the glory of resurrection is promised also to our bodies? As the soul is immortal, salvation is properly ascribed to it, as Paul sometimes is accustomed to say—'That the soul may be saved in the day of the Lord' (I Cor. 5.5). It is the same as though he had said 'Eternal salvation'. There is an implied comparison with the mortal, fading life which belongs to the body. At the same time, the body is not excluded from participation in glory in so far as it is connected to the soul.

Concerning which salvation the prophets sought and searched diligently, who prophesied of the grace that should come unto you: searching what time or what manner of time the Spirit of Christ which was in them did point unto, when it testified beforehand the sufferings of Christ, and the glories that should follow them. To whom it was revealed, that not unto themselves, but unto you, did they minister these things, which now have been announced unto you through them that preached the gospel unto you by the Holy Ghost sent forth from heaven; which things angels desire to look into. (10-12)

He commends the value of salvation from the fact that the prophets had their minds intently fixed on it. It must have been a great matter, and one of peculiar excellency, which could have kindled in the prophets such a spirit of inquiry. God's goodness toward us shines forth still more clearly because much more is now made known to us than what all the prophets attained by their long and careful inquiries. At the same time he confirms the certainty of salvation by this very antiquity since from the beginning of the world it has received a clear testimony from the Holy Spirit.

These two things ought to be distinctly noticed: he declares that more has been given to us than to the fathers of old, in order by this comparison to amplify the grace of the Gospel; and secondly that what is proclaimed to us about our salvation cannot be suspected of any novelty, for the Spirit has already testified to it by the prophets. Therefore when he says that the prophets searched and diligently inquired, this does not refer to their writings or doctrine, but to the private desire with which every one was filled. What follows is to be taken as referring to their public office.

In order that each particular may be more evident, the passage must be arranged under certain propositions. The first is this—that the prophets who foretold the grace which Christ showed at his coming diligently inquired as to the time when full revelation would be made. The second is that the Spirit of Christ predicted through them the future condition of Christ's kingdom, partly as it is at present seen, and partly as it is expected to be, namely that it is destined that Christ and His whole body should through manifold sufferings enter into glory. The third is that the prophets have ministered to us more richly than to their own age, and that this has been revealed to them from above, because in Christ alone is the full revelation of those things of which God at that time presented only a faint image. The fourth is that not only is there a clear confirmation of prophetic doctrine contained in the Gospel, since it is the same Spirit which speaks, but also a much fuller and plainer explanation, because the salvation which He formerly proclaimed at a distance by the prophets He now reveals openly to us, and as it were before our eyes. The last proposition is that it is made clear from this how wonderful is the glory of the salvation promised to us in the Gospel, because even the very angels, though they enjoy God's presence in heaven, burn with the desire of seeing it. All these things tend to show this one thing, that Christians, elevated to the height of happiness, ought to surmount all the obstacles of the world. What is there which this incomparable benefit does not reduce to nothing?

10. *Of which salvation.* Did not the fathers have the same salvation as we have? Why then does he say that the fathers *inquired*, as if they did not possess what is today offered to us? The answer to this is plain, that salvation is to be taken here in the sense of that clear manifestation

of it which we have reached through the coming of Christ. These words of Peter mean simply the same as those of Christ when he said, 'Many kings and prophets have desired to see the things which ye see, and have not seen them. Blessed therefore are your eyes' etc. (Matt. 13.17) Therefore since the prophets had but a limited experience of the grace brought by Christ, as far as revelation was concerned they rightly desired something more. When Simeon, after seeing Christ, prepared himself calmly and with a quiet mind for death, he showed that he had previously been dissatisfied and anxious. Such was the feeling of all the godly.

He points out the nature of their inquiry when he adds, *Searching what, or what manner of time.* There was a difference between the Law and the Gospel, as if there were a veil between them, so that they might not see more closely the things that are now revealed to our eyes. Indeed, it was not proper that while Christ, the Sun of righteousness, was not yet there the full light should shine as at mid-day. Though of necessity they had to confine themselves within the prescribed limits, yet it was no superstition to sigh with the desire to have a closer view. In wishing for redemption to be hastened, and desiring daily to see it, there was nothing in such a wish to prevent them patiently waiting as long as it pleased the Lord to postpone the time. Moreover, to seek particular time in prophecies seems to me unprofitable. What is spoken of here is not what the prophets taught, but what they wished. Where the Latin interpreters render, 'of future grace', the words mean literally, 'of the grace which is towards you'. But as the meaning remains the same, I have not been disposed to make any change.

It is more worth observing that he does not say that the prophets searched according to their own understanding for the moment of time when Christ's kingdom would come, but that they applied their minds to the revelation of the Spirit. Thus they have taught us by their example a sobriety in learning, for they did not go beyond what the Spirit taught them. Certainly there will be no limits to human curiosity, unless the Spirit of God governs their minds, so that they do not desire anything but to learn from Him. Further, the spiritual kingdom of Christ is something higher than the human mind can succeed in investigating, unless it has the Spirit as its guide. We must also therefore submit to His guidance.

11. *The Spirit of Christ which was in them.* First, '*who was in them*', and secondly, '*testifying*', that is, 'giving a testimony', by which expression he means that the prophets were endued with the Spirit of knowledge, and that in no ordinary way, as those who have been our teachers and witnesses, and that yet they did not share in that light

which is made clear to us. At the same time high praise is given to their doctrine, for it was the testimony of the Holy Spirit. Although the preachers and ministers were men, He was the Teacher. He does not say without reason that the Spirit of Christ then ruled, and he makes the Spirit, sent from heaven, the Lord of the teachers of the Gospel. He shows that the Gospel has come from God, and that the ancient prophecies were dictated by Christ.

The sufferings of Christ. In order that they may bear with greater equanimity their afflictions, he reminds them that they had been long ago foretold by the Spirit, but he includes much more than this. He teaches us that the government of the Church of Christ has been so divinely constituted from the beginning that the Cross has been the way to victory, death the way to life, and that this had been clearly testified. There is, therefore, no reason why afflictions should unreasonably depress us, as though we were miserable under them, since the Spirit of God declares us blessed.

The order is to be noticed. He mentions sufferings first, and then adds the glories which are to follow. He means that this order cannot be changed or subverted, but rather afflictions must precede glory. A twofold truth is therefore to be understood in these words, that Christians must suffer many troubles before they enjoy glory, and that afflictions are not evils, because they have glory attached to them. Since God has ordained this connexion, it is not for us to separate one from the other. It is unique consolation, that our condition, such as we find it to be, has been foretold so many ages ago.

From this we conclude that it is not in vain that a happy issue is promised to us. Again we further conclude that we are not afflicted by chance, but by the sure providence of God, and lastly, that prophecies are like mirrors setting forth to us in tribulations the image of celestial glory.

Peter, indeed, says that the Spirit had testified of the coming afflictions of Christ, but he does not separate Christ from His body. This, then, is not to be confined to the person of Christ, but a beginning is to be made with the Head, so that the members may follow in due order, as Paul also teaches us, that we must be conformed to Him who is the Firstborn among His brethren (Rom. 8.29). In short, Peter does not speak of what is peculiar to Christ, but is describing the universal state of the Church. It is much more relevant in confirming our faith, when he sets forth our afflictions as viewed in Christ, for we thereby see better the connexion of death and life between us and Him. Certainly it is the privilege and manner of the holy union, that He suffers daily in His members, so that after His sufferings have been completed in us, glory also may have its completion. See further on this subject in the third chapter of the Epistle to the Colossians, and in the fourth of the first Epistle to Timothy.

12. *Unto whom it was revealed.* This passage has been strangely perverted by fanatics, so as to exclude the fathers, who lived under the Law, from the hope of eternal salvation. It does not deny that the prophets usefully ministered to their own age, and edified the Church, but teaches us that their ministry is more useful to us, because we have fallen on the ends of the world. We see how highly they extolled the kingdom of Christ, how assiduous they were in adorning it, how diligently they encouraged all to seek it, but they were deprived by death of seeing it as it now is. What else was this, but a spreading of the table, so that others might afterwards feed on the food laid on it? They indeed by faith tasted those things which the Lord has passed on by their hands to us to enjoy, and they also partook of Christ as the real food of their souls. What is spoken of now is the showing forth of this. We know that the prophetic office was confined as it were within limits, in order that they might support themselves and others with the hope of the coming Christ. They therefore possessed Him as one hidden, and as it were absent; I say absent not in power of grace, but because He was not yet manifested in the flesh. Therefore His kingdom also was as yet hid as it were under coverings. In descending to earth, He in a manner opened heaven to us, so that we might have a near view of those spiritual riches, which before were exhibited under types at a distance. This fruition of Christ as manifested discloses the difference between us and the prophets. From this we learn how they ministered to us rather than to themselves.

Though the prophets were told from above that the grace which they proclaimed would be deferred to another age, yet they were not slow in proclaiming it, so far were they from being tired with waiting. If their patience was so great, we should certainly be twice and three times ungrateful, if the enjoyment of the grace denied to them does not sustain us under all the evils which are to be endured.

Which are now reported to you. He again marks the difference between ancient doctrine and the preaching of the Gospel. As the righteousness of God is revealed in the Gospel, having a testimony from the Law and the prophets, so also the glory of Christ, of which the Spirit testified formerly, is now openly proclaimed. At the same time he proves from this the certainty of the Gospel, because it contains nothing but what had been long ago testified by the Spirit of God. He further reminds them, that it was under the auspices of the same Spirit and by His dictation and guidance that the Gospel was preached, in case they might think of anything human here.

Which things the angels desire to look into. It is indeed the highest praise to the Gospel, that it contains treasures of wisdom, as yet concealed and hidden from angels. But someone may object, that it is not reasonable that things should be open and known to us which are hidden from angels, who always see the face of God and are His ministers in ruling the Church, and in the administration of all His blessings. To this I answer that these things are open to us in so far as we see them in the mirror of the Word, but our knowledge is not said to be higher than that of angels. Peter only means that such things are promised to us as angels desire to see fulfilled. Paul says (Eph. 3.8-10) that by the calling of the Gentiles the won derful wisdom of God was made known to angels. It was a new sight for them, when Christ gathered into one body the lost world, which had been alienated for so many ages from the hope of life. Thus they see daily with admiration the wonderful works of God in the government of His Church. How much greater will their wonder be at seeing the final display of divine justice, goodness and wisdom, when the kingdom of Christ is completed. This revelation which they still expect and justly wish to see, is hidden.

The meaning of this passage can be twofold, either that the treasure we have in the Gospel fills the angels with a desire to see it, because it is a spectacle which gives them the greater joy; or that they anxiously desire to see the kingdom of Christ, the living image of which is set forth in the Gospel. This latter seems to me to be the most suitable meaning.

Wherefore girding up the loins of your mind, be sober and set your hope perfectly on the grace that is to be brought unto you at the revelation of Jesus Christ; as children of obedience, not fashioning yourselves according to your former lusts in the time of your ignorance: but like as he which called you is holy, be ye yourselves also holy in all manner of living; because it is written, Ye shall be holy; for I am holy. (13-16)

From the greatness and excellency of grace he draws an exhortation, that it was their duty to receive the grace of God more readily, as the more bountifully He bestows it upon them. We must notice the context. He had said that the kingdom of Christ, to which the Gospel calls us, was so high that even angels in heaven desire to see it. What ought we who are in the world to do? Surely, as long as we live on earth the distance between us and Christ is so great that He invites us to Himself in vain. It is therefore necessary for us to put off the image of Adam and to cast aside the whole world and all hindrances, so that being thus set at liberty we may rise upwards to Christ. He exhorts those to whom he writes to be prepared and sober, and to hope for the grace offered to them, and also to renounce the world and their former life, and to be conformed to God.

The first part of the exhortation is, therefore, to gird up the loins of their mind and to direct their thoughts to the hope of grace which is given them. In the second part, he defines the manner, so that their minds may be changed and they may be conformed to the image of God.

13. *Wherefore gird up the loins of your mind.* This is a metaphor taken from an ancient custom. Since they had long garments, they could not make a journey, nor conveniently do any work, without being girded up. Hence these expressions, to gird up oneself for work or for an undertaking. He therefore bids them remove all hindrances, so that they may be set free and go on to God. Those who philosophize too subtly about the loins, as though he were commanding that lusts ought to be restrained and checked, depart from the real meaning of the Apostle, for these words mean the same as those of Christ, 'Let your loins be girded about, and your lamps burning in your hands' (Luke 12.35), except that Peter doubles the metaphor by ascribing loins to the mind. He means that our minds are held entangled by the passing cares of the world and by vain desires, so that they do not rise up to God. Therefore anyone who really wants to have this hope must learn in the first place to disentangle himself from the world, and gird up his mind so that he does not turn aside to vain affections. For the same reason he enjoins sobriety, which immediately follows. He commends not only temperance in eating and drinking, but rather spiritual sobriety, when we contain all our thoughts and affections so as not to be inebriated with the allurements of this world. Since even the least taste of them draws us away stealthily from God, when anyone plunges himself into these, he must of necessity become sleepy and stupid, and he forgets the things of God.

Hope to the end. He implies that those who let their minds loose on vanity do not really and sincerely hope for the grace of God as they should. Though they had some hope of grace, yet as they vacillated and were tossed to and fro in the world, there was no solidity in their hope. Then he says, *for the grace that is to be brought to you,* so that they may be more quick to receive it. God may be sought far off, but He comes of His own will to meet us. How great, then, is our ingratitude if we neglect the grace that is thus graciously set before us! This amplification is especially intended to stimulate our hope.

The addition, *at the revelation of Jesus Christ,* may be explained in two ways: that the doctrine of the Gospel reveals Christ to us; and that, as we see Him yet only through a glass and enigmatically full revelation is put off to the last day. The former meaning is preferred by Erasmus, and I do not reject it. The second seems, however, to be more suitable to the passage. The object of Peter is to call us away beyond the world, and for this purpose the most fitting thing was the remembrance of Christ's coming. If we direct our eyes to this, this world is crucified to us, and we to the world. Besides, Peter has used the expression shortly before with this meaning. It is no new thing for the apostles to employ the preposition ἐν in the sense of εἰς. So I explain the passage thus—'You have no need to make a long journey to attain the grace of God, for God anticipates you, inasmuch as He brings it to you.' But as the fruition of it will not be until Christ appears from heaven, for in Him is hid the salvation of the godly, there is need in the meantime for hope, since the grace of Christ is offered to us now in vain, if we do not patiently wait until the coming of Christ.

14. *As obedient children.* He means first of all that we are called by the Lord through the Gospel to the privilege and honour of adoption, and, secondly, that we are adopted on the ground that He should in turn have us as His obedient children. Although obedience does not make us His children, since the gift of adoption is gratuitous, yet it distinguishes children from foreigners. How far this obedience extends is shown by Peter when he forbids God's children to conform to or to comply with the desires of this world, and when he exhorts them rather to conform to the will of God. The sum of the whole law and of all that God requires of us has this end in view, that His image should shine forth in us, so that we should not be degenerate children. This cannot happen unless we are renewed and put off the image of old Adam.

From this we learn what object Christians ought to set before themselves throughout their lives, namely, to resemble God in holiness and purity; but since all the feelings of our flesh are against God, and the whole bent of our mind is inimical to Him, Peter begins with the renunciation of the world. Certainly whenever the Scripture speaks of the renewal of God's image in us, it begins from the point where the old man with his lusts is destroyed.

In your ignorance. By the time of ignorance he means the time before they were called into the faith of Christ. We learn from this that the fount of all evils is unbelief. He does not use the word ignorance, as we commonly do; for the assertion of Plato that ignorance alone is the cause of sin is false. Yet, however much conscience may reprove the unbelieving, they nevertheless go astray as blind men in darkness, because they do not keep to the right way, and they are without the true light. It is in this sense that Paul says, 'Ye henceforth no longer walk as the Gentiles, in the vanity of their mind, being darkened in

their understanding, alienated from the life of God because of the ignorance that is in them' (Eph. 4.17). Where the knowledge of God is
not strong, darkness, error, vanity, and destitution of light and life
prevail. These things, however, do not make it impossible for the
ungodly to be conscious of doing wrong when they sin, and to know
that their judge is in heaven, and to feel the executioner within them.
In short, as the kingdom of God is a kingdom of light, all who are
alienated from Him must necessarily be blind and wander in a labyrinth.

In the meantime we are reminded that we are enlightened with the
knowledge of God, so as not to be carried away any more by roving
lusts. Hence, whatever progress anyone has made in newness of life
he has made the same amount in the knowledge of God.

Here the question arises, why, since he is addressing Jews, who had
always been acquainted with the law, and brought up in the worship
of the only true God, does he charge them with ignorance and blindness, as though they were heathens? I reply, that it is abundantly clear
from this how profitless all knowledge is without Christ. When Paul
wants to expose the vain boasting of those who wished to be wise
apart from Christ, he rightly says in one short sentence that they do not
hold fast the head (Col. 2.19). Such were the Jews, in that being
wrapped up in numberless corruptions, they had a veil over the eyes,
so that they did not see Christ in the Law (II Cor. 3.14-15). The
doctrine in which they had been brought up was indeed a true light,
but they were blind in the midst of light, as long as the Sun of Righteousness was hidden from them. If Peter declares that even the literal
followers of the Law were in darkness like the heathen, as long as they
were ignorant of Christ, the only true wisdom of God, how much
greater care must we take to strive towards the knowledge of Him.

15. *He which called you is holy.* He argues from the purpose for
which we are called. God sets us apart as a peculiar people for Himself,
and therefore we ought to be free from all stains. He quotes a sentence
which is often repeated by Moses. As the people of Israel were surrounded on every side by heathen tribes, from whom they might
easily have adopted the worst examples and innumerable corruptions,
the Lord frequently recalls them to Himself, as though He said, 'It is
with me that you have to do; you are mine; therefore abstain from the
pollutions of the Gentiles.' We are too ready to look to men, so as to
follow their common way of living, and it thus happens that some
lead others in a body to all kinds of evil, until the Lord separates us by
His calling.

In bidding us to be *holy* like Himself, the comparison is not that of
equals, but we ought to advance in this direction as far as our con-

dition will take us. Since even the most perfect are always very far
from coming up to the mark, we ought daily to strive more and more.
We ought to remember that we are not only told what our duty is,
but that God also adds, 'I am he who sanctifies you.'

He adds, *In all manner of living*, so that there should be no part of
our life which is not to savour of this good odour of holiness. We
see that in the smallest and most insignificant things the Lord has
accustomed His people to the practice of holiness, in order that they
may have a more earnest care for themselves.

*And if ye call on him as Father, who without respect of persons judgeth
according to each man's work, pass the time of your sojourning in fear:
knowing that ye were redeemed, not with corruptible things, with silver
or gold, from your vain manner or life handed down from your fathers;
but with precious blood, as of a lamb without blemish and without spot,
even the blood of Christ: who was foreknown indeed before the foundation of the world, but was manifested at the end of the times for your
sake. Who through him are believers in God, which raised him from
the dead, and gave him glory; so that your faith and hope might be in
God. Seeing ye have purified your souls in your obedience to the truth
unto unfeigned love of the brethren, love one another from the heart
fervently. (17-22)*

17. *And if ye call on him as Father.* Those who are said here to call
on God the Father are whose who profess themselves to be His children, as Moses says in Genesis 48.16, that the name of Jacob was named
on Ephraim and Manasseh, so that they might be counted as his
children. The sense is the same as that in which we use the French
reclamer. He refers back to what he has said before, 'As obedient
children', and from the character of the Father Himself he shows what
sort of obedience ought to be rendered. He *judges*, he says, *without
respect of persons*; that is, no outward mask is of any account with Him,
as it is with men, but He sees the heart (I Sam. 16.17), and His eyes look
on faithfulness (Jer. 5.3). This is also what Paul means when he says
that God's judgment is according to truth (Rom. 2.2); for he is there
attacking hypocrites, who hope that God can be deceived by a vain
pretence. The meaning is that we do not by any means discharge our
duty towards God when we obey Him only in appearance, for He is
not a mortal man whom the outward appearance pleases, but He reads
us for what we are inwardly in our hearts. He not only sets down laws
for our feet and hands, but He also requires spiritual righteousness.

By saying, *According to each man's work*, he does not refer to merit or
to reward. Peter is not concerned here with the merits of works, nor

with the cause of salvation, but is simply reminding us, that there will be no place before the tribunal of God for personal status, but that regard will only be paid to real sincerity of the heart. In this passage faith is included in work. It is abundantly clear from this how foolish and puerile is the inference that is drawn, that God is such that He judges every one of us by the integrity of his conscience, not by the outward appearance, and therefore we obtain salvation by works.

The *fear* which he mentions, stands in opposition to the carelessness that is wont to creep in when there is a hope of deceiving with impunity. As God's eye is so keen as to penetrate into the hidden recesses of the heart, we ought to walk with Him carefully and not negligently. He calls the present life a *sojourning*, not in the sense in which at the beginning of the Epistle he called the Jews to whom he writes sojourners, but because all the godly are pilgrims in this world (Heb. 11.13).

18. *Knowing*. There is another reason, drawn from the price of our redemption, which ought always to be remembered when our salvation is spoken of. To the person who repudiates or despises the grace of the Gospel, not only is salvation worthless and rejected, but also the blood of Christ, by which God has shown us its value. We know how dreadfully sacrilegious it is to hold the blood of the Son of God cheaply. There is hence nothing which ought to stimulate us to the practice of holiness more keenly than the memory of this price of our redemption.

Silver and gold. He sets these in contrast to amplify his argument so that we may know that the whole world and all things deemed precious by men are nothing compared with the excellency of this price.

He says that they were *redeemed from* their *vain manner of life*, so that we may know that the whole life of man is a ruinous labyrinth of wanderings until he has been converted to Christ. He shows us that it is not through our merits that we are restored to the right way, but because it is God's will that the price which He has paid for our salvation should be effectual in our behalf. Therefore the blood of Christ is not only the pledge of our salvation, but also the reason for our calling.

Moreover, Peter warns us to beware lest our unbelief should render this price void or reduce it to be of no effect. When Paul boasts that he worshipped God with a pure conscience from his forefathers (I Tim. 1.3), and as he likewise commends to Timothy for his imitation the piety of his grandmother Lois, and of his mother Eunice (II Tim. 1.5), and as Christ also said of the Jews that they knew whom they worshipped (John 4.22), it may seem strange that Peter should assert that the Jews of his time had learned nothing from their fathers but mere vanity. My answer to this is that, when Christ declares that the way or the knowledge of true religion belonged to the Jews, He is referring to the Law and the commandments of God rather than to the common people. The temple had not been built at Jerusalem without purpose, nor was God worshipped there according to the fancies of men, but according to what was prescribed in the Law. Therefore he says that the Jews are not going astray in their keeping of the Law. As to Paul's forefathers, and as to Lois, Eunice, and similar cases, there is no doubt that God always had at least a small remnant among the people, in whom sincere piety was still to be found, while the main body of the people had become wholly corrupt, and had plunged themselves into all kinds of errors. Innumerable superstitions held sway, hypocrisy prevailed, the hope of salvation was built on I know not what trifles. They were not only soaked in evil ideas, but also fascinated with the grossest delusions, and those who had been scattered to various parts of the world were ensnared by still greater corruptions. In short, the greater part of that nation had either wholly fallen away from true religion, or had greatly degenerated. Therefore Peter, when he condemns the tradition of the fathers, differentiates it from Christ, who is the soul and the truth of the Law.

We learn from this that as soon as men depart from Christ, they go fatally astray. It is vain to hide behind the pretext either of the authority of the Fathers or of ancient custom. The prophet Ezekiel cried to the Jews, 'Walk ye not in the statutes of your fathers' (Ezek. 20.18). This ought also to have equal force for us in the present day, for, in order that the redemption of Christ may be effectual and useful to us, we must renounce our former life, even though it derives from the teaching and practice of our fathers. Therefore the Papists are thrice foolish in thinking that the name of Fathers alone is sufficient defence for all their superstitions, so that they reject whatever is brought forward from the Word of God without regard to the consequences.

19. *As of a lamb.* He means by this analogy that in Christ we have everything that has been foreshadowed by the ancient sacrifices, though he especially alludes to the Paschal lamb. From this we are to learn what benefit the reading of the Law brings us in this respect. Although the rite of sacrificing is abolished, it yet greatly assists our faith to compare the reality with the types, so that we may seek in the one what the other contains. Moses ordered that the lamb which was to be sacrificed at the Passover was to be whole and without blemish (Exod. 12.5). The same thing is often repeated about the sacrifices—cf. Lev. 3.6, 4.3, 22.20-25; Num. 28.3, 9, 11, 19, 31; and elsewhere. By applying this to Christ Peter teaches us that He was a suitable victim, approved by God, for He was perfect, without any blemish. Had He had any defect in Him, He could not have been rightly offered to God, nor could He pacify His wrath.

20. *Who was foreknown.* Again by a comparison he amplifies the grace of God, with which the men of that age were particularly favoured. It was not a common or a small favour that God put off the manifestation of Christ to their time, when He had ordained Him by His eternal counsel for the salvation of the world. At the same time, however, he reminds us that from the side of God it was not a new or a sudden thing that Christ appeared as a Saviour; and this is what ought to be specially understood. In addition to the fact that novelty is always suspicious, what foundation would our faith have if we believed that a remedy for mankind had suddenly occurred to God at last after some thousands of years? In short, we cannot confidently put trust in Christ unless we are convinced that eternal salvation is in Him, and always has been. Besides, Peter is addressing the Jews, who heard that He had already been long ago promised, and though they understood nothing true or clear or certain about His power and office, yet there remained among them a conviction that a Redeemer had been promised by God to the fathers.

It may, however, be asked, as Adam did not fall before the creation of the world, how was Christ appointed to be the Redeemer? For a cure ought to come after the disease. My reply is, that this is to be referred to God's foreknowledge, for doubtless before He created man, God foresaw that he would not stand firm for long in his integrity. Hence, according to His wonderful wisdom and goodness, He ordained that Christ should be the Redeemer, who would deliver the lost race of man from ruin. In this there shines forth more clearly the unspeakable goodness of God, in that He anticipated our disease by the remedy of His grace, and provided a restoration to life before the first man had fallen into death. If the reader wishes any more information on this subject, he may find it in my *Institutes.*

But was manifested at the end of the times. Included in these words, I think, is not only the personal appearance of Christ, but also the proclamation of the Gospel. By the coming of Christ God has carried out what He had decreed, and what He had obscurely indicated to the fathers is now clearly and fully made known to us by the teaching of Gospel. He says that this was done *in these* last times, in the same sense as when Paul says, 'In the fulness of time' (Gal. 4.4), this being the mature season and the perfect moment God in His counsel had appointed. *For your sake.* He does not exclude the fathers, to whom the promise had been useless, but as God has favoured us more than them, he means that the greater the measure of grace towards us, the more reverence and ardour and care are required of us. He adds, *Who believe,* because the manifestation of Christ does not refer to all indiscriminately, but belongs only to those whom He illumines by the

Gospel. We must notice the words, *Who through him are believers in God*, by which he expresses concisely what faith is. Since God is incomprehensible, faith can never reach to Him, unless it has immediate regard to Christ. There are two reasons why faith cannot be in God, unless Christ intervenes as a Mediator. First, the greatness of the divine glory must be taken into account, and at the same time the littleness of our capacity. Our acuteness is very far from being capable of ascending so high as to comprehend God. Hence all thinking about God without Christ is a vast abyss which immediately swallows up all our thoughts. There is clear proof of this not only in the Turks and the Jews, who worship their own dreams under the name of God, but also in the Papists. It is a common axiom of the schools that God is the object of faith (*objectum fidei*). Thus they extensively and carefully speculate about His hidden majesty, leaving out Christ, but with what success? They entangle themselves in astounding delusions, so that there is no end to their wanderings. They think that faith is nothing but imaginative speculation (Col. 1.15). Let us, therefore, remember, that Christ is not called the image of the invisible God in vain, but this name is given to Him for this reason, that God cannot be known except in Him.

The second reason is that, as faith ought to unite us to God, we shun and dread every access to Him, unless a Mediator comes who can deliver us from fear, for sin, which reigns in us, renders us hateful to God and Him in turn to us. Hence, as soon as mention is made of God, we must necessarily be filled with dread, and if we approach Him, His justice is like fire, which will utterly consume us.

It is evident from this that we cannot believe in God except through Christ, in whom God in a manner makes Himself little (*quodammodo parvum facit*), in order to accommodate Himself to our comprehension (*ut se ad captum nostrum submittat*), and it is Christ alone who can make our consciences at peace, so that we may dare to come in confidence to God.

That raised him up from the dead. He adds that Christ was raised from the dead in order that our faith and hope might have a firm foundation to support them. Here again the remark about universal and indiscriminate faith in God is refuted, for if there had been no resurrection of Christ, God would still remain in heaven. But Peter says that it is not possible for faith to be put in Him unless Christ has risen. It is then evident that faith is something other than beholding the naked majesty of God. Peter speaks rightly in this manner, for it belongs to faith to penetrate into heaven, in order to find the Father there. How could it do so, unless it has Christ as a leader? 'By him,' says Paul, 'we have confidence of access' (Eph. 3.12). He also says in Heb. 4.14-16, that, relying on our high priest, we can come with confidence to the throne of grace. Hope is the anchor of the soul, which enters into the inner part of the sanctuary; but not unless Christ goes before (Heb. 6.19). Faith is our victory against the world (I John 5.4), and what is it that makes it victorious, except that Christ, the Lord of heaven and earth, has us under His guardianship and protection?

Therefore since our salvation depends on the resurrection of Christ and His supreme power, faith and hope find here what can support them. Unless He had triumphed over death by rising again, and now held the highest sovereignty to protect us by His power, what would become of us, exposed to such great a power of our enemies, and to such violent attacks? Let us, therefore, learn to what goal we ought to direct our aim, so that we may really have faith in God.

22. *Seeing ye have purified your souls.* Erasmus renders the words badly, 'You, who have purified,' etc. Peter does not declare what they are but reminds them of what they ought to be. The participle is certainly in the past tense, but it may be rendered as a gerund, 'By purifying,' etc. The meaning is that our souls would not be capable of receiving grace until they have been purified, and by this our uncleanness is proved. But so as not to appear to ascribe to us the power of purifying our souls, he immediately adds the qualification, *through the Spirit*; as though he were saying, 'Your souls are to be purified, but as you cannot do this, offer them to God, that He may take away your uncleanness by His Spirit.' He only mentions souls although we need to be cleansed as well from the defilements of the flesh, as Paul tells the Corinthians (II Cor. 7.1), but as the principal uncleanness is within, and necessarily draws with it that which is outward, Peter thought it sufficient to mention only the former, as though he were saying that not only ought outward actions to be corrected, but our very hearts ought to be thoroughly reformed.

Lastly he points out the manner; for purity of soul consists in our obedience to God. *Truth* is to be taken in the sense of the role which God prescribes for us in the Gospel. He is not concerned only with works, but rather with faith which holds here the chief place. Paul specially teaches us in the first and last chapter of the Epistle to the Romans that faith is that by which we obey God; and Peter in Acts 15 bestows on it this eulogy, that by it God purifies the heart.

Unto love of the brethren. He briefly reminds us what God especially requires in our life, and of the mark to which all our endeavours should be directed. Thus Paul in Ephesians 1.4, when speaking of the perfection of the faithful, makes it to consist in love. We ought to notice this more carefully, because the world makes its own sanctity consist in all kinds of trifles, and almost overlooks this, the chief thing. We see how the Papists weary themselves beyond measure with a thousand invented superstitions, while all the time the ultimate is that love which God especially commends. This, then, is the reason why Peter calls our attention to it, when speaking of a rightly formed life.

He has already spoken of the mortification of the flesh, and of our conformity with the will of God; but he now reminds us of what God would have us to cultivate through life, namely mutual love towards one another, for by that we testify that we also love God, and by this evidence God proves who are those who truly love Him.

He calls it *unfeigned* (ἀνυπόκριτον), like Paul in I Tim. 1.5, for nothing is more difficult than sincerely to put our mind to love our neighbours. The love of ourselves which is full of hypocrisy holds sway, and besides everyone measures the love which he shows to others by the advantage he gets for himself rather than by the eagerness to do good. He adds, *fervently*; for the more slothful we are by nature, the more everyone ought to stimulate himself to fervour and earnestness, and that not only once, but more and more every day.

Having been begotten again, not of corruptible seed, but of incorruptible, through the word of God, which liveth and abideth. For, All flesh is as grass, And all the glory thereof as the flower of grass, The grass withereth, and the flower falleth: But the word of the Lord abideth for ever. And this is the word of good tidings which was preached unto you. (23-25)

23. *Having been begotten again.* Here is another cause for exhortation, that since they are new men and born again of God, it behoves them to shape their lives worthily of God and of their spiritual rebirth. This seems to be connected with a verse in the next chapter about seeking the milk of the Word, so that their way of living might correspond with their birth. It may, however, be extended further, so as to refer also to what has gone before, for Peter is bringing together into one category those things which can lead us to an upright and a holy life. Peter's object is to teach us that we cannot be Christians without regeneration, for the Gospel is not preached only in order to be heard by us, but that it may radically reform our hearts as a seed of immortal life. The *corruptible seed* is set over against God's Word, in order that the faithful may know that they ought to renounce their former nature, and so that it may be more evident how much difference there is between the children of Adam who are only born as men into the world, and the children of God who are renewed into a heavenly life. Because the construction of the Greek text is doubtful, we may read 'the living word of God', as well as 'the word of the living God'; but since this latter reading is less forced, I prefer it, though it must be noted that the term is applied to God in the context of the character of

the passage. As in Heb. 4.12 the apostle argues that because God sees all things, and nothing is hid from Him, the Word of God penetrates into the inmost marrow, so as to discern thoughts and feelings, so, when Peter in this passage calls him the living God, who abides for ever, he is referring to the Word, in which the perpetuity of God shines forth as in a living mirror.

24. *For all flesh.* He aptly quotes the passage from Isaiah to prove both clauses, that is, to make it clear how transient and miserable is the first birth of man, and how great is the grace of the new birth. Since the prophet is there speaking of the restoration of the Church, in order to prepare the way for it, he reduces men to nothing in case they should flatter themselves. I know that these words are wrongly twisted by some to another sense. Some explain them as referring to the Assyrians, as though the prophet were saying that there was no reason for the Jews to fear so much from flesh, which is like a fading flower. Others think that the vain confidence which the Jews put in human aids is being reproved. But the prophet himself refutes both these views by adding that the people are as grass. He expressly condemns the Jews for vanity, but he promises them restoration in the name of the Lord. This, then, is what I have already said, that until men have been shown their own emptiness, they are not prepared to receive the grace of God. In short, the meaning of the prophet is something like this: as exile was like death to the Jews, he promised them a new and fresh consolation, to wit, that God would send prophets with a command of this kind. (40.2, 3); the Lord, he says, will yet say, 'Comfort ye my people'; and in the desert and the wilderness the prophetic voice will yet be heard, for a way to be prepared for the Lord.

Since the obstinate pride which fills them must of necessity be purged from their minds, so that an access may be open for God, the prophet adds what Peter quotes about the vanishing glory of the flesh. What is Man? and he answers, grass; what is the glory of man? the flower of the grass. Since it was difficult to believe that man, in whom so much excellency appears, is like grass, the prophet makes a form of concession, as though he were saying, 'Granted that flesh has some glory, in case that should dazzle your eyes, know that the flower soon withers.' He afterwards shows how suddenly everything that gives pleasure to men vanishes through the blowing of the Spirit of God. By this he means that man seems to be something until he comes to God, but that his whole brightness is as nothing in God's presence; that, in a word, his glory is rooted in this world, and has no place in the heavenly kingdom.

The grass withereth. Many think that this refers only to the outward man, but they are mistaken, for we must consider the comparison between God's Word and man. If he meant only the body and what belongs to this present life, he ought to have said in the second clause that the soul was far more excellent. But what he sets in opposition to the grass and its flower is the word of God. It follows, therefore, that in man nothing but vanity is found. Therefore, when Isaiah speaks of the flesh and its glory, he means the whole man, such as he is in himself, for his purpose is to deny to man what he ascribes as peculiar to God's Word. In short, the prophet is dealing with the same truth as Christ in John 3.3, that man is wholly alienated from the kingdom of God, that he is nothing but an earthly, fading, and empty creature, unless he is born again.

25. *But the word of the Lord.* The prophet does not show what the word of God is in itself, but what we ought to think of it. Since man is vanity in himself, it remains for him to seek life elsewhere. Hence Peter ascribes power and efficiency to God's Word, on the authority of the prophet, to bring to us what is solid and eternal. What the prophet had in mind was that there is no permanent life but in God, and that this is communicated to us by the Word. However fading the nature of man may be, he is made eternal by the Word, for he is remade into a new creature.

This is the word of good tidings which was preached unto you. He first reminds us that when the Word of God is mentioned, we are very foolish if we imagine it be to remote from us in the air or in heaven, for we ought to realize that it has been revealed to us by the Lord. What, then, is this Word of the Lord, which gives us life? It is the Law, the Prophets, and the Gospel. Those who wander beyond these limits of revelation, find nothing but the impostures of Satan and his delusions instead of the Word of the Lord. We ought to notice this more carefully, because impious men of Lucifer craftily allow God's Word its own honour, while at the same time attempting to draw us away from the Scriptures, like that unprincipled man, Agrippa, who highly extols the eternity of God's Word, and yet scurrilously mocks the prophets, and thus indirectly scorns the Word of God.

In short, as I have already reminded you, no mention is made here of the Word which lies hid in the bosom of God, but of that which has proceeded from His mouth, and has come to us. Thus again it ought to be borne in mind that God has purposed to speak to us by the apostles and prophets, and their lips are the mouth of the one true God.

When Peter says, *Which was preached, to you,* he means that the Word is not to be sought anywhere else but in the Gospel preached to us, and indeed we do not know the power of eternal life except by faith.

Yet there will be no faith, unless we know that the Word is destined for us.

What Moses said to the people has the same purpose, 'Say not in thine heart,' 'Who shall ascend into heaven,' etc.; 'the word is with thee in thy mouth and in thy heart' (Deut. 30.12). That these words agree with what Peter says is shown by Paul in Rom. 10.8, where he teaches us that it was the Word of faith which he preached.

Peter gives no ordinary eulogy on outward preaching, in declaring that it is the life-giving Word. It is God alone who regenerates us, but for that purpose He employs the ministry of men. On this account Paul glories that the Corinthians had been spiritually begotten by him (I Cor. 4.15). It is indeed certain that those who plant and those who water, are nothing, but whenever God is pleased to bless their labour, he makes their doctrine efficacious by the power of His Spirit, and the Voice which is in itself mortal is an instrument of eternal life.

CHAPTER TWO

Putting away therefore all wickedness, and all guile, and hypocrisies, and envies, and all evil speakings, as newborn babes, long for the spiritual milk which is without guile, that ye may grow thereby unto salvation: If ye have tasted that the Lord is gracious: unto whom coming, a living stone, rejected indeed of men, but with God elect, precious, ye also, as living stones, are built up a spiritual house, to be a holy priesthood, to offer up spiritual sacrifices, acceptable to God through Jesus Christ. (1-5)

Now that he has taught that the faithful are regenerated by the Word of God, he exhorts them to lead a life corresponding with their birth. If we live in the Spirit, we ought also to walk in the Spirit, as Paul says (Gal. 5.25). It is not sufficient for us to be once called by the Lord, unless we live as new creatures. This is the long and short of it. In the words he uses the apostle continues the same metaphor. As we have been born again, he requires from us a life like that of infants, by which he means that we are to put off the old man and his works. This verse agrees with what Christ says, 'Except ye become like this little child, ye shall not enter into the kingdom of God' (Matt. 18.3).

Infancy is here set by Peter over against the old age of the flesh, which leads to corruption; and by the word *milk* he includes all the feelings of spiritual life. In this bit there is a contrast between the vices which he enumerates and the sincere milk of the Word; as though he had said, 'Malice and hypocrisy belong to those who have conformed to the corruptions of the world, and have imbibed these vices; while what pertains to infancy is honest simplicity, free from all guile. When men live for a while they become imbued with envy, they learn to slander one another, they are taught the arts of mischief; in short, they become hardened in every kind of evil: infants, owing to their age, do not yet know what it is to envy, to do mischief, and the like'. He then compares the vices, in which the old age of the flesh indulges, to strong food, and milk is called that way of living which is suitable to innocent nature and simple infancy.

1. *All wickedness.* This is not a complete enumeration of all the things which we ought to lay aside, but when the apostles speak of the old man, they lay down as examples some of those vices which mark his whole character. Paul says, 'works of the flesh are manifest which are these' (Gal. 5.19), yet he does not enumerate them all, but in those few things, we may see, as in a mirror, that immense mass of evil

which proceeds from our flesh. So also in other passages, where he speaks of reforming the whole life of man, he touches only on a few examples, by which we can understand the whole character.

What he says then amounts to this, that having laid aside the works of your former life, such as malice, deceit, pretences, envyings, and other things of this kind, you are to devote yourselves to things of an opposite nature, cultivate kindness, and honesty. He urges this, so that new morals may follow a new life.

2. *The spiritual milk.* This passage is commonly expounded according to the translation of Erasmus, 'Milk not for the body but for the soul'; as though the apostle reminded us by this expression that he spoke metaphorically. I rather think that this passage agrees with the saying of Paul, 'Be not children in mind, but in malice' (I Cor. 14.20). In case anyone thinks that he is commending an infancy that is void of understanding but full of fatuity, he meets this objection in due course. Thus he bids them to desire milk free from guile, but drawn from right understanding. We now see for what purpose he joins these two words λογικὸν and ἄδολον. Simplicity and quickness of understanding are two things apparently opposite, but they ought to be mixed together, in case simplicity becomes insipid, and malicious craftiness creeps in in the place of understanding. This well regulated mingling is in line with what Christ says, 'Be ye wise as serpents, and harmless as doves' (Matt. 10.16). Thus the question is solved which might have been otherwise raised.

Paul reproves the Corinthians because they are like children, and therefore they cannot take strong food, but are to be fed with milk (I Cor. 3.1.) Almost the same words are found in Heb. 5.12. But in these passages those who are compared to children remain always novices and ignorant scholars in the doctrine of religion, stick at the first elements, and never penetrate into the higher knowledge of God. *Milk* is called the simpler mode of teaching, and one suitable to children, when there is no progress made beyond the first rudiments. Paul then rightly charges this as a fault, equally with the author of the Epistle to the Hebrews. But milk, here, is not elementary doctrine, which one perpetually learns, and never comes to the knowledge of the truth, but a mode of living which has the savour of the new birth, when we surrender ourselves to be brought up by God. In the same manner *infancy* is not set in opposition to manhood, or to the full-grown man in Christ (as Paul calls him in Eph. 4.13), but to the old age of the flesh and of the old life. Moreover, as the infancy of the new life is perpetual, so Peter recommends milk as a perpetual nourishment for he wishes those nourished by it to grow.

3. *If ye have tasted.* He refers to Ps. 34.8, 'Taste and see that the Lord

is good.' He means that this taste is to be had in Christ, as our souls can find no sure rest anywhere but in Him. But he has drawn the ground of his exhortation from the goodness of God, because His kindness, which we experience in Christ, ought to allure us.

What follows, *To whom coming*, does not refer simply to God, but describes Him as He is revealed to us in the person of Christ. Now, it must be the case that the grace of God draws us all to Himself and inflames us with the love of Him by whom we obtain a real perception of it. If Plato affirms this of his Beautiful, of which he saw only a shadowy idea from far off, this is much more true with regard to God.

It is to be noticed that Peter connects access to God with the taste of His goodness. Just as the human mind necessarily dreads and shuns God, as long as it imagines Him to be rigid and severe, so, as soon as He makes known His paternal love to the faithful, it immediately follows that they disregard everything and even forget themselves and hasten to Him. In short, the only person who makes progress in the Gospel is the one who comes to God with his heart.

He also shows for what purpose and on what condition we ought to come to Christ, namely that we may have Him as our foundation. Since He is constituted a stone, He ought to provide us with this power, so that nothing is supplied to Him by the Father in vain or to no purpose. He anticipates the offence in allowing that Christ is rejected by men, for, as a great part of the world reject Him, and many even abhor Him, He might for this reason be despised by us, since we see that some of the ignorant are alienated from the Gospel, because it is not everywhere popular, and does not confer favour on those who profess it. But Peter forbids us to think any less of Christ, however despised He may be by the world, because He nevertheless retains His own worth and honour before God.

5. *Ye also, as living stones, are built up*. The verb may be in the imperative as well as in the indicative mood, for the ending in Greek could mean either. But whichever way it is taken, there is no doubt that Peter means to exhort the faithful to consecrate themselves as a spiritual temple to God, for he aptly infers from the purpose of our calling what our duty is. We must further observe that he makes one house of the whole number of the faithful. Though every one of us is said to be the temple of God and is so described, yet all must be united together in one, and joined together by mutual love, so that one temple may be made of us all. Since it is true that each one is a temple in which God dwells by His Spirit, so all ought to be so fitted together, that they may form the structure of one universal temple. This happens when every one, content with his own lot, keeps himself

within the limits of his own duty, but when all at the same time bring whatever gifts they have, into the common service.

By calling us *living stones* and a *spiritual house*, just as he had already said that Christ is a living stone, he implies a comparison between us and the ancient temple, a fact which serves to amplify divine grace. The same purpose lies behind what he adds about *spiritual sacrifices*. The more excellent the reality is than the types, so much the more excellent are all things in the kingdom of Christ, for we have that heavenly examplar, which the ancient sanctuary and everything instituted by Moses under the Law foreshadowed.

A holy priesthood. It is a singular honour that God should not only consecrate us as a temple to Himself, in which He dwells and is worshipped, but that He also wills to make us priests. Peter mentions this double honour in order to stimulate us to serve and worship God more earnestly. Among the spiritual sacrifices, he gives first place to the offering of ourselves, of which Paul speaks in Romans 12.1, for we can offer nothing to God until we offer to Him ourselves as a sacrifice, which is done by denying ourselves. Then, afterwards follow prayers, thanksgiving, alms, and all the duties of religion.

Acceptable to God. It ought also to add not a little to our keenness, when we know that the worship we perform to God is pleasing to Him, just as doubt necessarily brings with it slackness. Here, then, is the third stimulus in his exhortation, that he declares that our offerings are acceptable to God, in case fear should make us slack. Idolaters are indeed influenced by great enthusiasm in their fictitious forms of worship, but this is so, because Satan drugs their minds in case they come to consider their works. But whenever their consciences are led to an examination they begin to stagger. It is indeed certain that it is impossible for anyone seriously and from the heart to devote himself to God, unless he is fully persuaded that he does not labour in vain.

The apostle adds, *through Jesus Christ*. There is never such purity found in our sacrifices that they are of themselves acceptable to God. Our self-denial is never entire and complete, our urge to pray is never so sincere as it ought to be, we are never so zealous and so diligent in doing good, but that our works are imperfect, and mingled with many vices. Nevertheless, Christ gains favour for them. Peter here faces that want of faith which we may have with regard to the acceptability of our works, when he says that they are accepted, not for the merit of their own excellency, but through Christ. It ought to kindle the ardour of our efforts all the more when we hear that God deals so indulgently with us as to set a value on our works in Christ, which in themselves deserve nothing. At the same time, the preposition *through Christ* may be fitly connected with the verb 'offer', for a

similar phrase is found in Heb. 13.15, 'Through him let us offer the
sacrifice of praise to God.' The sense, however, will remain the same,
for we offer sacrifices through Christ, that they may be acceptable to
God.

> *Because it is contained in scripture, Behold, I lay in Zion a chief corner-*
> *stone, elect, precious: And he that believeth on him shall not be put to*
> *shame. For you which believe is the preciousness: but for such as dis-*
> *believe, The stone which the builders rejected, The same was made the*
> *head of the corner; and, A stone of stumbling, and a rock of offence; for*
> *they stumble at the word, being disobedient; whereunto also they were*
> *appointed. (6-8)*

6. *Because it is contained in Scripture.* Those who refer the verb
'contain' (περιέχειν) to Christ and render it 'embrace', because it is
through Him that all these unite together, wholly depart from the
meaning of the apostle. The exposition that Christ excels others is no
more acceptable. Peter simply intended to quote the testimony of
Scripture. He means that what he adds has been taught by the Holy
Spirit in the Scriptures, or (which is the same thing) that it is contained
in them. It is not an unsuitable confirmation of the preceding verse,
for we see for what slight reasons, and almost for none, many reject
Christ, and some fall away from Him. This is a stumbling block
which above all others stands in the way of some. They are drawn
away, because not only the common people despise and reject Christ,
but also those who are high in dignity and honour, and seem to excel
others. This evil has almost always prevailed in the world, and it does
so greatly today, for a great many judge Christ according to the false
opinion of the world. Moreover, such is the ingratitude and impiety
of men, that Christ is everywhere despised. Thus it is that while they
regard one another few pay Him His due honour. Hence Peter reminds us of what had been foretold of Christ, so that the contempt or
the rejection of him may not move us from a true faith.

The first passage which he quotes is taken from Isaiah 28.16, where,
after the prophet has attacked the desperate wickedness of his own
nation, he finally adds, 'Your perfidy will not prevent God from
restoring His Church, which now through you lies wholly in ruins.'
He thus describes the manner of restoration, 'I will lay in Sion a stone.'
We learn from this that there is no building up of the Church without
Christ; for there is no other foundation, as Paul testifies (I Cor. 3.11).
This is no wonder, for all our salvation is found in Him. Whoever,
then, turns away from Him even in the slightest will find he has a
precipice for his foundation.

Therefore the prophet not only calls Him a corner-stone, on which the whole weight of the edifice rests, but also a stone of testing, according to which the building is to be measured and regulated. Further, he calls Him a solid foundation, which sustains the whole edifice. He is a corner-stone of such a kind as to be the standard of the whole building, as well as the only foundation. Peter has taken from the words of the prophet what was specially suitable to his present argument, namely that He was a chosen stone, full of honour and value, and also that on Him we ought to build. This honour has this in view, that however much Christ may be despised by the world, He may not be despised by us, for He is regarded as very precious by God. In calling Him a *corner-stone*, he means that those who do not rest on Christ have no concern for their salvation. The subtle meaning that some have given to the word 'corner', as though it meant that Christ joins together Jews and Gentiles, as two distinct walls, is not well founded. Let us be content with the simple explanation, that He is so called, because the weight of the building rests on Him.

We must further observe, that the prophet introduces God as the speaker, for He alone is the maker and architect of His own Church, as it is put in Psalm 78.69, that His hand had founded Sion. He, indeed, employs the labour and ministry of men in building it; but this does not prevent Him from saying that it is truly His own work. Christ, then, is the foundation of our salvation, because He has been ordained for this end by the Father.

He says *in Sion*, because there God's spiritual temple was to have its beginning. In order that our faith may rest firmly on Christ, we must come to the Law and the Prophets. Although this stone extends to the uttermost parts of the world, it must of necessity be first located in Sion where the seat of the Church then was. 'It is said to have been laid when the Father revealed Him for the purpose of restoring His Church. In short, we must take it that only those who rely on Christ keep the unity of the Church, for He is not set as a foundation-stone except in Sion. Since the Church went forth from Sion and is now spread in all directions, so also it is from Sion that our faith has derived its beginning, as Isaiah says, 'From Sion shall go forth the Law, and the word of the Lord from Jerusalem' (Isa. 2.3). This corresponds to what is said in the Psalms, 'The sceptre of thy power will the Lord send forth from Sion' (Ps. 110.2).

He that believeth. The prophet does not emphasize *in him*, but declares generally, 'He that believeth shall not make haste.' However, since there is no doubt that God sets forth Christ there as the object of our faith (*in scopum fidei*), the faith of which the prophet speaks must look to Him alone, and no one can rightly believe except he who has set Christ before him as the One he ought wholly to trust.

The words of the prophet may be taken in two ways, either as a promise or as an exhortation. The future tense would render, 'He shall not make haste'; but in Hebrew the future is often to be taken for an imperative, 'Let him not make haste'. Thus the meaning would be, 'Be not moved in your minds, but hold on quietly to your desires, and check your feelings, until the Lord will be pleased to fulfil his promise.' So he says in another place, 'In silence and in quietness shall be your strength' (Isa. 30.15). But as the other reading seems to come nearer to Peter's interpretation, I prefer it. Then the sense would be that he who believes will not waver nor vacillate, because he has a firm and lasting foundation. This is a valuable truth, that if we rely on Christ, we are beyond the danger of falling. To be ashamed (*pudefieri*) means the same as to be afraid. Peter has retained the real sense of the prophet, though he has followed the Greek version.

7. *For you therefore which believe.* Since God has pronounced Christ to be a precious and a chosen stone, Peter draws the conclusion that He is so to us. Christ is here described as we apprehend Him by faith, and as He proves himself to be by real evidence. We ought, then, to notice carefully this conclusion. Christ is a precious stone in the sight of God, and therefore He is such to the faithful. It is faith alone which shows us the value and excellency of Christ.

Since the design of the apostle is to meet the offence which the multitude of the ungodly creates, he immediately adds another clause about unbelievers, to the effect that by rejecting Christ they do not take away the honour given Him by the Father. For this purpose Ps. 118.22 is quoted, that the stone which the builders rejected is become nevertheless the head of the corner. It follows from this that in spite of His enemies Christ continues in the dignity to which He has been appointed by the Father. We must take note of two things that are said here; the first is that Christ was rejected by those who bore rule in the Church of God; and the other, that their efforts were in vain, because God's decree must needs be fulfilled, that He as the corner-stone should sustain the building.

Moreover, the fact that this passage ought truly and properly to be understood of Christ, is borne out not only by the witness of the Holy Spirit but also by Christ himself, who has thus explained it (Matt. 21.42); and it also appears evident from this, that it was commonly understood in this sense before Christ came into the world. There is no doubt that this exposition had been delivered as it were from hand to hand from the fathers. We see, then, that this was, as it were, a common saying even among children about the Messiah. I shall, therefore, no longer discuss this point. We may take it for granted that David was thus rejected by his own time, so that he might typify Christ.

Let us now return to the first clause. Christ was rejected by the builders, an event which was first foreshadowed in David; for those who were in power counted him as condemned and lost. The same thing was fulfilled in Christ, for those who ruled in the Church rejected Him as far as they could. It might have greatly disturbed the weak, when they say that Christ's enemies were so many, including the priests, elders and teachers, in whom alone the image of the Church was clearly seen. In his desire to remove this offence Peter reminds the faithful that this very thing had been predicted by the evidence of David. He specially addresses the Jews, to whom this properly applied, although this admonition is no less useful today. Those who arrogate to themselves the place of prime authority in the Church are Christ's most inveterate enemies, and persecute His Gospel with diabolical fury.

The Pope calls himself the vicar of Christ, and yet we see how fiercely he opposes Him. This spectacle frightens the simple and ignorant. Why is this? Surely because they do not consider that what David has predicted is now happening. Let us, then, remember that not only those who saw Christ rejected by the scribes and Pharisees were worried by this prophecy, but that we are also fortified by it against the daily offences, which might otherwise upset our faith. Whenever, I declare, we see those who glory in the title of prelates, rising up against Christ, let it come to our minds, that the stone is rejected by the builders, according to the prediction of David. As the metaphor of building is a common one, when political or spiritual government is spoken of, so David calls 'builders' those to whom is committed the care and power of governing, not because they build rightly, but because they have the name of builders, and possess due power. It follows from this that those in office are not always God's true and faithful ministers. It is, therefore, doubly ridiculous of the Pope and his followers to arrogate to themselves supreme and indubitable authority on this sole pretence, that they are the ordinary governors of the Church. In the first place, their vocation to govern the Church is in no way more just or more legitimate than that of Heliogabalus to govern the empire. Even though we allow them what they unblushingly claim, that they are rightly called, yet we see what David declares respecting the ordinary rulers of the Church, namely, that they rejected Christ, so that they built a stye for swine rather than a temple for God. The next part follows, that all those great men who are proud of their power and dignity will not cause Christ to be moved from His place.

8. *And a stone of stumbling.* Now that he has reassured the faithful that they will have in Christ a firm and permanent foundation, even

though the greater part of men and the chief among them allow Him no place in the building, he now announces the punishment which awaits all the unbelieving, in order that they may be terrified by their example. For this purpose he quotes the testimony of Isaiah (8.14). The prophet declares that the Lord would be a stone of stumbling and rock of offence to the Jews. This properly refers to Chri.t, as may be seen from the context, and Paul applies it to Christ (Rom. 9.32), for in Him the God of hosts has clearly manifested Himself.

Here, then, the terrible vengeance of God on all the ungodly is announced, because Christ will be to them an offence and a stumbling, inasmuch as they refuse to make Him their foundation. As the firmness and stability of Christ are such as to sustain all who depend on Him in faith, so His hardness is so great that it will break and tear in pieces all who resist Him. For there is no middle way between these two; we must either build on Him, or be dashed against Him.

For they stumble at the word. He points out here the way in which Christ becomes a stumbling-block, that is when men perversely oppose the word of God. This is what the Jews did, for though they professed themselves willing to receive the Messiah, yet they furiously rejected Him when He was given to them by God. The Papists do the same today; they worship the mere name of Christ, while they cannot endure the doctrine of the Gospel. Peter means here that all who do not receive Christ as revealed in the Gospel, are adversaries to God, and resist His Word, and further that Christ is a destruction only to those who, through headstrong wickedness and obstinacy, rush against the Word of God.

This especially deserves to be noticed in case the blame for our fault should be imputed to Christ, for, as He has been given to us as a foundation, it is incidental that He becomes a rock of offence. In short, His proper office is to fit us to be a spiritual temple to God, but it is the fault of men that they stumble at Him, because unbelief leads men to contend with God. Therefore in order to set forth the character of the conflict, Peter has said that they are the unbelieving.

Whereunto also they were appointed. This passage may be explained in two ways. It is certain that Peter is speaking of the Jews, and the common interpretation is, that they were appointed to believe, for the promise of salvation was destined for them. But the other sense is equally suitable, that they had been appointed to unbelief, as Pharaoh is said to have been put into the position of resisting God (Exod. 9.16), and all unbelievers are destined for the same purpose. What inclines me to this latter meaning is the particle καί which is put in. However, if the first view be preferred, then it is a violent upbraiding, for Peter heightens the sin of unbelief in the people who had been chosen by

God, because they rejected the salvation that had been peculiarly ordained for them. This circumstance renders them doubly inexcusable, that, having been called in preference to others, they have refused to listen to God. By saying that they were appointed to believe, he refers only to their outward call, thereby having regard to the covenant which God had made generally with the whole nation, although the ingratitude of men (as it has been said) was sufficiently proved, when they rejected the word preached to them.

But ye are an elect race, a royal priesthood, a holy nation, a people for God's own possession, that ye may shew forth the excellencies of him who called you out of darkness into his marvellous light: which in time past were no people, but now are the people of God: which had not obtained mercy, but now have obtained mercy. (9-10)

9. *But ye are an elect race.* Here again he separates them from the unbelieving, in case they are driven by their example (as it is often the case) and fall away from the faith. Since it is unreasonable that those whom God has separated from the world should have fellowship with the ungodly, Peter here reminds the faithful of the great honour to which they have been raised, and also to what purpose they have been called. It was with the same high titles which he confers on them that Moses honoured the ancient people (Exod. 19.6), but the apostle's purpose is to show that they had recovered again through the goodness of Christ the great dignity from which they had fallen. At the same time it is true that God gave to the fathers only an earthly taste of these blessings, and that they are given solid manifestation in Christ.

The meaning then is as though he had said, 'Moses of old called your fathers a holy nation, a priestly kingdom, and God's peculiar people; now all these high titles more justly belong to you; therefore you ought to beware lest your unbelief should rob you of them.'

In the meantime, however, since the greater part of the nation did not believe, the apostle by implication sets the believing Jews in opposition to all the rest, though they exceeded them in number, as though he were saying that the true children of Abraham were only those who believed in Christ, and that they only retained possession of all the blessings which God had by a singular privilege bestowed on the whole nation.

He calls them *an elect race,* because God, passing by others, adopted them as it were in a special manner. They were also *a holy nation,* for God had consecrated them to Himself, and destined that they should lead a pure and holy life; and *a people for God's own possession,* that they might be to Him a peculiar possession or inheritance. I take the words simply in this sense, that the Lord has called us, in order to possess us as His own people, devoted to Him. This meaning is proved by the words of Moses, 'If ye keep my covenant, ye shall be to me a peculiar treasure beyond all other nations' (Exod. 19.5).

In the words *a royal priesthood* there is a striking inversion of the words of Moses. He says, 'a priestly kingdom', but the same thing is meant. What Peter means is this: Moses called your fathers a sacred kingdom, because the whole people enjoyed as it were a royal freedom, and from their body the priests were chosen; both dignities were therefore joined together; but now you are royal priests, and that in a more excellent way, because you are each consecrated in Christ to be both the associates of His kingdom, and partakers of His priesthood. Though the fathers had something like what you have, yet you far excel them. After the wall of partition has been pulled down by Christ, we are now gathered from every nation, and the Lord bestows these high titles on all whom He makes his people.

In the matter of these benefits, there is a contrast between us and the rest of mankind to be considered, from which it is clearer how incomparable is God's goodness towards us, because He sanctified us, who are by nature polluted. He has chosen us, when He could find nothing in us but evil and vileness; He makes us His peculiar possession from being worthless dregs; He confers the honour of priesthood on the profane; He brings the vassals of Satan, of sin, and of death, to royal liberty.

That ye may shew forth. He carefully points out the end of our calling, in order to stimulate us to give the glory to God. The sum of what he says is, that God has favoured us with these immense benefits and constantly manifests them, that His glory may be shown forth by us. By excellencies, he understands wisdom, goodness, power, righteousness, and everything else in which the glory of God shines forth. It behoves us to declare these excellencies not only by our tongue, but also by our whole life. This doctrine ought to be a subject of daily meditation, and it ought to be remembered by us every moment that all God's blessings with which He favours us are intended for this end, that His glory may be proclaimed by us.

We must also notice his phrase, that we have been *called* out of darkness into God's wonderful light, for by these words he enlarges the greatness of divine grace. If the Lord had given us light on our journey, while we were seeking it, it would have been a favour, but it was a much greater favour to draw us out of the labyrinth of ignorance and the abyss of darkness. We must learn from this what man's condition is before he is translated into the kingdom of God. This is what Isaiah says, 'Darkness shall cover the earth, and gross darkness the people; but over thee shall the Lord be seen, and his glory shall in thee

266

shine forth' (Isa. 60.2). Certainly we cannot be other than sunk in darkness, after we have departed from God, who is our only light. See more fully on this subject in the second chapter of the Epistle to the Ephesians.

10. *Which in time past were no people.* He quotes for confirmation a passage from Hosea, and uses it well for his own purpose. After having declared in God's name that the Jews were repudiated, Hosea gives them a hope of a future restoration. Peter reminds us that this was fulfilled in his own age, for the Jews were scattered here and there, as the torn members of a body; indeed, they seemed to be cut off from God's people, no worship remained among them, and they were entangled in the corruptions of the heathens. It could only be said of them, that they were repudiated by the Lord. Therefore when they are gathered together in Christ, from being no people they really become the people of God. Paul applies also this prophecy to the Gentiles in Rom. 19.26, and not without reason, for from the time the Lord's covenant was broken, from which alone the Jews derived their superiority, they were put on a level with the Gentiles. Hence it follows that God's promise to make a people of no people belongs in common to both.

Which had not obtained mercy. This was added by the prophet, in order that the gratuitous covenant of God, by which He takes them to be His people, might be more clearly set forth; as though he had said, 'There is no other reason why the Lord counts us His people, except that He has mercy on us and graciously adopts us.' It is then God's free goodness, which makes us of no people to be a people to God, and reconciles those who are alienated.

> *Beloved, I beseech you as sojourners and pilgrims, to abstain from fleshly lusts, which war against the soul; having your behaviour seemly among the Gentiles; that, wherein they speak against you as evil-doers, they may by your good works, which they behold, glorify God in the day of visitation.* (11-12)

11. *As sojourners.* There are two parts to this exhortation, first that their souls are to be free within from wicked and vicious lusts, and secondly, that they were to live honestly among men, and by the example of a good life not only to confirm the godly, but also win over the unbelieving to God.

First, to call them away from the indulgence of carnal lusts, he uses the argument that they are sojourners and strangers. He calls them this not because they were banished from their country, and scattered into various lands, but because the children of God, wherever they may go on the earth are only guests in this world. He called them sojourners in the true sense at the beginning of the Epistle, as it appears from the context, but what he says here is common to them all. The lusts of the flesh hold us entangled, because mentally we dwell in the world, and do not realize that heaven is our native land, but when we pass as strangers through this life, we are not in bondage to the flesh.

By the *lusts of the flesh* he means not only those gross desires which we have in common with animals, as the sophists hold, but also all those passions of the soul to which we are by nature guided and led. For it is certain that every thought of the flesh, that is, of unredeemed nature, is enmity against God (Rom. 8.7).

Which war against the soul. Another argument is that they could not comply with the desires of the flesh, except to their own ruin. He is not referring here to the battle described by Paul in the seventh chapter of Romans, and in the fifth of Galatians, where he makes the soul the antagonist of the flesh, but what he says here is that the desires of the flesh lead to perdition, whenever the soul consents to them. He reveals our carelessness in this respect, in that while we anxiously avoid enemies from whom we fear danger to the body, we willingly allow enemies hurtful to the soul to destroy us, indeed, we as it were stretch forth our neck to them.

12. *Your behaviour.* The second part of the exhortation is that they are to conduct themselves honestly towards men. Logically what precedes this is that their minds should be cleansed before God, but regard must be paid to human reason, so that we do not become a hindrance to them. He expressly says, *among the Gentiles, wherein they speak against you*, for the Jews were not only hated everywhere, but were also almost abhorred. Therefore they ought to have laboured all the more carefully to wipe off the odium and infamy attached to their name by a holy life and a well-regulated conduct. The admonition of Paul ought to be attended to, 'To give no occasion to those who seek one' (II Cor. 11.12). Therefore the evil speakings and the wicked talk of the ungodly ought to stimulate us to lead an upright life, for this is no time for living listlessly and carelessly, when they watch us closely, in order to find out whatever we do amiss.

That they may glorify God. He means that we ought not to strive for our own sake, so that men may think and speak well of us, but that we ought to seek the glory of God, as Christ also teaches us. Peter shows how this would happen, namely by the unbelieving, led by our good works, becoming obedient to God, and thus by their own conversion giving glory to Him. This is what he means by the words, *in the day of visitation.* I know that some refer this to the last coming of Christ, but I take it otherwise, to mean that God employs the holy and honest life of His people as a preparation to bring back the wandering to the right way. The beginning of our conversion is when God is pleased to look on us with a fatherly eye, but when His face is turned away from us, we perish. Hence the day of visitation may justly be said to be the time when He invites us to Himself.

Be subject to every ordinance of man for the Lord's sake: whether it be to the king, as supreme; or unto governors, as sent by him for vengeance on evil-doers and for praise to them that do well. For so is the will of God, that by well-doing ye should put to silence the ignorance of foolish men: as free, and not using your freedom for a cloke of wickedness, but as bond-servants of God. (13-16)

13. *Be subject.* He comes now to particular exhortations, and as obedience towards magistrates is a part of honest behaviour, he draws this inference, *be subject therefore.* By refusing the yoke of government, they would have given to the Gentiles no little occasion for reproaching them. Indeed, the Jews were especially hated and notorious for this very reason, that they were regarded as ungovernable on account of their perverseness. As the commotions which they raised up in the provinces were the cause of great calamities, everyone of a quiet and peaceable disposition dreaded them like the plague, and for this reason Peter was forced to speak so strongly on subjection. There is the further fact that many thought the Gospel was a proclamation of such liberty that everyone might think of himself as free from servitude. It seemed an unworthy thing that God's children should be servants, and that the heirs of the world should not have free possession, even of their own bodies. Then there was another difficulty since all the magistrates were Christ's adversaries, and they so abused their authority, that no image of God, which secures especial reverence, was seen in them. We now perceive the design of Peter; he exhorted the Jews, especially for these reasons, to show respect to the civil power.

To every ordinance of man. Some render the words 'to every creature'; but from a rendering so obscure and ambiguous, many have twisted the sense to elicit some meaning. I have no doubt but that Peter meant to point out the distinct manner in which God governs mankind. The verb κτίζειν in Greek (from which κτίσις comes) means to form and to construct a building. It corresponds to the word 'ordinance'; by which Peter reminds us that God the Maker of the world has not left the human race in a state of confusion, so that they live after the manner of beasts, but has given them as it were a building regularly formed, and divided into several compartments. It is called a *human ordinance,* not because it has been invented by man, but because it is a mode of living, well arranged and duly ordered, appropriate to men.

Whether it be to the king. In my opinion he is naming Caesar, whose empire extended over all those countries mentioned at the beginning of the Epistle. Though 'king' was a name extremely hated by the Romans, yet it was in use among the Greeks; indeed they often called him αὐτοκράτωρ, but sometimes he was also called by them βασιλεύς. By adding the reason that he ought to be obeyed because he excels or is supreme, he is not comparing Caesar along with other magistrates. He held the supreme power; but that eminence which Peter extols is common to all who exercise public authority. So Paul, in Rom. 13.1, extends it to all magistrates. The meaning is, that obedience is due to all who rule, because they have been raised to that honour not by chance, but by God's providence. Most people are in the habit of inquiring too closely by what right power has been attained, but we ought to be satisfied with this alone, that we see that they exercise power. Thus Paul cuts off the handle of useless objections when he declares that there is no power but from God. It is for this reason that Scripture so often says that it is God who girds kings with a sword, who raises them on high, and who transfers kingdoms as He pleases.

Since Peter refers especially to the Roman Emperor, it was necessary to add this admonition, for it is certain that the Romans penetrated into Asia and subdued these countries more by unjust guiles than by any legitimate way. Besides, the Caesars who then reigned had snatched possession of the monarchy by tyrannical force. Peter, therefore, forbids all these things to be brought into debate, for he shows that subjects ought to obey their rulers without hesitation, because they are only made eminent by being raised by God's hand.

14. *Or unto governors.* He describes every kind of magistrate as though he were saying that there is no kind of government to which we ought not to submit. He confirms this by saying that they are God's ministers; and those who refer the pronoun *him* to the king are greatly mistaken. There is a common reason, which extols the authority of all magistrates, to wit, that they rule by the command of God, and are sent by Him. It hence follows (as Paul also teaches us) that those who do not obediently submit to a power ordained by Him resist God.

For vengeance. This is the second reason why we ought to regard and to respect civil authority, and that is, because it has been appointed by the Lord for the common good of mankind, for we must be utterly barbarous and brutal, if the public good is not close to our hearts. This, in short, is what Peter means, that since God keeps the world in order by the ministry of magistrates, all those who detract from their authority are the enemies of mankind.

He puts together the two things which Plato says are the marks of a state, that is, reward to the good and punishment to the wicked; for, in ancient times, not only was punishment allotted to evil-doers, but also rewards to the good. Though it often happens that honours are not rightly distributed, nor rewards given to the deserving, yet it is an honour not to be despised that the good at least live under the care and protection of magistrates, that they are not exposed to the violence and injuries of the ungodly, and that they live more quietly under laws and retain their reputation more easily than if everyone lived as he pleased without any restraint. In short, it is a particular blessing of God, that the wicked are not allowed to do what they like.

It may be objected here that kings and other magistrates often abuse their power, and exercise tyrannical cruelty rather than justice. Almost all the magistrates were like that when this Epistle was written. To this I answer that tyrants and those like them do not do such things by their abuse, without the ordinance of God still remaining in force, just as the perpetual institution of marriage is not subverted even though the wife and the husband behave in an unseemly way. However men may go astray, the end fixed by God is unchanged in its place.

If anyone objects and says that we ought not to obey princes who, as far as they can, pervert the holy ordinance of God, and thus become savage wild beasts, while magistrates ought to bear the image of God, I reply that the order established by God ought to be so highly valued by us as to honour even tyrants when in power. There is yet another reply still more evident, that there has never been a tyranny, nor can one be imagined, however cruel and unbridled, in which some portion of equity has not appeared. God never allows His just order to be destroyed by the sin of men without some of its outlines remaining unobscured. And finally, some kind of government, however deformed and corrupt it may be, is still better and more beneficial than anarchy.

15. *For so is the will of God.* He returns to his former doctrine, in case opportunity is given to the unbelieving to speak evil, though he expresses less than what he had said before, for he says only that the mouths of the foolish ought to be stopped. The phrase which he adopts, *to put to silence the ignorance,* though it may seem harsh on account of its novelty, does not however obscure the sense. Apart from the fact that he calls the unbelieving foolish, he is concerned to point out why they slander, in fact because they are ignorant of God. In depriving the unbelieving of understanding and reason, we conclude that a right understanding cannot exist without the knowledge of God. Therefore however much the unbelieving may be satisfied with their own acuteness, and may even seem to others to be wise and prudent, yet the Spirit of God condemns them for their folly, in

order that we may know that, apart from God, we cannot be really wise, as without Him there is nothing firm.

He lays down the way in which the evil-speaking of the unbelieving is to be restrained, namely *by well-doing*. In this expression he includes all the duties of humanity and kindness which we ought to perform towards our neighbours. Among these is included obedience to magistrates, without which peace among men cannot be cultivated. If anyone objects that the faithful will never be so careful to do good, that they will not be evil spoken of by the unbelieving, the obvious answer is that the apostle here does not in the least exempt them from insults and reproaches. He means that they will have no occasion to slander, however much they may desire it. In case anyone objects further that unbelievers are not worthy of so much regard that God's children should form their life to please them, Peter expressly reminds us that we are bound by God's command to shut up their mouths.

16. *As free*. This is said by way of anticipation, to meet those objections which are usually raised with regard to the liberty of God's children. As men are naturally ingenious in laying hold on what is for their advantage, many at the commencement of the Gospel thought that they were free to live only for themselves. This deluded opinion is what Peter corrects by showing briefly how far the liberty of Christians differs from unbridled licentiousness. In the first place, he denies that there is any cloak or pretext for wickedness, by which he means that we are not given liberty to hurt our neighbours, or to do any harm to others. True liberty is that which harms or injures no one. To confirm this, he declares that those who serve God are free. The immediate conclusion is that we obtain liberty in order that we may more promptly and more readily obey God. That is simply freedom from sin, and the dominion is taken away from sin, so that men may become obedient to righteousness.

In short, it is a free servitude, and a serving freedom. As we ought to be the servants of God, in order to enjoy this benefit, so moderation is required in the use of it. In this way, our consciences become free; but this does not prevent us from serving God, who requires us also to be subject to men.

Honour all men. Love the brotherhood. Fear God. Honour the king. (17)

This is a brief summary of what is gone before. He means that God is not feared, nor justice done to men, unless civil order prevails among us, and magistrates retain their authority. His command that honour is to be rendered to all, I explain as an order that none are to be neglected. It is a general command, which refers to the fostering of human

fellowship. The word *honour* has a wide meaning in Hebrew, and we
know that the apostles, although they wrote in Greek, followed the
meaning of the former language. Therefore, this word conveys to me
the simple idea that regard ought to be had for all men, since we ought
to cultivate, as far as we can, peace and friendship with all; there is,
indeed, nothing more inimical to concord than contempt.

What he adds respecting the love of brethren is a special instance of
what he has just said, for he is speaking of that particular love which
we are bidden to have towards the household of faith, because we are
connected with them by a closer relationship. Peter did not omit this
connexion, but yet he reminds us that though our brethren are to be
specially regarded, yet this ought not to prevent our love from being
extended to the whole human race. The word brotherhood I take
collectively for the brethren.

Fear God. I have already said that all these clauses are applied by
Peter to the subject in hand. He means that the honour that is paid to
kings has its origin in the fear of God and the love of man, and that,
therefore, it is connected with them, as though he had said, 'Whoever
fears God, loves his brethren and extends his feelings to embrace the
whole human race as he ought, and will also give honour to kings.'
At the same time, he mentions Caesar by name, because that form of
government was more than any other disliked, and in it all other forms
are included.

*Servants, be in subjection to your masters with all fear; not only to the
good and gentle, but also to the forward. For this is acceptable, if for
conscience toward God a man endureth griefs, suffering wrongfully.
For what glory is it, if, when ye sin, and are buffeted for it, ye shall
take it patiently? but if, when ye do well, and suffer for it, ye shall take
it patiently, this is acceptable with God.* (18-20)

18. *Servants, be in subjection.* Though this is a particular admonition,
yet it is connected with what has gone before, as well as the other
things which follow, for the command to servants to obey their
masters, and to wives to obey their husbands, forms a part of civil
subjection.

First of all he wants servants to be subject *with all fear*, by which
expression he means that sincere and willing feeling of reverence,
because they acknowledge it to be due in their station. He then sets
this fear in opposition to pretence as well as to forced subjection, for
an ὀφθαλμοδουλεία, as Paul calls it (Col. 3.21), is the opposite of this fear.
If servants clamour against severe treatment, and are ready to throw
off the yoke if they can, they cannot properly be said to fear. In short,
this fear arises from a right knowledge of duty. Although no ex-

s   273

ception is added in this passage, yet, according to others, it is to be understood, for the subjection that is due to men is not to be extended so far that it lessens the authority of God. Servants are therefore to be subject to their masters, but only in God, or so far as the altars, as they say. Since the word here is not δοῦλοι but οἰκέται, we may understand freemen as well as the bond-servants to be meant, though it is a difference of little moment.

Not only to the good. Although it is the duty of servants to obey their masters only so far as their conscience allows, yet if they are unjustly treated, as far as they themselves are concerned, they ought not to resist authority. Whatever kind of people their masters may be, there is no excuse for servants not faithfully obeying them. When a superior abuses his power, he must hereafter render an account to God, but he does not for the present lose his right. For this law is laid on servants, that they are to serve their masters, even though they are unworthy. He contrasts *the forward* with the humane, and by this word he describes the cruel and the perverse, or those who have no humanity or mercy.

It is a wonder what could have induced an interpreter to change one Greek word for another, and turn it into 'wayward'. I should say nothing of the gross ignorance of the doctors of the Sorbonne, who commonly understand by 'wayward' the dissolute or dissipated, were it not for the fact that they try to build it up as an article of faith on this absurd rendering, that we ought to obey the Pope and his horned wild beasts, however grievous and intolerable a tyranny they may exercise. This passage, then, shows how boldly they trifle with the Word of God.

19. *For this is acceptable.* The word *gratia* has the meaning of praise, for he means that no grace or praise will make us acceptable before God, if we bear the punishment which we have deserved by our faults, but that those who patiently bear injuries are worthy of praise and do what is acceptable to God. To testify that it was acceptable to God if anyone from conscience towards God persevered in doing his duty, even though men treated him unjustly and unworthily, was at that time very necessary. The condition of servants was very hard; they were despised and counted no better than cattle, and such indignity could have driven them to despair. The only thing left for them was to look to God.

Conscience towards God means this, that one performs his duty, not from a regard for men, but for God. When a wife is submissive and obedient to her husband, in order to gain favour with him, she has her reward in this world, as Christ says of the ambitious, who looked to the praise of men (Matt. 6.16). The same view is to be taken of other cases. When a son obeys his father in order to secure his favour and bounty, he will have his reward from his father, not from God. In short, it is a general truth that the performance of our duty is approved by God, if our object be to serve Him, and if we are not influenced by a regard for man alone. Moreover, he who keeps in mind that he has to do with God must necessarily endeavour to overcome evil with good, for God not only requires that we should be such to everyone as He in turn is to us, but also that we should be good to the unworthy and to such as persecute us.

This assertion is not without its difficulty, when he says that there is nothing praiseworthy in a man who is justly punished, for when the Lord punishes our sins, patience is certainly a sacrifice of sweet odour to him, if we bear our punishment with equanimity. To this I reply that Peter is not here speaking simply but comparatively. It is small and slender praise to bear with submission a just punishment, in comparison with that of an innocent man, who willingly bears the wrongs of men only because he fears God. At the same time he seems to refer implicitly to the motive, because those who suffer punishment for their faults, are influenced by the fear of men. But the reply I have already given will suffice.

> For hereunto were ye called: because Christ also suffered for you, leaving you an example, that ye should follow his steps: who did no sin, neither was guile found in his mouth: who, when he was reviled, reviled not again; when he suffered, threatened not; but committed himself to him that judgeth righteously. (21-23)

21. *For hereunto were ye called.* Though his discussion was about servants, yet this passage ought not to be confined to that subject. The apostle here reminds all the godly in common what the condition of Christianity is, as though he were saying that we are called by the Lord on condition that we patiently bear wrongs, and, as he says in another place, that we are appointed to this. In case this should seem grievous to us, he consoles us with the example of Christ. Nothing seems more unworthy, and therefore less tolerable, than undeservedly to suffer, but when we turn our eyes to the Son of God, this bitterness is mitigated, for who would refuse to follow Him as He goes before us?

We must notice the phrase, *Leaving you an example.* Since he is speaking of imitation, it is necessary to know what Christ has set before us as our example. He walked dry-shod on the sea, He cleansed the leper, He raised the dead, He restored sight to the blind. If we try to imitate Him in these things, it would be absurd, for when He gave these evidences of His power, it was not His purpose that we should imitate Him this way. It has happened as a consequence that His fasting for forty days has been made an example without reason. What He had in view was something quite different. We ought, therefore, to exercise in this respect a right judgment, as also Augustine somewhere reminds us, when explaining the following passage, 'Learn of me, for I am meek and lowly in heart' (Matt. 11.29). The same thing may be learnt from the words of Peter, for he notes the need for differentiating by saying in so many words, 'I have given you an example of the suffering of Christ, which we ought to follow.' This subject is handled at greater length by Paul in Romans 8.29, where he teaches us that all the children of God are foreordained to be conformed to the image of Christ, in order that He might be the firstborn among many brethren. Hence in order that we may live with Him, we must first die with Him.

22. *Who did no sin.* This belongs to the subject in hand, for, if anyone boasts of his own innocence, Christ did not suffer as a punishment for his misdeeds. At the same time, he shows how far we come short of what Christ was, when he says that there was *no guile found in his mouth*, for he who offends not by his tongue, as James says, is a perfect man (James 3.2). He declares that there was in Christ the highest perfection of innocency, such as no one of us can dare claim for himself. It appears from this more clearly how unjustly He suffered beyond all others. There is therefore no reason why any one of us should refuse to suffer after His example, since no one is so conscious of having acted rightly, that he does not labour under some sin.

23. *When he was reviled.* Here Peter points out what we ought to imitate in Christ, to wit, that we should calmly bear wrongs, and not think of avenging them, for such is our disposition that when we receive injuries, our minds immediately boil over with the desire for revenge. But Christ abstained from every kind of retaliation. Our minds, therefore, ought to be bridled, so that we should not seek to render evil for evil.

But committed himself. The word *cause* is not expressed, but it is easily understood. Peter adds this for the consolation of the godly, that if they patiently endure the reproaches and violence of the wicked, they will have God as their defender. It would be a very hard thing for us to be subjected to the will of the ungodly, and not to have God caring for our wrongs. Peter therefore adorns God with this high attribute, that He *judgeth righteously*, as though he were saying, 'It is for us to bear evils calmly; God in the meantime will not neglect His part, but will show Himself to be a righteous Judge.' However wanton the ungodly may be for a time, yet they will not go unpunished for the wrongs done now to the children of God. There is no cause for the godly to fear, as though they were without any protection, for since it belongs to God to defend them and to undertake their cause, they will possess their souls in patience.

As this doctrine brings no little consolation, so it has the force of allaying and subduing the inclinations of the flesh. Nobody can rely on the fidelity and protection of God, except the man who in a meek spirit waits for His judgment. Anyone who jumps at vengeance intrudes into what belongs to God, and does not allow God to perform His own office. It is with reference to this that Paul says, 'Give place to wrath' (Rom. 12.19), meaning that the way is closed up against God, so that He does not Himself judge, when we anticipate Him. He confirms what he had said by the testimony of Moses, 'Vengeance is mine' (Deut. 32.35). Peter in short means this, that if we follow the example of Christ we shall be more ready to endure injuries if we give to God His own honour, that is, if we believe Him to be a righteous judge, and refer our right and our cause to Him.

It may be asked how Christ has committed His cause to the Father. If He required vengeance from Him, He Himself says that this is not lawful for us; for He bids us to do good to those who injure us, to pray for those who speak evil of us (Matt. 5.44). To this my reply is that it appears evident from the Gospel history that Christ did thus refer His judgment to God, and yet did not demand vengeance to be taken on His enemies, but that, on the contrary, He offered His prayers for them. 'Father,' he said, 'forgive them' (Luke 23.34). Certainly the feelings of our flesh are far from being in harmony with the judgment of God. For anyone to commit his cause to Him who judges righteously, it is necessary that he should first put a check on himself, so that he does not ask anything inconsistent with the righteous judgment of God. Those who indulge themselves in looking for vengeance fail to concede to God His office of Judge, but in a manner wish to make Him an executioner. Anyone who is so calm in his spirit as to wish those who are now his adversaries to become his friends, and who tries to bring them to the right way, rightly commits to God his own cause, and prays something like this—'Thou, O Lord, knowest my heart, how I wish those who seek to destroy me to be saved. If they are converted, I shall congratulate them, but if they continue obstinate in their wickedness, for I know that thou watchest over my safety, I commit my cause to thee.' Christ held to this meekness, and therefore it is the rule to be observed by us.

Who his own self bare our sins in his body upon the tree, that we, having died unto sins, might live unto righteousness; by whose stripes ye were healed. For ye were going astray like sheep; but are now returned unto the Shepherd and Bishop of your souls. (24-25)

If he had commended nothing in Christ's death except its example, he would have been too narrow in his views, and he now refers to a much more excellent fruit. There are three things to be noticed in this passage. The first is that by His death Christ has given us an example of patience; the second, that by His death He has redeemed and restored us to life, from which it follows that we are so bound to Him, that we ought gladly to follow His example. In the third place, he refers to the general purpose of His death, that we, being dead to sins, ought to live to righteousness. All these things confirm his previous exhortation.

24. *Who his own self bare our sins.* This form of speaking is a fitting one to set forth the efficacy of Christ's death. As under the Law in order to be released from guilt the sinner substituted a victim in his own place, so Christ took on Himself the curse due to our sins, so that He might atone for them before God. He expressly adds, *upon the tree,* because He could not offer such an expiation except on the Cross. Peter therefore well expressed the truth that Christ's death was a sacrifice for the expiation of our sins, for when He was fixed to the Cross and offered Himself as a victim for us, He took on Himself our sin and our punishment. Isaiah, from whom Peter has taken the substance of his doctrine, employs various forms of expression—that He was smitten by God's hand for our sins, that He was wounded for our iniquities, that He was afflicted and broken for our sake, and that the chastisement of our peace was laid on Him (Isa. 53.5). Peter's intention has been to set forth the same truth by the words of this verse, namely that we are reconciled to God on this condition, that Christ made Himself the surety and the guilty one for us before His judgment-seat in order to suffer the punishment due to us.

The Sophists in their schools obscure this great benefit as much as they can. They chatter that we are only freed from guilt after baptism by the sacrifice of the death of Christ, but that punishment is redeemed by our giving satisfaction. But when Peter says that He bore our sins, he means not only that guilt was imputed to Him, but also that He suffered its punishment, that He might thus be an expiatory victim, according to the saying of the prophet, 'The chastisement of our peace was upon him'. If they object that this only avails before baptism, the context of this passage disproves them, for the words are addressed to the faithful.

This clause and that which immediately follows, *by whose stripes ye were healed,* can also be applied to the subject in hand, to the effect that it behoves us to bear on our shoulders the sins of others, not indeed to expiate for them, but only to bear them as a burden laid on us.

Having died unto sins. He had already pointed out another purpose in the example of patience, but here it is made more clear (as has been stated) that we are to live a holy and righteous life. The Scripture sometimes mentions both; that the Lord tries us with troubles and adversities, so that we may be conformed to the death of Christ (Phil. 3.10), and also secondly that the old man has been crucified in the death of Christ, that we may walk in newness of life (Rom. 6.10), although this purpose of which he speaks differs from the former as the general from the particular. In patience there is simply an example, but when he says that Christ suffered, that we being dead to sins should live to righteousness, he means that there is power in Christ's death to mortify our flesh, as Paul explains more fully in the Epistle to the Romans, chapter 6. He has brought to us this great benefit, that God justifies us freely, not only by not imputing to us our sins, but also because we die to the world and to the flesh, that we may rise again to a new life; not that one day makes this death complete, but because the death of Christ is universally efficacious for the expiation of sins, and likewise for the mortification of the flesh.

25. *For ye were gone astray like sheep.* Peter borrowed this too from Isaiah, except that the prophet makes it a universal statement, 'All we like sheep have gone astray' (Isaiah 53.6). There is no particular stress on the word *sheep*. He certainly compares us to sheep, but the emphasis is on the simile which the prophet develops when he adds, that every one had turned to his own way. The meaning is that we are all going astray from the way of salvation, and running in the direction of ruin, until Christ brings us back from this wandering.

This appears still more clearly from the contrasting clause, when he says, *but are now returned with the Shepherd.* He declares that all those who are not ruled by Christ are wandering like lost sheep in the ways of error. Thus, the whole wisdom of the world, which does not submit to the government of Christ, is condemned. The two titles given here to Christ are outstanding, that he is the *Shepherd and Bishop of souls.* There is no cause to fear that he will not faithfully watch over the safety of those who are in His fold and under His care. Although it is His office to keep us safe both in body and soul, Peter mentions only souls, because this heavenly Shepherd keeps us under His own spiritual protection to eternal life.

CHAPTER THREE

In like manner, ye wives, be in subjection to your own husbands; that, even if any obey not the word, they may without the word be gained by the behaviour of their wives; beholding your chaste behaviour coupled with fear. Whose adorning let it not be the outward adorning of plaiting the hair, and of wearing jewels of gold, or of putting on apparel; but let it be the hidden man of the heart, in the incorruptible apparel of a meek and quiet spirit, which is in the sight of God of great price. (1-4)

He proceeds now to another instance of subjection, and bids wives to be subject to their husbands. Since those who are married to men who are unbelievers seem to have more reason for shaking off the yoke, he expressly reminds them of their duty, and shows particular reason why they ought to obey more faithfully, so that by their honesty they may attract their husbands to the faith. If wives ought to obey ungodly husbands, those who have believing husbands ought to obey even more readily.

It may seem strange that Peter should say, that a husband might be *gained* to the Lord *without the word*, for why is it said, that 'faith cometh by hearing' (Rom. 10.17)? To this I reply that Peter's words are not to be understood as though a holy life alone could lead the unbelieving to Christ, but because it softens and pacifies their minds, so that they might have less dislike of religion. As bad examples create stumbling-blocks, so good ones afford no small help. Peter means that wives can by a holy and pious life do much to prepare their husbands to embrace the faith of Christ, even without saying anything.

2. *Beholding.* However alienated men's spirits are from the true faith, they are subdued when they see the good conduct of believers, for, because they do not understand the doctrine of Christ, they form an opinion of it by our life. It must therefore have the result of commending Christianity, which teaches purity and fear.

3. *Whose adorning.* The second part of his exhortation is that wives are to adorn themselves sparingly and modestly. We know that in this respect they are much more painstaking and ambitious than they ought to be, so that Peter does not seek to correct them for this vanity without reason. Though he reproves generally costly adorning, he points out some things in particular—that they were not artificially to curl or crisp their hair, as was usually done by curling-pins, or otherwise to form it into waves, nor were they to set gold

around their head, for these are the things in which excesses especially appear.

It may be now asked whether the apostle is completely condemning the use of gold in adorning the body. If anyone presses these words, it may be argued that he prohibits precious garments no less than gold, for he immediately adds, *putting on apparel.* But it would be an immoderate strictness simply to forbid neatness and elegance in clothing. If the material is said to be too sumptuous, the Lord has created it, and we know that skill in art has proceeded from Him. Peter did not intend to condemn every sort of ornament, but the evil of vanity, to which women are subject. Two things are to be regarded in clothing, usefulness and decency, and what decency requires is moderation and modesty. Therefore if a woman goes about with her hair wantonly curled and braided, and makes an extravagant display, her vanity cannot be excused. Those who object that to clothe oneself in this or that way is a matter of indifference and freedom may be easily confuted, for excessive elegance and superfluous display, and in fact all excesses, arise from a corrupted mind. Besides ambition, pride, affectation of display, and other things of this kind, are not matters of indifference. Therefore those whose minds are pure of all vanity, will duly order everything, so as not to exceed moderation.

4. *But let it be the hidden man of the heart.* The contrast here ought to be carefully observed. Cato said that those who are anxiously engaged in adorning the body neglect the adorning of the mind, and so Peter, to restrain this desire in women, introduces as a remedy that they are to devote themselves rather to the cultivation of their minds. The word *heart* no doubt means the whole soul. At the same time he shows in what the spiritual adorning of women consists, namely in *the incorruptness of a meek and quiet spirit. Incorruptness* in my opinion is set in opposition to the things which fade and vanish away, which are the things which serve to adorn the body. The version of Erasmus therefore departs from the real meaning. In short, Peter means that the ornament of the soul is not like a fading flower, and does not consist in vanishing splendour, but is incorruptible. By saying a *meek* and a *quiet spirit,* he marks what especially belongs to women, for nothing more becomes their sex than a placid and a sedate temper. We know what an outrageous being an imperious and a self-willed woman is, and, moreover, nothing is more fitted to correct the vanity of which Peter speaks than a placid quietness of spirit.

What follows next, that it is *in the sight of God of great price,* may be referred to the whole previous sentence as well as to the word *spirit,* for the meaning will remain the same. Why do women take so much care to adorn themselves, except to turn the eyes of men on themselves?

Peter, on the contrary, bids them to be more anxious for what is of a great price in the sight of God.

For after this manner aforetime the holy women also, who hoped in God, adorned themselves, being in subjection to their own husbands: as Sarah obeyed Abraham, calling him lord: whose children ye now are, if ye do well, and are not put in fear by any terror. (5-6)

He sets before them the example of pious women, who sought for spiritual adorning rather than the fineries of outward ornaments. He mentions Sarah above all others, because, as the mother of all the faithful, she is especially worthy of honour and imitation on the part of her sex. He returns again to the principle of subjection, and confirms it by the example of Sarah, who, according to the words of Moses, called her husband Lord (Gen. 18.12). God indeed does not regard such titles, and it may sometimes be that someone especially petulant and disobedient should use such a word with her tongue; but Peter means that Sarah usually spoke thus, because she knew that the command had been given her by the Lord, to be subject to her husband. Peter adds that those who have imitated her fidelity would be her daughters, that is, they would have a place among the faithful.

6. *And are not put in fear.* The weakness of their sex makes women suspicious and timid, and therefore morose, because they are afraid in case by their subjection to men they are more rudely treated by them. It is this that Peter seems to have in view in forbidding them to be disturbed by any fear, as though he were saying, 'Submit willingly to the authority of your husbands, and do not let fear prevent your obedience, as though your condition would be worse if you obeyed.' The sentence may be more general, 'Do not raise up commotions at home.' Since they are liable to be frightened, they often make much of a little thing, and thus disturb themselves and the family. Others think that the timidity of women, which is contrary to faith, is in general reproved, as though Peter were exhorting them to perform the duties of their calling with a brave and fearless spirit. However, the first explanation is what I prefer, though the last is not very different from it.

Ye husbands, in like manner, dwell with your wives according to knowledge, giving honour unto the woman, as unto the weaker vessel, being also joint-heirs of the grace of life; to the end that your prayers be not hindered. (7)

7. *Ye husbands, in like manner dwell with them.* From husbands he requires prudence, for dominion over their wives is given them only on this condition, that they exercise prudence to do their duty properly. Doubtless many foolish things must be endured by them, many un-

pleasant things must be borne with, and at the same time they must take care that their indulgence should not foster folly. Hence the admonition of Peter is not in vain, that the husbands ought to live with them knowledgeably, *as with a weaker vessel.* He means that part of the prudence which he has mentioned is that the husbands honour their wives, for nothing destroys the fellowship of life more than contempt, and we cannot really love any but those whom we esteem, so that love must be connected with respect.

He uses a twofold argument, to persuade husbands to treat their wives honourably and kindly. The first is derived from the weakness of sex; the other from the honour with which God favours them. These things seem in a way to be contrary, that honour ought to be given to wives, because they are weak, and because they excel, but, where love abounds, these things well agree together. It is evident that God is despised for His gifts, unless we honour those on whom He has conferred any excellency. When we consider that we are members of the same body, we learn to bear with one another, and to cover our infirmities with forgiveness to one another. This is what Paul means when he says that greater honour is given to the weaker members (I Cor. 12.23), because we are more careful to protect them from shame. Peter does not unreasonably order women to be cared for, and be honoured with a gentle treatment, because they are weak. Further, just as we forgive children more easily, when they offend through inexperience of age, so the weakness of the female sex ought to make us not too rigid and severe towards our wives.

It is sufficient to note that the word *vessel,* as is well known, means in Scripture any sort of instrument.

Being joint-heirs of the grace of life. Some MSS have 'of manifold grace'; others instead of 'life' have the adjective 'living'. Some read 'co-heirs' in the dative case, which makes no difference in the sense. By others a conjunction is put between manifold grace and life, and this is the reading which suits best. Since the Lord bestows the same grace alike on husbands and wives, he invites them to seek an equality in them, and we know that those graces which wives share with their husbands are manifold. Some belong to the present life, and some to God's spiritual kingdom. Afterwards he adds that they are co-heirs also of life, and that is the main thing. Though some are strangers to the hope of salvation, yet as it is offered by the Lord to them no less than to their husbands, it is a sufficient honour to the sex.

That your prayers be not hindered. God cannot be rightly called upon, unless our minds be calm and peaceable. There is no place for prayer among strifes and contentions. Peter addresses both the husband and the wife, when he bids them to be at peace one with another, so that they may pray to God with one mind. Hence we may gather this general doctrine, that no one can come to God unless he is united to his brethren. As this reason ought to quieten all domestic quarrels and strifes, in order that each one of the family may pray to God, so in common life generally, it ought to be as it were a bridle to check all contentions, for we are more than insane, if we knowingly and wilfully close up the way to God's presence by prayer, since this is the only refuge of our salvation.

Some give this exposition, that intercourse with the wife ought to be sparing and temperate, in case too much indulgence in this prevents attention to prayer, according to Paul's 'Defraud not one another, unless by consent for a time, that ye may give your selves to fasting and prayer' (I Cor. 7.5). But the doctrine of Peter extends further, and Paul does not mean that prayers are interrupted by mutual cohabitation. Therefore the explanation which I have given ought to be retained.

Finally, be ye all likeminded, compassionate, loving as brethren, tender-hearted, humble minded: not rendering evil for evil, or reviling for reviling; but contrariwise blessing; for hereunto were ye called, that ye should inherit a blessing. (8-9)

Now follow general precepts which belong to all without distinction. He summarizes some things which are especially necessary to foster friendship and love. The first is, *Be ye all likeminded.* Though friends are at liberty to think differently, yet to do so is a cloud which obscures love, and indeed from this seed hatred easily arises. Sympathy (συμπάθεια) extends to all our faculties, when concord flourishes between us, so that everyone condoles with the adversities of his neighbours no less than his own, and rejoices in prosperity, and thereby not only cares for himself, but has regard to the benefit of others.

What follows next, *Loving as brethren,* belongs peculiarly to the faithful. Where God is known as a Father, there and only there brotherhood really exists. *Be tenderhearted,* which he adds, means that we are not only to help our brethren and relieve their miseries, but also to bear with their infirmities. In what follows there are two readings in Greek, but the one that seems to me the most probable is the one I have put as the text. We know that the chief bond in preserving friendship is when everyone thinks modestly and humbly of himself, just as there is nothing which produces more discords than when we think too highly of ourselves. Peter is wise to bid us to be *humble minded* (ταπεινόφρονες) in case pride and haughtiness lead us to despise our neighbours.

9. *Not rendering evil for evil.* In these words every kind of revenge is forbidden. In order to preserve love, we must bear with many

things, although at the same time he is not speaking here of mutual benevolence, but he wants us to endure wrongs, when provoked by ungodly men. Although it is commonly thought that it is an instance of a weak and abject mind not to avenge injuries, yet it is counted before God as the highest magnanimity as has been said already. It is not enough to abstain from revenge, but Peter requires also that we should pray for blessing on those who reproach us. To *bless* here means to pray, because it is set in contrast to the second clause. Peter teaches us as a general principle that evils are to be overcome by acts of kindness. This is indeed very hard, but we ought to imitate our heavenly Father in this because He makes His sun to rise on the unworthy. What the sophists imagine to be the meaning is a futile evasion, for when Christ said, 'Love your enemies,' He at the same time confirmed His teaching by saying, 'That ye might be the children of God' (Matt. 5.44-45).

For hereunto were ye called. He means that this condition was required of the faithful when they were called by God, that they were not only to be so meek as not to revenge injuries, but also to bless those who cursed them. Because this condition may seem hard and almost unjust, he calls their attention to the reward, as though he were saying that there is no reason why the faithful should complain, because they will turn wrongs to their own benefit. In short, he shows what a gain patience will be, for if we submissively bear injuries, the Lord will bestow on us His blessing.

The verb κληρονομεῖν seems to express perpetuity, as though Peter had said that the blessing would not be for a short time, but perpetual, if we are submissive in bearing injuries. God blesses in a different way from men, for it is for us to express our wishes to Him, but He has the power to make them effective. On the other hand, Peter means that they who seek to revenge injuries are trying to do something that will bring them no good, because by so doing they deprive themselves of God's blessing.

For, he that would love life, and see good days, Let him refrain his tongue from evil, and his lips that they speak no guile: And let him turn away from evil, and do good; Let him seek peace, and pursue it. For the eyes of the Lord are upon the righteous, And his ears unto their supplication: But the face of the Lord is upon them that do evil. And who is he that will harm you, if ye be zealous of that which is good? But and if ye should suffer for righteousness' sake, blessed are ye: and fear not their fear, neither be troubled; But sanctify in your hearts Christ as Lord: being ready always to give answer to every man that asketh you a reason concerning the hope that is in you, yet with meekness and fear. (10-15)

10. *For he, etc.* He confirms the last sentence by the testimony of David. The passage is taken from Psalm 34.12, where the Spirit testifies that it will be well with all those who keep themselves from all evil-doing and wrong. Common feeling tends toward something quite different, for men think that they will expose themselves to the insolence of enemies if they do not strenuously defend themselves, but the Spirit of God promises a happy life only to the meek, and those who endure evils. We cannot be happy unless God prospers our ways, and it is the good and the benevolent, and not the cruel and inhuman, that He will favour.

Peter has followed the Greek version, though there is little difference in the sense. David's words are literally these, 'He who loves life and desires to see good days' (Ps. 34.12). It is indeed a desirable thing, since God has placed us in this world, to pass our time in peace. He indicates that the way of obtaining this blessing is to conduct ourselves justly and harmlessly towards all.

The first thing he takes note of is the avoidance of the vices of the tongue, that we are not to be rude and insolent, nor speak deceitfully and with duplicity. From this he comes to deeds, that we are not to injure or cause loss to anyone, but to endeavour to be kind to all, and to exercise the duties of humanity.

11. *Let him seek peace.* It is not enough to embrace it when it is offered to us, but it ought to be followed even when it seems to escape us. It often happens that when we seek it as much as we can, others will not give us it. On account of these difficulties and hindrances he bids us to seek and pursue it.

12. *For the eyes of the Lord are upon the righteous.* It ought to be a consolation to us, enough to mitigate all evils, that we are looked upon by the Lord, so that He will bring us help in due time. The meaning then is that the prosperity which he has mentioned depends on the protection of God. Unless the Lord cares for His people, they would be like sheep exposed to the prey of wolves. The fact that we raise storms in teacups, that we suddenly flare up in anger, and that we burn with the passion of revenge, all happens because we do not remember that God cares for us, and because we do not rely on His aid. We shall be taught patience in vain unless our minds are first steeped in this truth, that God exercises such care over us, that He will in due time succour us. On the contrary, when we are fully persuaded that God defends the cause of the righteous, we shall first give our minds simply to innocence, and then, when we are molested and hated by the ungodly, we shall flee to the protection of God. When he says that the *ears* of the Lord are open to our prayers, he encourages us to pray.

But the face of the Lord. By this clause he means that the Lord will be our avenger, because He will not always suffer the insolence of the ungodly to prevail, and at the same time he shows what will happen if we want to defend our life from injuries, to wit, that God will be against us. On the other hand, it may be objected that our daily experience is quite different, for the more righteous anyone is, and the greater lover of peace he is, the more he is harassed by the wicked. To this I reply that no one is so attentive to righteousness and peace that he does not sometimes sin in this regard. It ought to be especially observed that the promises about this life do not extend further than to what is expedient for us to be fulfilled. Our peace with the world is often disturbed, in order that our flesh may be brought into obedience to God, and also for other reasons, so that nothing may be lost to us.

13. *Who is he that will harm you.* He further confirms the previous sentence by an argument drawn from common experience. It commonly happens that the ungodly bother us, either because they are provoked by us, or because we do not labour to do them good as we ought, for those who seek to do good soften minds which are otherwise hard as iron. Plato uses the same argument in book 1 of the *Republic* (351d): στάσεις γάρ που ἥ γε ἀδικία καὶ μίση καὶ μάχας ἐν ἀλλήλοις παρέχει, ἡ δὲ δικαιοσύνη ὁμόνοιαν καὶ φιλίαν. That is: 'Injustice causes strife and hatred and battles with one another; justice brings concord and friendship.' Though this commonly happens, it is not always the case, for however much the children of God strive to pacify the ungodly by their kindnesses, and show themselves friendly towards all, they are still often assailed undeservedly by many.

14. *But and if ye should suffer for righteousness.* The meaning is that the faithful will do more towards obtaining a quiet state of life by kindness than by violence and promptitude in taking revenge, but that when they have neglected nothing to gain peace, if they then suffer, they are still blessed, because they suffer for the sake of righteousness. This latter clause is greatly at variance with the judgment of our flesh, but Christ has not said so without reason, nor has Peter repeated the sentence from the Master's lips without good cause. God will come as the deliverer, and what now seems incredible will then openly appear, that is, that the miseries of the godly have been blessings when endured with patience.

To suffer *for righteousness* means not only to submit to some loss or disadvantage in defending a good cause, but also to suffer unjustly, when anyone is innocently harassed by men on account of his fear of God.

Fear not their fear. He again points out the source and cause of impatience, that we are troubled beyond measure when the ungodly rise up against us. Such fear either disheartens us, or degrades us, or kindles within us the desire for revenge. In the meantime, we do not trust the defence of God. The best remedy therefore for checking the turbulent emotions of our minds will be if we can conquer unreasonable terrors by trusting in divine aid.

Peter no doubt meant to allude to a passage in the eighth chapter of Isaiah, which is found at Ch. 8.12. When the Jews in the face of the prohibition of God sought to fortify themselves by the aid of the Gentile world, God warns his prophet not to be afraid like them. At the same time Peter seems to have turned *fear* into a different meaning, for the prophet uses it passively in accusing the people of unbelief, because, at a time when they ought to have relied on the aid of God and to have boldly despised all dangers, they became so prostrate and broken with fear, that they summoned unlawful help from all around. But Peter takes fear in another sense, as meaning the terror with which the ungodly are wont to fill us by their violence and cruel threatenings. He thus departs from the meaning of the prophet; but there is nothing unreasonable in this, for his object was not to expound the words of the prophet, but only to show that nothing is more apt to produce patience than what Isaiah prescribes, to wit, to ascribe to God His honour by relying with full confidence on His power.

If anyone prefers to render Peter's words thus, *Fear ye not their fear*; as though he had said, 'Be ye not afraid as the unbelieving, or the children of this world are wont to be, because they understand nothing of God's providence,' I do not have any strong objection, but this, I think, would be a forced explanation. There is, indeed, no need for us to labour this point, since Peter did not intend to explain here every word used by the prophet, but only referred to this one thing, that the faithful will firmly stand, and can never be moved from a right course of their duty by any dread or fear, if they will sanctify the Lord of hosts.

This sanctification ought to be confined to the circumstances of this case in hand. How is it that we are overwhelmed with fear, and think ourselves lost, when danger is impending, unless because we ascribe to mortal man more power to injure us than to God to save us? God promises that He will be the guardian of our salvation, while the ungodly, on the other hand, attempt to subvert it. Unless God's promise sustains us, do we not deal unjustly with Him, and to some degree profane Him? The prophet therefore teaches us that we ought to think honourably of the Lord of hosts, because however much the ungodly may contrive all kinds of things to destroy us, and whatever power they may possess, He alone is more than sufficiently powerful to secure our safety. Peter adds, *in your hearts*. If the conviction takes full possession of our minds, that the help promised by the Lord is sufficient for us, we shall be best fortified to repel all the fears of unbelief.

But sanctify in your hearts Christ as Lord: being ready always to give answer to every man that asketh you a reason concerning the hope that is in you, yet with meekness and fear: Having a good conscience; that, wherein ye are spoken against, they may be put to shame who revile your good manner of life in Christ. (15-16)

Though this is a new piece of advice, it yet depends on what has gone before, for he requires constancy in the faithful, so that they can boldly give a reason for their faith to their adversaries. This is a part of that sanctification which he has just mentioned, because we really honour God when neither fear nor shame hinders us from making a true profession of our faith. Peter does not expressly bid us to assert and proclaim what has been given us by the Lord everywhere, and always and among all indiscriminately, for the Lord gives His people the spirit of discretion, so that they may know when and how far and to whom it is expedient to speak. He bids them only to be ready to give an answer, in case by their reluctance or their cowardly fear of the flesh they expose the doctrine of Christ to the derision of the ungodly by their silence. The gist is, then, that we ought to be prompt in avowing our faith, so as to set it forth whenever there is need, in case the unbelieving through our silence should condemn the whole religion which we follow.

It should be noted that Peter is not commanding us to be prepared to solve any question about any matter that may be raised, for it is not the duty of everyone to speak on every subject. It is the general doctrine that is meant, which applies to the ignorant and the simple. Peter has in view simply that Christians should make it plain to un-believers that they truly worship God, and have a holy and true religion. There is no difficulty in this, for it would be absurd if we could make no defence of our faith when anyone makes inquiries about it. We ought always to take care that all may know that we fear God, and that we regard His rightful worship with piety and reverence.

This was also required by the state of the times, for the name Christian was much hated and notorious, in that many thought the sect wicked and guilty of many sacrileges. It would have been the highest betrayal of God, if, when asked, they had neglected to give testimony to their religion. This, I think, is the meaning of the word *apology*, which Peter uses, that the Christians were to make it evident to the world that they were far from every impiety, and that they did not corrupt true religion, of which they were suspected by the ignorant. *Hope* here is to be taken for faith by synecdoche. As has been said, Peter does not require them to be able to discuss carefully and scholastically every article of the faith, but only to show that their faith in Christ was consistent with genuine piety. From this we learn how all those who understand nothing for certain about their faith, and have nothing to give as an answer for it, misuse the name of Christian.

We ought again carefully to consider what he says, in the phrase *the hope that is in you*. He means that it is the confession which flows from the heart alone which is acceptable to God, for unless faith dwells within, the tongue prattles in vain. It must therefore have its roots within us, so that it may afterwards bring forth the fruit of confession.

With meekness. This is a most necessary admonition, for unless our minds are endued with meekness, strife will immediately break out. Meekness is set in contrast both to pride and vain ostentation, as well as to excessive zeal. To this he rightly adds *fear*, for where reverence for God prevails, it tames all the fierceness of our minds, and it will especially make us speak calmly of the mysteries of God. Contentious disputes arise from the fact that many think less honourably than they ought of the greatness of divine wisdom, and are carried away by profane audacity. If we want to make the confession of our faith acceptable to God, all boasting must be put aside, and all contention must be relinquished.

16. *Having a good conscience.* What we say has little weight without a corresponding life, and he therefore joins to confession a good conscience. We see that most people are sufficiently ready with their tongue, and chatter lots of things very freely, and yet with no fruit, because their life does not correspond. Besides, integrity of conscience alone is that which gives us confidence to speak as we ought, for those who chatter a lot about the Gospel, but whose dissolute life is a proof of their impiety, not only make themselves objects of ridicule, but also expose the truth itself to the slanders of the ungodly. Why has he already bidden us be ready to defend the faith, if anyone requires from us a reason for it, except that it is our duty to defend the truth of God against those false suspicions which the ignorant entertain about it? The defence of the tongue will be of little avail unless the life corresponds with it.

He therefore says *that they may be put to shame*, who blame your good behaviour in Christ, because they speak against you as evil-doers; as though he were saying, 'If your adversaries have nothing to allege against you, except that you follow Christ, they will at length be ashamed of their malice, or, at least, your innocence will be sufficient to confound them.'

For it is better, if the will of God should so will, that ye suffer for well-doing than for evil-doing. Because Christ also suffered for sins once, the righteous for the unrighteous, that he might bring us to God; being put to death in the flesh, but quickened in the spirit. (17-18)

17. *For it is better.* This has reference not only to what follows but to the whole context. He has spoken of profession of faith, which at that time was very dangerous, and he now says that it is much better, if they sustain a loss in defending a good cause, to suffer unjustly rather than to be punished for their evil deeds. This consolation is understood rather by secret meditation than by a long argument of many words. One meets this sentiment everywhere in secular writers, that there is a sufficient defence in a good conscience, whatever evils may happen and must be endured. These authors have spoken courageously, but the only truly brave man is he who looks to God. Therefore Peter has added this clause, *If the will of God should so will.* In these words he reminds us that if we suffer unjustly, it is not by chance, but rather according to the divine will, and he takes it for granted that God wills nothing or appoints nothing but for the best reason. The faithful have therefore always this comfort in their miseries, that they know that they have God as their witness, and further that they also know that they are led by Him to the contest, in order that under His protection they may give a proof of their faith.

18. *Because Christ also.* It is another comfort that, if in our affliction we are conscious of having done well, we suffer according to the example of Christ, and it thus follows that we are blessed. At the same time he proves from the purpose of Christ's death, that it is by no means consistent with our faith that we should suffer for our evil deeds, for he teaches us that Christ suffered in order to bring us to God. What does this mean, except that we have been consecrated to God by Christ's death, so that we may live and die to Him?

There are then two parts in this sentence; the first is that persecutions ought to be borne with equanimity, because the Son of God shows us the way; and the second is that since we have been brought to obedience to God by the death of Christ, it behoves us to suffer, not for our faults, but for righteousness' sake.

A question may, however, be raised here. Does not God chastise the faithful, whenever He allows them to be afflicted? To this I answer that it does often happen that God punishes them according to their deserts, and this Peter does not deny. But he reminds us what a comfort it is to have our cause conjoined to God. We shall see in the next chapter how God does not punish sins in those who endure persecution for the sake of righteousness, and in what sense they are called innocent.

Being put to death in the flesh. It is a great thing for us to be made conformable to the Son of God when we suffer without cause, but there is an additional cause for consolation in that the death of Christ had a happy issue, because though He suffered through the weakness of the flesh He yet rose again through the power of the Spirit. Therefore neither the Cross nor His death were hurtful to Christ, since life won the victory. This is said (as Paul also reminds us in II Cor. 4.10) so that we may know that we bear in our body the dying of Christ, in order that His life may be manifested in us. *Flesh* here means the outward man, and *Spirit* the divine power, by which Christ emerged from death as the conqueror.

> *In which also he went and preached unto the spirits in prison, which aforetime were disobedient, when the longsuffering of God waited in the days of Noah, while the ark was a preparing, wherein few, that is, eight souls, were saved through water: which also after a true likeness doth now save you, even baptism, not the putting away of the filth of the flesh, but the interrogation of a good conscience toward God, through the resurrection of Jesus Christ; who is on the right hand of God, having gone into heaven; angels and authorities and powers being made subject unto him.* (19-22)

19. *In which also.* Peter adds this so that we might know that the life-giving power of the Spirit of which he spoke, was not only exerted in the Person of Christ Himself, but is also poured out upon us, as Paul says in Rom. 5.5. He says therefore that Christ did not rise only for Himself, but to make known to others the same power of His Spirit, so that it penetrates even to the dead. It follows from this that we shall feel it no less life-giving to whatever in us is mortal.

Since the obscurity of this passage has produced, as usual, various explanations, I shall first refute some of the views that have been brought forward, and then we shall seek its true and proper meaning.

There has been a common opinion that it is Christ's descent into hell that is here referred to. But the words mean something quite different, for there is no mention made of the soul of Christ, but only that He came in the Spirit. These are two very different things, that Christ's soul went, and that Christ preached by the power of His Spirit. Peter expressly mentions *the Spirit*, so as to take away the notion of what may be called a real presence.

Others explain this passage as referring to the apostles, that Christ by their ministry appeared to the dead, that is, to unbelievers. I certainly allow that Christ through His apostles went by His Spirit to those who were imprisoned in the flesh, but this exposition appears incorrect for several reasons. First, Peter says that Christ went *to* *spirits*, by which he means souls separated from their bodies, for living men are never called spirits. Secondly, what Peter repeats in the fourth chapter, in the same sense, does not admit of such an allegory; therefore the words must be properly understood of the dead. Thirdly, it seems very strange that Peter, in speaking of the apostles, should immediately go back to the time of Noah, as though he forgot himself. Certainly this manner of speech would be illogical and inept, so that this explanation cannot be right.

Moreover, the strange notion of those who think that unbelievers were freed from their sin by the coming of Christ after His death needs no long refutation, for it is indubitably the teaching of Scripture that we do not obtain salvation in Christ except by faith; therefore then those who continue unbelieving to death have no hope left. Those who say that the redemption obtained by Christ availed the dead who in the time of Noah were unbelieving, but who repented a short time before they were drowned by the deluge, have a more likely point. Their understanding is that such people suffered in the flesh the punishment due to their perverseness, but were saved by Christ, so that they did not perish for ever. But this interpretation is too shaky, for it is inconsistent with the context of the passage, since Peter ascribes salvation only to the family of Noah, and gives over to ruin all who were not within the ark.

I therefore have no doubt that Peter is speaking generally, to the effect that the manifestation of Christ's grace was made to godly spirits, and that they were thus endued with the life-giving power of the Spirit. Hence there is no reason to fear that it will not be poured out on us. It may be asked why he puts in prison the souls of the godly after they have quitted their bodies? It seems to me that φυλακή rather means a watch-tower in which watchmen stand for the purpose of watching, or the act of watching itself. It is often so taken by Greek authors, and would give the best sense, that godly souls were watching in hope of the salvation promised them, as though they saw it afar off. There is no doubt that the holy fathers both in life and after death directed their thoughts to this object. If it is preferred to retain the word *prison*, it would not be too unsuitable, for, as the Law (according to Paul, Gal. 3.23) was a sort of confining prison in which they were kept in life, so after death they must have felt constrained by the same desire for Christ, because the spirit of liberty had not as yet been fully given. Hence this anxiety of waiting was to them a kind of prison.

So far the Apostle's words seem to agree with the facts and with the thread of the argument, but what follows is of some difficulty. He makes no mention here of the faithful, but only of the unbelieving, and this seems to overturn the foregoing exposition. For this reason some have been led to think that what is being said here is simply that unbelievers, who had formerly been the enemies and persecutors of the godly, discovered the Spirit of Christ to be their Judge, as though Peter were consoling the faithful with the argument that Christ, even when dead, punished them. This mistake is exposed by the fact, as we shall see in the next chapter, that the Gospel was preached to the dead, so that they might live according to God in the spirit, which applies particularly to the faithful. It is also certain that he repeats there what he now says. Besides, they have not noticed that what Peter meant was especially this, that as the power of the Spirit of Christ shows itself to be life-giving in Him, and was known as such by the dead, it will be so towards us.

However, let us see why it is that he mentions only the unbelieving. He seems to say that Christ in Spirit appeared to those who were once unbelieving; but I understand him otherwise in the sense that at that time the true servants of God were mixed together with the unbelieving, and were almost hidden on account of their number. I allow that the Greek construction is at variance with this meaning, for Peter, if he meant this, ought to have used the genitive absolute. But as it was not unusual for the apostle to put one case instead of another, and as we see that Peter is here piling many things together, and no other suitable meaning can be elicited, I have no hesitation in giving this explanation of this intricate passage, so that readers may understand that those called unbelieving are different from those to whom he said the Gospel was preached.

After saying that Christ was manifested to the dead, he immediately adds, *which aforetime were disobedient,* by which he means that no injury was done to the holy fathers in being almost overrun by the vast number of the ungodly. He meets, in my opinion, a doubt which might have harassed the faithful of that day. They saw almost the whole world filled with unbelievers, that they enjoyed all authority, and that life was in their power. This trial might have shaken the confidence of those who were shut up, as it were, under the sentence of death. Therefore Peter reminds them, that the condition of the fathers was the same, and that though the multitude of the ungodly then covered the whole earth, their life was kept safe by the power of God.

He comforts the godly, in case they are cast down or discouraged because they are so few, and he chooses the most remarkable example in all antiquity, that of the world drowned by the deluge. In the common ruin of mankind, the family of Noah alone escaped. He points out how this happened, and says that it was a kind of baptism. There is then nothing odd about this.

The sum of what is said is this, that the world has always been full of unbelievers, but that the godly ought not to be frightened by their vast number. Though Noah was surrounded on every side by the ungodly, and had very few friends, he was nevertheless not drawn aside from the true course of his faith.

20. *When the long-suffering of God waited.* This ought to be applied to the ungodly, whom God's patience renders more slothful. When God defers His vengeance and does not execute it immediately, the ungodly carelessly disregard all threatenings, but Noah on the contrary being warned by God by a prophecy had the deluge in mind for a long time, hence his assiduity in building the ark, because in his fear of God's judgment he shook off all slackness.

21. *Which also after a true likeness.* I think on the whole that the relative pronoun ought to be read in the dative case, and that the mistake has been made of putting ὅ instead of ᾧ. The meaning, however, is in no doubt, that Noah was saved by water, in a figure of baptism. The apostle mentions this so that the likeness between him and us might be more apparent. It has already been said that the design of this clause is to prevent us from being led away by wicked examples from the fear of God, and the right way of salvation, and mixing with the world. This is made evident in baptism, in which we are buried together with Christ, so that we may become dead to the world and to the flesh, and may live to God. For this reason he says that our baptism is an antitype (ἀντίτυπον) of the baptism of Noah, not that Noah's baptism was the first pattern, and ours an inferior figure, as the apostle uses this word in the Epistle to the Hebrews, where the ceremonies of the law are said to be ἀντίτυπα of heavenly things (Heb. 9.4). Greek writers apply the same word to sacraments, when they speak of the mystical bread of the Holy Supper, calling it the ἀντίτυπον of Christ's body. But here there is no comparison made between the greater and the less, and the apostle only means that there is a mutual likeness, and (as they commonly say) a correspondence. Perhaps it might more properly be described as a counterpart (ἀντίστροφον), as Aristotle makes dialectics to be the ἀντίστροφον of rhetoric. We do not need to labour about words, when the fact itself is not in doubt. As Noah obtained life through death, when he was buried in the ark just as if in a grave, and among the total ruin of the world he was preserved together with his small family, so today the death which is set forth in baptism is to us an entrance into life, and no salvation can be hoped for, unless we be separated from the world.

Not the putting away of the filth of the flesh. This was added because it could happen that the majority of men would profess the name of Christ, and so it is with us, that almost all are introduced into the fellowship of the Church by baptism. In these circumstances what he has previously said—that few at this day are saved by baptism, as God saved only eight by the ark—would be inappropriate. Peter anticipates this objection when he affirms that he is not speaking of the naked sign, but that the result must also be connected with it, as though he were saying that what happened in the age of Noah would always be the case, that mankind would rush to their own destruction, but that the Lord would in a wonderful way deliver His little flock.

We see now what this correction means, for someone might object that our baptism is far different from that of Noah, for it happens that most people today are baptized. To this he replies that the external symbol is not sufficient, unless baptism be received really and effectually. The reality (*veritas*) of it will be found only in a few. It follows from this that we ought to look carefully to see how men commonly act when we rely on examples, and that we ought not to fear though we may be few in number.

Fanatical men like Schuencfeldius pervert this testimony ridiculously by wanting to take away from sacraments all their power and effect. Peter here did not mean to teach that Christ's institution is vain and inefficacious, but only to exclude hypocrites from the hope of salvation, since, as far as they can, they deprave and corrupt baptism. Moreover, when we speak of sacraments, two things are to be considered, the sign and the thing itself. In baptism the sign is water, but the thing is the washing of the soul by the blood of Christ, and the mortifying of the flesh. The institution of Christ includes these two things. The fact that the sign often appears inefficacious and fruitless happens through the abuse of men, but it does not take away the nature of the sacrament. Let us learn then not to divorce the thing signified from the sign. At the same time we must beware of another evil, such as prevails among the Papists, because in not distinguishing as they ought between the thing and the sign, they stop at the outward element, and fix on that their hope of salvation. Therefore the sight of the water takes away their thoughts from the blood of Christ and the power of the Spirit. They do not regard Christ as the only Author of all the blessings offered to us in it, but they transfer the glory of His death to the water, and tie the secret power of the Spirit to the visible sign.

What then ought we to do? Not to put asunder what has been joined together by the Lord. We ought to acknowledge in baptism a spiritual washing, we ought to embrace therein the testimony of the remission of sin and the pledge of our renewal, and yet leave to Christ and also to the Holy Spirit each His own honour, so that no part of our salvation should be transferred to the sign. Doubtless when Peter, having mentioned baptism, immediately made this exception, that it is not the putting off of the filth of the flesh, he gives a sufficient indication that baptism to some is only the literal act, and that the outward sign of itself avails nothing.

But the interrogation of a good conscience. The word interrogation is to be taken here for answer or testimony. Now Peter briefly defines the efficacy and use of baptism, when he calls attention to conscience, and expressly requires that confidence which can bear the sight of God and can stand before His tribunal. In this passage he teaches us that baptism in its main part is spiritual, and that it includes the remission of sins and renovation of the old man. How can there be a good and pure conscience until our old man is reformed, and we are renewed in the righteousness of God? and how can we answer before God, unless we rely on and are sustained by the free pardon of our sins? In short, Peter had in mind to set forth the effect of baptism, that no one might glory in a bare and dead sign, as hypocrites are wont to do.

But we must notice that he says *through the resurrection of Jesus Christ.* By these words he teaches us that we are not to cleave to the element of water, but that what is thereby typified flows from Christ alone, and is to be sought from Him. When he refers to the resurrection, he looks back at the foregoing doctrine, that Christ was raised to life by the Spirit, for the resurrection was victory over death and the completion of our salvation. We learn from this that the death of Christ is not excluded, but is included in His resurrection. We cannot otherwise derive benefit from baptism, except by having all our thoughts fixed on the death and the resurrection of Christ.

22. *Who is on the right hand of God.* He commends to us the ascension of Christ to heaven, in case our eyes look for Him in the world, and this is especially the concern of faith. He commends to our notice His session on the Father's right hand, in case we doubt His power to save us. What is meant by His *sitting* at the right hand of the Father we have explained elsewhere, namely that Christ exercises supreme power everywhere as the representative of God. What follows is by way of explanation of this, *angels being made subject unto him.* He adds *powers* and *authorities* only for the sake of amplification, it being usual to describe angels by such words. It was thus Peter's object to extol the sovereignty which Christ has obtained by these great titles.

CHAPTER FOUR

Forasmuch then as Christ suffered in the flesh, arm ye yourselves also with the same mind; for he that hath suffered in the flesh hath ceased from sin; that ye no longer should live the rest of your time in the flesh to the lusts of men, but to the will of God. For the time past may suffice to have wrought the desire of the Gentiles, and to have walked in lasciviousness, lusts, winebibbings, revellings, carousings, and abominable idolatries: wherein they think it strange that ye run not with them into the same excess of riot, speaking evil of you: who shall give account to him that is ready to judge the quick and the dead. (1-5)

1. *Forasmuch then as Christ.* When he set forth Christ before us earlier, he only spoke of the suffering of the Cross, for sometimes the Cross means mortification, because the outward man is wasted by the trials of his afflictions, and our flesh is also subdued. Now he ascends higher, and speaks of the reformation of the whole man. Scripture commends to us a twofold likeness to the death of Christ: first that we are to be conformed to Him in reproaches and troubles (Phil. 3.6), and secondly that the old man being dead and extinct in us, we are to be renewed to a spiritual life (Rom. 6.4). Christ is not simply to be viewed as our example, when we are concerned with the mortification of the flesh, but it is by His Spirit that we are really made conformable to His death, so that it becomes effectual in us to the crucifying of our flesh. In short, as Peter at the end of the last chapter exhorted us to patience by the example of Christ, because death was to Him a passage to life, so now from the same death he leads to a higher doctrine, that we ought to die to the flesh, and to the world, as in the Epistle to the Romans, chapter 6, where Paul follows out this discussion more fully. He therefore says, *arm yourselves*, meaning that we are really and effectually supplied with invincible weapons to subdue the flesh, if we recognize as we ought the power of Christ's death.

For he that hath suffered. I do not think that the particle ὅτι here denotes the cause, but that it is rather to be taken as explanatory, for Peter is describing what that thought is with which Christ's death arms us, to wit, that the reign of sin ought to be abolished in us, so that God may rule in our life. Erasmus, I think, has made a bad rendering in applying the word 'suffered' to Christ. This is an indefinite sentence, which extends generally to all the godly, and these words have the same meaning as those of Paul in the Epistle to the Romans 6.7. 'He

298

who is dead is justified or freed from sin.' Both the apostles mean that, when we become dead to the flesh, we have no more to do with sin, that it should reign in us, and exercise its power in our life.

It may, however, be objected, that Peter is here speaking unsuitably in making us to be conformable to Christ in that we suffer in the flesh, for it is certain that there was nothing sinful in Christ which required to be corrected. The answer is obvious, that it is not necessary that a comparison should correspond in every part. It is enough that we should be made conformable to the death of Christ to some extent. In the same way Paul's phrase that we are planted in the likeness of His death (Rom. 6.5) is suitably explained in that the manner is not altogether the same, but His death is in a way the type and pattern of our mortification.

We should further notice that the word *flesh* is used here twice, but in a different sense, when he says that Christ suffered in the flesh, he means that the human nature which Christ had taken from us was made subject to death, that is, that Christ as a man died naturally. In the second clause, which refers to us, *flesh* means the corruption and the sinfulness of our nature, and thus suffering in the flesh means the denying of ourselves. We now see what is the likeness and what is the difference between Christ and us; in fact, that as He suffered in the flesh taken from us, so the whole of our flesh ought to be crucified.

2. *That ye no longer.* He sets out here the way of ceasing from sin, namely that by renouncing the greed of men we should try to form our life according to the will of God. He therefore includes here the two things in which renovation consists, the destruction of the flesh and the life of the spirit. The course of good living is to begin with the former, and then we are to advance to the latter.

Peter further defines here what is the rule of right living, that is when man depends on the will of God, from which it follows that nothing is right and well ordered in life as soon as anyone strays from this rule. We ought further to notice the contrast between the *will of God* and the *lusts of men*. From this we understand how great our depravity is, and how we ought to strive to become obedient to God. When he says, *the rest of your time in the flesh*, the word *flesh* means the present life, as in Heb. 5.7.

3. *For the time past may suffice.* Peter does not mean that we ought to be wearied with pleasures, as those usually are who fill themselves with them to saturation point, but that on the contrary the memory of our past life should stimulate us to repentance. It ought to be the sharpest goad to make us run well to recollect that we have been wandering from the right way for the greatest part of our life. Peter

reminds us that it would be stupid if we did not change our life for the better, after we have been enlightened by Christ. He makes a distinction here between the time of ignorance and the time of faith, as though he were saying that it was right that they should become new and different men from the time that Christ had called them. Instead of the greed of men, he now mentions *the desire of the Gentiles*, by which he reproves the Jews for having mixed with the Gentiles in all kinds of pollutions, although the Lord had separated them from the Gentiles.

In what follows he says that those vices which show the blindness and ignorance of God among men ought to be put off, and there is emphasis in the phrase, *the time past of our life*. He means that we ought to persevere to the end, as when Paul says that Christ, being raised from the dead, dies no more (Rom. 6.9). We have been redeemed by the Lord for the purpose of serving Him all the days of our life.

In lasciviousness. He does not give a complete list of sins, but only mentions some of them, by which we may briefly learn what those things are which men not renewed by the Spirit of God desire, and to which they are inclined. He names the grosser vices, as is the custom when examples are cited. I shall not stop to explain the words, for there is no difficulty in them.

But a question arises here, that Peter seems to have done wrong to many in making all men guilty of lasciviousness, dissipation, lusts, drunkenness, and revelling, for certainly not everyone is involved in these vices; indeed we know that some among the Gentiles lived honourably and without any taint of infamy. To this I reply that Peter does not attribute these vices to the Gentiles with the purpose of charging every individual with all of them, but because we are by nature inclined to all these evils, and not only so, but that we are so much under the power of depravity that these fruits which he specifies necessarily proceed from an evil root. There is no one who has not within him the seed of all vices, but they do not all germinate and grow up in every individual. Yet the contagion is so spread and scattered through the whole human race, that the whole community appears infected with innumerable evils, and no member is free or pure from the common corruption.

The last clause can give rise to another question, for Peter addressed the Jews, and yet he says that they had been involved in abominable idolatries. But wherever the Jews went in every part of the world, they carefully abstained from idols. A twofold answer may be given here; either that by using a synecdoche he postulates of all in common what referred only to a few (for there is no doubt that the Churches to which he wrote were made up of Gentiles mixed with Jews), or that he gives the name of idolatries to those superstitions in which the Jews were then involved. Though they professed to worship the God of Israel, yet we know that no part of divine worship was genuine among them. How great must have been the confusion in barbarous countries and among the scattered dispersion, when Jerusalem itself, from whose rays they borrowed their light, had fallen into the extreme of impiety! We know that delusions of every kind prevailed unchecked, so that the high-priesthood, and the whole government of the Church, were in the power of the Sadducees.

4. *Wherein they think it strange.* Literally Peter is saying: 'In which they are strangers, you not running with them into the same excess of riot, blaspheming.' The phrase, *to be strangers,* is used in the sense of stopping to look at something new and unusual. This is a way of speaking which the Romans sometimes use, as when Cicero says that he was a stranger in the city, because he did not know what was going on there. In this passage Peter is warning the faithful not to allow themselves to be disturbed or corrupted by the perverse judgments or words of the ungodly. It is no light temptation, when those among whom we live charge us that our life is out of conformity with that of mankind in general. A new world (they say) must be made for people like that, who differ from all mankind. So they accuse the children of God, as though they are trying to engineer a split in the world.

The apostle anticipates this, and tells the faithful not to be discouraged by such reproaches and calumnies. He sets before them, as a support, the judgment of God, for the thing that can sustain us against all assaults is patiently to wait for that day in which Christ will punish all those who now brashly condemn us, and will show that we and our cause are approved by Him. He expressly mentions *the quick and the dead,* in case we think that we shall suffer any loss, if they remain alive when we are dead, because they will not on any account escape the hand of God. In what sense he calls them the living and the dead, we may learn from I Corinthians, ch. 15.

> For unto this end was the gospel preached even to the dead, that they might be judged according to men in the flesh, but live according to God in the spirit. But the end of all things is at hand: be ye therefore of sound mind, and be sober unto prayer: above all things being fervent in your love among yourselves; for love covereth a multitude of sins: using hospitality one to another without murmuring: according as each hath received a gift, ministering it among yourselves, as good stewards of the manifold grace of God; if any man speaketh, speaking as it were oracles of God; if any man ministereth, ministering as of the strength which God supplieth: that in all things God may be glorified through

*Jesus Christ, whose is the glory and the dominion for ever and ever.
Amen.* (6-11)

6. *For unto this end was the gospel preached even to the dead.* We see
in what sense he takes the former passage, which we had in chapter 3,
that death does not hinder Christ from being always our defender.
It is a remarkable consolation to the godly that death itself brings no
loss to their salvation. Even if Christ does not appear as Deliverer in
this life, yet His redemption is not void, or without effect, for His
power extends even to the dead. As the Greek word is ambiguous, it
may be rendered in the masculine or in the neuter gender, but the
meaning is almost the same, that is, that Christ has been revealed as
Redeemer to the dead, or that salvation has been revealed to them by
the Gospel. If the grace of Christ has once penetrated to the dead,
there is no doubt that we shall experience it even when dead. We set
for it limits that are much too narrow, if we confine it to the present
life.

That they might be judged. I omit the explanations of others, because
they seem to me to be far removed from the apostle's meaning. This
has been said, I think, by way of anticipation, because it could be
objected that the Gospel is of no benefit to the dead, since it does not
restore them to life. Peter concedes part of this objection, yet in such
a way, that they are not deprived of the salvation made available by
Christ. In the first clause, when he says, *that they might be judged in the
flesh, according to men,* it is a concession; and *judged* here means, as often
elsewhere, condemned. *Flesh* is the outward man. So that the meaning
is that, though according to the way of the world the dead suffer
destruction in their flesh, and are thought of as condemned in the out-

ward man, yet they do not cease to live with God, and in the spirit,
because Christ quickens them by His Spirit.

We must add what Paul teaches us in Rom. 8.10, that the Spirit is
life, and it will come about that He will at last absorb the relics of
death which still cleave to us. The sum of what he says is, that though
the condition of the dead in the flesh is humanly speaking worse, yet
it is enough that the Spirit of Christ revives them, and will eventually
lead them to the perfection of life.

7. *But the end of all things is at hand.* Though the faithful hear that
their blessedness is elsewhere than in the world, yet because they think
that they will live long, this false thought makes them lazy, and even
careless, so that they do not direct their thoughts to the kingdom of
God. Hence in order to rouse them from the drowsiness of the flesh,
the apostle reminds them that the end of all things is nigh, by which he
means that we ought not to become rooted in this world, from which

we must soon remove. He does not speak only of the end of individuals, but of the universal renovation of the world; as though he were saying that Christ will shortly come, and He will put an end to all things.

It is, therefore, no wonder that the cares of this world overwhelm us, and make us drowsy, if present things dazzle our eyes, because almost all of us promise ourselves an eternity in this world; at least, an end never occurs to us. But if the trumpet of Christ were to sound in our ears, it would rouse us with alacrity, and not allow us to lie slothfully.

It could be objected that a long series of ages has passed away since Peter wrote this, and yet that the end is not in sight. My reply to this is that the time seems long to us, because we measure its length by the extent of this fleeting life, but if we could understand the eternity of the life to come many ages would appear to us like a moment, as Peter will also tell us in his next letter. Besides, we must remember this principle, that from the time when Christ once appeared there is nothing left for the faithful except to look forward to His second coming with minds alert.

The *watchfulness* and the *sobriety* to which he exhorted them belong in my opinion more to the mind than to the body. The words are similar to those of Christ: 'Watch ye, for ye know neither the day nor the hour wherein the Son of Man cometh' (Matt. 25.13). As indulgence in drink and sleep renders the body unfit for its duties, so the vain cares and pleasures of the world drug the mind and make it drowsy.

By adding *unto prayer*, or prayers, he points to an exercise that is specially necessary, and in which the faithful ought to be particularly occupied, since their whole strength depends on the Lord; as though he were saying, 'Since you are in yourselves very weak, pray to the Lord to strengthen you.' He reminds them too, that they are to pray earnestly, not perfunctorily.

8. *And above all things.* He commends love as the first thing, because it is the bond of perfection. And he says it should be *fervent*, or vehement, which is the same thing, for anyone who is immoderately fervent in loving himself loves others coldly. He commends it on account of its fruit, because it buries innumerable sins, than which nothing is more desirable.

The sentence is taken from Solomon, whose words are found in Prov. 10.12, 'Hatred stirs up strife; but love covers a multitude of sins.' What Solomon meant is quite clear, for the two clauses contain things which are set in contrast with one another. As he says in the first clause that hatred is the reason why men ridicule and defame one another, and bring in everything that is reproachful and dishonourable, so it follows that a contrary effect is ascribed to love, that is, that men who love one another kindly and courteously forgive one another, and hence it happens that they willingly bury each other's vices, and each one seeks to preserve the honour of the other. Peter confirms his exhortation with the view that nothing is more necessary then to cherish mutual love. Who is there who has not many faults? Therefore all stand in need of forgiveness, and there is no one who does not wish to be forgiven.

This is the singular benefit that love brings to us when it exists among us, so that innumerable evils are covered in oblivion. On the other hand, where a loose rein is given to hatred, men must necessarily consume one another by mutual biting and wounding, as Paul says (Gal. 5.15).

It ought to be noted that Solomon does not say that only a few sins are covered, but a multitude of sins, in accordance with the saying of Christ, when He bids us to forgive our brethren seventy times seven (Matt. 18.22). The more sins love covers, the more evident its usefulness appears for the wellbeing of mankind.

This is the plain meaning of the words. It appears from this how absurd the Papists are, in seeking to deduce from this passage their own satisfactions, as though almsgiving and other duties of charity were a kind of compensation to God for blotting out their sins. It is enough to point out in passing their gross ignorance, for in a matter so clear it would be superfluous to add many words.

9. *Using hospitality*. After having exhorted them to love in general, he specially mentions one of the duties of love. At that time hospitality was a common custom, and it was considered in a way a sacred kind of humanity, as we have stated elsewhere. He therefore bids them to exercise it mutually, so that no one might require more from others than he himself was prepared to render. He adds, *without murmuring*, because it is a rare example for anyone to spend himself and his own on his neighbour without any disparaging reflection. The apostle wants us to show kindness willingly and with a cheerful mind.

10. *According as each hath received*. He reminds us what we ought to bear in mind when we do good to our neighbours; for nothing is better suited to correct our murmurings than to remember that we do not give our own, but only dispense what God has committed to us. When therefore he says, *ministering the gift which every one has received*, he means· that to each one has been distributed what gifts he has, on the condition that in helping their brethren they are the ministers of God. Thus the second clause is an explanation of the first, for instead of ministry he mentions stewardship. In saying, *as each one hath received a gift*, he mentions the many different graces which God

variously distributes to us, so that each might bring his own share into
the common pool. If we excel others in any gift, let us remember
that we are the stewards of God, to the extent that we may kindly
share it in friendship with our neighbours as their necessity or benefit
may require. Thus it comes about that we are disposed and ready to
share.

The consideration is also very important that the Lord has so
divided His manifold graces among men, that no one is content with
one thing and with his own gifts, but everyone needs the help and aid
of his brother. This, I say, is a bond which God has appointed for
preserving fellowship among men, for they cannot live without
mutual assistance. Thus it comes about that he who seeks the aid of
his brethren in many things ought to share with them more freely
what he has received. This bond for promoting unity has been observed by heathens. Peter teaches us here that God had done this on
purpose to bind men one to another.

11. *If any man speaketh.* As he had spoken of the right and honest
use of gifts, he specifies two things as examples, and chooses those
which are more excellent or especially renowned. The office of
teaching in the Church is a remarkable instance of God's favour, and
he therefore expressly commands those called to it to fulfil it faithfully,
though he is not speaking here only of what we owe to men, but also
of what we owe to God, so that we do not deprive Him of His glory.

He who speaks, that is, he who is rightly appointed by public
authority, *let him speak as it were oracles of God*; that is, let him reverently
in the fear of God and in sincerity seek to perform the charge committed to him, regarding himself as engaged in God's work, and as
ministering God's Word and not his own. He is still founding on the
doctrine that when we confer anything on our brethren, we minister
to them by God's command what He has bestowed on us for that
purpose. If all those who profess to be teachers in the Church would
duly consider this one thing, there would be much more fidelity and
devotedness in them. For how great a thing it is that, in teaching the
oracles of God, they are representatives of Christ! So much carelessness
and rashness comes from the fact that the sacred majesty of the Word
of God is only borne in mind by a few, and so they indulge themselves
as if in a secular stewardship.

In the meantime, we learn from these words of Peter that it is not
lawful for those who are engaged in teaching to do anything else but
faithfully to deliver into the hands of others the doctrine they have
received from God. He forbids anyone to go forth, except one who is
instructed in the Word of God and who proclaims sure oracles from
his mouth. He leaves no room for human inventions, for he briefly

defines the doctrine which ought to be taught in the Church. No particle of comparison is introduced here which might modify the sentence, as though it were sufficient to profess that it is the Word of God that is taught. This was commonly the case formerly with false prophets, and we see today how arrogantly the Pope and his followers cover all their impious traditions with this pretence. Peter did not intend to set up pastors in the hypocrisy of pretending that they had from God whatever doctrine it pleased them to announce, but he takes his argument from the subject itself, in order to exhort them to sobriety and meekness, to a reverence for God, and to an earnest attention to their work.

If any man minister. This second example extends further, and includes the office of teaching. Since it would take too long to enumerate each of the ministries, he preferred to sum them up all together, as though he had said, 'Whatever part of the burden you bear in the Church, know that you can do nothing but what has been given you by the Lord, and that you are nothing but an instrument of God; therefore take heed not to abuse the grace of God by exalting yourself; take heed not to suppress the power of God, which exerts and manifests itself in your ministry for the salvation of the brethren.' Let him then minister *as of the strength that God supplieth*, let him regard nothing as his own, but let him humbly render obedience to God and His Church.

That in all things God may be glorified. When he says, *In all*, the word may be taken as masculine or neuter gender, and thus men or gifts may be meant, and both meanings are equally suitable. The meaning is that God does not adorn us with His gifts in order to rob Himself and make Himself as it were an empty idol by transferring His own glory to us, but on the contrary so that His own glory may shine forth everywhere. It is therefore a sacrilegious profanation of God's gifts when men propose to themselves any other object than to glorify God. He says *through Jesus Christ*, because whatever power we have to minister, He alone bestows it on us, for He is the Head, with whom the whole body is connected by joints and bindings, and grows in the Lord, according as He supplies strength to every member.

Whose is the glory. Some refer this to Christ, but the context of the passage requires that it should be rather applied to God. He confirms the last exhortation, that God justly claims glory for Himself, and, therefore, men wickedly take away from Him what is his own, when they obscure His glory in any thing or any part.

Beloved, think it not strange concerning the fiery trial among you, which cometh upon you to prove you, as though a strange thing happened unto you: but insomuch as ye are partakers of Christ's sufferings, rejoice; that at the revelation of his glory also ye may rejoice with exceeding joy. If ye are reproached for the name of Christ, blessed are ye; because the Spirit of glory and the Spirit of God resteth upon you. For let none of you suffer as a murderer, or a thief, or an evil-doer, or as a meddler in other men's matters: but if a man suffer as a Christian, let him not be ashamed; but let him glorify God in this name. For the time is come for judgment to begin at the house of God: and if it begin first at us, what shall be the end of them that obey not the gospel of God? (12-17)

12. *Beloved, think it not strange.* Mention is frequently made in this Epistle of afflictions, the reason for which we have elsewhere explained. But this difference is to be observed, that when he exhorts the faithful to patience, he is sometimes speaking generally of the troubles that are common to human life, but here he is speaking of the wrongs which the faithful suffer for the name of Christ. First, indeed, he reminds them that they ought not to wonder at it as something sudden or unexpected, meaning thereby that they ought to have been previously prepared by long meditation to bear the cross. Anyone who has resolved to fight under Christ's banner will not be dismayed if persecution comes, but will patiently bear it, as one who is used to it. In order to be in a prepared state of mind when the floods of persecutions roll over us, we ought to get used to such an event in good time by meditating continually on the Cross.

He shows the usefulness of the Cross to us by two arguments, first that God makes trial of our faith in this way, and secondly that we become partakers with Christ. In the first place, therefore, let us remember that this trial by which our faith is tested is more than necessary, and that we ought gladly to obey God because He is concerning Himself for our salvation. The chief consolation is to be looked for from fellowship with Christ. Peter not only tells us not to think it strange when he sets this before us, but also bids us to rejoice. It is, indeed, a cause of joy when God forces us to show our faith by persecutions, but this other joy far surpasses it, that the Son of God gathers us into the same course of life as Himself, so as to lead us with Himself to a blessed fellowship of heavenly glory. We must hold on to this truth, that we bear the dying of Christ in our flesh, so that His life may be manifested in us. The wicked indeed bear many afflictions, but as they are separated from Christ, they achieve nothing but God's wrath and curse. So it happens that sorrow and dread overwhelm them utterly.

The whole consolation of the godly comes from this, that they are sharers with Christ for this purpose, that hereafter they may be partakers of His glory. We are always to bear in mind this transition from the Cross to the resurrection. As this world is like a labyrinth, in which no end of evils is apparent, Peter refers to the future revelation of Christ's glory, as though he were saying that it is not to be overlooked because it is at present hidden, but ought to be waited for. He mentions a twofold joy, one which we now enjoy in hope, and the other the full fruition of which the advent of Christ will bring to us. Because the first is mingled with grief and sorrow, the second is connected to exultation. It is not fitting in the midst of afflictions to think of joy, which can free us from all trouble, but the consolations of God temper the feelings of evil, so that we can rejoice at the same time.

14. *If ye are reproached.* He mentions reproaches, because there is often more bitterness in them than in the loss of goods, or in the torments or agonies of the body. There is nothing which is harder on ingenuous spirits. We see many people who are brave in bearing want, courageous in torments, and bold in the face of death, who yet succumb under reproach. To meet this evil, Peter declares blessed, according to what Christ says (Mark 8.35), those who are reproached for the sake of the Gospel. This is quite against what men commonly think and feel, but he gives as the reason, *Because the Spirit of God*, which is also the *Spirit of glory, rests on* them. Some read the words separately, 'that which belongs to glory', as though he had said, 'glory and the Spirit of God'; but the former reading is more appropriate to the sense, and simpler as far as the language is concerned. Peter shows that it is no hindrance to the happiness of the godly that they suffer reproach for the name of Christ, because they nevertheless retain glory unspoiled in the sight of God, while the Spirit, who has glory ever connected with Him, dwells in them. What seems a paradox to the flesh the Spirit of God establishes in their minds with a sense of certainty.

On their part. This is confirmation of the last sentence, for he means that it ought to be enough for the godly, that the Spirit of God testifies to them that the reproaches endured for the sake of the Gospel are blessed and full of glory. The wicked, however, try to effect something quite different, as though he were saying, 'You can boldly despise the insolence of the ungodly, because the testimony of glory, which God's Spirit gives you, remains firmly within.' He says that the *Spirit* of God suffers reproach, because the unbelieving ridicule whatever He suggests and lays down for our consolation. But this is κατὰ πρόληψιν; for although the world in its blindness may see nothing but what is disgraceful in the reproaches of Christ, he would not have the eyes of the godly to be dazzled by this false opinion, because they ought rather to look up to God. He does not hide what men commonly think, but he sets the hidden perception of faith, which God's children possess in their own consciences, against their presumption. Thus Paul boasts that he carried the marks of Christ, and he gloried in his bonds (Gal. 6.17), when at the same time he had sufficiently found out what the judgment of the world was about them. He indicates that those to whom the slander of the flesh is not glorious are foolish in their thinking and blind along with the rest of the world.

15. *For let none of you.* Here again he anticipates an objection. He had exhorted the faithful to patience, if they happened to be persecuted for the cause of Christ. He now adds the reason why he has only spoken of that kind of trouble, to wit, because they ought to have abstained from all evil-doing. Therefore, this second exhortation is included in case they do anything for which they might seem to be justly punished. The causal particle is not superfluous here, since the apostle wished to give a reason why he so much exhorted the faithful to fellowship with the sufferings of Christ, and at the same time to take occasion to remind them to live justly and harmlessly, in case they bring on themselves a just punishment through their own faults. It is as though he were saying that it is the mark of Christians to deserve well of all, even when they are badly and cruelly treated by the world.

If anyone objects that no one can be found who is so innocent that he does not deserve to be chastised by God for many faults, I reply that Peter is here speaking of sins from which we ought to be entirely freed, such as thefts and murders; and I give this second reply, that the apostle commands Christians to be the kind of people they ought. It is, therefore, no wonder that he points out a difference between us and the children of this world, who because they are without God's Spirit abandon themselves to every kind of wickedness. He does not want God's children to be in the same condition as to draw on themselves by a wicked life the just punishments of the law. We have already said elsewhere that though there are always many sins in the elect, which God might justly punish, he spares His own children according to His paternal indulgence, so that He does not inflict the punishment they deserve, and that in the meantime, for honour's sake, He adorns them with His own tokens and those of His Christ, when He suffers them to be afflicted for the testimony of the Gospel.

The noun ἀλλοτριοεπίσκοπος seems to me to indicate one who covets what belongs to another. Those who gape after plunder or fraud, look at other people's affairs with tortuous or crooked eyes, as Horace says, but the despiser of money, as he also says elsewhere, looks on vast heaps of gold with a straight eye.

16. *But if any man suffer as a Christian.* After having forbidden the Christians to do any hurt or harm, in case, like the unbelieving, they

should earn the hatred of the world for their evil deeds, he now bids them to give thanks to God if they suffer persecutions for the name of Christ. It is in truth no common kindness of God, that He calls us, freed and exempted from the common punishment of our sins, to so honourable a warfare as to undergo for the testimony of His Gospel either exile, or prison, or reproaches, or even death itself. He means that those who clamour or murmur in time of persecutions are ungrateful to God, as though they were unworthily treated, since on the contrary they ought to regard it as gain and to acknowledge God's favour.

When he says, *as a Christian*, he has regard not so much to the name as to the cause. It is certain that the adversaries of Christ omit nothing to degrade the Gospel. Therefore, whatever reproachful words they use, it is enough for the faithful that they suffer for nothing else but for the defence of the Gospel.

On this behalf. Since all afflictions derive their origin from sin, this thought ought to occur to the godly, 'I am indeed worthy to be visited by the Lord with this and even with greater punishment for my sins, but now He would have me to suffer for righteousness, as though I were innocent.' However much the saints may acknowledge their own faults, yet since they look to a different end in persecutions, such as the Lord sets before them, they feel that their guilt is blotted out and abolished before God. *On this behalf*, they have reason to glorify God.

17. *For the time is come.* He amplifies the consolation which the goodness of the cause for which we suffer brings to us while we are afflicted for the name of Christ. The fate, he says, awaits the whole Church of God, not only to be subject to the common miseries of men, but especially and mainly to be chastised by the hand of God. Persecutions for Christ's sake ought therefore to be endured with more equanimity. Unless we want to be blotted out from the number of the faithful, we must submit our backs to the scourges of God. It is a sweet consolation, that God does not execute His judgments on us as on others, but that He marks us with the personality of His own Son, so that we only suffer for His cause and for His name.

Peter has taken this sentence from the common and constant teaching of Scripture, and this seems more probable to me than the idea of some that a particular passage is referred to. It was the custom of the Lord of old, as all the prophets testify, to find the first examples of His chastisements in His own people, as the head of a family corrects his own children rather than those of strangers. Although God is the Judge of the whole world, yet He wishes His providence to be especially acknowledged in the government of His own Church. Hence, when

He declares that He will rise up to be the Judge of the whole world, He adds that this will be after He has completed His work on Mount Sion (Isa. 10.12). He puts forth His hand indiscriminately against His own people and against strangers, for we see that both are in common subjected to adversities; and if a comparison be made, He seems in a manner to spare the reprobate, in contrast to His severity towards the elect. Hence the complaints of the godly, that the wicked pass their life in continual pleasures, delight themselves with wine and the harp, and at length descend without pains in an instant into the grave; that fatness covers their eyes; that they are exempt from troubles and that they securely and joyfully spend their life, looking down with contempt on others, so that they dare to set their mouth against heaven (Job. 21.7-13; Ps. 73.3). In short, God so regulates His judgments in this world that He fattens the wicked for the day of slaughter, and therefore passes by their many sins, as though He connived at them. In the meantime, He recalls by corrections His own children, for whom He has a care, to the right way, whenever they depart from it.

It is in this sense that Peter says that judgment begins at the house of God, for judgment includes all those punishments which the Lord inflicts on men for their sins, and whatever refers to the reformation of the world.

But why does he say that now is *the time*? He means (I think) what the prophets declare concerning their own time, that it belongs especially to Christ's kingdom, that the beginning of the reformation should be in the Church. Hence Paul says that Christians, without the hope of a resurrection, would of all men be the most miserable (I Cor. 15.19), and justly so, because, while others indulge themselves without fear, the faithful continually sigh and groan, while God connives at the sins of others, and suffers them to continue inactive, He deals more strictly with His own people under the discipline of the Cross.

And if it begin first at us, what shall be the end of them that obey not the gospel of God? And if the righteous is scarcely saved, where shall the ungodly and sinner appear? Wherefore let them also that suffer according to the will of God commit their souls in well-doing unto a faithful Creator. (17-19)

When the faithful see that it is well with the wicked, they are necessarily tempted to be envious, and this is a very dangerous trial, for present happiness is what all desire. Hence the Spirit of God dwells carefully on this in many places, particularly in the thirty-seventh Psalm in case the faithful should envy the prosperity of the ungodly. This is what Peter now deals with, showing that afflictions ought to be calmly borne by the children of God, if they compare the lot of others with their own. He takes it for granted that God is the Judge of the world, and that, therefore, no one can escape His hand with impunity. He infers from this that a dreadful vengeance will soon overtake those whose condition now seems more favourable. The gist of what he says (as I have already said) is to show that the children of God should not fall short under the bitterness of present evils, but that they ought on the contrary to bear their afflictions calmly for a short time, as the issue will be their salvation, while the ungodly will have to exchange a fading and fleeting prosperity for eternal perdition.

The argument is from the less to the greater; for if God does not spare His own children whom He loves and who obey Him, how much more dreadful will be His severity against enemies and rebels. There is nothing better, therefore, than to obey the Gospel, so that God in His mercy may correct us by His paternal hand for our salvation.

18. *And if the righteous.* Some think that this sentence is taken from Prov. 11.31, and the Greek translators have thus rendered what Solomon says, 'If the righteous shall be recompensed on the earth, how much more the ungodly and the sinner?' Whether Peter intended to quote this passage, or was repeating a common proverbial saying (which seems to me more probable), the meaning is that God's judgment would be dreadful against the ungodly, since the way to salvation was so thorny and difficult to the elect. This is said so that we should not carelessly indulge ourselves, but carefully proceed in our course, and further in case we should also seek the smooth and easy road, the end of which is a terrible precipice.

When he says that the *righteous is scarcely saved,* he refers to the difficulties of the present life, for our course in the world is like a dangerous sailing between many rocks, exposed to many storms and tempests, and so no one arrives at the port, except the one who has escaped from a thousand deaths. Meantime it is certain that we are guided by God's hand, and that we are in no danger of shipwreck as long as we have Him as our Pilot.

Those interpreters who think that we shall only be saved hardly and with difficulty, when we shall come before God in judgment, are quite absurd, for it is the present and not the future time that Peter refers to. He does not speak of God's strictness or rigour, but shows how many and what arduous difficulties must be surmounted by the Christian man before he reaches the goal. *Sinner* here means a wicked man, just as he describes as the righteous not those who are altogether perfect in righteousness, but who strive to live righteously.

19. *Wherefore let them also that suffer.* He draws this conclusion, that persecutions ought to be borne with equanimity, because the condition of the godly in them is much happier than that of the un-

believing, who enjoy prosperity to their utmost wishes. He reminds us that we suffer nothing except by the permission of God, which greatly tends to comfort us. When he says, *Let them commit their souls,* it is the same as though he had said, 'Let them deliver themselves and their life to the trust of God.' He calls Him a *faithful protector,* because He faithfully keeps and looks after whatever is under His protection of power. Some render the word 'Creator', and the term κτίστης means both in Greek, but I prefer the former meaning, for by bidding us to deposit our life with God, he makes him its safe keeper. He adds, *in well-doing,* so that the faithful should not retaliate the wrongs done to them, but that they might rather contend with the ungodly, who injure them, by well-doing.

CHAPTER FIVE

The elders therefore among you I exhort, who am a fellow-elder, and a witness of the sufferings of Christ, who am also a partaker of the glory that shall be revealed: tend the flock of God which is among you, exercising the oversight, not of constraint, but willingly, according unto God; nor yet for filthy lucre, but of a ready mind; neither as lording it over the charge allotted to you, but making yourselves ensamples to the flock. And when the chief Shepherd shall be manifested, ye shall receive the crown of glory that fadeth not away. (1-4)

In exhorting pastors to their duty, he points out three vices especially which are often to be found, namely sloth, desire for gain, and lust for power. Against the first vice he sets alacrity or a willing attention; against the second, liberality; and against the third, moderation and meekness, by which they are to keep themselves in their proper place.

He is therefore saying that pastors ought not to exercise care over the flock of the Lord, only so far as they are compelled, for they who seek to do no more than what constraint compels do their work superficially and negligently. He wants them to do what they do willingly, as those who are really devoted to their work. To correct avarice, he bids them exercise their office with a ready mind, for anyone who does not have it in view as his purpose to spend himself and his labour disinterestedly and gladly in behalf of the Church will not be a minister of Christ, but a slave to his own stomach and his purse. The third vice which he condemns is a lust for exercising power or dominion. It may be asked what kind of power he means. This, it seems to me, may be gathered from the contrasting clause, in which he bids them to be examples to the flock. It is the same as though he were saying that they are to excel for the purpose of being eminent in holiness, which cannot be the case unless they humbly subject themselves and their life to the same common rule. The thing that stands opposed to this virtue is tyrannical pride, when the pastor exempts himself from all subjection, and oppresses the Church with tyranny. It was for this that Ezekiel condemned the false prophets, because they ruled cruelly and tyranically (Ezek. 34.4). Christ also condemned the Pharisees, because they laid intolerable burdens on the shoulders of the people which they would not touch, no, not with a finger (Matt. 23.4). This imperious strictness, then, which ungodly pastors exercise over the Church, can only be corrected, if their authority is restrained, so that they may rule by the example of a godly life.

1. *The elders.* By this word he means pastors and all those who are appointed for the government of the Church. They called them presbyters or elders for the sake of honour (*seniores honoris causa*), not because they are all old in age, but because they were mainly chosen from the aged, for old age for the most part has more prudence, authority and experience. But because sometimes hoariness is not wisdom (as the Greek proverb has it), and as young men are found more suitable, such as Timothy, it was accepted practice that these were also called presbyters, after having been elected into that order. Since Peter similarly calls himself a *presbyter*, this would seem to be a common name, a fact which is still more evident from many other passages. Moreover, he secures for himself more authority by this title, as though he were saying that he had a right to admonish pastors, because he was one of themselves, for there ought to be mutual liberty between colleagues. If he had the right of primacy he would have claimed it, and this would have been most suitable on the present occasion, but although he was an apostle, he knew that authority over his colleagues was by no means delegated to him, but that on the contrary he was joined with the others in the sharing of the same office.

A witness of the sufferings of Christ. This may be explained with reference to teaching, yet I prefer to regard it as referring to his own life. Although both are likely, I am more disposed to take the latter, because these two clauses will be more in harmony, that Peter shows the sufferings of Christ in his own flesh, and that he would be also a partaker of His glory. The passage agrees with that of Paul, 'If we suffer together, we shall also reign together' (II Tim. 2.12). Besides, it is no little incentive to make us believe His words, that He gave a proof of His faith by enduring the Cross. It appears evident from this that He spoke in earnest, and in thus proving His people the Lord as it were seals their ministry, so that it may have more honour and reverence among men. Peter, then, probably had this in view, so as to be heard as the faithful minister of Christ, proof of which he gave in the persecutions he had suffered, and in the hope of the life to come.

We must observe that Peter confidently declares that he will be a partaker of that glory which was not yet revealed, for it is the character of faith to have trust in hidden blessings.

2. *Tend the flock of God.* We learn from this what force the word *presbyter* has, that it includes the office of feeding. The Pope makes presbyters for the quite different purpose of daily slaying Christ, and no mention is made of feeding in their ordination. Let us then remember to distinguish the institution of Christ from the confusion of the

Pope, as light is different from darkness. We must also bear in mind the definition of the word, for the flock of Christ cannot be fed except with pure doctrine, which alone is our spiritual food. Hence pastors are not silent spectres, nor men who spread their own imagination, which destroy the souls of men like deadly poison.

The phrase, *as much as in you lies*, means the same as though he had said, 'Apply all your strength, and whatever power God has conferred on you to this.' The old interpreter has rendered it, 'Which is among you'; and this may be the sense of the words. The rendering of Erasmus, which I have followed, is, however, more accurate, though I do not reject nor disapprove of the other.

Whether you read *the flock of God*, or of the Lord, or of Christ, it matters little, for the three readings are found in different MSS.

Exercising the oversight. Erasmus renders the words, 'Taking care of it', but as the Greek word is ἐπισκοποῦντες, I have no doubt that Peter meant to set forth the office and title of the episcopate. We can understand from other passages of Scripture that these two names, bishop and presbyter, are synonymous. He is thus showing how they rightly perform the pastoral office, though the word ἐπισκοπεῖν generally means to preside or to oversee. What I have rendered *not of constraint* is, literally, 'not necessarily', for when we act according to what necessity prescribes, we progress in our work slowly and feebly, as though by constraint.

3. *Neither as lording it.* The preposition κατά in Greek is almost always used in a bad sense. Peter is here condemning unreasonable exercise of power, as the case is with those who do not think of themselves as the ministers of Christ and His Church, but seek something else. He calls particular churches *charges* (*cleros*) for since the whole body of the Church is the Lord's heritage, so the churches are scattered through towns and villages like so many farms, the cultivation of which he assigns to individual presbyters. Some very ignorantly think that the so-called clergy are meant here. It was, indeed, an ancient way of speaking, to call the whole order of ministers clergy, but I wish that it had never occurred to the Fathers to speak thus, because it was by no means right to confine to a few men what Scripture ascribes in common to the whole Church. This way of speaking was misleading, or at least it was a departure from apostolic usage.

Peter expressly gives the churches this title, so that we may know that whatever men ascribe to themselves is robbed from the Lord, as in many places He calls the Church His peculiar treasure, and the rod of His heritage, when He intends to claim entire dominion over it. He never delivers to pastors the government (*regnum*), but only the care (*curam*), so that His own right remains unimpared.

4. *When the chief Shepherd shall be manifested.* Unless pastors keep this end in view, it can never come about that they will proceed in the course of their calling in earnest, but on the contrary they will often fail, because there are innumerable hindrances which can discourage the most prudent. They have often to do with ungrateful men, from whom they receive an unworthy reward; long and great labours are often in vain; Satan sometimes prevails with his wicked devices. So then, to prevent the faithful servant of Christ from being cast down, there is this one and only remedy, to turn his eyes to the coming of Christ. By this it will come about that he, who seems to derive no encouragement from men, will faithfully go on with his labours, knowing that a great reward is prepared for him by the Lord. Moreover, in case delayed expectation produces weariness, he sets forth at the same time the greatness of the reward, which is sufficient to compensate for all delay. *A crown of glory that fadeth not away* awaits you.

It ought also to be observed that he calls Christ the *chief Shepherd,* because we are to rule the Church under Him and in His name, so that He Himself is really the Pastor. The word *chief* here does not only mean the principal, but Him to whose power all others ought to be subject, as they do not represent Him except by His command and authority.

Likewise, ye younger, be subject unto the elder. Yea, all of you gird yourselves with humility, to serve one another: for God resisteth the proud, but giveth grace to the humble. Humble yourselves therefore under the mighty hand of God, that he may exalt you in due time; casting all your anxiety upon him, because he careth for you. (5-7)

5. *Likewise ye younger.* He uses the word *elders (seniores)* here in a different sense from before, for it is necessary, when a comparison is made between them and the younger, that the two clauses should correspond. When he spoke earlier about the office, he refers to the elders in age *(aetate senes).* Now he comes from the particular to the general. In short, he bids everyone that is inferior in age to obey the counsels of his elders *(maiorum),* and to show himself teachable and humble. The age of youth is inconstant and needs a bridle. Besides, pastors cannot perform their duty unless this feeling of reverence is strong and is cultivated, so that the younger allow themselves to be ruled. If there be no subjection, government is overturned. When those who ought by right or order of nature to rule have no authority, everyone will immediately become insolent and wanton.

Yea all. He shows the reason why the young ought to submit to the old *(senes),* namely that things between them should be duly stable and well ordered. When authority is granted to the elders *(senibus),* they

317

are not given the right or the liberty of throwing over the rein, but they are also themselves to keep their due order, so that there may be a mutual subjection. The husband is the head of the wife, and yet he in his turn is to be in some things subject to her. The father has authority over his children, and still he is not free from all subjection, but something is due to them. The same thing is true of the rest. In short, all ranks in society have to look after the whole body, and this cannot be done unless all the members are joined together by the bond of mutual subjection. *Gird yourselves with humility*. Nothing is more contrary to the disposition of man than subjection. It was once very truly said that everyone has within him the soul of a king. Until the high spirits with which the human nature of men boils are subdued, no man will give way to another, but, on the contrary, each one will despise the others, and claim everything for himself.

Therefore, in order that humility may find a place among us, the apostle wisely reproves this haughtiness and pride. The metaphor he uses is very appropriate, as though he were saying, 'Surround yourselves with humility on every side, as your clothes cover the whole body.' He means that no ornament is more beautiful or more becoming than when we submit one to another.

For. It is a most severe threat, when he says that all those who try to elevate themselves, will have God as their enemy, and He will lay them low. On the other hand, God will be kindly and favourable to the humble. We are to imagine that God has two hands, one which like a hammer beats down and breaks in pieces those who raise up themselves, and the other which raises up the humble who willingly bow themselves down, and sustain them like a firm prop. If we were really convinced of this, and had it deeply rooted in our minds, who of us would dare to urge war on God in pride. The hope of impunity now makes us fearlessly raise up our horn to heaven Let this sentence of Peter be as a celestial thunderbolt, to make men humble.

He calls *humble* those who empty themselves of all trust in their own power and wisdom, and righteousness, and who seek every good from God alone. Since there is no coming of God except in this way, who ought not to forget his own glory, and willingly humble himself?

6. *Humble yourselves therefore*. We must always bear in mind the purpose for which he bids us be humble before God, to wit, that we may be more courteous and kind to our brethren, and not refuse to submit to them as far as love demands. Therefore he says that those who are haughty and refractory towards men are acting insolently towards God. Thus he exhorts all the godly to submit to God's authority. He invokes *the mighty hand of God* in order to make them more afraid. Though 'hand' is often applied to God, yet it is to be

understood here in the context of the passage. As we are commonly
used to being afraid in case our humility is a disadvantage to us, and
others might for this reason grow more insolent, Peter meets this
objection by promising eminence to all who humble themselves.

He adds, *in due time*, in order at the same time to prevent too much
haste. He means that it is necessary for us to learn humility now, but
that the Lord well knows when it is expedient for us to be elevated.
It is proper for us to yield to His counsel.

7. *Casting all your anxiety.* He sets forth here more expressly the
providence of God. What is the meaning of these proverbial sayings,
'We shall have to howl among wolves', or 'They are foolish who are
like sheep, exposing themselves to wolves to be devoured', unless we
shall think that by our humility we let loose the reins to the audacity of
the ungodly, so that they insult us more wantonly? This fear arises
from our ignorance of divine providence. On the other hand, as soon
as we are convinced that God cares for us, our minds are easily composed to patience and humility. In case the wickedness of men should
incite us to fierceness, the apostle prescribes a remedy for us, as does
David in Psalm 37, so that, having cast our care on God, we may
calmly rest. All those who do not rely on God's providence must
necessarily be in constant turmoil and rush violently up against others.
We ought to dwell all the more on this thought, that God cares for us,
first, in order to have peace within, and, secondly, in order that we
may be humble and meek towards men.

We are not bidden to cast all our care on God, as though God
wished us to have stony hearts, and to be void of all feeling, but in
case fear or too much anxiety should drive us to impatience. In like
manner, the knowledge of divine providence does not free men from
every care, so that they can indulge themselves carelessly, for it ought
not to encourage the laziness of the flesh, but to give rest to faith.

> *Be sober, be watchful: your adversary the devil, as a roaring lion,*
> *walketh about, seeking whom he may devour: whom withstand stedfast*
> *in your faith, knowing that the same sufferings are accomplished in your*
> *brethren who are in the world. And the God of all grace, who called*
> *you unto his eternal glory in Christ, after that ye have suffered a little*
> *while, shall himself perfect, stablish, strengthen you. To him be the*
> *dominion for ever and ever. Amen.* (8-11)

8. *Be sober.* This explanation extends further, to the extent that as
we are at war with a most fierce and most powerful enemy, we are to
be strenuous in resisting him. He uses a twofold metaphor, that they
were to be sober, and that they were to be watchful. Surfeiting produces laziness and sleep, so those who indulge in earthly cares and

pleasures think of nothing else, oppressed as they are by spiritual lethargy.

We now see what the meaning of the apostle is. He says that we must carry on a warfare in this world, and he reminds us that we have to do with no common enemy, but with one who, like a lion, runs here and there, ready to devour. He concludes from this that we ought to watch carefully. Paul encourages us with the same argument in Ephesians, chapter 6, where he says that we have a contest not with flesh and blood, but with spiritual wickedness, etc. We too often turn peace into sloth, and hence it comes about that the enemy then surrounds and overwhelms us, because we indulge ourselves according to the will of the flesh, as though we were beyond the reach of danger.

He compares the devil to a lion, as though he were saying that he is a savage wild beast. He says that he walks about to devour, in order to rouse us to careful watching. He calls him the *adversary* of the godly, so that they know that they worship God and profess faith in Christ on the condition that they have a continual warfare with the devil, for he who fights with the Head will not spare the members.

9. *Whom withstand.* Just as the power of an enemy ought to make us keener and more careful, so there would be danger that our hearts might fail by the occupation of immoderate fear, unless the hope of victory were set before us. This is what the apostle speaks of, so that we know that the issue of the war will be favourable, if we indeed fight under the banner of Christ. He declares that anyone who comes to this contest endued with faith will certainly be a conqueror.

He says *withstand.* If anyone asks how, he answers there is sufficient strength in faith. Paul, in the passage which I have already quoted, enumerates the various parts of our armour (Eph. 6.13). The meaning is the same. John testifies that faith alone is our victory over the world.

Knowing that the same sufferings. There is this consolation, that we have the same battle as all the children of God. Satan tries us dangerously, when he separates us from the body of Christ. We hear how he attempted to attack the courage of Job, 'Look to the saints, has any one of them suffered such a thing?' (Job 5.1). The apostle on the other hand, reminds us here that nothing happens to us but what we see happening to other members of the Church. Moreover a fellowship or a similar condition, with all the saints, is not to be refused by us.

When he says that *the same sufferings are accomplished,* he means what Paul says in Col. 1.24, that what is lacking of the sufferings of Christ is daily fulfilled in the faithful.

The phrase, *who are in the world,* may be explained in two ways, either that God tries His faithful people indiscriminately everywhere in the world, or that the necessity of fighting remains with us as long as we are in the world. We must note that as he has already said that we are assailed by Satan, he then goes on to include in that every kind of affliction. We gather from this that we have always to do with our spiritual enemy, however adversities may come, or whatever they may be, whether diseases oppress us, or the barrenness of the land threatens us with famine, or men persecute us.

10. *The God of all grace.* After having sufficiently dwelt on his admonitions, he now turns to prayer, for doctrine is vanity poured forth into the air, unless God works by His Spirit. This example ought to be followed by all the ministers of God, that He may grant success to their labours, for otherwise they effect nothing either by planting or by watering.

Some MSS have the future tense, as though it were a promise, but the other reading is more commonly accepted. At the same time, the apostle, by praying God, confirms those to whom he was writing, for when he calls God the Author of *all grace*, and reminds them that they are called to eternal glory his purpose no doubt is to confirm them in the conviction that the work of their salvation, which he has begun, would be completed.

He is called the *God of all grace* from this effect, according to Hebrew meaning. He mentions expressly *all grace*, first so that they may learn to look on every blessing as the gift of God, and secondly that one grace is connected with another, so that they may hope in future for the addition of those graces in which they have been hitherto wanting.

Who called you. This (as I have said) serves to increase confidence, because God is led not only by His goodness, but also by His benefits, to help us more and more. He does not simply mention calling, but he tells us why they are called, namely to obtain eternal glory. He establishes the foundation of calling in Christ. Both these things lead to perpetual confidence, for if our calling is founded on Christ, and reaches to the celestial kingdom of God and a blessed immortality, it follows that it is not transient nor fading.

It may also be right to observe in passing, first, that when he says that we are called *in Christ*, our calling is established, because it is rightly founded, and secondly, that all regard to our worthiness and merit is excluded. The fact that God, by the preaching of the Gospel, invites us to Himself is wholly gratuitous, and it is still a greater grace that He effectively touches our hearts so that we obey His voice. Peter is especially addressing the faithful, and he therefore connects the efficacious power of the Spirit with the outward doctrine.

As to the three words which follow, some MSS have them in the ablative case, so that they may be rendered by gerunds, that is, *by supporting, by strengthening, by establishing,* but there is not much importance in this as far as the meaning goes. Peter means the same thing by all these words, simply to confirm the faithful, and he uses them in this way, so that we may know that to follow our course is a matter of extraordinary difficulty, and that therefore we need the special grace of God. The phrase *suffered a little while*, which is inserted here, shows that the time of suffering is short, and this is no small consolation.

11. *To him be the dominion.* In order to give more confidence to the godly, he breaks out at once into thanksgiving. Although this can be read in the indicative as well as in the optative mood, the meaning is almost the same.

> *By Silvanus, our faithful brother, as I account him, I have written unto you briefly, exhorting, and testifying that this is the true grace of God: stand ye fast therein. She that is in Babylon, elect together with you, saluteth you; and so doth Mark my son. Salute one another with a kiss of love. Peace be unto you all that are in Christ.* (12-14)

12. *By Silvanus.* At the conclusion of the epistle he exhorts them to constancy in the faith, and declares that his design in writing has been to keep them in obedience to the doctrine which they had embraced. First he commends the brevity of his epistle, in case the reading of it should be tedious to them, and, secondly, he adds a short commendation of his messenger, so as to add the living voice to what was written. This is the purpose of the testimony he bears to his fidelity. The exception, *as I account him*, was added, either for the sake of modesty or to let them know for certain that he spoke according to the conviction of his own mind, and that it was unreasonable for them not to assent to the judgment of so great an apostle.

Exhorting and testifying. How difficult it is to continue in the faith is shown by the evidence of the daily defections of many. Indeed there is no great wonder at this, when we consider how great is the levity and inconsistency of men, and how great is their inclination to vanity. As no doctrine can have firm and lasting roots in human hearts, if it is accompanied with any doubt, he bears witness that God's truth, in which they had been taught, was certain. Unless its certainty is clear to our minds, we must of necessity continually vacillate, and be easily turned to every wind of new doctrine. By the *grace of God*, he means faith with all its effects and fruits.

13. *That is at Babylon.* Many of the old commentators thought that Rome is here symbolically denoted. The Papists gladly lay hold on this comment, so that Peter seems to have been head of the Church of Rome. The infamy of the name does not deter them, provided they can pretend to the title, nor do they care greatly about Christ, pro-

vided Peter is left to them. Provided they can retain only the name of Peter's chair, they will not refuse to locate Rome in the infernal regions. But this old comment has no colour of truth, nor do I see why it was approved by Eusebius and others, except that they were already led astray by the error that Peter had been at Rome. Add the fact that they are inconsistent with themselves. They say that Mark died at Alexandria, in the eighth year of Nero, but they imagine that Peter, six years after this, was put to death at Rome by Nero. If Mark (as they say) founded the Alexandrian Church, and had been long a bishop there, he could never have been at Rome with Peter. The theory of Eusebius and Jerome which extends the time of Peter's presidency at Rome to twenty-five years can be easily disproved by what is said in the first and the second chapter of the Epistle to the Galatians.

Since Peter had Mark as his companion when he wrote this Epistle, it is very probable that he was at Babylon; and this was in accordance with his vocation, for we know that he was appointed an apostle especially to the Jews. He therefore visited chiefly those parts of the world where there was the greatest number of that nation.

In saying that the Church there was a partaker of the same election, his object is that others should be confirmed more and more in the faith, for it was a great thing that the Jews were gathered into the One Church in such remote parts of the world.

My son. He calls Mark that for the sake of honour, but the reason is that he had begotten him in the faith, as Paul did Timothy. I have spoken elsewhere of the *kiss of love.* He wants this kiss of love to be given, so that the sincerity of the heart might correspond with the external act.

THE THEME OF THE
SECOND EPISTLE OF PETER

THE fact that Eusebius says that he had doubts about this epistle ought not to keep us from reading it. If they are based on purely human authority, since he does not say by whom this doubt was expressed, we need not pay any more regard to this than to unknown men. Afterwards he adds that it was universally received without dispute. Jerome moves me much more when he writes that there were some who were led by the diversity of style to think that Peter was not the author. Although some affinity can be traced, I admit that there is a clear difference, which argues for different writers. There are other probable conjectures, from which we can deduce that it is by some other than Peter.

At the same time it is unanimously agreed that it contains nothing unworthy of Peter, and that it shows throughout the power and grace of the apostolic spirit. If it is received as canonical, we must admit that Peter is the author, not only because it bears his name, but also because he testifies that he lived with Christ. It would have been a fiction unworthy of a minister of Christ to pretend to another personality. Therefore I conclude that if the epistle is trustworthy it has come from Peter; not that he wrote it himself, but that one of his disciples composed by his command what the necessity of the times demanded.

It is probable that at the time he was very old; he says he is near to death, and it could be that at the request of the godly he allowed this testament of his mind to be signed and sealed just before his death, because it might have some force after he was dead to encourage the good and repress the wicked. Certainly since the majesty of the Spirit of Christ expresses itself in all parts of the epistle, I have a dread of repudiating it, even though I do not recognize in it the genuine language of Peter. Since there is no agreement as to the author, I shall allow myself to use the name Peter or the apostle indiscriminately.

I come now to the theme which can be sufficiently stated shortly.

The aim is to show that those who have once professed a true faith in Christ answer to their calling to the last. After he has extolled in noble terms the grace of God, he commends to them. holiness of life because God habitually punishes hypocrites for their false profession of His Name with terrible blindness, while on the other hand He increases His gifts to those who have truly and from the heart accepted the teaching of holiness. He encourages them, therefore, to make proof of their calling by godly living. To give greater weight to his advice, he says that he himself is near to death, and at the same time he excuses himself for repeating the same things so often, on the ground that when he is dead those who remain alive on the earth should have more deeply fixed in their minds what he wrote when he was alive.

Since the root of all godliness is the certainty of the Gospel, he shows first how undoubted its truth is from the fact that he was an eye-witness of everything that it contains, and especially that he heard Christ declared from heaven to be the Son of God; and further that God willed that it should be testified to and approved by the sayings of the prophets.

At the same time he predicts that danger will arise both from false teachers, who will spread ungodly inventions, and from mockers of God who will despise all religion, so that the faithful will be instructed and warned to beware. He seems to say this of set purpose, in case they expected that the course of true doctrine in the kingdom of Christ would be peaceable and even free from all strife. Thereafter as if in a picture he portrays the character and manners of those who will stain Christianity by their corruptions. The description which he gives fits our present age most admirably as a comparison will reveal. He unsheathes his pen particularly against Lucianic men who abandon themselves to every wickedness, and introduce their profane licentiousness to show contempt for God, who even make fun of the hope of a life to come. We see that the world is full of such a rabble of men today.

He goes on to exhort the faithful not only to wait for the return of Christ with eager and expectant minds, but also to regard that day as if it were present to their sight, and in the meantime to keep themselves unspotted unto the Lord. He cites Paul as his ally and his supporter in this doctrine, and to defend what he has written from the libels of the ungodly, he severely condemns all those who pervert his writings to other purposes.

CHAPTER ONE

Simon Peter, a servant and apostle of Jesus Christ, to them that have obtained a like precious faith with us in the righteousness of our God and Saviour Jesus Christ: grace to you and peace be multiplied in the knowledge of God and of Jesus our Lord; seeing that his divine power hath granted unto us all things that pertain unto life and godliness, through the knowledge of him that called us by his own glory and virtue; whereby he hath granted unto us his precious and exceeding great promises; that through these ye may become partakers of the divine nature, having escaped from the corruption that is in the world by lust. (1-4)

1. *Simon Peter.* A prayer takes first place at the beginning of this epistle, and there follows an act of thanksgiving to encourage the Jews to gratitude, so that they do not forget the kind and number of the benefits which they have received from God's hand. We have said elsewhere why it is that he calls himself the *servant and apostle of Jesus Christ,* namely because no one is to be listened to in the Church unless he speaks as in the name of Christ. The word *servant* has a more general meaning because it includes all the ministers of Christ who perform any public office in the Church, while apostleship ranks as a higher place of honour. His meaning is that he is not just anyone from the rank and file of the ministers, but one placed by the Lord in the apostolic order (*in ordine apostilico*), who held a higher place than the rest.

To them that have obtained a like precious faith. This has the effect of commending the grace which God has bestowed without distinction on all His elect. It was no ordinary gift that they had all been called into one and the same faith, since faith is the outstanding and highest good of mankind. He calls it a *like precious* faith, not because it is the same in everyone, but because by faith everyone possesses the same Christ and His righteousness, and the same salvation. Although the measure of faith varies, that does not prevent the knowledge of God and the fruit that comes from it being common to all. Thus we have a real fellowship of faith with Peter and the apostles.

He adds *in the righteousness of our God* so that they will know that they have not obtained faith by their own efforts or power, but that they have it by the sheer gift of God. The righteousness of God (in the sense in which it is taken here) and the merits of man are things which are opposed to each other. The righteousness of God is called the

effective cause of faith because no one is capable of conferring it on
himself. This righteousness is therefore to be understood not as that
which remains inherently in God, but as that which imparts itself to
men, as in Romans 3.22. He further attributes this righteousness in
common to God and to Christ, because it proceeds from God, and is
channelled down to us through Christ.

2. *Grace to you and peace.* The word *grace* indubitably denotes the
fatherly favour of God towards us. We have been reconciled to God
once for all by the death of Christ, and we have entered into possession
of this great benefit by faith; but because we perceive this grace of God
only in proportion to the measure of our faith, it is said to increase
according as our appreciation of it comes more fully to consciousness
in us. He adds *peace*, because, just as the beginning of our happiness is
when God receives us into His grace, so the more He confirms His love
in our hearts, the more richly we are endowed with His blessing so as
to be happy and prosperous in everything.

Through the knowledge; literally, 'in the knowledge', but the preposition ἐν has the force of 'with'. Although either meaning will suit
the context I prefer the former. The more one progresses in the knowledge of God, the more every kind of blessing increases along with the
sense of the Divine love. Therefore let anyone who aspires to the full
fruit of the life of blessedness remember to keep to this way, as laid
down by Peter. He connects together the knowledge of God and of
Christ because God can only be properly known in Christ, as the saying
testifies, 'No one knoweth the Father, save the Son, and he to whom-
soever the Son willeth to reveal him' (Matt. 11.27).

3. *Seeing that his divine power.* He refers to the boundless goodness of
God which they had already experienced, so that they may place a
greater reliance on Him in future. It is a consistent mark of God that
He prosecutes His course of benevolence right to the end, unless we
ourselves interrupt it by our faithlessness. His power is inexhaustible,
and His desire of beneficence equally so, and hence the apostle rightly
encourages the faithful to good hope on the basis of God's former
benefits. His words of amplification are to the same purpose. He
could have said more simply, 'as He has fully given us everything',
but by using the expression 'divine power' he lifts his argument to the
higher consideration of how God has fully unfolded the vast resources
of His power. This latter clause may refer equally well to Christ as to
the Father, and both references are appropriate; but it applies more
fittingly to Christ, as if he said that the grace which is conveyed to us
by Him is evidence of His Godhead, because humanity could not do
this.

That pertains unto life and godliness. Some think that this denotes this present life, since godliness follows life as the more excellent gift, as though Peter wanted to prove with these two witnesses how beneficent and bountiful God is towards the faithful, because He has brought them into light, supplies them abundantly with everything that they need to support their earthly life, and finally has given them rebirth into a spiritual life and endowed them with godliness. But this distinction is foreign to the mind of Peter, because as soon as he has made mention of life he immediately adds godliness as if it were the soul of life. God truly revives us when He re-forms us in obedience to His righteousness. Peter is not speaking here about the natural gifts of God, but he is describing only those which He bestows particularly on His elect over and above the common natural order. The fact that we are born men, that we are endowed with reason and understanding, and that our life is sustained by the necessary provisions is all due to God. Yet since men, being as they are perverse and ungrateful, do not reckon all these varied gifts of nature (as they call them) as the mercies of God, so it is not the general condition of human life that is touched on here, but the special gifts of the new spiritual life which take their origin from the kingdom of Christ. Since everything that makes for godliness and salvation is reckoned to be included among the supernatural gifts of God, men must learn not to claim as of right, but humbly to ask from God whatever they seem to need, and to give credit to Him whatever blessing they receive. By claiming the whole total of godliness and all the helps to salvation as originating in the divine power of Christ, Peter here removes them from the common nature of man, thereby leaving us without the merest scrap of any virtue.

Through the knowledge of him. He now describes the way in which God makes us sharers of these great blessings, namely by revealing Himself to us in the Gospel. Knowledge of God is the basis of life and the first doorway to godliness. None of the spiritual gifts can be of any use for salvation until we are enlightened with the knowledge of God by the teaching of the Gospel. He makes God the source of this knowledge because we never approach Him unless we are called, and it is therefore the calling of God and not the perception of our own minds that is the effective cause of faith. He is not speaking only of outward calling which by itself is ineffectual, but of inward calling which consists of the hidden power of the Spirit, for God does not only speak to our ears by human voice, but He inwardly draws our heart to Him by His Spirit.

By his own glory and virtue. 'Through glory' is the more generally accepted reading, but since some MSS have ἰδίᾳ δόξῃ that is, 'by his own glory', and the old commentator so renders it, I prefer to accept this latter reading, because the sense seems to flow more easily. Peter's purpose is to ascribe expressly to God alone the whole credit for our salvation, so that we know that we owe everything to Him, and this is expressed more clearly in the words that He has called us 'by His own glory and power'. The other reading, though more obscure, is to the same effect. He is saying that we are covered with shame and are utterly sinful, until God clothes us with His glory and endows us with His power. He means that the effect in the elect of this calling is that the glorious image of God is restored in them, and they are reformed in holiness and righteousness.

4. *Whereby he hath granted unto us.* It is not certain whether he is referring only to glory and power, or to the other things that have been mentioned above as well. The difficulty lies in the fact that this verse does not fit in with the glory and power which God confers on us. But if we read 'by His own glory and power' there is no difficulty or confusion. Everything promised to us by God can rightly and fittingly be thought of as the result of His power and glory. MSS vary here, some having δι' ὅν, 'on account of whom', to make the reference to Christ. Whichever reading you choose, the sense remains the same, that the promises of God are to be given the highest possible value, and that they are free, because they are offered to us as gifts. He points out that the excellence of the promises arises from the fact that they make us partakers of the divine nature, than which nothing more outstanding can be imagined.

We must take account whence it is that God raises us to such a peak of honour. We know how worthless is the condition of our nature, and the fact that God makes Himself ours so that all His possessions become in a sense ours is a grace the magnitude of which our minds can never fully grasp. This thought alone ought to give us abundant cause to renounce the world entirely and be borne aloft to heaven. We should notice that it is the purpose of the Gospel to make us sooner or later like God; indeed it is, so to speak, a kind of deification.

The word *nature* does not denote essence but kind. The Manicheans used to dream that we took our roots from the stem of God and that when we have finished the course of our life we shall revert to our original state. Likewise today there are fanatics who imagine that we cross over into God's nature so that His nature absorbs ours. This is how they explain Paul's words in I Cor. 15.28—'that God may be all in all'. They take this passage in the same sense. This kind of madness never occurred to the minds of the holy apostles. They were simply concerned to say that when we have put off all the vices of the flesh we shall be partakers of divine immortality and the glory of blessedness, and thus we shall be in a way one with God so far as our capacity allows.

This teaching was not unfamiliar to Plato, because he defines the highest human good in various passages as being completely conformed to God. But he was wrapped up in the fog of errors, and afterwards he slid away into his own invented ideas. We, however, must leave aside these empty speculations and be content with this one thing, that the image of God in holiness and righteousness is reborn in us on the condition of our sharing in eternal life and glory, so far as is necessary for complete blessedness.

Having escaped. We have already explained that it is the apostle's purpose to set before us the worth of the heavenly glory to which God invites us, and thereby to wean us away from the vanity of this present world. He sets the corruption of the world over against the divine nature. He shows this to be not only in the environment which surrounds us, but also in our own hearts, because it is there that the vicious, depraved desires hold sway, of which he describes the source and root by the word *lust*. Corruption is set in the context of the world so that we know that the world is in us.

Yea, and for this very cause adding on your part all diligence, in your faith supply virtue; and in your virtue knowledge; and in your knowledge temperance; and in your temperance patience; and in your patience godliness; and in your godliness love of the brethren; and in your love of the brethren love. For if these things are yours and abound, they make you to be not idle nor unfruitful unto the knowledge of our Lord Jesus Christ. For he that lacketh these things is blind, seeing only what is near, having forgotten the cleansing from his old sins. (5-9)

5. *Yea, and for this very cause.* Since this task is hard and one of immense labour, he bids us put off the corruption that is in us, and strive earnestly to this purpose. He means by this that there is no place for laziness or for following the calling of God easily or carelessly, but keen zeal is a necessity, as though he were saying, 'Put forth every effort and let everyone see it.' This is the force of the participle which he uses.

In your faith supply. He shows that what the faithful ought to strive towards is to have a faith consisting in upright morality, prudence, tolerance and love. He means, therefore, that faith should not be bare or empty, but that these should be its inseparable companions. To supply to your faith is to add to your faith. There is no particular climax in the sense here, though there appears to be one in the words. Love does not follow tolerance in sequence, nor does it proceed from it. The passage can be simply explained in this way: Take care that virtue, prudence, temperance and the other things which follow are added to your faith.

I take *virtue* in the sense of an honest and well-ordered life, not in the sense of power (ἐνέργεια) but of goodness (ἀρετή). *Knowledge* means acting prudently. After setting down the general term, he enumerates some of the main endowments of the Christian man. Φιλαδελφία is mutual love between the sons of God. *Charity* has a wider application and extends to all mankind.

At this point it may be asked whether by allotting to us the task of supplying virtue Peter is to that extent commending the force and the power of free-will. Those who are concerned to establish free-will in man, certainly allow a prior place to God in that He begins to work in us, but they imagine that we co-operate at the same time, and that therefore it is to our credit that the movements of God are not in vain or ineffective. On the other hand the whole teaching of Scripture is against this error, for it bears clear testimony to the fact that proper feelings are formed in us by God, and made effective by Him; that our progress and perseverance are from God alone. Moreover it specifically declares that prudence, charity and patience are the gifts of God's Spirit. In demanding these qualities the apostle is by no means maintaining that they are possible for us, but is only showing what we ought to have and to do. When godly men are conscious of their own weakness and see that they fail in their duty, they have no alternative but to take refuge in the help of God.

8. *For if these things are yours.* You will give proof, he says, that Christ is really known to you at the point when you are endowed with virtue, temperance and the other gifts, for the knowledge of Christ is something efficacious, a living root which results in fruit.

When he says that these things *make you to be not idle nor unfruitful* he means that those who boast about their knowledge of Christ without love, patience and similar gifts, glory in it falsely and without foundation, as Paul says in Ephesians 4.20f, 'Ye did not so learn Christ, if so be that ye heard him and were taught in him, even as truth is in Jesus and that ye put away the old man which waxeth corrupt,' etc. His purpose is not only to build up the faithful in patience, godliness, temperance and love, but he also demands continual progress and improvement to be made in these gifts, and rightly so, for we are as yet far off from the goal. We ought, therefore, to be always going on so that the gifts of God increase in us.

9. *For he that lacketh these things.* He now puts more clearly the fact that those who plead that they have faith by itself are utter strangers to true understanding. He says that they wander in darkness like blind men because they do not keep to the way shown to us by the light of the Gospel. He confirms this by adding as the reason for this that they have forgotten that as such they have been cleansed from sin by the

mercy of Christ. This is the basis of our Christianity, from which it follows that those who have no concern for a pure and holy life do not even keep the elementary rules of faith.

Peter takes it for granted that those who still wallow in the dirt of the flesh have *forgotten the cleansing*. The blood of Christ has not made us clean simply to be stained by our dirt again. He mentions the *old sins*, by which he means that our life is to be differently ordered, because we have been cleansed from our sins.

He does not mean that anyone can be pure from all evil as long as he lives in this world, or that the cleansing that we achieve through Christ consists simply of pardon alone, but he does mean that we ought to differ from unbelievers by the fact that God has chosen us out for Himself. Even though we sin daily, and God pardons us daily, and the blood of Christ makes us clean from our sins, yet sin ought not to reign over us, but the sanctification of the Spirit should prevail. Thus Paul in I Cor. 6.11—'And such were some of you: but ye were washed', etc.

Wherefore, brethren, give the more diligence to make your calling and election sure: for if ye do these things, ye shall never stumble: for thus shall be richly supplied unto you the entrance into the eternal kingdom of our Lord and Saviour Jesus Christ. Wherefore I shall be ready always to put you in remembrance of these things, though ye know them, and are established in the truth which is with you. And I think it right, as long as I am in this tabernacle, to stir you up by putting you in remembrance; knowing that the putting off of my tabernacle cometh swiftly, even as our Lord Jesus Christ signified unto me. Yea, I will give diligence that at every time ye may be able after my decease to call these things to remembrance. (10-15)

10. *Wherefore, brethren, give the more diligence.* He finishes by saying that one argument whereby we may prove that we are truly elected by God and not called in vain is that our profession of faith should find its response in a good conscience and an upright life. He draws the conclusion that more zeal and diligence should be given to this because he has already said that faith ought not to be barren. Some MSS have 'by good works', an addition which makes no alteration to the sense, because it is to be understood even if it is not specifically expressed.

He mentions *calling* first, though it comes later in sequence. The reason is that election is of greater importance and the proper order of a sentence is to put the most important words at the end. The meaning is therefore this: take pains to give proof of the fact that you have not been called or elected in vain. He uses *calling* here in the sense of the result or evidence of election. If anyone prefers to give the two words the same meaning, I do not object, because Scripture does sometimes ignore the difference that there is between these two terms. I have, therefore, given what is to me the more likely exposition.

The question now arises whether the stability of our calling and election depends on good works. If so, it follows that it depends on us. On the other hand the unanimous teaching of Scripture is that our election is founded first and foremost on the eternal decree of God, and that our calling is thereafter begun and perfected by His gratuitous goodness. The sophists are in the habit of perverting this evidence by transferring to us what belongs properly to the grace of God, but their nonsense can be easily refuted. If anyone understands his calling to be made firm by men, there is nothing absurd in that. One can even go further and say that everyone confirms his calling by living a good and holy life. But I maintain that it is ridiculous to conclude the sophists' contention from this, for this is a proof adduced not from the cause, but from the sign or the result. This is no reason why election is not free, nor does it follow from this that the validation of our election is in our power or in our hands.

The truth of the matter is this. God effectually calls those whom He has fore-ordained to life from before the foundation of the world by His secret purpose, and in the same way He follows through His continuous course of calling by His sheer grace. But because He chooses and calls us for the purpose of being pure and spotless in His sight, purity of life is rightly regarded as the illustration and evidence of election, whereby the faithful not only show to others that they are the sons of God, but also confirm themselves in this faith, but in such a way that they place their sure foundations elsewhere.

This assurance of which Peter speaks should not, in my opinion, be referred to conscience, as though the faithful acknowledged themselves before God to be elect and called. I take it simply of the fact itself, that calling is shown to be confirmed by a holy life. One could read thus: take pains that your calling becomes sure; for the verb $\pi o\iota\epsilon\hat{\iota}\sigma\theta\alpha\iota$ is the middle voice.

Whichever way you take it, the meaning is much the same. The gist of it is that the sons of God are distinguished from the reprobate by this mark, that they live holy and godly lives. Because this is the aim of divine election. From this it is clear how wrongly some of these wicked dogs make mockery of God that when they make His free election the excuse for every kind of licence, as though they had permission to sin with impunity because they are predestined to righteousness and holiness.

For if ye do these things. Peter again seems to ascribe it to the merits of our works that God promotes the course of our salvation and that we continue unwaveringly in His grace. The answer is simple. He has simply wanted to show that there is no firmness in hypocrites, but that on the contrary those who prove that their calling is sure by their good works are in no danger of falling, because the grace of God by which they are supported is a sure foundation. In this way the foundation of our salvation is certainly not placed in ourselves, and its cause is assuredly outside us. Peter is encouraging those who feel the effective working of the Spirit in themselves to be of good heart for the future, because the Lord has laid in them the sure foundation of a true and certain calling.

When he says, *there shall be richly supplied to you the entrance*, he is describing the means of persevering. The meaning of this phrase is that God will lead you into His kingdom by supplying you richly with new graces. This is added because although we have already passed from death to life, that passage is one of hope. As far as the ultimate completion of our lives is concerned, we have still a long way ahead of us. Meantime we are not left without many necessary helps. Peter is therefore meeting any doubt with these words: the Lord will supply your needs enough and more than enough until you have entered His eternal kingdom. He calls it the kingdom of Christ because we only reach heaven by His guidance and favour.

12. *Wherefore I shall be ready always.* Because when we often remind people of something we seem to show a lack of trust in their memory or their attention, the apostle discreetly makes the excuse that he has persisted in pressing on the faithful something that was well known to them and deeply rooted in their minds because the importance and the greatness of the subject demanded it. 'You do indeed,' he says, 'hold firmly to the truth of the Gospel, and I am not strengthening you as if you were wavering, but in such a vital matter warnings and exhortations are never wasted, and they are not to be thought of as annoying.' Paul uses a similar form of apology in Romans 15.14, where he says, 'I am persuaded of you, my brethren, that ye yourselves are filled with all knowledge, able also to admonish one another. But I write the more boldly unto you, as putting you again in remembrance.' What they have already entered in to possess with sure faith he calls *the truth which is with you.* Thus he commends their faith so that they will remain more firmly fixed in it.

13. *And I think it right.* He now expresses more clearly the usefulness and indeed the necessity of his advice, in that it serves to encourage the faithful who are otherwise overcome by the laziness of the flesh. He says that, although they had no lack of teaching, yet the stimulus of these exhortations is useful so that carelessness and self-indulgence do not overthrow and finally obliterate what they have properly learned

(as is so often the case). He adds a further reason why he has this purpose all the more in his mind, namely, because he knows that he has only a short time left. 'I must employ my time earnestly,' he says, 'for the Lord has made it clear to me that my life in this world will not be long.'

From this we learn that exhortations are so to be delivered that the people for whose advantage they are uttered should not think that they are being put in the wrong. We must beware against giving offence, and yet at the same time give full rein to our teaching and not give up admonition. Such moderation is to be used in the case of those to whom a sharper form of command would not be appropriate, but who are rather to be tactfully encouraged because they have the inclination in themselves to do their duty.

We are further taught by Peter's example that the shorter the span of life which remains to us, the more zealous we ought to be in carrying out our responsibility. It is not usually given to us to foresee our end, but those who are given intimation of the shortness of their life by such indications as advanced age or failing health ought to spur themselves on more eagerly to carry out in good time what the Lord has laid upon them. Indeed even those who are in the most robust health and who flourish at the prime of their years, and who yet do not give God such daily obedience as is to be desired, ought to provoke themselves to the same kind of solicitude by remembering the approach of death, so that they do not miss the opportunity of doing good by giving only negligent and thoughtless attention to their work.

At the same time I have no doubt that Peter's purpose was to gain more weight of authority to his teaching by saying that it would be his concern to make them remember these things after his death, which was then imminent. When anyone addresses us shortly before his departure from this life, his words have the force of a kind of last will and testament and are usually received by us with a greater reverence.

14. *The putting off of my tabernacle.* Literally, 'soon is the putting off of this tabernacle'. By this phrase and by the word decease which comes later, he means death; and this is worth noticing because we can see from this the difference between dying and perishing. The fear of death disturbs us unduly because we do not give enough thought to the transience and the impermanence of this life, nor do we set before ourselves the stedfast eternity of the life to come. What does Peter say? He declares that death is the exit from the world, by which we move on elsewhere, in fact, to the Lord. It ought not to be a terrifying event for us, as if when we die, we perished. He says that it is the laying down of a covering in which we have been clothed for a short time. There is no reason why we should take its removal from

us badly. There is an implied antithesis between the failing tabernacle and the eternal dwelling-place, which Paul explains in II Cor. 5.1.

When he says that it has been revealed to him by Christ, he is referring not to the kind of death but to the time. If he received the revelation of his approaching death at Babylon, how was he crucified in Rome? Unless he flew over sea and land in the blink of an eye, it must be held for certain that he died far from Italy. We shall refute in its proper place the practice of the Papists to make out that they are the Babylonians and that Rome is called Babylon by Peter, so as to vindicate their claim to Peter's body. What he says about keeping these things in remembrance after his death is with the intent that those who come after should learn from him even when dead, for the apostles did not look to their own age alone, but intended us also to have the benefit. Therefore, although they are dead, their teaching still lives on and flourishes. It is for us to profit by their writings as though they themselves were present before our very eyes.

For we did not follow cunningly devised fables, when we made known unto you the power and coming of our Lord Jesus Christ, but we were eyewitnesses of his majesty. For he received from God the Father honour and glory, when there came such a voice to him from the excellent glory, This is my beloved Son, in whom I am well pleased: and this voice we ourselves heard come out of heaven, when we were with him in the holy mount. (16-18)

16. *For we did not follow fables.* It adds a great deal to our confidence to know that we are engaged in something that is certain. In case the faithful should think that they were beating the air by their labours, he now proceeds to set forth the certainty of the Gospel, and says that he has handed on nothing but what was undoubtedly certain and undeniably trustworthy. By this they are encouraged to persevere, in that they are assured of a happy issue of their calling.

To begin with Peter declares that he was an eyewitness, because he has seen with his own eyes the glory of Christ which he describes. He contrasts this knowledge with the kind of cunningly devised fables which astute men are in the habit of inventing to entangle the minds of the simple. The old commentator renders the word 'feigned' (*fictas*), while Erasmus has it 'formed by craft'. It seems to me that what is meant is a subtle invention with intent to deceive. This is sometimes the meaning of the Greek σοφίζεσθαι. We know what energy men put out on frivolous arguments solely to get some enjoyment out of them. Our minds ought, therefore, to be applied no less seriously to truth which is not deceiving and teaching which is not worthless, but which reveals to us the glory of the Son of God and our salvation.

The power and coming of Christ. I have no doubt that his purpose is to embrace with this phrase the sum of the Gospel, since it certainly contains nothing but Christ in whom are hidden all the treasures of wisdom. He distinguishes two parts: first, that Christ was shown forth in the flesh, and second, the nature and efficacy of His power. We have the Gospel in its entirety, when we know that He who had long been promised as Redeemer came down from heaven, put on our flesh, lived in the world, experienced death and then rose again; and secondly when we see the purpose and the fruits of all these things in the fact that He was God with us, that He gave us in Himself a sure pledge of our adoption, that by the grace of His Spirit He has cleansed us from the stains of our carnal iniquities and consecrated us to be temples to God, that He has raised us up from the depths to heaven, that by His sacrificial death He has made atonement for the sins of the world, that He has reconciled us to the Father, and that He has been the source of righteousness and life for us. Whoever holds to these things has rightly grasped the Gospel.

We were eyewitnesses. We conclude from this that those who brashly leap into the pulpit to chatter about speculations of which they are ignorant do no service to Christ nor have anything in common with the apostles. The true minister of God is he who bears witness to the truth of the teaching which he passes on; not that certainty comes in the same way to everyone. Peter says that he was present when Christ was declared to be the Son of God by a voice from heaven. Only three were present, but they were nevertheless sufficient witnesses because they had seen the glory of Christ in so many miracles, and had the outstanding proof of His divinity in the resurrection. We must obtain our certainty in a different way. Granted that Christ did not rise again before our eyes, yet we know from those by whom His resurrection has been handed down to us from hand to hand. There is also the inner testimony of our consciences, that seal of the Spirit (as I call it) which far excels all the proofs of the senses. Let us remember that from the beginning the Gospel was not made up of vague rumours, but that the apostles were the authentic heralds of those things which they had seen.

17. *He received from God the Father.* He chooses the one example, outstanding above all others, by which Christ was adorned with heavenly glory and thereby afforded a conspicuous vision of His divine excellence to the three disciples. Although Peter does not recount all the historical circumstances, he points to them in a single phrase when he says that *there came a voice to Him from the excellent glory.* The mean-

ing is that nothing earthly was seen there, but heavenly majesty shone all around. We may take from this what the signs of excellence were of which the evangelists tell. It was fitting that it should be so, so that the authority of the voice which came should be the more awesome, as we have seen done by God from time to time. When He spoke to the fathers, for example, He did not allow His words only to sound through the air, but He bore witness to His commands by adding symbols of His presence.

This is my Son. Peter makes mention of this voice as if it alone were sufficient to give full support for the Gospel, and rightly so, for when Christ is recognized, as the Father gives Him to us, this is the ultimate goal of our wisdom.

This sentence has two clauses. When He says, 'This is', He puts great emphasis on the fact that He is that Messiah who had been promised so often. Whatever is said about the Messiah in the law and the prophets is now applied by the Father by means of this demonstration to the Person of Him whom He commends by this pronouncement. In the second clause He declares that Christ is His Son, in whom all His love dwells and abides. It follows from this that we are loved only in Him, and that the love of God is not to be sought anywhere else. It is sufficient for me simply to touch on these matters in passing.

18. *In the holy mount.* He calls the mountain 'holy' for the same reason that the ground where God appeared to Moses is called holy. Wherever God appears, He sanctifies everything by the savour of His presence inasmuch as He is the source of all holiness. From these words we learn not only to receive God with reverence wherever He shows Himself, but also to dispose ourselves to holiness as soon as He draws near us, just as the people were commanded to do when the law was given on Mount Sinai. This is a universal principle: Be ye holy, for I am holy, who dwell in the midst of you. (Lev. 11.44, 19.2)

And we have the word of prophecy made more sure; whereunto ye do well that ye take heed, as unto a lamp shining in a dark place, until the day dawn, and the daystar arise in your hearts: knowing this first, that no prophecy of scripture is of private interpretation. For no prophecy ever came by the will of man: but men spake from God, being moved by the Holy Ghost. (19-21)

19. *And we have.* He now goes on to show that the certainty of the Gospel is also based on the sayings of the prophets, in case those who have embraced it have doubts about pledging themselves wholly to Christ. If men hesitate, it can only be that they are spiritually negligent. When he says, 'We have', he may be referring to himself and the other

teachers as well as to the disciples. The apostles had the prophets as the patrons, as it were, of their teaching, and the faithful sought confirmation of the Gospel from the same source. I am more inclined to this view because he is speaking of the whole Church, and he includes himself as one among others, although he means the Jews particularly who were familiar with the teaching of the prophets. It is for this reason, in my humble opinion, that he says that their word is *made more sure*.

Those who take the comparative to be used in place of the positive do not sufficiently comprehend the whole context. It does violence to the meaning to say that the word of prophecy is made more sure because it was from it that God in fact completed what He had promised therein concerning His Son. What we have here is simply the truth of the Gospel proved by a twofold evidence; that Christ has been highly approved by the solemn declaration of God, and secondly that all the oracles of the prophets have this same end in view. At first sight it seems absurd that the word of the prophets is said to be more sure than the Word that came forth from the sacred lips of God Himself. First of all, the authority of the Word of God is the same as it was in the beginning, and then it was given further confirmation than before by the advent of Christ, as has been said at length in the Epistle to the Hebrews.

The answer to this problem is not difficult, because the apostle is having regard here to his own nation who were acquainted with the prophets, so that their teaching was accepted without dispute. Therefore since the Jews were in no doubt that everything that the prophets taught came from God, it is no wonder that Peter says that their word is more sure. Its very antiquity brings with it a measure of reverence. Furthermore, there are other circumstances to be noted, especially the fact that no suspicion could attach to those prophecies in which the Kingdom of Christ was so long foretold.

The question here, therefore, is not whether the prophets are more trustworthy than the Gospel. Peter is simply having regard to the deference which the Jews paid to those who looked on the prophets as without any doubt true ministers of God, and who had been brought up from childhood in their school.

Whereunto ye do well. This passage is one of some greater difficulty. It may be asked what that *day* is to which Peter refers. To some it seems to be the clear recognition of Christ when men fully accept the Gospel. They explain *darkness* as the state of hesitating in indecision when the teaching of the Gospel is not yet accepted as self-evident (αὐτόπιστος), as if Peter were praising the Jews who look for Christ in the Law and the prophets, and who are striving towards Christ as the Sun of righteousness as if led by a lamp shining in front of them, such as were praised by Luke (Acts 17.11) who having heard Paul's arguments searched the scriptures to see whether it was so.

To take the passage in this sense, however, implies an inconsistency, in that it would seem to restrict the usefulness of the prophets to a short period, as though they became superfluous when the light of the Gospel is apprehended. If anyone objects that this does not necessarily follow, because the conjunction *until* does not always denote finality, I would say that in the case of imperatives it cannot be taken any other way. 'Walk, until you have finished the road; fight until you have won.' In expressions like these we see that a certain length of time is certainly specified. Even if I concede the point that the reading of the prophets is not wholly cast away by this method, everyone can see that it is cold recommendation that the prophets are useful until Christ is revealed to us, when all the time their teaching is necessary to the very end of our lives.

Secondly, we must bear in mind who it is that Peter is addressing. He is not instructing ignorant novices who are still engaged with the first rudiments, but those whom he has already testified as having received the same precious faith and as being confirmed in the present truth. This gross darkness of ignorance does not fit such people. I know that some take the view that not all make equal progress, and that here he is dealing particularly with beginners who were still looking for Christ.

Yet since it is clear from the context that these words are addressed to the same audience, this passage must necessarily be applied to the faithful who have already taken service under Christ and have been given their share in the true light. Therefore I extend this darkness of which Peter speaks to cover the whole span of life, and I understand the day to dawn upon us when we see face to face what we now perceive through a glass darkly. Christ, the Sun of righteousness, does indeed shine forth in the Gospel, but in such a way that the darkness of death always partly possesses our minds until we are released from the work-house of the flesh (*e carnis ergastulo*) and carried off into heaven. The brightness of the day will be when no clouds or mists of ignorance veil the clear sight of the sun. Certainly we are as far from the full day as our faith is from perfection. It is therefore no wonder if the present state of our life is called darkness, since we are far distant from that knowledge to which the Gospel calls us.

To sum up: Peter is reminding us that as long as we are on pilgrimage through this world we need the teaching of the prophets to be as a guiding light, which if it is quenched we can do nothing but wander in darkness. He does not separate prophecy from Gospel in saying that the former gives us light to show us the way. His only purpose is to show that the whole course of our life ought to be ruled by the Word of God, because otherwise we are surrounded on every side by the darkness of ignorance, and the Lord only gives us light when we look at His Word as our lamp.

He does not use the simile of a lamp to mean that the light is feeble and thin, but in order to make the two clauses balance each other. We lack the proper light, and we can no more keep to the proper way than a man who goes astray with darkest night all around him; but the Lord provides the remedy for our ills by lighting a torch to guide us in the midst of the darkness.

It does not seem to fit in with this exposition that he immediately connects his argument to the rising of the daystar, for the firm knowledge to which we progress through all our life cannot be called the beginning of the day. I reply that he is not comparing parts of the day with one another, but that the whole day with all its parts is contrasted with the darkness which completely overwhelms all our senses unless the Lord comes to our help with the light of His Word.

This is a notable passage, for from it we learn how God governs us. The Papists are always saying that the Church cannot err, and they imagine that it is ruled by the Spirit even though the Word has been lost. But Peter on the contrary declares that all are immersed in darkness who do not look to the light of the Word. Therefore unless you want to cast yourself of your own accord into a labyrinth, you must take the utmost care not to deviate even a hair's breadth from the direction of the Word. Even the Church can only follow God as its Guide by observing this form of government.

In this verse, too, Peter condemns all human wisdom so that we may learn humbly to seek the true rule of understanding elsewhere than in our own power of perception, for apart from the Word nothing is left for men but darkness.

It is worth noticing further what he says about the clarity of Scripture. This would be a false commendation if Scripture were not a fit and proper guide to show us clearly the way. Therefore anyone who opens his eyes by the obedience of faith will see by that very experiment that Scripture has not been called a lamp for nothing. To the unbelieving it is obscure, but those who wilfully give themselves over to death are blind anyway. It is therefore a damnable blasphemy of the Papists to imagine that the light of Scripture does nothing but dazzle the eyes, so that they frighten off the simple from reading it. It is no wonder that proud men, puffed up by the wind of their false self-confidence, do not see that light which the Lord bestows only on the humble and the little children (Matt. 11.25). David commends the Law of God in similar terms in Psalms 19 and 119.

20. *Knowing this first.* Peter begins to show here how we ought to dispose our minds if we want to make proper use of Scripture. There are two possible interpretations of the words, one if you read, as some do, ἐπηλύσεως, that is, 'approach' or 'attack', but I have preferred to read ἐπιλύσεως, which means 'interpretation'. The meaning which almost all accept is that we ought not to rush at our reading of Scripture rashly, trusting in our own understanding. They think that there is support for this meaning in the fact that the Spirit who spoke by the prophets is His own true interpreter. This exposition certainly contains a true, godly and profitable lesson, to the effect that the prophets are only read with advantage when we put aside our carnal understanding and subject ourselves to the teaching of the Holy Spirit, and that it is an unholy profanation of Scripture when we presumptuously bring our own native shrewdness to the understanding of it, since it contains the mysteries of God which are hidden from our flesh, and the sublime treasures of life which far surpass our human measure. This is what we have said above, that the light which shines in it comes only to the humble.

The Papists are doubly stupid in concluding from this that no interpretation of private individuals ought to be looked on as authentic. They pervert this testimony of Peter to arrogate to their councils the final authority to interpret Scripture, and in so doing they act childishly indeed. Peter speaks of *private interpretation* not to prohibit any individual from handling Scripture by himself, but he is saying that whatever men bring to it of their own is profane. Let the whole world be unanimously agreed, and let all the minds of men be of one united opinion, what results would still be private and their own, because the subject is contrasted here with divine revelation, in that the faithful are enlightened by the Holy Spirit and acknowledge only what God wills in His Word.

However, the other meaning seems to me simpler, namely that Peter is saying that Scripture was not handed down from man or by human desire. You will never come to read it well prepared unless you bring to it reverence, obedience, and willingness to learn. A proper reverence arises from the conviction that it is God who speaks with us and not mortal men. Peter especially bids us trust the prophets as the undoubted oracles of God, because they did not give way to any private, human impulse.

What immediately follows is to the same effect, that holy men of God spoke *being moved by the Holy Ghost*. They did not blab their inventions of their own accord or according to their own judgments. The gist of all this is, that the beginning of a proper understanding is when we give His holy prophets the same trust that is due to God. He calls them the holy men of God because they faithfully carried out the task imposed on them and upheld the divine Person by their ministry. He says that they were *moved*, not because they were out of their minds (as the heathen imagine ἐνθουσιασμός in their prophets), but because they dared nothing by themselves but only in obedience to the guidance of the Spirit who held sway over their lips as in His own temple. The prophecy of Scripture means what is contained in the Holy Scriptures.

CHAPTER TWO

But there arose false prophets also among the people, as among you also there shall be false teachers, who shall privily bring in destructive heresies, denying even the Master that bought them, bringing upon themselves swift destruction. And many shall follow their lascivious doings; by reason of whom the way of the truth shall be evil spoken of. And in covetousness shall they with feigned words make merchandise of you: whose sentence now from of old lingereth not, and their destruction slumbereth not. (1-3)

1. *But there arose, etc.* Since the rise of false teachers who corrupt or pervert sacred doctrine usually shakes weak consciences grievously and dangerously, it was necessary for the apostle to remove this kind of stumbling-block by trying to encourage the faithful to persevere. He encourages and strengthens those to whom he writes with the argument that God has always disciplined His Church with this kind of trial so that their hearts may not be disturbed by its novelty. He says that the condition of the Church under the Gospel will be no different from what it was under the Law; false prophets upset the old Church, and we must expect the same. It was necessary to say this specifically because there were many who thought that the state of the Church under the reign of Christ would be peaceful. Because the prophets promised that at His coming there would be lasting peace, the fullest light of heavenly wisdom and full restoration of all things, they did not think that the Church would be exposed to any more conflicts. Let us, therefore, remember that the Spirit of God has declared once and for all that the Church will never be free from this internal trouble, and let this image be kept in mind that the trial of faith is common both to us and to our fathers, because it has the same purpose, namely to make clear by this means whether we truly love God, as is written in Deuteronomy 13.3.

It is not necessary to refer here to individual examples. It is enough to remember in general that like our fathers we must fight against unholy doctrines, and that our faith ought not to be shaken by divisions and heresies, because the truth of God will firmly prevail over all the turbulent upsets by which Satan has so often tried to overthrow everything.

Notice too that Peter mentions no particular time when he says that *there shall be false teachers*, but rather includes all ages. He is comparing

Christians with the people of old. We should apply this teaching to our own time in case temptation should overcome us when we see false teachers rise up to attack the truth of God. The Spirit of God warns us to take heed and beware, and the whole description that immediately follows is to the same effect, although he does not depict individual sects in their own colours, but directs his homily particularly at unbelieving men, who show contempt for God. The general sense is that we must beware of false teachers, but he has chosen out one example from which greater danger arose. This will be seen more clearly in the words of Jude who develops the same argument.

Who shall privily bring in. By this phrase he points out the craftiness of Satan and of all wicked men who war under the same banner in infiltrating by flanking attacks and by underground tunnellings. The godly ought to be all the more on their guard to escape their hidden traps, for however they wriggle their way in, they cannot circumvent those who are wide awake.

He speaks of *destructive heresies* so that anyone who has any concern for his salvation may shun such heresies as the most poisonous pestilences. As far as the name 'sects' or 'heresies' is concerned, it has always been notorious and hateful to the people of God, and not without reason. The bond of holy unity is the simple truth of God, and whenever that is discarded nothing remains but dreadful disintegration.

Even the Master that bought them. Though Christ is denied in all kinds of ways, Peter is here referring (in my opinion) to that which is expressed by Jude when he refers to the grace of God being turned into lasciviousness. Christ redeemed us to have us as a people separated from all the iniquities of the world, devoted to holiness and purity. Those who throw over the traces and plunge themselves into every kind of licence are not unjustly said to deny Christ, by whom they were redeemed. Therefore, in order that the teaching of the Gospel may remain pure and undefiled in us, let it be firmly fixed in our minds that we have been redeemed by Christ, that He may be the Lord both of our life and death, and thus it will be our object and purpose to live and die to Him. He goes on to say that *swift destruction* comes upon them so that others do not involve themselves with them.

2. *And many shall follow.* It is no small stumbling-block to those who are weak to see false teachings received by the common approbation of the world, and a huge number of men led astray, so that only a few remain in the pure obedience of Christ. There is nothing that disturbs godly minds so violently today as such defection. Scarcely one in ten of those who enlist under Christ keep the purity of their faith to the very end. Almost all fall away into corruption, are led astray by the teachers of licentiousness and betray their faith. To prevent this

destroying our faith, Peter interposes with the timely prediction that this very thing will happen, and ungodly teachers will drag many to perdition.

There is a double reading here, even in the Greek MSS. Some read 'lasciviousness', others 'perditions', but I have followed what the majority accept.

By reason of whom the way of the truth. I understand this to have been said because, just as religion is adorned when men are brought up into the fear of God, integrity of life, and chaste and honest behaviour, or when at least the mouth of the wicked is shut up so that they do not malign the Gospel, so when the reins are thrown over to every kind of licentiousness the name and teaching of Christ are exposed to the insults of the ungodly.

Others give a different sense, and hold that those false teachers will bark at sound doctrine like dirty dogs. To me the words of Peter rather mean that they will give opportunity to the enemy to assault the truth of God shamelessly. Although they will not themselves assail the Christian faith with insults, they arm others with the means to do so.

With feigned words. Peter studies in every way to make the faithful hostile to the evil teachers so that they may resist them more keenly and constantly. It is particularly hateful that we are exposed for sale like cheap slaves. He bears witness that this happens when anyone suborns us from our freedom in Christ. He calls those *feigned words* that are artfully designed to deceive. Therefore, unless anyone is so mad as to want of his own accord to sell his soul's salvation to false teachers for a price, let him shut up every approach to their perverted inventions. With the same purpose as before, namely, to frighten the good away from their company, he repeats that their destruction has not passed from them. Since they are ordained to an imminent destruction, anyone who associates with them cannot help perishing miserably.

For if God spared not angels when they sinned, but cast them down to hell, and committed them to pits of darkness, to be reserved unto judgment; and spared not the ancient world, but preserved Noah with seven others, a preacher of righteousness, when he brought a flood upon the world of the ungodly; and turning the cities of Sodom and Gomorrah into ashes condemned them with an overthrow, having made them an example unto those that should live ungodly; and delivered righteous Lot, sore distressed by the lascivious life of the wicked (for that righteous man dwelling among them, in seeing and hearing, vexed his righteous soul from day to day with their lawless deeds). (4-8)

4. *For if.* We have said how much it helps us to know that the un-

godly who corrupt the Church by their wicked teachings cannot escape the vengeance of God. He gives evidence of this by three notable examples of divine judgment—that He did not even spare the angels, that He once obliterated the whole world at the Flood, and that He reduced Sodom and other neighbouring cities to ashes. Peter takes for granted what should be axiomatic for us, that God is the Judge of the whole world. It follows from this that the punishments He exacted of old from the ungodly and the wicked He will also exact nowadays from others of their kind. He cannot deny Himself, nor does He have respect of persons that He should pardon the same offence in one case, and punish it in the other. He hates unrighteousness equally wherever it may be found. We must always bear in mind this difference between God and men, that men judge inequitably, but God keeps the same constant scale of judgment. In forgiving the sins of the elect He does so because He blots them out by reason of repentance and faith. He only reconciles us to Himself on the basis of justifying us. Until sin is taken away there is always cause of tension between us and Him.

As far as *angels* are concerned, the argument is from the greater to the less. Although they were far more exalted, yet their dignity did not save them from the hand of God. Much less, therefore, will mortal men who have followed their impiety escape. Since Peter has touched briefly here on the fall of the angels, but does not specify the time or manner of other circumstances, we must speculate carefully on this matter. There are many curious men who never stop probing into these things, but since God has only rarely touched on them in Scripture, and then only in passing, this fact warns us to be content with a modicum of knowledge. Those who inquire further in their over-anxiety have no regard to edification but want to feed their minds on empty speculations. God has made known what is useful for us to know, that the devils were originally created to obey God, that they fell from grace through their own fault because they did not submit to God's rule; and therefore that the wickedness which cleaves to them was accidental and not organic to their nature, so that it cannot be attributed to God.

Peter describes this quite clearly when he makes the angels who fell superior to men, and Jude still more so when he writes that they did not hold to their origin or to their principality. Those who are dissatisfied with these evidences can have the theology of the Sorbonne which will teach them about angels till they have had more than enough and will thrust them down to the depths along with the devils.

To chains of darkness. This metaphor means that they are held bound in darkness to the last day. This comparison is drawn from criminals, who, after they are condemned, suffer half their punishment in the harshness of imprisonment until they are dragged out for the final penalty. Hence we may conclude not only what punishment the wicked endure after death, but also what is the condition of the children of God. They rest peacefully in the sure hope of blessedness, even though they do not yet enjoy it, just as the others endure terrible torture at the thought of the vengeance in store for them.

5. *The ancient world.* The sense of this phrase is that after God had submerged the human race He founded as it were a new world over again. The argument here is from the greater to the less. How will the wicked escape the flood of divine anger when the whole world was once overwhelmed by it? When he says that eight were saved, he means that a crowd will not be any kind of a shield to protect sinners before God. As many as have sinned will pay the penalty, whether they are few in number or many.

It may be asked why he calls Noah *a preacher of righteousness.* Some understand this as a preacher of the righteousness of God, as Scripture commends the righteousness of God in that He looks after His own and restores them to life when they have been carried off by death. I would rather take him as being called a preacher of righteousness because he tried to bring a degenerate world to a sound state of mind, and because he did so not only by teaching and exhortations to holiness but by his constant and anxious toil for a hundred and twenty years in building the ark. The apostle's purpose is to place before our very eyes the wrath of God against the wicked so as to encourage us to imitation of the saints.

6. *The cities of Sodom.* This was such a notable example of divine vengeance that whenever Scripture speaks of the universal destruction of the ungodly, it refers to this as the type. So Peter says that these cities were designed to be an example. This could indeed be said of others, but Peter refers to this in particular because it is an outstanding and vivid picture. Because the Lord has willed that His wrath against the ungodly should be made known to all generations, just as when He redeemed His people from Egypt, so He has depicted for us in this one act of grace the eternal safety of the Church. This is what Jude has expressed in speaking of the punishment of eternal fire.

8. *In seeing and hearing.* The common exposition is that Lot was righteous in seeing and hearing because all his senses shrank from the crimes of Sodom. But hearing and sight may have another reference, the sense being this, that when he lived justly among the people of Sodom he tormented his soul by seeing and hearing. We know that he was forced to hear and see many things that tortured his soul

terribly. In short it comes to this, that although the holy man was surrounded on every side with every kind of monstrous vice, he was never distracted from the right course.

Peter expresses more than he did before in that Lot as a righteous man underwent his torments voluntarily, for just as it is right that all the godly should be affected by no little grief when they see the world rushing into every kind of evil, it is the more necessary that we should groan over our own sins. The apostle has declared this specifically so that when impiety rages everywhere we should not be caught and intoxicated by the enticements of vice and so perish with the rest, but that we should prefer this grief which is blessed of the Lord to all the pleasures of the world.

The Lord knoweth how to deliver the godly out of temptation, and to keep the unrighteous under punishment unto the day of judgment; but chiefly them that walk after the flesh in the lust of defilement, and despise dominion. Daring, selfwilled, they tremble not to rail at dignities: whereas angels, though greater in might and power, bring not a railing judgment against them before the Lord. (9-11)

9. *The Lord knoweth.* The first cause of stumbling to the weak is that when the faithful sigh anxiously for help they are not immediately relieved by the ever-present aid of God, but rather the Lord sometimes allows them as it were to pine away in daily weariness and languor; and secondly that the wicked have their licence with impunity while God is silent as though He connived at their wickednesses. Peter now removes this double offence. He testifies that the Lord knows when the time is ripe to remove the godly from temptation. In saying this he instructs us that these are matters to be left to Him, and therefore we must hold on patiently in times of temptation and not give way when He puts off His vengeance on the ungodly.

This consolation is very necessary for us, for the idea is apt to insinuate itself that if the Lord wants to keep His people unspotted, why does He not gather them all together into some corner of the earth where they can encourage each other in holiness? Why does He mix them in with the wicked, by whom they are defiled? But when God appropriates to Himself the responsibility for helping and protecting His own, so that they do not fail in the struggle, we take heart to fight the harder. The gist of the first clause is that this principle is laid down by the Lord for all believers, that they are tested by all kinds of temptations, but they must have good hope of a happy issue because they are never bereft of His help.

The unrighteous. This clause is to show that God adjusts His judgment so as to bear with the wicked for a time, but not leave them unpunished.

In this way he corrects the over-impatience by which we are often carried away especially when the grievousness of evil hurts us deeply. We want God to thunder on the spot, and if He delays He does not seem to be the Judge of the world any longer. Therefore in case this temporary impunity of wickedness disturbs us, Peter reminds us that the day of judgment is fixed by the Lord, and that the wicked will by no means escape their punishment, even if it is not immediately enforced.

There is emphasis on the word *keep* as if he were saying that they have not slipped out of God's hand, but are held bound by hidden chains to be brought forth at the appointed time to judgment. The participle κολαζομένους, though in the present tense, is to be translated in the sense that they are kept as requiring to be punished or in order to be punished. He bids us depend on the hope of ultimate judgment so that we may soldier on to the bitter end in patient hope.

10. *Chiefly them that walk, etc.* He comes now to his particular thesis and applies the general principle to his particular proposition. He has to do with men of grossest wickedness, and he therefore shows that a terrible vengeance inevitably awaits them. Since God will exact punishment from all, how will they escape who throw themselves into every kind of iniquity like wild beasts?

That walk after the flesh. This means to be given up to the flesh just as brute beasts do not behave rationally or responsibly but are guided entirely by their fleshly desires. By *lust of defilement* we must understand lewd and uncontrolled lusts, when men throw away every honest motive and give up any sense of shame and are carried off into degradation.

The first mark by which he brands them is that they are men of impurity, given over to villainy. Other marks follow, for example, that they disregard authority and that they are not afraid to insult and reproach men to whom God has given honour and prestige. I take these two words to refer to the same thing. After saying that they hold authority in contempt, he goes on to show that the source of this evil is that they are *daring and self-willed.* Finally to heighten their pride even more, he says that they do not tremble even to rail insultingly at dignities. It is monstrous presumption to hold in no regard the prestige which adorns those set in high positions by God. There is no doubt that he means by this emperors and magistrates. Although there is no lawful station of life that is not worthy of regard, yet we know that the office of magistrate excels all others, because in governing the human race they act as the viceroys of God. That power is indeed glorious in which God Himself is shown forth.

We can now grasp what the apostle means in the second clause, namely, that those men of whom he speaks were madmen, stirring up troubles and creating confusion, because no one can bring anarchy (ἀναρχία) into the world without introducing disorder (ἀταξία). These men unblushingly belched forth abuse against the magistrates to take away all respect for public law and order, and this was openly to attack God with their blasphemies. There are many turbulent men of this kind today who boast that all the power of the sword is heathen and unlawful and who busy themselves furiously to overthrow the body politic. Such ragings which upset the progress of the Gospel are stirred up by Satan. But the Lord has dealt favourably with us not only in warning us to beware of this deadly poison, but also in strengthening us against stumbling by the example of days of old. The Papists therefore, act wholly dishonestly when they charge us with providing arms for rebellious men by our teaching, as though they could not have once laid this to the charge of the apostles, who were far from being guilty of this.

11. *Whereas angels.* He displays their rash presumption in the fact that they dared to assume more freedom than the very angels themselves. It is strange that he says that the angels do not bring a railing charge against the magistrates, for how could they oppose the sacred order (*sancto ordine*) whose author they knew to be God? Why should they rise up against rulers whom they knew to exercise the same ministry as they themselves? For this reason some have come to think that what is said refers to the devils, but they do not escape the difficulty this way. How would Satan be so reasonable in sparing men when he is the source of all blasphemy against God? Their opinion is refuted by the words of Jude.

If we think of the circumstances of the time, what is said is said very properly of the holy angels, for at that time almost all the magistrates were ungodly and bloody enemies of the Gospel. They must, therefore, inevitably have been hateful to the angels as guardians of the Gospel. Nevertheless he says that men who had earned their hatred and execration were damned by them in such a way as to preserve respect for power divinely instituted. He says that although there is this restraint in the angels, these men rush on boldly in their wicked, unrestrained blasphemies.

But these, as creatures without reason, born mere animals to be taken and destroyed, railing in matters whereof they are ignorant, shall in their destroying surely be destroyed. Suffering wrong as the hire of wrong-doing; men that count it pleasure to revel in the day-time, spots and blemishes, revelling in their love-feasts while they feast with you. Having eyes full of adultery, and that cannot cease from sin; enticing un–

stedfast souls; having a heart exercised in covetousness; children of cursing; forsaking the right way, they went astray, having followed the way of Balaam the son of Beor, who loved the hire of wrong-doing; but he was rebuked for his own transgression: a dumb ass spake with man's voice and stayed the madness of the prophet. (12-16)

12. *But these.* He continues what he had begun to say about the ungodly and wicked corrupters. First of all he reproaches them for their debased morals and the impure wickedness of their whole life, and then he says that they are audacious and perverse in worming their way into the favour of many people by their scurrilous chatter. He compares them first to *brute animals*, which seem to be born to be caught in snares and carried to their death by their own violence, as though he were saying that they are not baited by any allurements but of their own accord hasten to throw themselves into the snares of Satan and of death. What we have translated as *born mere animals*, Peter has literally 'born natural', but there is little difference in the meaning whether one of these two has been supplied by some other hand or whether he wanted to express his meaning more fully by having both expressions.

The addition, *railing in matters whereof they are ignorant*, refers to the pride which has just been referred to. He says that every kind of excellence is wantonly despised by them because they have become so utterly stupid that they are indistinguishable from cattle. What I have rendered *in their destroying*, or alternatively *in corruption* in either case represents the word φθορᾶς which can be taken in either meaning. By saying that they will perish in their own corruption he means that their corruptions will be fatal for them.

13. *That count it pleasure.* This is as though he were saying, 'They find their happiness in their present enjoyments.' We know that men are better than mere animals in the fact that they turn their minds to things further ahead. It is therefore unworthy of a man to busy himself with his present state. He means by this that unless we want to sink to the level of animals, our minds ought to be disentangled from their present enjoyments. What follows has the sense of saying that these people defile you and your friends with dirty stains, because while they feast with you they luxuriate in their errors and show by their faces and their actions lustful desires and a debased lack of control. Erasmus renders this 'They mock you by feasting in their errors', but this is too forced. It could possibly be suitably expounded, 'As they feast with you they make fun of you with their errors', but I have rendered it as seems to me most likely.

Those who have *eyes full of adultery* means the lustful, and those who are incessantly carried away by unrestrained sinfulness, such as he goes on to describe.

14. *Enticing unstedfast souls.* The metaphor of baiting warns the faithful to beware of their hidden and beguiling deceptions. He compares their impostures to hooks which can catch the unwary to their destruction. By adding *unstedfast souls* he shows that the way of caution is for us to plant our roots firmly in the faith and fear of God and at the same time he declares that those who allow themselves to be enticed by such blandishments have no excuse worthy of the name, because it must be ascribed to their rootlessness. Therefore let there be a stable faith, and we shall be safe from the snares of the ungodly.

A heart exercised in covetousness. Erasmus renders this 'rapines' but the meaning of the Greek is uncertain. I prefer 'covetousness' because just as he has already condemned the lust of their eyes, so now he seems to remark on the vices that are hidden in the heart. This ought not to be restricted simply to avarice. The phrase *children of cursing* which he uses can be taken equally well in the active or the passive sense, either that wherever they go they bring a curse with them, or that they are themselves accursed.

Up to this point he has described the harm that they do by their example of a perverted and evil life, and now he reiterates that by their teaching they spread the deadly poison of godlessness, by which they destroy the simple. He compares them to Balaam the son of Beor who used his venal tongue to curse the people of God. To show that they are not worth a long refutation, he says that Balaam was rebuked by an ass and his madness was thereby demonstrated. By the same token he warns off the faithful from all association with them. It was a dreadful judgment of God that the angel revealed himself to the ass before the prophet, and that the ass seeing that God was displeased did not dare to go further but rather retraced its steps, while the prophet under the blind impulse of his own avarice pressed on in the face of the clear prohibition of God. The answer to go on that was finally given him was a sign of divine indignation rather than permission. As a final, crowning indignity the mouth of the ass was opened, so that he who had refused to submit to the rule of God had to accept the orders of the ass. The purpose of the Lord in this miracle was to show what a monstrous thing it is to change the truth to a lie.

It may be asked at this point by what right Balaam was distinguished with the name of a prophet, since it is evident that he was involved in many evil superstitions. I reply that the gift of prophecy is a particular possession, so that even a man who offers his worship to others than the true God, and who does not keep to the true religion may yet be endowed with it. Moreover it has sometimes been the will of God for

354

prophecy to exist in the midst of idolatry so that men may have less excuse.

Anyone who ponders the tenor of what Peter is saying will see that this warning is no less relevant to our own age. Everywhere there flourishes this disease of men using scurrilous raillery to mock God and Christ, undermining all religion under the cloak of wit, and with their addiction to the flesh like beasts yet mingling with the faithful. They chatter a bit about the Gospel, but all the time they debase their tongue to the service of the devil so as to bring the whole world to eternal ruin, as far as in them lies. In this regard they are worse than Balaam himself, because they pour out their curses quite gratuitously, while he was at least induced by a reward, when he broke forth into cursing.

These are springs without water, and mists driven by a storm; for whom the blackness of darkness hath been reserved. For uttering great swelling words of vanity, they entice in the lusts of the flesh, by lasciviousness, those who are just escaping from them that live in error; promising them liberty, while they themselves are bondservants of corruption; for of whom a man is overcome, of the same is he also brought into bondage. (17-19)

17. *These are springs without water.* By these two metaphors he shows that although they make a great outward show they have nothing behind it. A fountain draws men by its very appearance because it promises water both for drinking and for the other necessities of life. As soon as clouds appear they give a hope of rain approaching to water the earth. He says therefore that these people are like fountains because they make great boasts, show some shrewdness in their speech, and give an appearance of charm in their words, but within they are dry and barren, and hence the form of the fountain deceives.

He says *mists driven by a storm* without rain, or which burst forth into a disastrous storm. By this he means that they never bring anything beneficial, but often they are very harmful. He repeats the denunciation of the terrible judgment of God upon them so that fear of this may check the faithful. In describing the *blackness of darkness* he refers to clouds which darken the sky, as though he were saying that in place of the momentary darkness which they now cast there is prepared for them a much thicker and eternal one.

18. *Uttering great swelling words.* He means that they dazzle the eyes of the simple by bombasts of words, whereby they cannot notice the trickery, for it would not be easy for men's minds to be captivated by such nonsense unless they were first stupefied by some cunning deceit. He says that they have an inflated using of words and way of speaking, by the admiration of which they trap the unwary. This grandi-

loquence, which (as Perseus says) the large lungs of the soul breathes out, is a fit cover for their equivocations. We can see from the writings of Irenaeus that this kind of craftiness was to be found in Valentinus and his like. They made up words never previously heard of, by the empty sound of which the unskilled were struck and enslaved by their charms. There are similar madmen today who give themselves the plausible title of Libertines. They spill mouthfuls about the Spirit and the things of the Spirit as though thundering from above the clouds, and captivate many by their illusions, so that you would say that the apostle has fittingly prophesied of them. They treat everything jokingly and facetiously and although they are the greatest fools, yet because they indulge in every kind of vice, they find favour for their so-called drolleries. The upshot is that when the choice between good and evil is removed anything is possible, men are released from all obedience to law and they follow their own pleasures. This letter can therefore be of considerable advantage to our times.

They entice in the lusts of the flesh. He neatly compares the enticements of the ungodly when they make anything lawful to hooks, for as the avarice of men is blind and grasping, as soon as any licence is offered they grab at it with a greedy clutch, but then a little later the choking hook within is felt.

It is, however, worth while considering the whole sentence of the apostle. He says that those who had in fact escaped from the society of those who live in error are again deceived by a new error, in that the reins are loosened for them to fall into every kind of intemperance. By this he warns us how dangerous their wiles are. There was already the dreadful example that blindness, and thick darkness possessed almost the whole human race. There is now this double portent that men who have been freed from the general errors of the world after seeing the light of God are immersed in an animal insensibility. From this we are warned that our greatest threat after we have once seen the light is that Satan should on the pretext of liberty entice us to give ourselves to licentiousness to gratify the lust of the flesh. Those who give earnest heed to the pursuit of sanctification will be free from this danger.

19. *Promising them liberty.* By its very inconsistency he shows that those who by their own sin have surrendered themselves to the worst possible bondage falsely promise liberty to others. No one can give what he does not possess. This argument does not seem altogether valid, however, because it sometimes happens that evil men may preach acceptably about the benefits of Christ and yet be utter strangers to Him. It should be noted on the other hand that it is unwholesome doctrine joined with impurity of life that is condemned here. The apostle's aim is to meet cases of deceptive enticements by which the

foolish are ensnared. The name of liberty is sweet, but they have abused it to draw the hearer away from the fear of divine law and thrust him into uncontrolled licence. This is quite different from the liberty which Christ has gained for us, and which the Gospel offers us daily. He has released us from the yoke of the law in so far as it subjected us to damnation so that we might be free from the dominion of sin in so far as it delivers us to its lusts. Where lusts hold sway and therefore where the flesh occupies the throne, the liberty of Christ has no place. The apostle declares that to all the godly, so that they will not look for a liberty other than that which leads them when they are freed from sin to a willing obedience to righteousness.

From this we may conclude that there have always been evil men who have falsely pretended to the name of liberty, and this is an old trick of Satan, so that we should not be surprised that the same wiles are stirred up by frenzied men.

The Papists show their absurd impudence by the fact that they twist this passage against us. First of all men of the vilest life spew forth in their noissome public-houses and brothels the charge that we are the servants of corruption, we in whose lives they can point to no mark of reproach. Secondly, since we give no teaching about Christian liberty except what we have received from Christ and the apostles, and at the same time demand mortification of the flesh and a true practice of subduing it much more stringently than those who slander us, they belch out their curses not only at us but against the Son of God whom we have as our sure authority.

For of whom. This concept is taken from military law. It is, however, a common idea among pagan writers that no bondage is harder or more miserable than that where lusts reign. What, then, ought we to do, to whom the Son of God has given His Spirit, not only to be freed from the reign of sin, but also to be victors over the world and the flesh?

For if, after they have escaped the defilements of the world through the knowledge of the Lord and Saviour Jesus Christ, they are again entangled therein and overcome, the last state is become worse with them than the first. For it were better for them not to have known the way of righteousness, than, after knowing it, to turn back from the holy commandment delivered unto them. It has happened unto them according to the true proverb, The dog turning to his own vomit again, and the sow that had washed to wallowing in the mire. (20-22)

20. *For if, after.* He again shows the dangerous nature of this sect which takes men who are consecrated to God and drags them back again to their old impurity and the corruptions of the world. He

sharpens the gravity of the evil by a comparison, because it is no ordinary offence to fall away from the holy doctrine of God. It would have been better (he says) if they had never known the way of righteousness, for although there is no excuse in ignorance, nevertheless a servant who knowingly and willingly despises the commands of God deserves a double penalty. Added to this there is the ingratitude that of their own accord they quench the light of God, throw away the grace given to them, cast off the yoke and sin wantonly against God, indeed as far as in them lies they profane and destroy the inviolable covenant of God, ratified by the blood of Christ. We must therefore be all the more careful to go on reverently and earnestly in the course of our calling.

It is worth while considering more particularly the individual phrases. He mentions the *defilements of the world* to show that we wallow in filth and are wholly defiled until we renounce the world. There is no doubt that by the *knowledge of Christ* he means the Gospel. He bears witness that its purpose is to raise up and lead us far from the defilements of the world. In this sense a little later on he calls it the *way of righteousness*. Only he who faithfully learns Christ makes due progress in the Gospel, and he alone holds to Christ who has learned from Him to put off the old man and to put on the new as Paul advises in Ephesians 4.22.

When he says, *to turn back from the holy commandment delivered unto them* he indicates how inexcusable they are to return again to their old defilements, and then he reminds us that the doctrine of holy and righteous living, though it is common to all, and applies indiscriminately to everyone, is yet declared particularly to those on whom God bestows the light of His Gospel. Further he says that those who enslave themselves afresh to the defilements of the world revolt from the Gospel. The faithful certainly sin, but because they do not allow sin to reign over them, they do not fall from the grace of God, nor desert the profession of sound doctrine which they once embraced. Indeed they are not thought of as defeated, since they vigorously resist the flesh and its lusts.

22. *It has happened unto them.* Because many are disturbed by the sight of men who have given themselves to the obedience of Christ rushing headlong into vice without fear of shame, to remove the offence the apostle says that this happens as a result of their own wickedness, because they are pigs and dogs. It follows from this that no share of the blame can be ascribed to the Gospel.

To this end he cites two ancient proverbs, the former of which is found in the sayings of Solomon in Proverbs 26.11. Peter's purpose is in short to say this, that the Gospel is a medicine that purges us as a wholesome emetic, but there are many dogs who swallow again what they have brought up to their own ruin. Likewise the Gospel is a basin which cleanses us from all our dirt and stains, but there are many pigs who immediately after they have washed roll back again into the mud. Thus the godly are warned to beware of both dangers, if they do not want to be included in the ranks of the dogs and the pigs.

CHAPTER THREE

This is now, beloved, the second epistle that I write unto you; and in both of them I stir up your sincere mind by putting you in remembrance; that ye should remember the words which were spoken before by the holy prophets, and the commandment of the Lord and Saviour through your apostles: knowing this first, that in the last days mockers shall come with mockery, walking after their own lusts, and saying, Where is the promise of his coming? for, from the day that the fathers fell asleep, all things continue as they were from the beginning of the creation. (1-4)

In case they are wearied by a second letter, and think that the first was sufficient, he says that neither was written without a purpose, because they have frequent need of being aroused. To make this clearer he points out that they will not be free from danger unless they are well fortified, because they will be in conflict with wicked men who not only corrupt the purity of the faith with false dogmas, but, so far as they may, completely overturn all faith.

To say, *I stir up your sincere mind* is as if to say, 'I wish to arouse you to sincerity of mind', and the words ought to be translated, 'I stir up your mind so that it may be pure and clear.' The meaning is that when exhortations are given up the minds of the godly become dim and as it were attract rust. Hence we learn that even men who are endowed with learning tend to lie back and drowse unless they are constantly spurred on by admonitions. It is now clear what the advantage of such admonitions are, and how necessary they are for us. The laziness of the flesh smothers doctrine once it is accepted and makes it ineffective unless the urge of admonitions comes to its aid. For men to hold on to what they need it is not enough that they should be taught, but there is also a call to godly teachers to look to this second responsibility, namely to implant their teaching firmly in their hearers' memories.

Since men for the most part are naturally eager for novelty and so inclined to hyper-criticism, it is useful for us to bear in mind what Peter says, not only so that we gladly allow ourselves to be advised by others, but also so that each of us may exercise himself by constantly calling our teaching to mind, so that our minds may shine with the pure, clear understanding of it.

2. *That ye should remember.* He means by this that we have enough in the writings of the prophets and in the Gospel to stir us up, so long as we are suitably earnest in meditating on them. It is due to our

laziness that our minds sometimes get rusty or are clouded by darkness. We must therefore apply ourselves to this study, so that God may continually illumine us, and meantime our faith should rest on these sure and credible witnesses. If we are in agreement with the prophets and apostles, indeed if we have them as ministers of our faith, and God as its Author, and the angels in approval, then there is no reason why we should be moved from our position by any conspiracy of the ungodly. By *commandment* of the apostles he means the whole teaching by which they instructed the godly.

3. *Knowing this first.* The participle 'knowing' could be applied personally to the apostle, in the sense, 'I labour to stir you up because I know the nature and extent of the danger you are in from mockers', but I prefer to expound it otherwise, taking the participle as used in place of a verb, as if he had said, 'Know this above all'. It was necessary for them to be thus forewarned, because they could have been badly shaken if the ungodly had suddenly attacked them with this kind of mockery. He wants them to know this and to be assured so as to be ready to resist.

He recalls the faithful a second time to the teaching on which he has touched in chapter two. It is quite evident that by *the last days* he denotes the kingdom of Christ, as in St Paul (I Cor. 10.11), 'upon whom the ends of the ages are come'. The meaning is that the more pressingly God offers Himself to the world in the Gospel, and invites men into His Kingdom, the more boldly will wicked men belch forth the poison of their impiety.

According to the common usage of Scripture he calls *mockers* those who seek to appear clever by their despite of God and their blasphemous pride. It is the culminating evil of all for men to allow themselves to make fun of the awful Name of God in sport. The first Psalm speaks thus of the scorners' chair, and David in Psalm 119.51 complains that he was held in derision by the proud because he did not swerve from God's law. So, too, Isaiah in chapter 28 makes mention of them, describing their heedlessness and carelessness and their simplicity.

Let us, therefore, bear in mind that nothing is more to be feared than this battle with the mockers, about which we have said something in respect of Galatians 3. However, since the Holy Spirit has foretold their coming, and has put into our hands a shield whereby we can defend ourselves against them, we have no excuse for not standing firm whatever machinations they may employ.

4. *Where is the promise?* It is a dangerous piece of scoffing when they cast doubt on the resurrection of the last day, because if this is taken away nothing is left of the Gospel, the power of Christ is drained away, and all religion is destroyed. Satan directly attacks the throat of the

Church when he destroys faith in the return of Christ. Why did
Christ die and rise again if not to redeem us and to gather us sometime
or other to Himself in eternal life? Godliness is utterly destroyed unless
faith in the resurrection remains firm, and therefore it is in this quarter
that Satan attacks us more fiercely.

We must notice the nature of this piece of mockery. They set the
ongoing course of nature, such as it has been seen to flow on from the
beginning, in opposition to the promise of God, as though they were
contraries, or things incompatible with one another. Though the faith
of our fathers was the same, they say, yet nothing has been changed
since they died, and we know that many generations have passed since
then. From this they conclude that what was said about the end of the
world was just a story, because they imagine that because it has lasted
so long it will last for ever.

> For this they wilfully forget, that there were heavens from of old, and an
> earth compacted out of water and amidst water, by the word of God; by
> which means the world that then was, being overflowed with water,
> perished: but the heavens that now are, and the earth, by the same word
> have been stored up for fire, being reserved against the day of judgment
> and destruction of ungodly men. But forget not this one thing, beloved,
> that one day is with the Lord as a thousand years, and a thousand years
> as one day. (5-8)

5. *For this they wilfully forget.* He refutes this mockery of the ungodly
by the single argument that the world once perished in a flood of
water, when it yet consisted of waters. Since this history is sufficiently
well known and indeed famous, he says that they see *wilfully*, that is,
of their own free will, for those who deduce perpetuity from the daily
state of the world shut their eyes of evil intent in case they might see
so clear a judgment of God. The world certainly takes its origin from
the waters, for Moses calls the chaos out of which the earth was made
the waters (Gen. 1.2). Further, it was sustained by its waters, and the
Lord used the waters to destroy it. It is clear from this that the power
of nature is not enough to support and maintain the world, but rather
that it contains the material for its own ruin whenever it may so please
God.

It must always be remembered that the world does not properly
stand by any other power than that of the Word of God, that secon-
dary causes derive their power from Him, and that they have different
effects as they are directed. Thus the world was established on the
waters, but they had no power of themselves, but were rather subject
to the Word of God as an inferior element. As soon as it pleased God
to destroy the earth, that same water showed its obedience in a death-

carrying flood. We can now see how wrong people are who stop at the bare elements as though perpetuity was to be found in them, and not rather that their nature is amenable to the will of God.

In these few words there is abundant refutation of the capriciousness of those who arm themselves with physical arguments to fight against God. The history of the flood (Gen. 7.17ff) is full and sufficient witness to the fact that the whole order of nature is governed by the rule of God alone.

It seems odd that he says that *the world* perished in the flood when he had previously mentioned heaven and earth. My answer is that heaven was also overwhelmed by it, being the region of air which lay between the two waters. The division which Moses mentions (Gen. 1.6) was obliterated, and the name heaven is often taken in this sense. If anyone wishes more on this subject, he should read Augustine, *The City of God,* chapter 20.

7. *The heavens that now are.* He does not infer this as a consequence. It was not his purpose to do other than debunk the craftiness of the mockers about the perpetual state of nature, for we see many such men today who have a light smattering of the rudiments of philosophy, and who hunt after profane speculations simply to pass themselves off as great thinkers.

It is clearly evident from the foregoing that there is nothing absurd in the declaration by the Lord that heaven and earth will one day be consumed by fire, since the rationale of fire is the same as that of water. It was commonly agreed by the ancients that everything proceeded from these two prime elements. Since he was dealing with the ungodly, he speaks expressly of their destruction.

8. *But forget not this one thing.* He now turns his address to the godly, and bids them when the coming of Christ is being talked of to raise their eyes upwards, for by so doing they will not subject the time appointed by God to their own ridiculous wishes. The period of waiting seems over-long because we keep our eyes cast down at the shortness of this present life, and, further, we increase the weariness by counting up days and hours and minutes. When the eternity of the kingdom of God meets us, many ages vanish away like a moment of time.

The apostle recalls us to this truth so that we may know that the day of resurrection does not depend on the flow of the present time, but on the eternal decree of God. It is as if he were saying that men wish to anticipate God because they measure time by their carnal senses, and they are naturally inclined to be impatient, so that even speed is a delay to them. You, therefore, he says, must ascend to heaven in your minds, and thus time for you will be neither long nor short.

*The Lord is not slack concerning his promise, as some count slackness;
but is long-suffering to you-ward, not wishing that any should perish,
but that all should come to repentance. But the day of the Lord will
come as a thief; in the which the heavens shall pass away with a great
noise, and the elements shall be dissolved with fervent heat, and the
earth and the works that are therein shall be burned up. Seeing that
these things are thus all to be dissolved, what manner of persons ought ye
to be in all holy living and godliness, looking for and earnestly desiring
the coming of the day of God, by reason of which the heavens being on
fire shall be dissolved, and the elements shall melt with fervent heat?
But, according to his promise, we look for new heavens and a new earth,
wherein dwelleth righteousness.* (9-13)

9. *The Lord is not slack.* He checks haste that is overmuch and unreasonable by this other line of argument, that God puts off His advent
so as to call the whole human race to repentance. Our minds are always
itching, and there often creeps in the doubt why He does not come
more quickly. But when we hear that, when He delays, God is having
regard for our salvation, and delays because He is concerned for us,
there is no ground for further questioning His tardiness. He is said to
be slack who allows opportunity to slip by his laziness, but there is
nothing like this in God, who knows best how to accommodate the
pattern of time to our salvation. We must think in the same way about
the duration of the whole world as of any single human life. God sustains men by prolonging each man's time for him to repent. Likewise
He refrains from bringing forward the end of the world, so as to give
everyone time for repentance. This is a very useful admonition, so
that we may learn to use time properly, otherwise we shall justly pay
the penalty of our laziness.

Not wishing that any should perish. This is His wondrous love towards
the human race, that He desires all men to be saved, and is prepared to
bring even the perishing to safety. We must notice the order, that
God is prepared to receive all men into repentance, so that none may
perish. These words indicate the means of obtaining salvation, and
whoever of us seeks salvation must learn to follow in this way.

It could be asked here, if God does not want any to perish, why do
so many in fact perish? My reply is that no mention is made here of
the secret decree of God by which the wicked are doomed to their
own ruin, but only of His loving-kindness as it is made known to us
in the Gospel. There God stretches out His hand to all alike, but He
only grasps those (in such a way as to lead to Himself) whom He has
chosen before the foundation of the world.

Since the verb χωρῆσαι is often taken as middle in Greek, what I have put in parenthesis in this passage will be equally apt, in that God desires all who had formerly been wandering and scattered to come together to repentance.

10. *But the day of the Lord will come.* This is added so that the faithful may always be on the watch and not promise themselves tomorrow. Almost all of us labour under two very different evils, too much impatience and too much laziness. In our impatience we snatch at the day of Christ as something expected imminently, but in our carelessness we push it far off. Therefore just as the apostle has earlier corrected our reckless ardour, so now he shakes our sleepiness off us, so that we may look expectantly for the coming of Christ at any time, and not give up as we are accustomed to do. How does it come about that we indulge our flesh unless by reason of the fact that we have no thought of the near advent of Christ?

What follows after this about the burning of heaven and earth does not need any long exposition if we consider his intention. It is not his purpose to give a subtle disquisition about fire and storm and other things, but only to introduce the exhortation which immediately follows, that we too should strive to newness of life. He reasons this way, that as heaven and earth will be cleansed by fire so that they may be fit for the kingdom of Christ, so renewal is a far greater need in men. Those interpreters are, therefore, wicked, who take a great deal of trouble in abstruse speculations, since the apostle applies this whole teaching to godly exhortations. Heaven and earth, he says, will pass away for our sakes. Is is fitting, therefore, for us to be engrossed in the things of earth, and not rather to be thinking of living holy and godly lives? The corruption of heaven and earth will be purged by fire, although as the creatures of God they are pure. What, therefore, ought we to do, being as we are involved in so many evils?

The word *godliness* (*pietatibus*) is a plural used for the singular, unless you take it as duties of godliness.

I shall say just one thing about the elements of the world, that they will be consumed only in order to receive a new quality while their substance remains the same, as can easily be concluded from Romans 8.21 and other passages.

12. *Looking for and earnestly desiring.* I have preferred to render the words this way as though they were two participles. What we have considered separately above, he now gathers into one sentence, to the effect that we ought to wait quietly and in haste. This seeming contradiction has not a little neatness in it, as in the proverb 'Festina lente'.

When he says *looking for*, he refers to the endurance of hope, and he sets haste in contrast to sloth, and both fittingly. As quietness and calmness are the properties of hope, so we must beware that the care-

lessness of the flesh does not creep in, and likewise we must labour
earnestly in good works and run swiftly the race of our calling. What
we had earlier called the day of Christ (as it is customarily called
throughout Scripture) he now calls the day of God, and with justification, for Christ will then arise to restore the kingdom to the Father,
so that God may be all in all.

*Wherefore, beloved, seeing that ye look for these things, give diligence
that ye may be found in peace, without spot and blameless in his sight.
And account that the long-suffering of our Lord is salvation; even as our
beloved brother Paul also, according to the wisdom given to him, wrote
unto you; as also in all his epistles, speaking in them of these things;
wherein are some things hard to be understood, which the ignorant and
unstedfast wrest, as they do also the other scriptures, unto their own
destruction. Ye therefore, beloved, knowing these things beforehand,
beware lest, being carried away with the error of the wicked, ye fall from
your own stedfastness. But grow in the grace and knowledge of our
Lord and Saviour Jesus Christ. To him be the glory both now and for
ever. Amen.* (14-18)

14. *Wherefore.* He argues rightly from hope to its effect, which is
the practice of godly living. Hope is living and efficacious, and therefore it must draw us to itself. Anyone who hopes for new heavens
will begin renewal within himself, and will aspire to this with all his
energy, while those who stick to their own filthy ways will certainly
have no thoughts of the kingdom of God, and have no discernment of
anything but this corruptible world.

We must notice what he says about our being found *blameless* by
Christ. By this he means that while others are concerned with and
engaged by the appearance of the world we ought to cast our eyes to
the Lord. At the same time he shows what real integrity is, namely,
that which is approved by His judgment, and not what finds praise
among men.

The word *peace* seems to me to be taken in the sense of the state of a
conscience at peace, which has its roots in hope and endurance. The
fact that so few turn their attention to the judgment of Christ is because while they are carried along headlong by their own importunate
lust they are at the same time disquieted. This peace is the quietness
of a soul at ease which rests on the Word of God.

It may be asked how anyone can be found blameless by Christ when
we all labour under so many sins. Peter is here only showing the goal
to which the faithful should strive, even though they do not attain it,
until having put off the flesh they cleave wholly to Christ.

15. *The long-suffering of our Lord.* He takes it for granted that Christ

puts off the day of His coming because He has a concern for our salvation, and from this he encourages the faithful that in this long delay they have a sign of their salvation. Thus what habitually discourages others by delay he wisely turns to the opposite purpose.

Even as our beloved brother. We can easily see both from the Epistle to the Galatians and from other passages that good-for-nothing rascals who went around everywhere disturbing the churches misused as a pretext to detract from Paul's trustworthiness that he did not agree very well with the other apostles. It is therefore probable that Peter mentions Paul to bear witness to their agreement with one another, for it was more than necessary to remove any opportunity for such a libel. Yet when I consider everything more particularly, it seems more likely to me that this epistle was composed by someone else in accordance with the mind of Peter than that it was written by Peter himself. Peter would never have spoken like this. But it is enough for me to have this witness both of his teaching and of his good-will, who has produced nothing different from what he would have said himself.

16. *Wherein are some things.* This phrase does not agree with *epistles* for the pronoun is neuter in the Greek. The meaning is that in these things which he has mentioned, there is sometimes obscurity, which the unlearned take as occasion to wander off to their own destruction. We are warned in these words that we must speculate carefully in matters so exalted and obscure, and further we are strengthened against this kind of offence in case the foolish, stupid speculations of some men upset us, by which they entangle and pervert the simple doctrine which ought to serve for edification.

Let us note that we are not forbidden to read the epistles of Paul because they contain some things that are hard and difficult to understand, but rather they are commended to us provided we bring to them a calm and teachable mind. Peter condemns the trifling and superficial men who perversely turn to their ruin what is useful to everyone. He says that this generally happens in the whole of Scripture, but he does not conclude from that that we must abstain from it, but simply says that those vices which hinder advancement are to be corrected, because they render deadly what God has appointed for our salvation.

It may be asked whence this obscurity is, for Scripture shines for us like a lamp, and guides our steps with certainty. My answer is that it is not to be wondered at that Peter attributes obscurity to the mysteries of the kingdom of Christ, especially when we think how hidden they are from our carnal perception. The method of teaching which God adopts, however, is so arranged that those who do not refuse to follow the Holy Spirit as the guide of their way have in Scripture a clear light. There are many who are blind and stumble even at noonday, and others who are proud and wander through byways. They hasten over the rough places, and fall headlong.

17. *Ye therefore, beloved.* After he has shown to the faithful the dangers of which they must beware, he now concludes by saying that they are to be wise and take his advice. There is need of watchfulness in case they are overpowered. Certainly the subtlety of our enemy, the many, various traps with which he invests us, and the snares of ungodly men leave no place for carelessness. Therefore we must show vigilance so that the tricks of Satan and the ungodly do not succeed in overwhelming us. It seems that the assurance of our salvation stands on slippery ground and hangs suspended as if on a thread, since he warns the faithful to beware that they do not fall from their stedfastness.

What, then, will happen to us if we are exposed to the danger of falling? I reply that this exhortation and others like it are not made with the purpose of undermining the security of our faith which rests on God, but of correcting the idleness of our flesh. If anyone wishes more on this matter, I refer him to the tenth chapter of I Corinthians.

The sum of it all is this, that as long as we are in the flesh our laziness must be stirred up, and that is best done when our weakness and the variety of hazards that surround us are set before our eyes. But this will not shake the confidence that rests on the promises of God.

18. *But grow in grace.* He urges us to advance, because the only way of persevering is continually to go forward and not to stop and sit down in the middle of the journey. It is as though he were saying, that those who put their minds to making daily progress will be safe.

I take the word *grace* in the general sense of the spiritual gifts which we obtain through Christ. As we are partakers of the blessings of Christ according to the measure of our faith, knowledge is added to grace, as though he had said that, as faith grows, so the increase of grace will follow.

To Him be the glory, etc. This is an outstanding doxology for showing the divinity of Christ, for this cannot apply to any but God alone. The adverb of present time *now* means that we must not deprive Christ of His glory as long as we soldier on in the world. He adds immediately after *unto the day of eternity* so that we may now imagine in our minds His eternal kingdom, which will reveal to us His full glory.

INDEX OF SCRIPTURE REFERENCES

2 A

INDEX OF SCRIPTURE REFERENCES

INDEX OF NAMES

INDEX OF NAMES

GENERAL INDEX

Angels, 10ff, 18, 22, 242, 348, 352
  allegorically used, 13
Adoption, 123, 244
Atonement (*see also* Christ, sufferings of), 129-31
Authority
  in Church, 207, 212, 317
  of fathers, 39
  of husbands, 282f, 318
  of magistrates, 269f
Authorship
  of Hebrews, 20, 216
  of I Peter, 323

Baptism, 72f, 296
  of Noah, 295
Bishop, office of, 213
Blood, offering of, 119
Burning bush, 178

Calling, *v.s.* Election
Catechumens, 71
Childishness, 68f, 256
Christ
  as Advocate, 128
  coming of, 249, 361f, 364f
  compared with angels, 32
  compared with Melchizedek, 88-95
  compared with Moses, 96
  dispensation of, 199
  example of, 275
  Fore-runner, 87
  foreshadowed by David, 10
  Foundation, 208, 258, 260f
  functions of, 27
  glory of, 7
  Heir of all things, 6
  humiliation of, 16, 25

Image of God, 8
intercession of, 101
λόγος 9
lordship of, 23
masterbuilder, 35f
obedience of, 137
patience of, 188
priesthood of, 15, 54f, 58ff, 87, 97ff, 119ff, 129, 137-42, 211
resurrection of, 250
Shepherd, 30, 145, 279, 317
sufferings of, 26, 64f, 177, 240, 276, 278, 291, 298f
Teacher, 239f
transfiguration of, 338f
Wisdom of God, 11
Church, 112f, 143f, 155, 176, 177, 182, 185, 191, 196, 208, 242, 253, 261, 305, 314, 316, 345f, 350 (*v.s. also* Authority)
  brotherhood of, 204
  descended from Abraham, 167
  discipline of, 209
Corruption of flesh, 256
Covenant, 109-11, 113, 115, 123-8, 149
  ark of, 116
Creation, 22

David
  as type of Christ, 134, 135, 262f
  sacrifices of, 135
Death, 31
Devil, *v.s.* Satan

Elect, 76, 123, 201, 229
Election, 11, 177, 230, 249, 332-4
Exhortation, place of, 335f, 360

376